THE FATHERS OF THE CHURCH

A NEW TRANSLATION

VOLUME 37

THE FATHERS OF THE CHURCH

A NEW TRANSLATION

EDITORIAL BOARD

Hermigild Dressler, O.F.M.
Quincy College
Editorial Director

Robert P. Russell, O.S.A.
Villanova University

Thomas P. Halton
The Catholic University of America

Robert Sider
Dickinson College

Sister M. Josephine Brennan, I.H.M.
Marywood College

Richard Talaska
Editorial Assistant

FORMER EDITORIAL DIRECTORS

Ludwig Schopp, Roy J. Deferrari, Bernard M. Peebles

SAINT JOHN OF DAMASCUS

WRITINGS

Translated by
FREDERIC H. CHASE, JR.

THE CATHOLIC UNIVERSITY OF AMERICA PRESS
Washington, D.C.

NIHIL OBSTAT:

JOHN J. CONNELLY, S.T.D.
Censor Deputatus

IMPRIMATUR:

✠ RICHARD J. CUSHING
Archbishop of Boston

The *Nihil obstat* and *Imprimatur* are official declarations that a book or pamphlet is free of doctrinal or moral error. No implication is contained therein that those who have granted the *Nihil obstat* and *Imprimatur* agree with the contents, opinions, or statements expressed.

Copyright © 1958

THE CATHOLIC UNIVERSITY OF AMERICA PRESS

All rights reserved
Reprinted 1970, 1981
First short-run reprint 1999
Library of Congress Catalog Card No.: 59-792
ISBN 0-8132-0968-4
ISBN-13: 978-0-8132-0968-5 (pbk.)

INTRODUCTION

THE FOUNT OF KNOWLEDGE is one of the most important single works produced in the Greek patristic period, of which it marks the end, offering as it does an extensive and lucid synthesis of the Greek theological science of the whole period. It is the first great *Summa* of theology to appear in either the East or the West. And it is the last work of any theological importance to appear in the East. Of the life of its author, Yanah ibn Mansur ibn Sargun, better known as St. John of Damascus, very little is known. There are a few brief notices to be found in the acts of some Church councils and in some of the Byzantine chronicles,[1] but beyond such scattered and very limited information there is practically no certain source for the life of this man who was the last of the Fathers of the Church. The traditional source for the life of John of Damascus dates from no earlier than the eleventh century, a biography attributed to a Patriarch John of Jerusalem.[2] This John might be John VIII, who was Patriarch of Jerusalem toward the end of the eleventh century; or John IX, who came in the middle

---
1 Most of this material was gathered by Lequien and included in *PG* 94.503-514.
2 Published by Lequien, *PG* 94.429-490.

could be construed as a reference to his receiving instruction from some monk before entrance to the monastery. If there had been a monk Cosmas such as the *Life* describes, the 'Thou hast nourished me . . . with the milk of Thy sacred words' would be a very inadequate expression from such a writer as the Damascene. Had there been such a person, the Damascene would have made more explicit mention of him.

From the foregoing we may conclude that John Mansur, known to us as St. John of Damascus, was the son of Sergius, a Christian tax-collector for the Omayyad Caliph of Damascus, Abd-Al-Malik (685-705), and grandson of an important Christian official who had been given the surname of Mansur. He probably succeeded his father in office at a fairly early age and served under Abd-Al-Malik and his successor, Al-Walid (705-715). Al-Walid was not so lenient with his Christian subjects as his predecessors had been and in particular he imposed restrictions upon the Christian treasury officials. The harsh policy of Al-Walid towards the Christians may well have been the determining factor in John's decision to embrace the monastic life. Sometime, then, probably before 715, he entered the Monastery of St. Sabbas near Jerusalem. There he devoted himself to the practice of asceticism and the study of the Fathers, becoming a protege of John V, Patriarch of Jerusalem, by whom he was called to the priesthood and ordained sometime before the year 726.

In 726, Leo the Isaurian's first edict against the Holy Images was published. The enforcement of this edict led to the resignation of the then Patriarch of Constantinople, St. Germanus, in 729. It was of that time that Theophanes relates: 'At that time John Chrysorrhoas flourished at Damascus in Syria, a priest and monk and a teacher most noble in both life and speech . . . And John together with

of the following century; or one of the three Johns who were Patriarchs of Antioch in the eleventh and twelfth centuries. This *Life,* besides being bombastic and poorly written, is quite unreliable and contains so much legend that one can hardly separate the true from the false. It was based upon an Arabic *Life,* probably that composed by Michael, an eleventh-century monk from the Monastery of St. Simeon Stylites near Antioch. Michael wrote the *Life* as an expression of gratitude to St. John of Damascus, upon whose feast day he had been liberated from Saracen captivity.[3] The Arabic *Life* was based upon oral tradition and some scattered written records.

The *Life* of John of Jerusalem was so long accepted as genuine that the legend has become almost inseparably associated with the figure of St. John of Damascus. For that reason it will be necessary to give some account of it here. According to the *Life,* John came of a very pious Christian family of Damascus. His father held a high public office under the Mohammedan Caliph of Damascus. He was very anxious to obtain the best possible Christian education for his son, so, when Cosmas, a monk of extraordinary learning, was found among a group of Christian captives brought to Damascus from Italy, the father begged the caliph to turn him over to him. The request was granted and the monk Cosmas became the tutor of the young John and his adopted brother, also named Cosmas. John made great progress in theology in particular and in all the sciences. His learning and ability were such that, when his father died, he was chosen to succeed to his office and was almost immediately afterward appointed first counselor of the caliph. It was while John held this position that Leo the Isaurian initiated

---

[3] G. Graf, *Geschichte der christlichen arabischen Literatur* II (Vatican City 1947) 69-70.

his campaign against the cult of the holy images.[4] John immediately took up the defense in a series of discourses directed against the Iconoclasts. Leo was greatly angered, but, because John was in Saracen territory well out of his reach, he could do nothing about it. At length he had a letter forged, allegedly addressed to himself by John and in which it appeared that John informed him of the weak state of the defenses of the city of Damascus and begged him to come and liberate it from the Saracens. The letter was then forwarded to the caliph with a letter from Leo, explaining that this was only one of the many such letters that he was constantly receiving from the caliph's Christian subjects and suggesting that the caliph should know about it. John was summoned before the caliph and, in spite of his protestations of innocence, was judged guilty and punished by having his right hand cut off. The hand was hung in the public square, but at John's urgent request was restored to him toward the end of the day. He then spent the night in prayer before an ikon of the Mother of God. During the course of the night our Lady appeared to him and cured him. In the morning, when the caliph saw the hand perfectly restored to its proper place, with only a faint line of suture to suggest what had happened, he was so impressed that he became convinced of John's innocence and restored him to his former position of honor. John, however, requested permission to withdraw to a monastery. The permission was reluctantly granted and at length the former grand vizir entered the Monastery of St. Sabbas near Jerusalem, together with his adopted brother Cosmas. It was hard to find a spiritual father who would undertake the training of such an illustrious and learned man as John, but eventually a holy monk con-

---

[4] Leo III, Greek emperor from 717 to 741, published the first edict against the cult of the holy images in 726.

sented and took him into his cell. This spiritual father proved to be a very strict master. Among other things, he sent his pupil into the market place of Damascus to sell baskets at an exhorbitant price and thus subject himself to the derision of the city where he had once enjoyed such honor. Naturally, he acquitted himself very well in the performance of this task. Another test of his humility and obedience was the absolute prohibition to write. However, at the urgent request of one of the monks who had just lost his brother, he did finally consent to compose some verses of consolation.[5] Hearing of this, the spiritual father refused to continue his direction and expelled John from his cell. He was finally persuaded by the community to receive John back, but it was under the condition that he perfom the penance of cleaning all the monastery latrines with his bare hands. John's humble performance of this penance completely won over the old man, who a short time later was advised in a vision by the Blessed Virgin that he was being too hard upon John and should permit him to write. From then on a continuous stream of prose and poetical works flowed from his pen. Eventually, his adopted brother Cosmas was made Bishop of Maiuma and he himself ordained priest for the service of the Church in Jerusalem. He soon returned to the solitude of St. Sabbas, where he resumed his former life of asceticism and writing and so continued until his death. The author of the *Life* reports that during these last years John went over all his works carefully, correcting and revising them. This fact, at least, seems to be true, because many of the Damascene's writings do show definite signs of having been revised by the author himself. For instance, the shorter recension of the *Dialectica* seems to be a revision of the

---

5 The *Funeral Idiomela* (PG 96.1367-1370) are still sung in the funeral services of the Byzantine rite.

longer, while the treatise, *On the Virtues and Vices of the Soul and Body,* appears to be a later enlargement of *On the Eight Spirits of Evil.*

Much of the *Life* must be rejected, particularly the story of the severed hand. Even the single hint which it gives by which the chronology of the Damascene's life may be co-ordinated with known historical events is apparently wrong. For, according to the *Life,* Leo the Isaurian's first edict against the holy images must have been published while John was still a civil official; in which case the *Apologies* in defense of the holy images must have been written before he entered St. Sabbas. However, for reasons which will be explained further on, it is fairly certain that the *Apologies* were written not only after his entrance into the monastery but after his ordination to the priesthood.

What we do know with any certainty about the life of St. John of Damascus is very little indeed.[6] From the *Chronography* of Theophanes[7] we learn that John's father was Sergius, the son of a certain Mansur—an Arabic surname meaning 'victorious.' Mansur had evidently been one of the Greek officials of Damascus who were taken into the service of the Caliph Yazid when the city fell to the Arabs in 635. Sergius was 'a most Christian man' and Logothete General under the Omayyad Caliph of Damascus, Abimelech.[8] The logothete, or comptroller, was probably some sort of treasury official or collector of taxes. All such positions requiring some technical skill were usually held by Christians under the more or less benign rule of the Omayyads. However, Theophanes relates that Abimelech's successor, Al-Walid,[9]

---

[6] For what little there is, see M. Jugie, 'Jean Damascène,' *DTC* VIII cols. 693ff., and J. Nasrallah, *Saint Jean de Damas* (Harissa 1950).
[7] *PG* 108.741C.
[8] Abd-al-Malik (685-705).
[9] Al-Walid I (705-715); see *PG* 108.761B.

required the Christian public officials to keep their accounts in Arabic rather than in Greek—except for such of the more complicated as exceeded the potentialities of the Arabic language. This same caliph took several other measures against the Christians, such as taking away their permission to share the basilica of St. John the Baptist with the Moslems.[10] There is a strong tradition that John succeeded his father in office, and this would seem to be supported by the Acts of the Second Council of Nicea which compare him to St. Matthew the publican, saying that he considered the following of Christ to be of far more value than the treasures of Araby.[11] If the *Exposition and Declaration of Faith*[12] which has come down to us in an Arabic translation under the name of John of Damascus is authentic, then we have certain precious hints about his life which impugn the accuracy of the account given by the *Life*.[13] Thus in this profession of faith obviously made upon the occasion of his ordination to the priesthood he says about himself: 'Thou hast nourished me with spiritual milk, with the milk of Thy sacred words. Thou hast sustained me with the solid food of the body of our Lord Jesus Christ, Thy only-begotten and most holy Son, and hast intoxicated me with the sacred life-giving chalice which is His blood that He shed for the salvation of the world. Because, O Lord, Thou hast loved us and given Thy beloved only-begotten Son for our redemption, which He willingly undertook and without shrinking ... So truly, O Christ God didst Thou humble Thyself to bear

---

10 The Mosque of the Omayyads in Damascus. For this quasi-persecution, see also Nasrallah, *op. cit.* 73-74; but cf. C. Diehl and G. Marçais, *Le Monde Oriental de 395 à 1081* (Glotz, Histoire Générale, Moyen Age, III; Paris 1944) 338-339.
11 Mansi, *Sacrorum Conciliorum Nova et Amplissima Collectio* XIII, col. 357B.
12 Latin translation by Lequien in *PG* 95.417-438.
13 See Jugie, *op. cit.*, col. 694.

upon Thy shoulders the straying sheep that was I, and feed me in a verdant place and nourish me with the waters of right doctrine by the hands of Thy shepherds, who, once by Thyself fed, did forthwith feed Thy chosen and noble flock. And now, O Lord, by the hands of Thy pontiff Thou hast called me to minister to Thy children.'[14] Although Damascus was certainly one of the most verdant places in all Syria and Palestine, it is obvious enough that this 'verdant place' is of another kind: without any doubt, the Monastery of St. Sabbas. The 'shepherds' might well be the Bishop of Jerusalem and the priest of the monastery, but they are more probably the 'inspired Fathers'[15] teaching through their writings. We may conclude that, while St. John received at Damascus the normal religious training which any child of a devout Christian family would normally get—'Thou hast nourished me with the milk of Thy sacred words'—it was at Sabbas that he acquired his profound knowledge of the writings of the Fathers. The 'pontiff' referred to can only be John V of Jerusalem (706-735), whom John refers to in his letter, *On the Thrice Holy Hymn,* as one who 'in theology was in absolute agreeement with the holy Fathers' and of whom he himself was a devoted disciple.[16] In this, as in most professions of faith made upon the occasion of priestly ordination or episcopal consecration, there is the enumeration of the heresies to be anathematized. The iconoclastic heresy, however, is not mentioned at all, which is practically conclusive evidence of the fact that the ordination took place before the publication of Leo the Isaurian's first edict against the holy images in 726. Furthermore, there is nothing in the whole profession of faith which

---

14 *PG* 95.417-418.
15 The Damascene almost invariably refers to his predecessors the ecclesiastical writers as 'the inspired Fathers.'
16 *PG* 95.57AB.

the bishops of the East anathematized the impious [Leo].'[17] This was in 730 and it was about this time that the three *Apologies* were composed against the Iconoclasts in general and Leo in particular.[18] From the tone of these discourses and from what Theophanes says, it would seem that John was acting as the mouthpiece not only for John of Jerusalem but for all the bishops of the East beyond the territories of the Greek emperor. In them he spoke very plainly against secular interference in matters ecclesiastical. 'If an angel,' he says in the second *Apology,* 'if a king preach a gospel to you other than that which you have received, close your ears. For I still hesitate to say, as did the Apostle (Gal. 1:8), *let him be anathema,* as long as I see any possibility of resipiscence . . . It does not belong to kings to legislate for the Church . . . to kings belongs the maintenance of civil order, but the administration of the Church belongs to the shepherds and teachers.'[19] These *Apologetic Discourses* furnished such a complete defense of the veneration of sacred images based upon Scripture, tradition, and reason that in subsequent ages and down to the present day there has been no need to add to it. It is no wonder that John incurred the enmity and hatred of the Iconoclast emperors: Leo the Isaurian and his son and successor, Constantine V, Copronymus (741-775). Theophanes tells[20] how Constantine Copronymus called him, instead of Mansur, 'Manzer,' which in Hebrew means 'bastard,' and how he ordered him to be anathematized once a year. The Iconoclastic council, held in 753 in the Palace of the Hieria near Constantinople,[21] in anathematizing the three great opponents of the Iconoclasts —Germanus of Constantinople, George of Cyprus, and John

---

17 *PG* 108.824C.
18 Jugie, *op. cit.,* col. 705.
19 *PG* 94.1288C; 1296C.
20 *PG* 108.841B.

of Damascus—concludes thus: 'Anathema to Mansur, the man of evil name and Saracen sentiments! Anathema to Mansur, the worshiper of images and writer of falsehood! Anathema to Mansur, the insulter of Christ and traitor to the Empire. The Trinity has brought them down all three!'[22] John was by then already dead, but the impression which he had made upon the Iconoclasts was still very strong. The author of the *Life* and others have praised him for his courage in opposing the Iconoclastic emperors of Byzantium; others have indicated that John was quite safely beyond the reach of the Byzantine emperors and that it took no courage to oppose them. Nevertheless, it might be pointed out that the Damascene was living among Mohammedans, who themselves execrated every sort of picture or representation of any living creature, and that, furthermore, he wrote just as strongly against the Mohammedans as he did against the Iconoclasts.[23] We also know that Caliph Al-Walid II (743-744) ordered the tongue of Peter, Metropolitan of Damascus, to be cut out because of his preaching against the Moslems and the Manichaeans,[24] of which offense the Damascene was equally guilty. There is no doubt but that John of Damascus would have expressed himself just as forcefully against the enemies of the holy images, had he been living within the confines of the Greek Empire.

Theophanes refers to the Damascene as 'our holy father John, who has well been called Chrysorrhoas because of the golden grace of the Spirit that is reflected in his speech.'[25] Chrysorrhoas, 'golden-flowing,' was the name of the river

---

21 For this pseudo-council, see Hefele-Leclercq, *Histoire des Conciles* III.2 (Paris 1910) 693ff.
22 Mansi, *op. cit.* XIII, col. 356C.
23 Cf. in particular the chapter on the Ishmaelites, or Mohammedans, below p. 153ff.
24 *PG* 108.840B.
25 Ibid. 841A.

which irrigated the gardens of Damascus.[26] That this epithet was most fittingly applied to St. John has been well born out by his extant writings, particularly his sermons. The best example of his eloquence is to be found in the three homilies on the Dormition of our Lady. Internal evidence would indicate that these were delivered on the same day at the tomb of our Lady in Jerusalem, on the feast of her Dormition. They exemplify all that tradition has attributed to the Damascene—his eloquence, his theology, and his devotion to the Virgin Mother of God. In passing, it might be remarked that these three homilies contain most beautiful testimonies not only to the Assumption of our Lady, but to her Immaculate Conception and her universal mediation. There are others of his sermons extant, but unfortunately very few. What there is is sufficient to show that his traditional reputation as an eloquent, learned, and devout preacher is fully justified. They also show that his life was not spent entirely in the monastery, but that he was frequently called upon to serve in the churches of Jerusalem.

The monastery to which St. John retired from civil life was the famous Laura of St. Sabbas, the Great Laura, which is generallly known as Mar Saba. It is situated in a wild and inaccesible spot by the valley of the torrent of Cedron some ten miles southeast of Jerusalem. Here the anchorite St. Sabbas the Sanctified was living in solitude, when, in 483, a group of hermits attracted by his reputation for sanctity began to gather about him.[27] The group so grew that three years later the Bishop of Jerusalem, Salustius, ordained Sabbas a priest and appointed him abbot of the monastery. In his list of the monasteries in the Jerusalem dis-

---

26 Strabo XVI 2.16.
27 For the life of St. Sabbas the source is the *Life* by Cyril of Scythopolis. This has been published by E. Schwartz in *Texte and Untersuchungen* (Leipzig 1939).

trict restored by Justinian, Procopius names the monastery 'of the Lazians in the desert of Jerusalem.'[28] This was undoubtedly the monastery of St. Sabbas, who was still living at the time, and the restoration was probably not so much a restoration as a grandiose enlargement—the beginnings of the fortress-like structure which is the monastery today. The name 'of the Lazians' is accounted for by the large number of Armenian monks in St. Sabbas's community.[29] The Lazians were a people who lived just to the southeast of the Black Sea and who could easily be confused with their neighbors the Armenians. The monastery grew rapidly and soon became a very important center of Christian spirituality and learning. Among the monks were such figures as St. John the Silentiary, a bishop who retired to live as an unknown recluse at Mar Saba, where he died in the middle of the sixth century, and Cyril of Scythopolis, who came afterwards and composed the biographies of seven Palestinian monks including that of St. Sabbas.[30] Contemporaries or near contemporaries of St. John Damascene at Mar Saba were: St. Theodore of Edessa, an ascetic writer who later became Bishop of Edessa; St. Stephen the Wonderworker, who is said to have been the Damascene's nephew; and Stephen Melodus, who composed many canons and hymns and who also wrote the acts of the twenty Sabaite monks slain by the Saracens in the raid of 796, of which Stephen himself was an eye-witness. Also contemporary was Cosmas of Maiuma, called Melodus because of the beautiful ecclesiastical poetry which he composed. He became Bishop of Maiuma, the port of Gaza in southern Palestine, in 743.

---

28 Procopius, *Buildings* V 9.
29 The *Life* (ed. cit. 117) tells of the large number of Armenians in the community and how they celebrated the divine offices in their own language.
30 Schwartz, *op. cit.*

The *Life* calls him the adopted brother of St. John, but there is no evidence to support this contention; the most that can be said with any degree of certainty is that John and Cosmas were fellow monks and friends and that John composed his *Fount of Knowledge* at the request of Cosmas when this latter had become Bishop of Maiuma. In spite of many raids and massacres at the hands of marauding Bedouins (the last of which was as late as 1834), Mar Saba has survived to this day; one may still see the cell of St. John of Damascus where he lived and wrote for so many years and in or near which he was buried after his death.

It would seem that St. John spent the rest of his life at Mar Saba studying and writing and practicing the most strict asceticism. There were occasional short excursions to Jerusalem in the service of the Church, as when he preached the homilies on the Dormition of Mary. He was certainly alive in 743, when Cosmas was made Bishop of Maiuma, because, as has been noted, the *Fount of Knowledge* is dedicated to Cosmas as bishop. He was no longer living by 753, as the past tense used in the anathema of the iconoclastic council of the Hieria shows. Leontius, a Sabaite monk, in his life of Stephen the Wonderworker written about the beginning of the ninth century says that Stephen was brought to the monastery by his uncle, St. John of Damascus, in 735 and was under his guidance for fifteen years;[31] this would mean until 749 or 750, and may imply that John died at that time. The generally accepted date of his death is December 4, 749.[32] He was buried in the monastery. The relics were still there in the twelfth century, but by the fourteenth they had been translated to Constantinople.[33] As to the date

---

31 *Acta Sanctorum* (Bollandist) 30 (Julii Tom. III) 580C.
32 S. Vailhé, in *Echos d'Orient* (1906) 28-30.
33 *PG* 94.485-486 (note); Nasrallah, *op. cit.* 128-129.

of the Damascene's birth, nothing is known. Tradition, however, has it that he lived to old age and in the second *Homily on the Dormition* he refers to himself as having already arrived at the winter of his life,[34] so it may be assumed that he lived past seventy. If he reached seventy-five, then he would have been born in 674.

Besides the *Fount of Knowledge,* there are a great many other writings which bear the name of St. John of Damascus. Although many are of doubtful authenticity or definitely spurious, the number of extant writings attributed to him which are certainly authentic is considerable. Among the most important, after the *Fount of Knowledge,* are the three *Apologetic Discourses against the Attackers of the Holy Images* (*PG* 94.1231-1420). Internal evidence shows the first to have been written before 729, and the second and third not earlier than 729 or later than 730. These contain a sound dogmatic defense of the veneration of the holy images, each concluding with an impressive series of patristic testimonies. The last two are to some extent repetitions of the first. Besides these apologies against the Iconoclasts, the Damascene found it necessary to write other works against still other heresies. Monophysism, which had been suppressed under the imperial rule, was now free to flourish in Syria under the Arabs. The Monophysites of the time were known by several names: Jacobites, after the founder of their hierarchy;[35] Severians, from their great theologian;[36] and Acephali, or the headless, from the name of an originally extreme but very small group, which by the eighth century had become the dominating Monophysite party. The Nestorians had long been safely established in Persia, well out

---

34 See Nasrallah, *op. cit.* 126-127, and *PG* 96.724A.
35 James Baradeceus, who was clandestinely consecrated in 543 through the connivance of the Empress Theodora.

of the reach of the Greek emperors. Now, with the Arabs in Syria and Palestine, there was nothing to prevent them from penetrating into these former imperial territories. In the mountains of northern Syria there were still some Monothelites.[37] Finally, a dangerous revival of Manichaeism existed in Armenia, and these Neo-Manichaeans, known in history as Paulicians, were infiltrating all Asia Minor and the East. And there were always the Mohammedans and Jews to be contended with. Against these various sects the Damascene composed a number of works. The short *Disputation with a Manichaean* (*PG* 96.1319-1336) and the much longer *Dialogue against the Manichaeans* (*PG* 94.1505-1584) were directed against the Paulicians. Among other things they contain important discussions on the nature of God, the problem of evil, and the conciliation of God's foreknowledge with the freedom of the human will. Both are in the popular dialogue form. There also are two works against the Nestorians. The first is *A Most Exact Dissertation against the Heresy of the Nestorians* (*PG* 95.187-224), a very clear discussion and proof of the Catholic doctrine of the duality of natures and unity of person in Christ, based upon Scripture and the Creed. The second, *On the Faith against the Nestorians,* has only fairly recently been brought to light and published.[38] Against the Monophysites there is *On the Composite Nature against the Acephali* (*PG* 95.111-125), which shows how in Christ there is not one composite nature but one person in two natures. Also against the Monophysites is

---

36 Severus, Monophysite Patriarch of Antioch (512-518).
37 In the documents of the time these are frequently referred to as Maronites, but this does not mean that the Maronite Church or nation as a whole was tainted with this heresy. On the contrary, the perpetual orthodoxy of the Maronites is and always has been traditional.
38 F. Diekamp, in *Theol. Quartalschrift* (1901) 555-599.

the *Letter on the Thrice Holy Hymn* (*PG* 9.21-61), protesting the addition which the Monophysites had made to the Trisagion;[39] and the *Tome against the Jacobites* (*PG* 94.1435-1502), a long letter written by John Damascene in the name of Peter, Bishop of Damascus, to a certain Jacobite bishop in view of his conversion. It contains a clear demonstration of the truth of the Catholic doctrine of the two distinct natures in Christ and the absurdity of the Monophysite doctrine of one nature after the union. *On the Two Wills and Operations* (*PG* 95.127-186) is an outstanding work against the Monothelites, those who while admitting two natures in Christ, would not admit more than one will and operation; it is a concise and lucid discussion of person and nature and of the consequences of two natures in one person all upon purely philosophical grounds but with confirmation from Scripture. Finally, there is the *Disputation between a Saracen and a Christian* (*PG* 96.1335-1348), which is principally concerned with the refutation of fatalism and the defense of the doctrine of the Incarnation. There is another recension of this (*PG* 94.1585-1598) which is much shorter and of which the first may well be a revision made by the author himself.[40] Before leaving the works of a polemical nature it is necessary to mention two short but interesting fragments: *On Dragons* and *On Witches* (*PG* 94.1599-1604), which probably were a part of some more extensive work against the popular superstitions of the Saracens and the Jews. In these he appeals in a very natural way to ordinary common sense.

Dogmatic writings besides the *Fount of Knowledge* include an *Elementary Introduction to Dogma* (*PG* 95.99-112),

---

39 To 'Holy God, Holy Strong, Holy Immortal, have mercy on us' the Monophysites added 'who wast crucified for us,' thus applying the Trisagion not to the Trinity but to the Second Person alone.

40 For an English translation see *Moslem World* (July 1935) 266-273.

ten short chapters on such terms as *substance, nature, hypostasis, genus, species,* and the like. It much resembles the *Dialectica,* or *Philosophical Chapters,* of the *Fount of Knowledge,* but in an abridged and imperfect form. According to its full title it was dictated to one of John's disciples. The *Libellus on the Right Opinion* (*PG* 94.1421-1432) is a profession of faith composed at the request of Peter of Damascus for a Monothelite bishop who was returning to orthodoxy. Particular stress is laid upon the twofold nature and operation in Christ. The *Exposition and Profession of Faith* (*PG* 95.417-438) has come down to us only in an Arabic translation, of which Migne reproduces the Latin version given in Lequien's edition of the *Works*. The Arabic translation was made by a certain Anthony who was superior of the Monastery of St. Simeon Stylites near Antioch sometime during the twelfth century and who translated many of the Damascene's works into Arabic.[41] The authenticity of the *Exposition* has been questioned, but there seems to be no good reason for doubt. Internal evidence alone would seem to offer sufficient proof of the genuineness of its authorship. If it is genuine, then it is the profession of faith made by John of Damascus upon the occasion of his ordination to the priesthood. Its importance for determining the chronology of the Damascene's life has already been discussed. *On the Holy Trinity* (*PG* 95.9-18) is a concise summary of the Damascene's teaching on the Trinity, including that of the procession of the Holy Ghost from the Father through the Son. It is given in question and answer form.

Of a moral rather than of a dogmatic nature is the work which has come down to us in two recensions under the title of *Sacred Parallels*.[42] This was originally an immense and

---
[41] Graf, *op. cit.* II 41-45
[42] *PG* 95.1041-1588 and 96.9-442 give the longer recension; the shorter known as the *Parallela Rupefucaldina,* is in *PG* 96.441-544.

carefully arranged and indexed collection of scriptural and patristic texts illustrating almost every aspect of Christian moral and ascetic teaching. It may well have been composed as a moral companion to the dogmatic *Fount of Knowledge.* The patristic texts are drawn from almost all the Greek Fathers, both ante- and post-Nicene. Even the two great Jews, Philo and Josephus, are utilized. The two recensions which we have of this work do not represent the original work of the Damascene, but only that of compilers who have drawn upon the original as they saw fit; however, even in its present reduced and mutilated form, the work still has great practical value. Fortunately, we have the original introduction (*PG* 95.1041-1044) and from this we know the original plan of the whole work. It was divided into three books, of which the first treated of God, One and Triune; the second, of man and the human state; and the third, of the virtues and vices. The title given by the author himself was *Sacred Things,* that is, Sacred Sayings, but because of manner of presenting the virtues in Book 3, each with its parallel vice, the work came to be known as *Sacred Parallels.* Another moral work is the *Eight Spirits of Evil* (*PG* 95.79-84) which is addressed to monks and treats of the eight vices which so particularly beset them and with which the Greek ascetic writers have always been so particularly preoccupied. *The Virtues and Vices of the Soul and Body* (*PG* 95.85-98) seems to be an enlargement of the preceding work. It may be the result of the Damascene's practice of revising his works in later life. Still another work of a moral nature is the *Holy Fasts* (*PG* 95.63-78), written to a brother monk on the subject of the keeping of the Lenten fast.

The only extant exegetical work of John is an extensive commentary on the Pauline epistles, entitled *Chosen Selections from the Universal Commentary of John Chrysostom* (*PG*

95.439-1034). As its title indicates, the material for this is drawn principally from the homilies of St. John Chrysostom and, consequently, has little to offer which is the author's own.

Far more important than the moral and exegetical writings are his homilies. There are extant thirteen homilies which are attributed to him, but of these only nine are certainly authentic. The one authentic *Homily on the Nativity of Our Lady* (*PG* 96.661-680) and the three *Homilies on the Dormition* (*PG* 96.697-762) give most precious testimonies on the fundamental points of Mariological doctrine. They alone would merit for the Damascene the title of Doctor of Mary. On our Lord there are two authentic homilies, on the Transfiguration (*PG* 96.545-576) and on Holy Saturday (*PG* 96.601-644). In both of these the Damascene appears at his best as an eloquent preacher and profound theologian. The first, for instance, abounds in such happy turns of phrase as 'He had no father on earth who had no mother in heaven' and 'solitude is the mother of prayer.'[43] Of Peter it says: 'Not over tabernacles did the Lord appoint thee head, but over the universal Church.'[44] In the second he pauses, as it were, between the Passion and the Resurrection to review the whole field of theology: the Trinity, the Creation, the Fall, the Incarnation, and the Redemption. Of the other three definitely authentic homilies, two are encomia of saints, on St. John Chrysostom (*PG* 96.761-782) and on St. Barbara (*PG* 96.781-814), while the third is on the withered fig tree (*PG* 96.575-588). John of Damascus was a preacher of the first order and, although his style is at times more effusive and exalted, he may be said to rank with the great Chrysostom. His sermons have not only great literary value, but dogmatic as well. In them we find under a different form the same

---
43 *PG* 96.556C, 561A.
44 *Ibid.* 569D.

teachings on the Trinity, the Incarnation, and the Virgin Mother of God as we find in the more sober and didactic *Fount of Knowledge*.

The Damescene has been called 'golden-flowing' because of the elegance and eloquent beauty of his writings. The epithet is particularly suitable to him as the composer of some of the finest Greek liturgical poetry. This is to be found scattered through the various liturgical books of the Byzantine rite; a small portion has been reproduced in Migne (*PG* 96. 817-856).[45] The Damascene was not the originator of Greek liturgical poetry, but he is one of its greatest exponents. Tradition has attributed to him the composition of the entire *Oktoikhos*, or Book of the Eight Tones, which is an immense collection containing the ordinary office of the Byzantine rite from the end of the Easter season to the beginning of Lent. He is probably not responsible for the entire *Oktoikhos*, but there is no doubt that he composed a large part of it. There are also many hymns and canons[46] which can be definitely attributed to him. Some of these hymns are *metric*, that is, with the meter based upon quantity according to the old classical style; others have the meter based upon accent, and are called *rhythmic*.[47]

There are many other writings which have been attributed to the Damascene, of which some are doubtful and some definitely spurious. Most of these are in Migne (*PG* 94-96).

---

45 A metrical English translation of some of the Damascene's poetry is in John Mason Neale, *Hymns of the Eastern Church* (London 1882) 28-61. Naturally, this does not do justice to the originals. A more literal version of some specimens appears in Adrian Fortescue, *The Greek Fathers* (London 1908) 234-239.

46 The *canon* is a form of Greek liturgical poem based upon the nine scriptural odes, or canticles, of the Old and New Testaments, and celebrating some mystery, our Lady, or one of the saints.. They are sung at lauds as commemorations.

47 An example of a rhythmic hymn is that for Easter (*PG* 96.839-844); of a metric, that for Epiphany (*PG* 96.825-832).

There is no need to mention any except, perhaps, the *Life of Barlaam and Joasaph* (*PG* 96.859-1246), which has been traditionally ascribed to John of Damascus. The legend in its present form was certainly composed at the Monastery of St. Sabbas by a monk named John. It cannot be proved that this John was or was not the Damascene, so there is no reason why we should not continue to consider the Damascene as the author of this edifying christianized version of the story of Buddha.

The *Fount of Knowledge* (*PG* 94.521-1228) is one of the last works of John of Damascus and surely his greatest. It was written at the request of his good friend and former fellow monk at Mar Saba, Cosmas of Maiuma. Cosmas had been made Bishop of Maiuma in 743 and consequently, since the work is dedicated to him as bishop, it could not have been composed before 743. In his introduction the author explains what he intends to do: first, to give the best that Greek philosophy has had to offer; then, to describe the various aberrations from the truth during the course of the world's history, 'so that by recognizing the lie we may more closely follow the truth'; finally, to set forth the truth itself as contained in Scripture and tradition. 'I shall add nothing of my own,' he adds, 'but shall gather together those things which have been worked out by the most eminent teachers and make a compendium of them.'[48] Thus, he intended the entire work to consist of three parts: a philosophical introduction, an historical introduction, and an exposition of traditional Catholic teaching. Most authorities[49] are of the opinion that the Damascene succeeded quite well

---
48 *PG* 94.524C, 525A.
49 For example, K. Krumbacher, *Geschichte der byzantinischen Litteratur* (2nd ed., Munich 1897) 70; J. Tixeront, *Histoire des dogmes* III (8th ed., Paris 1928) 485.

in keeping his promise to add nothing of his own, but this is not entirely true. The *Fount of Knowledge* not only contains much that is original and a fresh viewpoint on many things, but it is in itself something new. It is the first real *Summa Theologica*.[50] Even the philosophical introduction is new, being the first attempt to present a complete manual of philosophy to serve as a basis for the study of Christian theology. The whole work is not a mere compilation; it is a new synthesis. It may be said, then, that although John of Damascus was undoubtedly sincere in his promise to add nothing of his own, he could not help injecting so much of himself as to be visible on almost every page.

The division of the *Fount of Knowledge* is as follows. First there is a short introduction to the entire work addressed to Cosmas of Maiuma. Then follows the philosophical introduction, entitled *Philosophical Chapters;* the historical introduction, called *On Heresies in Epitome;* finally, the main part of the work, of which the full title is *An Exact Exposition of the Orthodox Faith.*

In the West, the *Philosophical Chapters* (*PG* 94.525-676) are commonly called the *Dialectica* and are always so cited. This part contains sixty-eight chapters followed by an *Explanation of Expressions*. This last is probably the work of the Damascene—that is to say, he probably collected the various explanations—but it is entirely out of place, because the terms explained are not philosophical at all, but refer to purely natural phenomena such as the elements, the seasons, meteors, and so forth. It would be much more logically placed, were it inserted in Book 2 of the *Orthodox Faith* just after Chapter 11, that is, after the treatment of inanimate creation. In the *Philosophical Chapters* there is

---

50 This seems to have been forgotten by many Western theologians, e.g., P. Glorieux in 'Sommes Théologiques,' *DTC* XIV, cols. 2341ff., and W. Turner, 'Summae,' *Catholic Encyclopedia* XIV 333-334.

a collection of explanations of dialectical terms, but this appears in Chapter 65.

In accordance with his avowed intention of 'setting forth the best contributions of the philosophers of the Greeks,'[51] the author devotes himself in this philosophical part to a careful treatment of the Five Universals and Ten Categories of the Aristotelian system. His sources for what is Aristotelian are principally Porphyry's *Introduction to the Categories of Aristotle*[52] and Ammonius Hermeae, *Commentary on the Isagoge of Porphyry*. Actually, of the *Philosophical Chapters*, 10, 12-14, and 18-27 are taken directly from Porphyry with but little modification; 3, 5, 6, and 8 are taken from Ammonius' *Commentary on the Isagoge*. A few other chapters depend to some extent upon this work of Ammonius, but there are still others which may have drawn upon another work of Ammonius, his own *Commentary on the Categories of Aristotle*. The chapters depending upon Porphyry and Ammonius are chiefly concerned with the Five Universals and the dialectic method. But when it comes to the Categories themselves and such concepts as *prior, simultaneous, motion, having,* and the like, there is no dependence upon these two commentators. It is even probable that the Damascene used the *Categories* of Aristotle directly for these. At least, the first part of Chapter 62 reproduces *Categories* 15 almost verbatim.

All of the *Philosophical Chapters*, however, do not depend upon Aristotle and his commentators. Many of them are concerned with philosophical terms which had come to acquire very special meanings in theology and terms which had been used in various senses—terms which had played an important part in the development of the Christian

---
51 *PG* 94.524C.
52 Commonly cited as the *Isagoge*.

dogmatic tradition. Such are *hypostasis, person, enhypostaton, union, nature,* and so on. Here the source is not Aristotle and his commentators, but Christian tradition, which John calls 'the holy Fathers.' These, although not cited by name, are the Greek Fathers from Athanasius the Great to Anastasius the Sinaite. Naturally, he has presented nothing absolutely new here; what he has done is to give a concise and clear explanation of just what the Greek theological writers mean when they use certain fundamental but controverted terms. For instance, the term *enhypostaton* had long been used by the Greek theologians. At first it was used as meaning simply something that had existed as opposed to that which did not, but by the time of Leontius of Byzance it had acquired a very special meaning. Leontius defines it as something between the accident and the hypostasis. It is a substance which does not subsist in itself.[53] The Damascene not only explains the meaning given the term by Leontius, doing so even more clearly than Leontius had done, but he gives all the other shades of meaning, too.[54]

In the *Philosophical Chapters,* or *Dialectica,* we have the first example of a manual of philosophy especially composed as an aid to the study of theology. It is more than a curiosity. Useful in its own time and useful in the succeeding centuries, it has remained to the present day indispensable for a proper understanding of Greek theology. It is also interesting as showing to what extent Aristotle was known and used by the eight-century Christians under Arab rule and suggesting how Aristotle may have first been introduced to the Arabs. John of Damascus was not the first to put Aristotelian dialectic to the service of Christian theology. The first, or at least the one who is generally considered to have been the

---
53 Leontius, *Against the Nestorians and Eutychians* I (PG 86.1277D).
54 *Dialectica* 44.

first, was Leontius of Byzance, the Damascene's predecessor by two centuries.[55] Leontius, however, merely used Aristotelian dialectic. He did not compose any special manual devoted to philosophy and dialectic alone.

The *Philosophical Chapters* exist in two recensions, a longer and a shorter. It is only in Chapters 6 and 9-14 that the longer differs radically from the shorter. The shorter is more concise and is apparently the result of a revision made by the author himself. The *Life* tells us that he put much effort into going over and revising the books which he had written.[56] Both recensions are given by Lequien, whose text has been reproduced by Migne and serves as basis for the present translation.

The full title of the second part of the *Fount of Knowledge* is *Heresies in Epitome: How They Began and Whence They Drew Their Origin* (*PG* 94.677.780). It is usually cited as *Heresies* or *De haeresibus*. This part contains notices of varying length on 103 heresies, followed by an epilogue in the form of a profession of faith. The first eighty are taken verbatim from the *Panarion* of St. Epiphanius.[57] They are not, however, from the main text of the *Panarion,* but from the summaries which precede each of its seven parts and serve as tables of contents. The last notice taken from St. Epiphanius is that on the Massalians, or Euchites. To this short notice the Damascene has added from another source considerable material on the beliefs and practices of this sect. This is now one of the principal sources for our knowledge of the Massalians. He also added a chapter on

---

[55] Leontius (d. 543) has been called the first Scholastic. It is he who definitely clarified the concepts of nature and hypostasis. The Damascene owes much to him.

[56] *PG* 94.484B.

[57] The *Panarion,* or *Medicine Chest of Remedies against Eighty Heresies,* is in Migne (*PG* 41-42). A better edition is that of F. Oehler in *Corpus Haereseologicum* II-III (Berlin 1859-61).

the same sect taken from the *Ecclesiastical History* of Theodoret.[58] The next twenty notices, 81-100, begin with the Nestorians and cover the heresies from the time of Emperor Marcian (450-457) on. Lequien, in his introductory note to the *Heresies,* repeats a note which he found in one of the manuscripts to the effect that these twenty notices have been taken from Theodoret, Timothy of Constantinople, Sophronius of Jerusalem, and Leontius of Byzance.[59] Almost all subsequent writers on the subject have repeated this statement, but there is apparently no foundation for it. There is no evidence to show that any of the extant writings of those authors mentioned by Lequien has been utilized at all. Theodoret wrote a Compendium of *Heresies* (*PG* 83. 335-556) which ends with the heresies of Nestorius and Eutyches. These heresies are the only two which the *Compendium* and the *Heresies* have in common and even a cursory examination will show that there is absolutely no interdependence. Under the name of Timothy of Constantinople there has come down a treatise on *The Reception of Heretics* (*PG* 86.11-68) in which a number of the twenty heresies in question are described, but here again there is no sign of interdependence. The same is true of the *Synodic Letter* of Sophronius of Jerusalem (*PG* 87.3147-3200) and *On Sects* by Leontius of Byzance (*PG* 86.1193-1268), which are the only two works of these authors which could have any possible bearing upon the matter. However, internal evidence indicates that these twenty notices are not the work of John of Damascus. In all probability they were taken from some work of an author who as yet remains unknown. At any rate, they are of value to us as containing information on a number of obscure sects about which very little or

---

58 4.10 (*PG* 82.1141-1145).
59 *PG* 94.677-678.

nothing would otherwise be known. The even number of one hundred suggests that this unknown work had also included the eighty heresies from the *Panarion,* so that it was its author and not the Damascene who was the original borrower from Epiphanius.[60] It would seem, then, that all the Damascene is responsible for in the first hundred heresies is the addition of material on the Massalians to Heresy 80 and the inclusion of two important fragments of the *Arbiter* of John Philoponus in Heresy 83.[61] These fragments of the *Arbiter* are all that exists of the original Greek text, although the whole work is extant in a Syriac translation.

The only really original part of the *Heresies* is to be found in the last three heresies, 101-103: the Ishmaelites, or Mohammedans; the Christianocategori, or Iconoclasts; and the Aposchistae, a sect which rejected the sacraments and the priesthood, and for which this is our only source of information. Most important is the relatively long (four and one half columns of text in Migne) notice on the Mohammedans. Here the Damascene shows a thorough knowledge of the Koran, which he cites verbatim, and of the Hadith, or Moslem tradition. He bases his argument against Islam on the lack of authority of Mohammed, the inconsistency of the Mohammedans' beliefs and traditions, and their unnatural attitude toward women.

All in all *On Heresies in Epitome* deserves more attention than is usually granted. If one excepts the part borrowed from Epiphanius, which amounts to less than half of the whole text, we have in the *Heresies* much that is new, much

---

60 The 'century,' or group of one hundred sentences or chapters, was a popular literary form with Eastern ecclesiastical writers. It was first used by Evagrius Ponticus (d. 398). It was also used by St. Maximus the Confessor (d. 662). The third part of the *Fount of Knowledge* is itself a 'century' of dogmatic chapters.
61 See below, pp. 141-148.

that is original, and a great deal of information which otherwise we should not have had. Including the part taken from Epiphanius, the whole work represents the most complete listing of heresies that had been made up to the time.

The most important and best known part of the *Fount of Knowledge* is the *Exact Exposition of the Orthodox Faith* (*PG* 94.789-1228), which is usually cited as *De fide orthodoxa*. This consists of one hundred dogmatic chapters, which in the West are customarily divided into four books: Chapters 1-14; 15-44; 45-73; and 74-100. This division was probably made originally to correspond with that of the *Sentences* of Peter Lombard into four books. Book 1 of *The Orthodox Faith* treats of God in unity and trinity (*De Deo uno et trino*). The second treats of God's creation, both invisible and visible, with special attention given to man and his faculties. A large part of this book is no more than a presentation of the natural science of the time and for that reason is interesting only as a curiosity. However, the parts devoted to angels, providence, foreknowledge, and predestination are of considerable dogmatic importance. To a certain extent, Book 2 corresponds to the dogmatic tract *De Deo creante et elevante*. Book 3 is devoted entirely to Christology (*De Verbo Incarnato*). The division between Book 3 and 4 is purely arbitrary, for Chapters 1-8 of Book 4 are merely a continuation of the Christology of the third. The rest of Book 4 considers faith, baptism, the Eucharist, the genealogy of our Lord and our Lady, the veneration of saints and their relics, the cult of the holy images, and a number of other disparate subjects. It concludes with a chapter on the Resurrection. As can be seen, the general order of the work is that of the Nicene Creed, although two important articles have been omitted—those on the Holy Ghost and the Church. The Holy Ghost is given particular treatment in chapters 7-8 of

Book 1, in connection with the Holy Trinity, but the Church is entirely omitted. Indeed, the Church is mentioned only once in the entire work.[62] The whole is a surprisingly successful synthesis of traditional Catholic teaching as handed down by the Greek Fathers and the ecumenical councils. It represents an attempt to give a complete dogmatic exposition of the Catholic faith. Of course, it is not the first such attempt. There were the *De Principiis* of Origen and the *Catechetical Discourse* of Gregory of Nyssa; even the *Catecheses* of Cyril of Jerusalem might be included. The only other previous attempt at a dogmatic summa was that of Theodoret. To the four books of his *Compendium of the Evil Fictions of the Heretics* Theodoret added a fifth book entitled *Compendium of Divine Teachings*. It covers much the same ground as *The Orthodox Faith* and in much the same order. In fact, the whole *Compendium of Theodoret* with its dogmatic summa in Book 5 and its historical introduction on heresies in Books 1-4 may well have served as a model for the *Fount of Knowledge,* or at least have suggested it. However, all these works of the Damascene's predecessors were limited by the state of the theological development of their times. Furthermore, none of them pretended to the completeness of *The Orthodox Faith*. And their authors, great theologians though they were, did not possess the peculiar quality that made the Damascene such an apt synthesist. John Damascene's talent for synthesizing, together with his clear understanding of the great Christological controversies and his extensive acquaintance with the writings of the Greek Fathers made him eminently fit for the task which he had set for himself. Nevertheless, his acquaintance with the Fathers was apparently limited to the Greeks, because the only Western

---

62 4.10, where the author condemns as an infidel anyone 'who does not believe according to the tradition of the Catholic Church.'

writing which he uses is the letter of Pope St. Leo the Great to Flavian of Constantinople. This is the letter commonly known as the *Tome of Leo*, which was read at the Council of Chalcedon and acclaimed by the Fathers of the Council as expressing the traditional teachings of the Church on the Incarnation.[63] His chief authority, whom he frequently cites by name, is Gregory of Nazianzus. He depends particularly upon this theologian for the doctrine of God and the Trinity, although for the divine nature he draws considerably upon the Pseudo-Dionysius. In Book 1 he also uses to some extent the writings of Basil the Great, Cyril of Alexandria, and Athanasius. In Book 2 he depends for the creation much upon all three Cappadocians; and for the nature of man, upon Nemesius.[64] For Christology, in Book 3 and the first part of Book 4, besides Gregory of Nazianzus he principally utilizes his more immediate predecessors: Leontius of Byzance (d. 543), Maximus the Confessor (d. 662), and Anastasius the Sinaite (d. 700); but he also uses Basil the Great, Gregory of Nyssa, Cyril of Alexandria, Athanasius, John Chrysostom, and others. For the various other questions treated in Book 4 his main sources are the three Cappadocians and Cyril of Jerusalem. Conspicuously absent from *The Orthodox Faith* are the ante-Nicene writers. None seems to be used directly and only Origen is mentioned by name, but then only to be attacked. This does not mean that the Damascene was not acquainted with the earlier writers, because he certainly made abundant use of their writings in compiling the *Sacred Parallels*.

In spite of the imposing list of authorities used by St. John of Damascus for *The Orthodox Faith*—those already men-

---
63 2nd Session. See Mansi, *op. cit.* VI, col. 972AB.
64 Bishop of Emesa in the last half of the fourth century and known only for his remarkable treatise, *The Nature of Man* (PG 40.504-817).

tioned plus many more—he is much more than a simple compiler. *The Orthodox Faith* is, as has already been pointed out, not a compilation, but a synthesis, of Greek theology. It is a statement in very clear language of the teaching of the Greek Fathers in its most developed form. Of course, there is nothing new or original in the matter of doctrine, but there is something original in the treatment and in the clarity of this treatment. For instance, the chapters on psychology, providence, predestination, the divine Maternity, the Eucharist, and the cult of saints and sacred images show a fresh point of view clearly stated in a language that anyone can understand. This is also noticeable throughout the entire treatment of Christology, which makes for an extraordinarily complete and understandable exposition of the doctrine of the Incarnation. Naturally, the work is not perfect. There are weak spots: the proofs for the existence of God, for example, and the doctrine of the Holy Ghost. There are also many lacunae, as to the Church, grace, sacramental theology, and eschatology. These lacunae, however, are not entirely due to any failing on the part of the Damascene, for they are to a great extent the lacunae of Greek theology itself. Whatever defects *The Orthodox Faith* may have, it still remains an incomparable *summa* of theology and an indispensable aid to the study of the Greek Christian tradition.[65] And the *Fount of Knowledge* as a whole remains a fitting monument and landmark to mark the close of the patristic age, of which it is one of the greatest single achievements.

The earliest translations of the *Fount of Knowledge* were made in the East. The first was that of the *Dialectica* and *The Orthodox Faith* into Old Slavonic by John, Exarch of Bul-

---

65 For the theology of the Damascene see Jugie, *op. cit.*, col. 708-748; Tixeront, *op. cit.* III 484-513; B. Tatakis, *La philosophie byzantine* (Paris 1949) 105-126; and G. Florovsky, *The Byzantine Fathers* (Paris 1933), 228-254.

garia in the time of the Tsar Simeon, probably made at some time in the early part of the tenth century. The next translation of these same divisions was into Arabic by Anthony, superior of the Monastery of St. Simeon Stylites near Antioch, in the second half of the tenth century. The only other translations made in the East were a series of Russian translations which have appeared comparatively recently. Prince Andrew Kurbsky (d. 1583) made a new translation into Church Slavonic of the two. Another translation of *The Orthodox Faith* was made into Church Slavonic by the learned Kievan monk, Epiphanius Slavinetzky (d. 1676), and still another in the next century (Moscow 1765-81) by Ambrose (Zertis-Kamensky), Archbishop of Moscow. Then came a Russian translation published by the Moscow Theological Academy under the direction of P. S. Delitzyn (Moscow 1840). In 1877, a new edition of the Old Slavonic version of John the Exarch was brought out at Moscow by A. N. Popov. Finally, a Russian translation of *The Orthodox Faith* was published at Moscow in 1894 by Alexander Bronzov. In 1913 the publication of a new translation of the *Works* was started by the St. Petersburg Theological Academy. Only the first volume appeared, presumably containing the *Fount of Knowledge*.

In the West, a long series of Latin translations began with a twelfth-century Latin version of Chapters 1-8 of Book 3 of *The Orthodox Faith*. This was made in Hungary (*c.* 1134-1138) by a monk named Cerbanus. It was recently published by R. L. Szigeti (Budapest 1940). The entire *Orthodox Faith* was translated at the request of Pope Eugene III into Latin (*c.* 1148-1150) by Burgundio, a judge in Pisa. Burgundio may also be responsible for an abbreviated Latin version of the *Dialectica,* which was included with most of the early Latin editions of *The Orthodox Faith*. Another

Latin translation of these was made by Robert Grosseteste, Bishop of Lincoln (1235-1253). The next in chronological order was by a Carmelite, J. B. Panetius (d. 1497). During the sixteenth century two more appeared: the first of *The Orthodox Faith,* by Jacques Lefèvre d'Etaples (Paris 1507); the second of the *Fount of Knowledge* by Jacques de Billy O.S.B. (Paris 1577). In the seventeenth century, François Combefis, O. P., produced another version of *The Fount of Knowledge* in Latin (Paris 1672). Finally, there appeared at Paris in 1712 a completely new Latin translation of the *Fount of Knowledge* made by the learned Michel Lequien, O. P. This accompanied his new critical edition of the Greek text and is by far the best of any of the Latin translations.

After the Lequien version no more Latin translations appeared, but a number of translations of the *Fount of Knowledge* or parts of it have been made into several modern languages. The Russian translations have already been mentioned. An English one of *The Orthodox Faith* by S. D. F. Salmond was published in the Oxford edition of the *Nicene and Post Nicene Fathers,* 2nd ser., 9 (Oxford 1899), and a German by D. Stiefenhofer, *Bibliotek der Kirchenväter* 44 (Munich 1923). Excerpts from St. John of Damascus have been published in French in V. Ermoni's *Saint Jean Damascène* (Collection La Pensée Chrétienne, Paris 1904). And an English translation of the chapter on the Mohammedans (*Heresies* 101) by J. W. Voorhis appeared in *Moslem World* (October 1934) 391-398. At the present time a new critical edition of the Greek text is being worked upon at the Byzantine Institute of the Benedictine Abbey of Scheyern in Bavaria.

The Greek text of Lequien is the best available at the present time. For this he utilized not only the work of his predecessors, but twenty-four of the best manuscripts then available to him. This text, together with Lequien's Latin version, is reproduced in Migne (*PG* 94.521-1228), but because of some printer's omissions it must be controlled by the original Paris edition of the text. For the present translation the Migne text has been used, emendated, where necessary, from the Paris edition. Biblical citations are made from the Challoner revision of the Rheims-Douay version, with such changes and variations as have been occasionally necessary to make the English correspond with the Greek of the Damascene's text.

For valuable criticism and suggestions I wish to express my thanks to Rev. Francis X. Meehan and Rev. J. Joseph Ryan of the faculty of St. John's Seminary, Boston, Mass., and to Rev. Frederick J. Adelmann, S. J., of the faculty of the Graduate School of Boston College.

SELECT BIBLIOGRAPHY

Text:

Michel Lequien, ed., *Sancti Joannis Damasceni Opera omnia quae extant* (Paris 1712) I. (This is reproduced in Migne, *Patrologia Graeca* 94.)

Studies:

O. Bardenhewer, *Geschichte der altkirchlichen Literatur* V (Freiburg im Briesgau 1932).
G. Graf, *Geschichte der christlichen arabischen Literatur* I (Vatican City 1944).
G. Florovsky, *The Byzantine Fathers* (Paris 1933). (In Russian.)
M. Jugie, 'Jean Damascène,' *Dictionnaire de Théologie Catholique* VIII (Paris 1923) 693-751.
K. Krumbacher, *Geschichte der byzantinischen Litteratur* (2nd ed., Munich 1897).
J. Lupton, 'Joannes Damascenus,' *Dictionary of Christian Biography* III (London 1882) 409-423.
J. Nasrallah, *Saint Jean de Damas* (Harissa, Lebanon 1950).
B. Tatakis, *La Philosophie Byzantine* (Paris 1949).
J. Tixeront, *Histoires des Dogmes* III (8th ed., Paris 1928).

CONTENTS

INTRODUCTION v

THE FOUNT OF KNOWLEDGE

Preface 3
The Philosophical Chapters
  1 On Knowledge 7
  2 What the Purpose of This Work Is 10
  3 On Philosophy 11
  4 On Being, Substance, and Accident 13
  5 On Terms 15
  6 On Division 20
  7 On That Which Is by Nature Prior 25
  8 On Definition 26
  9 On Genus 29
 10 On Species 31
 11 On Individual 41
 12 On Difference 41
 13 On Accident 43
 14 On Property 44
 15 On Predicates 45
 16 On Univocal and Equivocal Predication 46
 17 On the Predication of the Essence of a Thing and on That of Its Sort 48
 18 What the Five Terms Have in Common and in What They Differ 49

19	What Genus and Difference Have in Common and in What They Differ	50
20	What Genus and Species Have in Common and in What They Differ	50
21	What Genus and Property Have in Common and in What They Differ	51
22	What Genus and Accident Have in Common and in What They Differ	51
23	What Difference and Species Have in Common and in What They Differ	52
24	What Difference and Property Have in Common and in What They Differ	52
25	What Difference and Accident Have in Common and in What They Differ	52
26	What Species and Property Have in Common and in What They Differ	53
27	What Species and Accident Have in Common and in What They Differ	54
28	What Property and Inseparable Accident Have in Common and in What They Differ	54
29	On Hypostasis, Enhypostaton, and Anhypostaton	54
30	On Substance, Nature, and Form; as Well as on Individual, Person, and Hypostasis	55
31	On Equivocals	56
32	On Univocals	59
33	On Mutinominals	59
34	On Things Which Are Different and on Heteronymus Things	60
35	On Conjugates	60
36	On the Ten Most General Genera	61
37	On Things Which are Generically the Same and Specifically the Same; and on Things Which Are Generically Different, Specifically Different and Numerically Different	62

38	On Being in Something	63
39	Again on Substance	64
40	On Nature	65
41	On Form	65
42	On Hypostasis	66
43	On Person	67
44	On Enhypostaton	68
45	On Anhypostaton	69
46	The Division of Being	69
47	The Division of Substance	70
48	Again on Things Which Are Generically the Same and Specifically the Same; and on Things Which Are Generically Different and Specifically Different; and on Things Which Are Hypostaticaly the Same and Things Which Are Numerically Different	72
49	On Quantum and Quality	77
50	On Relatives	80
51	On 'Being of Such a Sort' and Quality	80
52	On Action and Passion	84
53	On Position	86
54	On Place	87
55	On Time	87
56	On Having, or State	87
57	On Opposites	88
58	On Habit and Privation	90
59	On Prior and Posterior	91
60	On the Simultaneous	93
61	On Motion	94
62	On Having	96
63	On Statement, Negation, and Affirmation	97
64	On Term, Premise, and Syllogism	98
65	Various Definitions	99
66	Further on the Hypostatic Union	104
67	Six Definitions of Philosophy	105

68	On the Four Dialectical Methods	107
	Explanation of Expressions	108

ON HERESIES

1	Barbarism	111
2	Scythism	111
3	Hellenism	111
4	Judaism	113
5	The Pythagoreans, or Peripatetics	113
6	The Platonists	113
7	The Stoics	114
8	The Epicureans	114
9	Samaritanism	114
10	The Gorthenes	114
11	The Sebyaeans	114
12	The Essenes	114
13	The Dosthenes	114
14	The Scribes	115
15	The Pharisees	115
16	The Sadduccees	115
17	The Hemerobaptists	116
18	The Ossenes	116
19	The Nasaraeans	116
20	The Herodians	116
21	The Simonians	116
22	The Menandrianists	117
23	The Saturnilians	117
24	The Basilidians	117
25	The Nicolaitans	117
26	The Gnostics	118
27	The Carpocratians	118
28	The Cerinthians	118

29	The Nazarenes	119
30	The Ebionites	119
31	The Valentinians	119
32	The Secundians	119
33	The Ptolemaeans	120
34	The Marcoseans	120
35	The Colarbasaeans	120
36	The Heracleonites	120
37	The Ophites	121
38	The Cainites	121
39	The Sethians	121
40	The Archontics	121
41	The Cerdonians	121
42	The Marcionites	121
43	The Lucianists	122
44	The Apellians	122
45	The Severians	122
46	The Tatianists	123
47	The Encratites	123
48	The Cataphrygians, or Montanists, or Ascodrugites	123
49	The Pepuzians, or Quintillians	123
50	The Quartodecimans	124
51	The Alogians	124
52	The Adamians	124
53	The Sampsaeans, or Elkesaites	124
54	The Theodotians	124
55	The Melchisedechians	125
56	The Bardesanites	125
57	The Noetians	125
58	The Valesians	125
59	The Cathari	125
60	The Angelici	126
61	The Apostolici	126
62	The Sabellians	126

63	The Origenians	126
64	Other Origenians	126
65	The Paulianists	126
66	The Manichaeans	127
67	The Hieracites	127
68	The Meletians	127
69	The Arians, or Ariomanites, or Diatomites	127
70	The Audians	128
71	The Photinians	128
72	The Marcellians	128
73	The Semiarians	128
74	The Pneumatochi	129
75	The Aerians	129
76	The Aetians, or Anomaeans	130
77	The Dimoerites, or Apollinarists	131
78	The Antidicomarianites	131
79	The Collyridians	131
80	The Massalians, or Euchites	133
81	The Nestorians	138
82	The Eutychians	138
83	The Egyptians, or Schematics, or Monophysites	138
84	The Aphthartodocetae	148
85	The Agnoetae, or Themistians	148
86	The Barsanouphites, or Semidalites	149
87	The Hicetae	149
88	The Gnosimachi	149
89	The Heliotropites	149
90	The Thnetopsychites	150
91	The Agonyclites	150
92	The Theocatagonostae, or Blasphemers	150
93	The Christolytae	150
94	The Ethnophrones	150
95	The Donatists	150
96	The Ethicoproscoptae	151

97	The Parermeneutae	151
98	The Lampetians	151
99	The Monothelites	152
100	The Autoproscoptae	152
101	The Ishmaelites	153
102	The Christianocategori, or Iconoclasts	160
103	The Aposchistae, or Doxarii	160

THE ORTHODOX FAITH

BOOK ONE

1 (1)	That the Godhead is incomprehensible and that one should not search after or meddle in such things as have not been handed down to us by the holy Prophets, Apostles, and Evangelists	165
2 (2)	On things which can be expressed through speech and things which cannot, and on things which are knowable and things which are not	166
3 (3)	A proof of the existence of God	168
4 (4)	On what God is, and that He is incomprehensible	170
5 (5)	A demonstration of the fact that there is one God and not several	172
6 (6)	On the Word and Son of God—a demonstration from reason	174
7 (7)	On the Holy Ghost—a demonstration from reason	174
8 (8)	On the Holy Trinity	176
	[On the distinction of the three Persons, and on actuality and reason and thought]	185
9 (9)	On those things which are affirmed of God	189
10 (10)	On the divine union and distinction	190

11 (11)	On the things that are affirmed of God as if He had a body	191
12 (12)	On the same things	193
	[More on the names of God and more precisely]	194
13 (13)	On the place of God, and that only the Divinity is uncircumscribed	197
	[On the place of an angel and of the soul; and on the uncircumscribed]	198
	[A miscellany on God, and the Father, and the Son, and the Holy Ghost, and on the Word and the Spirit]	199
14 (14)	The attributes of the divine nature	201

BOOK TWO

1 (15)	On the term 'age'	203
2 (16)	On creation	205
3 (17)	On angels	205
4 (18)	On the Devil and evil spirits	209
5 (19)	On visible creation	210
6 (20)	On the heavens	210
7 (21)	On light, fire, luminaries, the sun, the moon, and the stars	215
8 (22)	On air and winds	222
9 (23)	On water	224
10 (24)	On the earth and the things that come from it	227
11 (25)	On paradise	230
12 (26)	On man	234
13 (27)	On pleasures	239
14 (28)	On pain	240
15 (29)	On fear	240
16 (30)	On anger	241
17 (31)	On the imagination	241
18 (32)	On sense	242

19 (33)	On thought	244
20 (34)	On memory	245
21 (35)	On mental and spoken speech	246
22 (36)	On passion and action	246
23 (37)	On act	252
24 (38)	On voluntary and involuntary	253
25 (39)	On what depends upon us, that is, on free will	255
26 (40)	On things done	257
27 (41)	On the reason for our having been created free	258
28 (42)	On those things which do not depend upon us	259
29 (43)	On providence	260
30 (44)	On foreknowledge and predestination . . .	263

BOOK THREE

1 (45)	On the divine dispensation and God's concern for us, and our salvation	267
2 (46)	On the manner of the conception of the Word and on His sacred Incarnation	269
3 (47)	On the two natures, against the Monophysites .	271
4 (48)	On the manner of the exchange of the properties	275
5 (49)	On the number of the natures	277
6 (50)	That the entire divine nature was united in one of its Persons to the entire human nature, and not a part of one to a part of the other . . .	278
7 (51)	On the one composite Person of God the Word	281
8 (52)	To those who ask whether the natures of the Lord are reducible to a continuous quantity or to a divided one	284
9 (53)	Answer to the question whether there is such a thing as a nature without subsistence . . .	286
10 (54)	On the Thrice-Holy Hymn	287

11 (55)	On the nature taken specifically and individually, on the difference between union and incarnation, and on how the expression 'the one incarnate nature of the Word of God' is to be understood	289
12 (56)	That the holy Virgin is Mother of God, against the Nestorians	292
13 (57)	On the properties of the two natures	295
14 (58)	On the wills and freedoms of our Lord Jesus Christ	296
15 (59)	On the operations which are in our Lord Jesus Christ	304
16 (60)	Against those who say that, if man has two natures and operations, then it is necessary to say that Christ has three natures and the same number of operations	314
17 (61)	On the deification of the nature of the Lord's flesh, and on that of His will	316
18 (62)	Further on wills and freedoms, minds and knowledges, and wisdoms	318
19 (63)	On the theandric operation	321
20 (64)	On the natural and blameless passions	323
21 (65)	On ignorance and servitude	324
22 (66)	On progress	326
23 (67)	On fear	327
24 (68)	On the prayer of the Lord	328
25 (69)	On appropriation	330
26 (70)	On the passibility of the Lord's body and on the impassibility of His divinity	331
27 (71)	On the divinity of the Word remaining inseparable from the body and soul, even in the Lord's death, and on the persistence of the one person	332
28 (72)	On destruction and corruption	333
29 (73)	On the descent into hell	334

BOOK FOUR

1 (74)	On the things that came after the resurrection	335
2 (75)	On the sitting at the right hand of the Father	336
3 (76)	Against those that say that, if Christ has two natures, either you adore the creature also by adoring a created nature, or you say that there is one nature that is adorable or one that is not	336
4 (77)	Why it was the Son of God that became man, and not the Father of the Holy Ghost; and what He accomplished, when He became man . . .	337
5 (78)	To them who inquire as to whether the Person of Christ is created or uncreated	339
6 (79)	On when He was called Christ	340
7 (80)	To them who inquire as to whether the holy Mother of God engendered two natures, and whether two natures hung upon the cross . .	341
8 (81)	How the only-begotten Son of God can be called first-born	342
9 (82)	On faith and baptism	343
10 (83)	On faith	348
11 (84)	On the cross, wherein still further on faith . .	351
12 (85)	On worshiping to the east	352
13 (86)	On the holy and undefiled sacrament of the Lord	354
14 (87)	On the genealogy of the Lord, and on the holy Mother of God	361
15 (88)	On the honor due to the saints and their relics	367
16 (89)	On images	370
17 (90)	On Scripture	373
18 (91)	On the things that are said about Christ . . .	376
19 (92)	That God is not the author of evil	383
20 (93)	That there are not two principles	385

21 (94)	Why God created those whom He foresaw were to sin and not repent	387
22 (95)	On the law of God and the law of sin	388
23 (96)	On the Sabbath, against the Jews	389
24 (97)	On virginity	393
25 (98)	On the circumcision	397
26 (99)	On Antichrist	398
27 (100)	On the resurrection	401
Index		407

SAINT JOHN OF DAMASCUS

WRITINGS

Translated by
FREDERIC H. CHASE, JR.
St. John's Seminary
Boston, Mass.

THE FOUNT OF KNOWLEDGE

Preface

THE MOST LOWLY MONK and priest John to the most saintly and honored of God, Father Cosmas[1] the most holy Bishop of Maiuma, greetings in the Lord.

Being fully conscious of the limitations of my intelligence and of the insufficiency of my language, your Beatitude, I have hesitated to undertake a task exceeding my capabilities and to presume to enter into the Holy of Holies like some bold and foolhardy person, for I am wary of the danger that threatens those who attempt such things. The divine Moses, the lawgiver, withdrew from all sight of human things and abandoned the turbulent sea of life. He purified the eye of his soul by wiping away every material reflection, and only then did he become fit to receive the divine vision. Only then was he found worthy to behold the benevolent

---

[1] Cosmas Melodus, a fellow monk and friend of the Damascene at the Monastery of St. Sabbas. He was reputedly his adopted brother, but there is no foundation for this. In 743 (or 742) he was made Bishop of Maiuma, the port of Gaza in southern Palestine. He is noted as a composer of liturgical poetry.

condescension of God the Word and His marvelous appearance in a bush and in immaterial fire, which, while it enkindled and burnt the tree and changed it into His splendor, did not consume or destroy it or alter its proper nature. He was the first to learn the name of HIM WHO IS and who truly is super-essential, and he was entrusted by God with the leadership of his own countrymen. Yet, if he considered himself as 'having impediment and slowness of tongue'[2]—and thus unable publicly to execute the divine will and to be appointed a mediator between God and man—then how am I, who am defiled and stained with every sort of sin, and who bear within myself the tumultuous seas of my conjectures, and who have purified neither my mind nor my understanding that they may serve as a mirror of God and His divine reflections; how am I, who have not sufficient power of speech to express such concepts, to utter those divine and ineffable things which surpass the comprehension of every rational creature? With these considerations in mind I have hesitated to undertake this book. Besides this, to tell the truth, I feared to accede to the request, lest I should incur ridicule on the double count of ignorance and of folly. The latter is quite serious, for the charge of ignorance may be excused—provided the ignorance is not from laziness; but to add to ignorance a false pretension to knowledge is serious, blameworthy, and quite unpardonable, and it is a sure sign of a greater, if not the greatest, ignorance. On the other hand, however, the fruit of disobedience is death, while the humble and obedient man, because he has shown himself to be an imitator of Christ, is led from the lowest place to the highest. He receives from God the grace that illuminates, so that in the opening of his mouth he is filled with the Spirit. He becomes purified in heart and enlightened in understanding. When he opens his mouth, he receives

---

2 Exod. 4.10.

the power of speech and has no concern as to what he shall say, because he is an instrument of the Spirit speaking within him. Therefore, in obedience through you to the Christ who in you exercises the pontifical office, I bow to your request and open my mouth, being confident that through your prayers it will be filled with the Spirit and that I, taking so much as He shall give and speaking this aloud, shall utter eloquently the fruit not of my own understanding but of the Spirit who giveth wisdom to the blind.

First of all I shall set forth the best contributions of the philosophers of the Greeks, because whatever there is of good has been given to men from above by God, since 'every best gift and every perfect gift is from above, coming down from the Father of lights.'[3] If, however, there is anything that is contrary to the truth, then it is a dark invention of the deceit of Satan and a fiction of the mind of an evil spirit, as that eminent theologian Gregory once said.[4] In imitation of the method of the bee, I shall make my composition from those things which are conformable with the truth and from our enemies themselves gather the fruit of salvation. But all that is worthless and falsely labeled as knowledge[5] I shall reject. Then, next, after this, I shall set forth in order the absurdities of the heresies hated of God, so that by recognizing the lie we may more closely follow the truth. Then, with God's help and by His grace I shall expose the truth—that truth which destroys deceit and puts falsehood to flight and which, as with golden fringes, has been embellished and adorned by the sayings of the divinely inspired prophets, the divinely taught fishermen, and the God-bearing shepherds and teachers—that truth, the glory of which flashes out from within to brighten with its radiance,

---
3 James 1.17.
4 Gregory of Nazianzus, *Sermon* 39.3 (*PG* 36.336C-337A).
5 1 Tim. 6.20.

when they encounter it, them that are duly purified and rid of troublesome speculations. However, as I have said, I shall add nothing of my own, but shall gather together into one those things which have been worked out by the most eminent of teachers and make a compendium of them, being in all things obedient to your command. But I beseech you, Honored of God, to be indulgent with me, who have been obedient to your commands, and, receiving my obedience, to give me in return of the abundance of your prayers.

PHILOSOPHICAL CHAPTERS

Chapter 1

NOTHING IS MORE ESTIMABLE than knowledge, for knowledge is the light of the rational soul. The opposite, which is ignorance, is darkness. Just as the absence of light is darkness, so is the absence of knowledge a darkness of the reason. Now, ignorance is proper to irrational beings, while knowledge is proper to those who are rational. Consequently, one who by nature has the faculty of knowing and understanding, yet does not have knowledge, such a one, although by nature rational, is by neglect and indifference inferior to rational beings. By knowledge I mean the true knowledge of things which are, because things which have being are the object of knowledge. False knowledge, in so far as it is a knowledge of that which is not, is ignorance rather than knowledge. For falsehood is nothing else but that which is not. Now, since we do not live with our soul stripped bare, but, on the contrary, have it clothed over, as it were, with the veil of the flesh, our soul has the mind as a sort of eye which sees and has the faculty of knowing and which is capable of receiving knowledge and having understanding of things which are. It does not, however, have knowledge and understanding of itself, but has need of one to teach it; so, let us approach that Teacher in whom there is no falsehood and who is the truth. Christ is the subsistent wisdom and truth and in Him are all the hidden treasures of knowledge.[1] In sacred Scripture let us hear the voice of Him who is the wisdom and power of God the Father,[2] and let us learn the true knowldege of all things that are. Let us approach with attention and in all sincerity and proceed without letting the spiritual eye of our soul be dulled by passions, for even the clearest and most limpid eye will hardly enable one to gain a clear view of the truth. 'If then the light that is in us (that is to say, the mind) be darkness: the darkness itself how great shall it be!'[3] With our whole soul and our whole understanding let us approach. And since it is impossible for the eye that is constantly shifting and turning about clearly to perceive the visible object, because for clear vision the eye must be steadily focused upon the object observed, let us put aside every anxiety of the mind and approach the truth unhampered by material considerations. And let us not be satisfied with arriving speedily at the gate, but rather let us knock hard, so that the door of the bridal chamber may be opened to us and we may behold the beauties within. Now, the gate is the letter, but the bridal chamber within the gate is the beauty of the thoughts hidden behind the letter, which is to say, the Spirit of truth. Let us knock hard, let us read once, twice, many times. By thus digging through we shall find the treasure of knowledge and take delight in the wealth of it. Let us seek, let us search, let us examine, let us inquire. 'For every one that asketh, receiveth: and he that seeketh,

---

1 Cf. Col. 2.3.
2 Cf. 1 Cor. 1.24.
3 Matt. 6.23.

findeth: and to him that knocketh, it shall be opened;'[4] and 'Ask thy father, and he will declare to thee: thy elders in knowledge and they will tell thee.'[5] If, then, we are lovers of learning, we shall learn much,[6] for it is of the nature of all things that they may be apprehended through industry and toil, and before all and after all by the grace of God, the Giver of grace.

Furthermore, since the divine Apostle says: 'But prove all things: hold fast that which is good,'[7] let us also find something in them worth carrying away and reap some fruit that will be of profit to our soul. For every craftman has need, also, of certain things for the prosecution of his works, and it is also fitting for the queen to be waited upon by certain handmaidens. So let us receive such sayings as serve the truth, while we reject the impiety which exercised an evil tyranny over them. And let us not belittle that which is good. Nor let us use the art of rhetoric for the deception of simpler folk. On the other hand, although the truth stands in no need of the service of subtle reasonings, let us definitely use them to overthrow both those who fight dishonestly and that which is falsely called knowledge.[8]

And so, having invoked Christ as our Guide, the subsistent Word of God by whom 'every best gift and every perfect gift'[9] is given, let us make our beginning with such principles as are adapted to those who are still in need of milk. May those who happen upon this work have it as their purpose to bring their mind safely through to the final blessed end—which means to be guided by their sense perceptions up to

---
4 Matt. 7.8; Clement of Alexandria, *Stromateis* 8.1 (*PG* 9.560A).
5 Deut. 32.7.
6 Isocrates, *To Demonicus* 4.
7 1 Thess. 5.21.
8 1 Tim. 6.20.
9 James 1.17.

that which is beyond all sense perception and comprehension, which is He who is the Author and Maker and Creator of all. 'For by the beauty of his own creatures the creator is by analogy discovered,' and 'the invisible things of him from the creation of the world are clearly seen, being understood by the things that are made.'[10] Thus, if we apply ourselves in a meek and humble spirit to the attainment of knowledge, we shall arrive at the desired end. 'You cannot believe in me,' said Christ, who is the truth, 'if you receive glory from men,' and, 'every one that exalteth himself shall be humbled; and he that humbleth himself shall be exalted.'[11]

Chapter 2

Anyone who begins something without a purpose is like someone fumbling in the dark, because he who labors with no end in view is entirely at loose ends. So, then, let us state at the very beginning what the proposed purpose of this work is, so that what we are to say may more easily be grasped. Our purpose, then, is to make a beginning of philosophy and to set down concisely in the present writing, so far as is possible, every sort of knowledge. For this reason let it be entitled a *Fount of Knowledge*. I shall say nothing of my own, but I shall set down things which have been said in various places by wise and godly men. First of all, then, it is best to know just what philosophy is.

---

10 Wisd. 13.5; Rom. 1.20.
11 John 5.44; Luke 14.11.

Chapter 3

Philosophy[1] is knowledge of things which are in so far as they are, that is, a knowledge of the nature of things which have being. And again, philosophy is knowledge of both divine and human things, that is to say, of things both visible and invisible. Philosophy, again, is a study of death, whether this be voluntary or natural. For life is of two kinds, there being the natural life by which we live and the voluntary one by which we cling lovingly to this present life. Death, also, is of two kinds: the one being natural, which is the separation of soul from body, whereas the other is the voluntary one by which we disdain this present life and aspire to that which is to come. Still again, philosophy is the making of one's self like God. Now, we become like God in wisdom, which is to say, in the true knowledge of good; and in justice, which is a fairness in judgment without respect to persons; and in holiness, which is to say, in goodness, which is superior to justice, being that by which we do good to them that wrong us. Philosophy is the art of arts and the science of sciences. This is because philosophy is the principle of every art, since through it every art and science has been invented. Now, according to some, art is what errs in some people and science what errs in no one, whereas philosophy alone does not err. According to others, art is that which is done with the hands, whereas science is any art that is practiced by the reason, such as grammar, rhetoric, and the like. Philosophy, again, is a love of wisdom. But, true wisdom is God. Therefore, the love of God, this is the true philosophy.

---

1 Ammonius, *In Isagogen*, pp. 2-9 (Definitions of Philosophy) and pp. 11-16 (Division of Philosophy). All references to Ammonius are to the pages of the edition of Adolf Busse, *Commentaria in Aristotelem Graeca* IV.3, *Ammonius in Porphyrii Isagogen sive V Voces* (Berlin 1891, and IV, *Ammonius in Aristotelis Categorias* (Berlin 1895).

Philosophy is divided into speculative and practical. The speculative is divided into theology, physiology, and mathematics. The practical is divided into ethics, domestic economy, and politics. Now, the speculative is the orderly disposition of knowledge. So, theology is the consideration of incorporeal and immaterial things—first of all, of God, who is absolutely immaterial; and then of angels and souls. Physiology, however, is the knowledge of the material things that are close at hand to us, such as animals, plants, stones, and the like. Mathematics is the knowledge of things which are in themselves incorporeal but which are found in corporeal beings—such, I mean, as numbers and musical notes, and, in addition, such things as geometrical figures and the movements of the stars. Thus it is that the logical consideration of numbers constitutes the science of arithmetic; that of the musical sounds, music; that of geometrical figures, geometry; that of the stars, astronomy. These stand midway between things that have bodies and things which have not, for, while number is in itself incorporeal, it is also found in material things, such as grain, for example, or wine, or any other such thing. Practical philosophy, moreover, is concerned with the virtues. It governs manners and shows how one must behave in society. If it lays down laws for the individual man, it is called ethics; but, if for the entire household, then it is called domestic economy; while, if for cities and countries, then it is called politics.

There are, however, some people who have endeavored to do away entirely with philosophy by asserting that it does not exist and that neither does any knowledge or perception exist. We shall answer them by asking: How is it that you say that there is neither philosophy, nor knowledge, nor perception? Is it by your knowing and perceiving it, or is it by your not knowing and perceiving it?. If you have perceived it, well, that is knowledge and perception. But if it is by your not knowing it, then no one will believe you, as long as you are discussing something of which you have no knowledge.

Since, then, there is such a thing as philosophy and since there is knowledge of things that are, let us talk about being. However, one should understand that we are beginning with that division of philosophy which concerns the reason and which is a tool of philosophy[2] rather than one of its divisions, because it is used for every demonstration. So, for the present, we shall discuss simple terms which through simple concepts signify simple things. Then, after we have explained the meanings of the words, we shall investigate dialectic.

Chapter 4

Being is the common name for all things which are. It is divided into substance and accident. *Substance* is the principal of these two, because it has existence in itself and not in another. *Accident,* on the other hand, is that which cannot exist in itself but is found in the substance. For the substance is a subject, just as matter is of the things made out of it, whereas an accident is that which is found in the substance as in a subject. Copper, for example, and wax are substance; but shape, form and color are accidents. And a body is a substance, whereas color is an accident. For the body is certainly not in the color; rather, the color is in the body. Nor is the soul in knowledge; rather, knowledge is in the soul. Nor are the copper and wax in the shape; rather, the shape is in the wax and the copper. Neither is the body said to belong to the color; rather, the color to the body. Nor does the wax belong to the shape; rather, the shape to the wax. What is more, the color and the knowl-

---

[2] *Ibid.* 23.

edge and the shape are subject to change, whereas the body and the soul and the wax remain the same, because substance is not subject to change. Also, the substance and the matter of the body is just one thing, while there are many colors. Similarly, in the case of all others things, the subject is substance, whereas that which is found in the substance as in a subject is accident.

Now, substance is defined as follows: *Substance* is a thing which exists in itself and has no need of another for its existence. *Accident,* however, is that which cannot exist in itself, but has its existence in another. God, then, is substance, and so is every created thing. God, however, even though He is substance, is super-substantial. There are also substantial qualities about which we shall have something to say.

Chapter 4 (variant)[1]

Being is the common name for all things which are. Now, this is divided into substance and accident. *Substance* is a thing existing in itself and having no need of another for existence, or, more precisely, that which is in itself and does not have its existence in another. *Accident* is that which cannot exist in itself, but has its existence in another. For the substance is a subject, just as matter is of the things made out of it, whereas an accident is what is found in a substance, as, for example, the body and its color. Certainly a body is not in the color; rather, the color is in the body. The body, then, is a substance, while the color is an accident. And it is the same way with the soul and prudence, for the

---

1 There are two recensions of the *Philosophical Chapters,* of which one is more prolix. Both are incorporated in the edition of Lequien. The entire variant versions of Chapters 4, 6, 9, and 10 are given separately, while the shorter variants are indicated by parentheses.

soul is not in the prudence; rather, the prudence is in the soul. For this reason the body is not said to belong to the color; rather, the color to the body. Neither is the soul said to belong to the prudence; rather, the prudence is said to belong to the soul. The soul, then, is a substance and prudence is an accident. For, when the soul is taken away, its prudence is likewise taken away, because, if there were to be no soul, in what would the prudence be? However, when prudence is taken away, the soul is not necessarily taken away, for it is quite possible for a soul to be without prudence. And similarly with all others beings, that which has existence in itself and not in another is substance, whereas that which cannot exist of itself but has its existence in another is accident.

Chapter 5

Since it is our purpose to discuss every simple philosophical term,[1] we must first of all know with what sort of terms it is that philosophy is concerned. So, we begin our discussion with *sound* itself. A sound is either meaningless or it has meaning. If it is meaningless, then it signifies nothing; but if it has a meaning, then it signifies something. Then, again, a meaningless sound is either articulate or inarticulate. Now, that sound which cannot be written is inarticulate, whereas that which can be written is articulate. Thus, for example, the sound made by a stone or a piece of wood is an inarticulate and meaningless one, because it is not written and has no meaning. But such a sound, for example, as *scindapsus* is meaningless, yet articulate; for it can be written, although it does not mean anything, because there never has been a *scindapsus,* nor is there any now. Now, philosophy is not

---

[1] φωνή means both *sound, voice, word,* and *term;* cf. Ammonius, *In Isagogen,* pp. 58-63.

concerned with the meaningless sound, whether it be inarticulate or articulate. Again, the sound which has meaning is either articulate or inarticulate. Thus, an inarticulate sound which does have meaning is one such as the barking of dogs, because this sound, since it is the sound made by a dog, signifies the dog. It also signifies the approach of some person. It is, however, inarticulate, because it is not written. And so, philosophy is not concerned with this kind of sound either. Now, the articulate sound which has meaning is either universal or particular. Man, for example, is universal, whereas Peter and Paul are particular. It is not with the particular term that philosophy is concerned; rather, philosophy is concerned with that sound which has meaning, is articulate, and is universal, or, in other words, common and predicated of several things.

Again, such a term is either *essential* or *non-essential*. Thus, that term is essential which signifies the essence,[2] or, to be more precise, the nature, of things. On the other hand, that is non-essential which signifies the accidents. For example: Man is a rational mortal animal. All of these terms are essential, for, should you remove one of them from the man, he would no longer be a man. If you say that he is not an animal, then, he is not a man. In the same way, if you say that he is not mortal, then he is not a man, because every man is at once animal, rational, and mortal. So, it is for this reason that these are called 'essential,' namely, that they complete man's nature, so that without them it is impossible for the man to be a man. And similarly with every individual thing, those elements which go to make up the nature are called essential. Non-essential, however, are the accidents which can be or not be in the subject—in a man, say, or a horse, or some such other thing. Take the color white, for instance. Whether one be white or black, one is by no means any less a man.

---

2 οὐσία: *substance, essence,* or *nature.*

Consequently, these and the like are non-essential, which is to say, they are accidents, and they or their opposites may inhere in us.

The essential term either shows what a thing is or of what sort it is. Thus, for example, when we are asked what a man is, we say that he is an animal. Then, when we are asked what sort of animal he is, we say a living and a mortal one. So, the essential term, which shows of what sort something is, is called *difference*. That term which shows what something is either signifies several species, in which case it constitutes the genus, or it signifies several individuals differing from one another numerically but by no means specifically, in which case it constitutes the species. An example of the former, that is to say, of genus, is substance. Substance signifies both man and horse and ox, because each one of them is termed a substance and is such, although each one is a different species. An example of the latter, that is to say, of species, is man, because this term signifies several men, or, more exactly, all numerically different men. Thus, Peter is one and Paul is another, and they are not one but two. In species, however, that is to say, in nature, they do not differ, for all are called men and are such.

Consequently, there is that which is more particular and is numerically different, as, for example, Peter, an individual, a person, and a hypostasis. This signifies a definite person. For, when we are asked who this man is, we say that he is Peter. The term 'other' signifies the same thing, for Peter is one and Paul is another. Likewise the terms 'he,' 'this,' and 'that'—these and such others as stand of themselves are applied to the individual. But that which includes the individuals is called *species* and is more general than the individual, because it does include several individuals. An example would be man, because this term includes both Peter and Paul and all individual men besides. This is what is called *nature* and *substance* and *form* by the holy Fathers.[3] Now, that which includes several species is called *genus,* an example of which is animal, for this includes man, ox, and horse, and is more universal than the species. Moreover, both species and genus were called *nature* and *form* and *substance* by the holy Fathers. Furthermore, the species—that is, the nature and the substance and the form—does not produce something which is 'other' or something which is 'of another sort,' but rather 'another' of the same sort. Thus, we may say that by nature man is one thing and the horse another, but we may not say that they are one and another of the same sort. Speaking specifically, one says 'this,' and 'it,' and 'that,' and the like, all of which declare in what something is. The *specific difference,* however, constitutes something 'of a different sort.' Thus, the rational animal is a thing of one sort, while the irrational animal is something of another sort. The specific difference furthermore constitutes 'such' a thing, and 'what kind' of a thing, and 'what sort' of a thing. The non-essential term may be applied either to one species or to several. If it applies to one, then it is called a *property*. For example, the property of laughter belongs to man alone and that of neighing to the horse alone. If, however, it is to be found in several species, then it is an *accident*. Take whiteness, for example. This exists both in man and in the horse, and in the dog and many other species.

Now, these are the five terms to which every philosophical term may be reduced. Accordingly, we must know what each one means and what they have in common with one another and in what they differ. They are *genus, species, difference, property,* and *accident.*

Genus is that which is predicated—that is, affirmed and

---

[3] Among others, see Gregory of Nyssa, *Against Eunomius* IV.8 (PG 45.672A), and Theodoret, *Dialogue I* (PG 83.73AC).

expressed (for to be predicated is to be affirmed in respect to something)—of several things that are specifically different in respect to what pertains to their essence. *Species,* on the other hand, is that in which something is, but which is predicated of several things that are numerically different. And *difference* is that which is predicated of several things specifically different in respect to their particular sort, and it is included in the definition as essential. This is that which cannot *be* and *not be* in the same species and cannot *not be* in the species to which it belongs. When present, it assures the existence of the species; when absent, the species is destroyed. Also, it is impossible for it and its opposite to be in the same species. Thus, for example, the rational cannot *not be* in man, because that which is irrational is not man. When it is present, it constitutes the nature of man; when it is absent, it destroys it, because that which is irrational is not man. Now, one must know that this is called essential, natural, constituent, and distinguishing, and specific difference, essential quality, and natural property of a nature. It is very properly said by the philosophers to be a difference which is presentative of the nature possessing it and most proper to this nature itself. A *property* is that which exists in one species and in the entire species, and which is always in it and is conversely predicable with it. Take, for example, the property of laughter. Thus, every man can laugh and everything that can laugh is a man. An *accident* is that in which something is of a certain sort and which is predicated of several things differing in species but which does not enter into the definition. It can either *be* or *not be*, for, when present, it does not assure the existence of the species, and when it is absent, the species is not destroyed. It is called a non-essential difference and quality. It is either separable or inseparable. That accident is separable which is sometimes present and sometimes absent in the same hypostasis, as would be sitting, lying, standing, sickness, or health. That, on the other hand, is inseparable which is not constituent of a substance because it is not found in the entire species, but which, nevertheless, when it does become present in some hypostasis, cannot be separated from it. Such, for example, are the having of a snub nose, being hook-nosed, being gray-haired, and the like. This inseparable accident is called a characteristic peculiarity. This is because such distinctiveness produces the hypostasis, which is to say, the individual—and an individual is that which subsists in itself of substance and accidents, is numerically distinct from the others of the same species, and does not signify *what* but *whom*. In the following we shall, with God's help, learn more accurately about these things.

Chapter 6

Division[1] is the first section of the thing. Thus, for example, the animal is divided into rational and irrational. *Redivision* is the second section of the same thing. For example, the animal is redivided into apod, biped and quadruped—apod, as a fish; biped as a man or a bird; quadruped, as an ox, horse, or other such. *Subdivision* is the section of the already divided-off branch. For example, the animal is divided into rational and irrational, and then the rational into mortal and immortal. Now, the first thing is divided into two branches: the rational and the irrational. It is the division of one of these branches, namely, the division of the rational into mortal and immortal, that is subdivision. Division and redivision are not used in all cases. However, when everything is not covered by the first division—as, for example, when the animal is divided into rational and irrational, the

---

1 Cf. Ammonius, *op. cit.*, pp. 9ff.

biped is found both among the rational and the irrational animals—then of necessity we redivide, that is to say, we make a second division of the same thing, and we say: 'The animal is divided into apod, biped, and quadruped.

For a similar reason, there are eight modes of division. Thus, everything that is divided is divided either according to itself, namely, according to substance, or according to accident. If it is divided according to itself, then it is either as a thing or as a term. If it is divided as a thing, then it is either as genus into species, as when you divide the animal into rational and irrational, or as species into individuals, as man into Peter and Paul and all other individual men, or as a whole into parts. This last division is twofold, being either into like or unlike parts. Now, a thing is of like parts whenever its sections admit of the name and the definition of the whole and of each other. For instance, when flesh is divided into several pieces, each portion is called flesh and admits of the definition of flesh. On the contrary, the thing is of unlike parts whenever the part cut off will not admit either of the name or of the definition, whether of the whole or of the parts. Thus, should you divide Socrates into hands and feet and head, the foot cut off from Socrates would neither be called Socrates nor his head, nor would it admit of the definition either of Socrates or of his head. Or division may be as that of an equivocal term into its various meanings. This, again, is of two kinds, because the term may signify either the whole of something or a part of it. It may signify the whole, as does the word 'dog,' since this last is used for land-dog, dog-star, and sea-dog, all of which are wholes and not part of an animal. On the other hand, it may signify a part, as when the name 'tongue' is given to the top part of a shoe, to a part of the flute, and to the organ of taste in animals, all of which are parts and not wholes.

The foregoing are the modes in which a thing is divided

according to itself. When it is divided according to accident, however, it may be divided as substance into accidents, as when I say that some men are white and some black—for men are substance, while white and black are accidents. Or it may be divided as an accident into substances, as when I speak of animate white things and inanimate white things—for the white is an accident, while the animate and inanimate things are substances. Or it may be divided as an accident into accidents, as when I say that some cold things are white and dry, while others are black and wet—for the cold and the white, the black, and the wet, and the dry are all accidents.

There is still another mode of division, which is that of things which are *derivative* (ἀφ' ἑνός, from one) and those which are *relative* (πρὸς ἕν, to one). Things are derivative as in the case of a medical book or a medical instrument deriving from medicine; for from one thing, medicine, medical things are named. On the other hand, a healthful drug or healthful food are *relative* because they relate to one thing, namely, health. Of the things which are *derivative*, some derive from some cause—as the man's image is said to be from the man as from a true cause; whereas others are as having being invented by someone, as the medical scalpel, and the like.

Now, this is the general division according to which everything that is divided is divided. It is either as genus into species, or as species into individuals, or as a whole into parts, or as an equivocal term into its various meanings, or as substance into accidents, or as accident into substances, or as accidents into accidents, or as the derivatives and relatives. There are some who deny the division of species into individuals, because they say that it rather is an enumeration, since all division is into two, or three, or, rarely, into four. But the species is divided into an unlimited number of individuals, because the number of individual men is unlimited.

One must furthermore know that that which is by nature prior and posterior, as well as that which is more and less, is not found to be divided into parts by any mode of division. However, that which is by nature prior and posterior, and that which is more and less, fall under derivatives and relatives—whence their classification.

Chapter 6 (variant)

Division is the first section of the thing. Thus, for example, the animal is divided into rational and irrational. *Subdivision* is the section and division of one part into two segments. Thus, for example, when the animal has been divided into rational and irrational, then we divide one part—say, the rational—into mortal and immortal. And we have *redivision* when we have made a division of a thing and then make another kind of division of the same thing over again. Thus, for example, man is divided into male and female—that is division. Then man is divided over again into soul and body—this is redivision. However, division and redivision is not always done, but only when everything is not covered by the first division. It is done in this case, because in both the male and the female body and soul are to be considered.

One should know that the two species into which the same genus is divided are said to be divided by dichotomy. For example, the animal is divided into rational and irrational; so, the rational and irrational are said to be divided by dichotomy.

There are, moreover, eight modes of division: either as genus into species, as the animal is divided into rational and irrational; or as species into individuals, as man is divided into Peter and Paul and all other individual men; or as the whole into parts. This last is of two kinds, for the parts are either alike or they are unlike. They are alike when they admit of the name and the definition of the whole and of one another, as when we cut up pieces of flesh into several pieces of flesh, for then each piece of the flesh is called flesh and admits of the definition of flesh. But they are unlike when they do not admit of the name or of the definition either of the whole or of each other, as when we divide Socrates into hands and head and feet. In this case neither the head, nor the hands, nor the feet admit of the name or of the definition of Socrates, nor do they of each other. Or division is that of an equivocal term divided into its various meanings. This is of two kinds, being either as a whole or as a part. It is as a whole as in the case of the term 'dog,' for this is used for a land-dog, and a dog-star, and a sea-dog, which precisely are wholes and not parts of an animal. It is, however, as a part, when the word 'tongue' is used for the top part of the shoe, for the endpiece of the flute, and for the organ of taste in animals —which are all some sort of parts and not wholes. Or, again, division is that of substance into accidents, as when I speak of some men being white and some black. Or it is as that of accidents into substances, as when I speak of some white things being animate and others inanimate. Or it is as that of accident into accidents, as when I speak of some cold things being dry and others wet. Or it is as the division of those things which are *derivative* and *relative*. We have *derivative* in the case of a medical book and a medical instrument, which derive from medicine; whereas we have *relative* in the case of a healthful drug and healthful food, for these relate to one thing, namely health. Now, according to this mode the being is divided into substance and accident.

One must know that that which is by nature prior and posterior and that which is more and less is not divided into parts by any mode of division except that of those things which are *derivative* and *relative*.

Chapter 7

That is by nature prior which is implied in something else, while in itself it does not imply this; and which takes something else away when it itself is taken away, but is not necessarily taken away when the other is. For example, animal is by nature prior to man, for when the animal is taken away so as not to exist, then man will necessarily not exist either, because man is an animal. But, when man is taken away and does not exist, there can still be an animal —for there would be the horse and the dog and such, which are certain kinds of animals. Again, when man is postulated, then animal is most certainly implied with him, because man is an animal. But, when the animal is postulated, man is not necessarily implied, because, on the contrary, it might be a horse, or a dog, or something of the sort, for these are animals, too. Therefore, Peter is not by nature prior to Paul, nor is the rational animal prior to the irrational. For, when Peter is taken away so as not to exist, there will still be Paul. Likewise, when Paul is postulated, Peter is not implied with him; nor, when Peter is postulated, will Paul be implied. And neither is Peter more, that is to say, more a man or more an animal than Paul, nor is Paul more so than Peter. However, a drug may be found which is more healthful than another drug, and a book which is more medical than some other book.

Chapter 8

A *definition*[1] is a concise statement setting forth the nature of the thing in question, that is to say, such statement as expresses in brief the nature of the thing in question. For example, man is a rational mortal animal capable of intelligence and knowledge. Now, many men have discoursed at length on the nature of man, that is, they have written long and extensive treatises on the subject. But these are not concise and, therefore, are not definitions. There are also consise statements, such as apophthegms, but, since they do not set forth the nature of a thing, they are not definitions. A name, too, oftentimes indicates the nature of the thing in question, but it is not a definition. For the name is one word, while the definition is a statement, and a statement is made up of at least two words. (Therefore, the definition is a name explained, whereas a name is a term of a proposition, when it is in conjunction.)

The definition is made up of genus and constituent, that is to say, essential differences. Thus it is with the definition of animal, for animal is an animate sentient substance. Here the genus is substance, while the constituent differences are the being animate and sentient. The definition may also be taken from matter and form, as, for example: A statue is that which is made of bronze and represents the form of a man. In this case the bronze is the matter, while the representation of the shape of the man is the form of the statue. The matter corresponds to the genus and the form to the specific difference. The definition may also be taken from subject and purpose. Medicine, for example, is concerned with human bodies and is productive of health. Here the subject of medicine is the human body, whereas its purpose is health.

---

1 Cf. Ammonius, *op. cit.,* pp. 34ff.

Now, the *description* is made up of non-essential elements, that is to say, of properties and accidents. For example, man is an animal which is able to laugh, walks erect, and has broad nails. These elements are non-essential. For this reason it is called description, since it outlines, bringing out not the essential substance but only the things consequential to it. The *descriptive definition* is a combination of essentials and non-essentials, as, for example: Man is rational animal walking erect and having broad nails.

Definition is the term for the setting of land boundaries taken in a metaphorical sense. For, just as the boundary separates that which belongs to one from that which belongs to another, so does the definition set off the nature of one thing from that of any other.

Now, the soundness of a definition lies in its having neither too few nor too many terms, while its vice lies in its having either too few or too many terms. A perfect definition is one which is convertible with the thing defined, while an imperfect one is one which is not. Neither is that which has too few terms convertible (nor that which has too many[2]), for, when it has too many terms, it covers too few things, whereas, when it has too few terms, it covers too many things. (And so one may say that nature has discovered a wonderful device—poverty that is wealthy and wealth feigning poverty.[3]) For example, the perfect definition of man is: Man is rational mortal animal. Notice how this is convertible, for every rational mortal animal is a man and every man is a rational mortal animal. Now, if one term were to be left out, the definition would cover too many things. Take it, for example, as 'rational animal.' Here there are too few terms, because I did not say 'mortal.' And it covers too many

---
2 Printer's omission from Migne text; cf. Lequien, *Damasceni Opera Omnia* I (Paris 1712) p. 19.
3 Not in some manuscripts.

things, because man is not the only rational animal; the angel is one, too. Therefore, it is not convertible. If, on the other hand, I should say 'a rational, mortal, literate animal,' again it is not convertible. For by my saying 'literate' it has received too many terms, while it covers too few things. This is because it has not defined every man, but only those men who are literate. Thus, every rational, mortal, and literate animal is a man, but not every man is a rational, mortal, and literate animal, because not every man is literate.

Therefore, those definitions are perfect which are convertible with the thing defined. Since, however, a property is also convertible with the thing of which it is a property—for, if anything is a man, it will be capable of laughter; and if anything is capable of laughter, it will be a man—then we must make an additional specification and say that perfect definitions are those which are taken from genus and constituent differences, which are neither deficient nor excessive in terms, and which are convertible with the thing defined. In the same way, those are perfect which are taken from the pairs of subject and purpose and of matter and form. Sometimes this is also true of those taken from the subject alone, as when the subject is not subject to any other art—as glass is not subject to any other art than that of the glass-maker. The same is also true of those taken from the purpose alone, in the case that that purpose is not the purpose of any other art—as with the art of shipbuilding. As a result of all this one must know that the perfection of a definition is in its convertibility.

Definition differs from *term* by the one being more particular and the other more general. For *term* is more general than *definition,* because it means the setting of limits. It also means a *decree,* as when we say that the king 'decreed.' It still further means that into which a proposition is resolved, as with God's help, we shall learn in that which is to follow. It also means *definition*. *Definition,* however, means only the concise statement setting forth the nature of the thing in question.

One must know, furthermore, that a definition is given only in the case of the substance and its species, and that we cannot give a definition of an individual or of accidents, but only a description, because of the fact that the definition is made up of genus and constituent differences, while the description is made up of non-essentials.

Chapter 9

One must know that in the matter of equivocal terms there are three things to be asked: whether the term is equivocal, how many meanings it has, and of which of these it is a question. Now, first of all, it must be explained what an equivocal term is. Terms are equivocal when two or more things have one name, while each one of them has a different meaning, that is to say, takes a different definition. Such is the case with the term *genus,*[1] for genus is of the number of equivocal terms. Thus, first of all, that is called a genus which is from a place of origin or from a progenitor, and both of these in two ways: either proximately or remotely. It is from the place of origin proximately, as when a person from Jerusalem is called a Hierosolymite, but remotely, as with a Palestinian from Palestine. Similarly, it is from the proximate progenitor, as when Achilles is called Peleides, because he was the son of Peleus; while it is from the more remote, as when Achilles is called Aeacides from his grandfather Aeacus—for the latter was the father of Peleus. Then, again, that relationship is called genus which exists between a person and his several descendants, as when all those descend-

---
1 Cf. Ammonius, *In Isagogen,* pp. 47ff.; Porphyry, *Isagoge* II.

ing from Israel are called Israelites. Now, these aforementioned kinds of genus are of no concern to the philosophers.

Again, that is called genus to which the species is subaltern. For example, under animal come man, the horse, and other species; hence, the animal is a genus. It is with this kind of genus that the philosophers are concerned and we define it by saying that *genus* is that which is predicated in respect to their essence of several things differing in species. Thus, animal, which is a genus, is predicated essentially of man, the horse, the ox, and a number of other things, all of which differ from one another in species. For the species of man is one thing, whereas that of the horse is another, and that of the ox is still another. The genus is predicated *as to what something is,* for, when we are asked what a man is, we reply that he is an animal. The same is true with the horse, because, when we are asked what it is, we reply that it is an animal. Thus, genus is that to which the species is subaltern. (And again, genus is that which is divided into species.[2]) For genus is divided into species, is more general than the species, contains the species, and is higher than they.

Now, one should know that the more general is said to be *superior,* while the more particular is said to be *inferior* and is subject to predication. Thus, there are things which are subject with respect to existence. Such is substance, because it is subject with respect to the existence of the accident, since the accident subsists in it. There is also that which is subject with respect to predication, and this is the particular. For the genus is predicated of the species as the species is of the individuals. It is clear, however, that the genus is more general than the species, as the species is more general than the individual. In what follows we shall with the help of God learn more accurately about these things. But, now that we have discussed genus, let us also discuss species.

---

2 Added by Lequien from shorter recension.

Chapter 10

Species[1] is also an equivocal term, since it is used in two different senses. Thus the form and appearance of anything is its species, as, for example, the species of the statue, in which sense it was once said: 'a first species worthy of sovereignty.'[2] There is another kind of species, which is substantial and subaltern to genus. And again, species is that of which genus is predicated in the category of substance. Still again, species is that which is predicated in respect to their common essence of several things which are numerically different. The first two of these descriptions differ only relatively, like 'ascent' and 'descent,' and they apply to every species. The third and last description, however, applies only to the *most specific species*,[3] which is that which is immediately above the individual and contains the individual substances—as we speak of the human species.

We have related how the term *genus* is used in three ways—genus from the progenitor and from the place of origin, each in two ways, and genus in a third way, in which the species is subaltern to it. The term *species* is used in two ways. In one way it is used for the form of anything. In the other way the genus is predicated of it and it is subaltern to genus, as being divided off from it. With this kind of genus and species the philosophers are concerned.

When we were discussing genus, we mentioned species, when we said that genus was that which was divided into species. And again, when discussing species, we mentioned genus by saying that species was that which was divided off from genus. Thus, one should know that when we speak of a father we must needs think of the son, too (for he is a

---
1 Porphyry, *Isagoge* II.
2 Quoted by Porphyry, *Isagoge* II 18, and from much-quoted fragment of Euripides' lost *Aeolus*. Cf. A. Nauck, *Tragicorum Graecorum fragmenta* (2nd ed., Leipzig 1926) 367.
3 The *infima species* or *species specialissima* of the Scholastics.

father who has a son), and when we discuss a son we must needs think of the father, too (for he is a son who has a father). And similarly, in this case, it is impossible to discuss genus without species or species without genus, for genus is definitely divided into species and that which does not have species divided off from it is not genus. In the same way, the species are divided off from a genus and those things which do not have a genus are not species.

Now, just as the first man—namely, Adam—is not called a son, because he had no father, but is called a father because he did have sons; and as Seth is both called the son of him who begot him, because he did have Adam for his father, and is also called the father of the one begotten by him, because he did beget Henoch; and as Abel is called a son, because he had Adam for father, but is not called a father, because he had no son—just as with these, so also it is with genus and species. The first genus, since it is divided off from no other genus and has no genus higher than itself, is genus only and not species. This is called the *most general genus* and we define it by saying that a most general genus is that which, while it is a genus, is not a species, because it has no genus higher than itself. Those things which are divided off from this, if they have other species inferior to themselves and divided from them, are at once species of those prior to them—that is to say, superior to themselves—from which they themselves have been divided off, and genera of those things divided off from them, which is to say, of those inferior to themselves. These are called *subaltern* genera and species. But the species which are the last and the lowest and which do not possess any lower species, that is, do not contain any species but just individuals—that is to say, individual substances—these are not called genera but just species, because of their not having, as I have said, any lower species divided off from themselves.

For it is impossible to call that a genus which neither contains any species nor has any lower species divided off from it. Therefore, that which does not contain any species, but only individual substances, is a *most specific species,* because, although it is a species, it nevertheless is not a genus. Similarly, the genus which is not a species is called a most general genus.

One should know furthermore that the species necessarily admit of both the name and the definition of their genus, and the genera of their genera up as far as the most general genus. The species, however, cannot admit of each others' definition. Now, to make the matter under discussion clearer, let us look at it in the following manner. Substance is the first and most general genus, for, although substance as well as accident is divided from being, being is not their genus. This is because, although they both admit of the name of being, they do not admit of its definition. A being is a thing which is either self-subsistent and without need of any other for its existence or which cannot exist of itself but has its existence in another. But, substance is a self-subsistent thing and has no need of another for its existence, and that is all. Thus, substance does not admit of the entire definition of being. Consequently, being is not the genus of substance, nor is substance [a species] of being, for the species admits of the definition of its genus in its entirety. What is more, accident is not a species of being either—because it does not admit of its entire definition, but only of half of it. This is because an accident is a thing which cannot exist of itself, but only has its existence in another. Thus, neither substance nor accident admit of the entire definition of being, but substance admits of one half and accident of the other. And so, even though being is divided into substance and accident, it is not their genus. Substance, however, is divided into corporeal and incorporeal substance. Here, the corporeal and the incorporeal are species of substance, because each of them admits of the name and the definition of substance. Thus, substance is not a species, because it has no genus higher than itself; rather, it is a first and most general genus. And again, the corporeal substance is divided into animate and inanimate. Here again, while the corporeal substance is a species of substance, it is the genus of the animate and inanimate. The animate is further divided into sentient and non-sentient. Now, the animal is sentient, because it has life and sensation; whereas the plant is non-sentient, because it does not have sensation. The plant, however, is called animate because it has faculties of assimilating food, of growing, and of reproducing. Again, the animal is divided into rational and irrational. The rational is divided into mortal and immortal, and the mortal into man, the horse, the ox, and the like, which admit no further division into other species, but only into individuals, that is to say, into individual substances. Thus, man is divided into Peter, Paul, John, and all other individual men, who are not species but hypostases. For the species, as we have said, do not admit of each other's definition. For example, the corporeal substance does not admit of the definition of the incorporeal, nor does man admit of the definition of the horse. Peter and Paul and John, however, do admit of one definition: that of man. It is the same for all other individual men; hence there are not various species of men, but individuals, that is to say, hypostases.

Again, when the species is divided, it communicates both its name and its definition to those inferior to itself. However, when Peter is divided into body and soul, he does not communicate his name and his definitions either to the soul or to the body. For Peter is not the soul alone or the body alone but both of them together.

Still further, every division of genus into species will go

as far as two or three or, very rarely, four species, because it is impossible for a genus to be divided into five or more species. Man, on the other hand, is divided into all individual men, and these are unlimited in number. For this reason there are some who say that that which is from species to individuals is not to be called division, but enumeration. Whence it is clear that Peter and Paul and John are not species but individuals, that is to say, hypostases. Nor is man the genus of Peter and Paul and John and the other individual men, but their species. Thus, man, too, is a most specific species, for he is a species belonging to the superior order in so far as he is contained under it; and he is the species of those inferior to himself, in so far as containing them. For, that which is contained by a genus is a species, and that which contains the individuals, or individual substances, is also species. This last, then, is the most specific species, which comes immediately above the individuals, and which they define by saying that it is a species which is predicated in the category of essence of several numerically different things. In the same way, the horse and the dog and other such species are most specific. Those which stand between the most general genus and the most specific species are subaltern genera and species—species of the superior order and genera of the inferior.

Then there are also the essential and natural differences and qualities which are called *dividing* and *constituent,* because they divide the superior and constitute the inferior. Thus, the corporeal and incorporeal divide substance. Similarly, the animate and the inanimate divide the body. Similarly, the sentient and the non-sentient divide the animate. These, then, go to make up the animal, for I take an animate sentient substance and I have an animal, because the animal is an animate sentient substance. Again, I take an inanimate non-sentient substance and I have a stone. Again, I take an animate non-sentient substance and I have a plant. Further still, the rational and the irrational divide the animal, and the mortal and the immortal divide the rational. So I take the animal, which is the genus of these last, and the rational and the mortal and I have a man, for man is a mortal rational animal. Then I take the animal and the irrational and the mortal and the terrestrial and I have a horse, a dog, and the like. Or I take the irrational and the mortal and the aquatic and I have a fish. Now, differences are called essential and natural, because they make one species differ from another and one nature and essence from another essence and nature.

Chapters 9-10 (variants)

The term *genus* is used in three senses: in one sense, as coming from the progenitor, as those descended from Israel are called Israelites; in the second sense, as coming from the place of origin, as those from Jerusalem are called Hierosolymites and those from Palestine Palestinians; and, in the third sense, that is called genus which is divided into species. With this last the philosophers are concerned, and they define it by saying that genus is that which is predicated in respect to their common essence of several things which are specifically different.

The term *species* has two meanings. Thus, appearance and form are called species, as for example, the species of the statue. That is also called species which is subordinate to genus, that is to say, divided off from a genus. With this last the philosophers are concerned.

Now, when we are discussing genus, we mentioned species by saying that genus was that which was divided into species. Again, when discussing species, we mentioned genus by saying that species was that which was divided off from genus. One should know that when we discuss the father we must needs think of the son, too (for he is a father who has a son), and when we discuss the son we must needs think of a father, too (for he is a son who has a father). And similarly in this case it is impossible to treat of the genus without the species, or the species without the genus, for the genus is definitely divided into the species and that which does not have species divided off from itself is not genus. In the same way, the species are divided off from the genus and those things which do not have a genus are not species. And just as the first man—that is to say, Adam—is not called a son, because he had no father, but is called a father because he did have sons; and just as Seth is called both son of him that begot him, for he had Adam for his father, and father of him begotten by him, for he did beget a son; and just as Abel is called a son, because he had Adam for his father, but is not called a father, because he had no son—so also is it with genus and species.

The first genus, which is not divided off from a genus and has no higher genus, is genus only and not a species. This is called a *most general genus* and they define it by saying that a most general genus is that which, while it is a genus, is not a species with a genus higher than itself. Those things which are divided off from this, if they have other species lower than themselves and divided off from themselves, are at once species of those before them—that is to say, higher than themselves—from which they are divided off, and genera of those divided off from themselves —that is to say, of those which are lower than they. These are called *subaltern* genera and species. However, the species which are the last and the lowest and which do not have any lower species are not called genera but only species, because they have no lower species divided off from them.

For it is impossible to call that a genus which neither contains any species nor has any lower species divided off from itself. Therefore, the species which has no species is called a most specific species.

One should know that the species must admit of the name and definition of their genus and that the genus must admit of those of its genus up as far as the most general genus. The species, however, cannot admit of each other's definition. Substance is a first and most general genus. For, even though substance and accident are divided from being, being is not their genus; and, although they do admit of the name of being, they do not admit of the definition. Being is defined as that which is either self-subsistent and without need of any other for its existence, or that which cannot exist of itself but has its existence in another. Now, substance is a thing which is self-subsistent and without need of another for its existence, and it is that alone; accident is a thing which cannot exist in itself, but has its existence in another, and it is that alone. Thus, neither substance nor accident admits of the entire definition of being, but substance admits of one half and accident of the other. Species, however, will admit of both the name and the entire perfect definition of their genus. And so, even though being is divided into substance and accident, it is still not their genus. Nor, indeed, is substance a species with a genus higher than itself. On the contrary, it is a first and most general genus.

This substance, then, is divided into corporeal and incorporeal. Hence, the corporeal and the incorporeal are species of substance. Again, corporeal substance is divided into animate and inanimate. Here again the corporeal, while it is a species of substance, is the genus of the animate and the inanimate. Again, the animate is divided into sentient and non-sentient. Now the sentient is the animal, because it has both life and sensation; but the non-sentient is the plant, because it does not have sensation. The plant is called animate because it has the faculties of assimilating food, of growth, and of reproduction. Again, the animal is divided into rational and irrational. The rational is divided into mortal and immortal. The mortal is divided into rational man and the irrational animals such as the horse, the dog, and the like. None of these last is divided into any further species; they are divided into individuals, that is to say, individual substances. Thus, man is divided into Peter and Paul and John and all other individual men, who are not species, because species, as we have said, do not admit of each other's definition. For example, the corporeal substance does not admit of the definition of the incorporeal. Man does not admit of the definition of the horse. But Peter and Paul and John do admit of one definition—that of man. And it is the same way with all other individual men. So, these last are not species of man. but they are individuals, that is to say, hypostases.

Again when the species is divided, it communicates both its name and its definition to those lower than itself. On the contrary, when Peter is divided into body and soul, he communicates neither his name nor his definition to the soul or the body. (For neither is the soul alone Peter, nor is the body; rather, he is both together.[1])

Still further, every division of genus into species will go as for as two or three, but very rarely to four species, because it is impossible for a genus to be divided into five or more species. But man is divided into all individual men, who are unlimited in number. For this reason there are some who say that that which is from species to individuals is not to be called division, but enumeration. Whence it is clear that Peter and Paul and John are not species but indi-

---

1 Not in some manuscripts.

viduals, that is to say, hypostases. Neither is man the genus of Peter and all of the other individual men, but their species. For this reason man is a most specific species, because he is a species in relation to the higher and species in relation to the lower. Similarly, the horse, the dog, and the like are species and not genera, for which reason they are most specific species. Those coming in between the most general genus and the most specific species are subaltern genera. They are species of the higher and genera of the lower.

Then, there are also the essential and natural specific differences and qualities which are called *dividing* and *constituent,* because they divide the higher and are constituent of the lower. Thus, the corporeal and incorporeal substances divide substance. Similarly, the animate and inanimate divide the corporeal substance. Similarly, the sentient and nonsentient divide the animate. These, then, go to make up the the animal, for I take an animate sentient substance and I have an animal, because the animal is an animate sentient substance. Then, I take an inanimate non-sentient substance and I have a stone. Again, I take an animate non-sentient substance and I have a plant. Then, again, the rational and the irrational divide the animal, and the mortal and the immortal divide the rational. So, I take the animal, which is the genus, and the rational and the mortal and I have a man, for a man is a mortal rational animal. And I take the animal and the irrational and the mortal and I have the horse, say, or the dog, or the like. Now, differences are called essential and natural, because they make one species differ from another and one nature and essence differ from another essence and nature.

Chapter 11

The term *individual*[1] is used in four senses. Thus, that which cannot be divided or partitioned is called individual, as the point, the instance of the time which is *now,* and the unit. These are said to be *quantitiless* (that is to say, *without quantity*[2]). That also is called individual which is hard to divide, that is to say, is difficult to cut up, as is the diamond and the like. That species is also called individual which is not further divisible into other species; in other words, the most specific species, such as man, the horse, and so forth. The term individual, however, is principally used as meaning that which, although it is divisible, does not maintain its species intact after the division. Thus, Peter is divided into soul and body, but neither is the soul by itself a perfect man or a perfect Peter, nor is the body. It is with this latter kind of individual—namely, that which shows the individuality of the substance—that the philosophers are concerned.

Chapter 12

Difference[1] and *quality* and *property* are all the same thing in relation to their subject, but in relation to their operation they are different. Thus, rationality is said to be both a quality and a property and a difference of man, but it is these in different ways. Thus, on the one hand, in so far as it makes and, as it were, forms the substance, it is said to be a quality. Then, in so far as it becomes peculiar to this substance, it is said to be a property. But, in comparison

---

1 ἄτομον: indivisible, that which cannot be cut.
2 Not in some manuscripts.

1 Porphyry, *Isagoge* III.

with the irrational—an ox, say, or a mule, or a dog—then it is said to be a *difference,* because in it man differs from the irrational animals.

The term difference is used in three senses: in a common sense, in a special sense, and in a very special sense. For it is impossible to find any two things which do not differ from each other in something. Thus, in some things species differ from species; in others an individual substance differs from another of the same species and substance; and in others an individual substance differs from itself. For the species of man differs from that of the horse by the rational and the irrational, the rational and the irrational being said to constitute an *essential difference.* Similarly, all things by which species differs from species are called natural and essential and constituent and specific difference and quality (and a natural property, as inhering unchangeably in the whole species). This is called by the philosophers a *very special difference,* as being indicative of the nature and more proper to it. Again, a man differs from a man, or a horse from a horse, or a dog from a dog (that is, an individual differs from an individual of the same species), according as one is large and the other small, or as one is old and the other young (or as one is flat-nosed and the other sharp-nosed),[2] or as one is intelligent and the other stupid. All these are called *non-essential* differences and qualities, which is precisely what an *accident* is, concerning which we shall speak directly.

---

2 The three passages enclosed in parenthesis are lacking in the shorter recension.

Chapter 13

An *accident*[1] is that which may either be present or absent without destroying the subject. Again, it is that which can be or not be in the same thing. Thus, it is possible for a man to be white or not, and also for him to be tall, intelligent, or flat-nosed or not. (For the presence of this does not save the species, because it does not belong to the definition of the species. Neither does its absence destroy the species. Thus, even though the Ethiopian is not white, this in no wise keeps him from being a man. And so, whether it is present or absent, it does not injure the subject substance—for we have said that the substance is a subject and sort of matter for the accidents.[2])

The accident is divided into two kinds: that which is commonly called a difference and that which is properly a difference. What is commonly called a difference is the *separable* accident. For example, one person is seated and another standing. Now, by the standing up of the one who is seated and the sitting down of the one who is standing it is possible for the original difference between the two to be removed and replaced by another difference. And one is also said to differ from oneself by a separable accident, for one does differ from oneself by sitting down and standing, by being young and growing old, by being sick and getting well, and so forth. A difference in the proper sense is the *inseparable* accident. For example, a person is snub-nosed and it is impossible to separate his snub-nosedness from him, and similarly with his being gray-eyed and the like. Thus, it is by these inseparable accidents that one individual, that is, one individual substance, differs from another. However, one's own self never differs from oneself. Now, the accidents

---
1 Porphyry, *Isagoge* V.
2 Lacking in the shorter recension.

do not enter into the definition (of the nature[3]), because it is possible for a man to be snub-nosed or not, and, just because a man does not have gray eyes, he remains no less a man.

Chapter 14

There are four ways in which a thing is said to be *property*.[1] In the first place, that is said to be a property which is in one species only but not in the entire species. Such, for example, is the ability which man has for land-surveying, for only man surveys land, yet not every man does have this ability. Secondly, that is said to be a property which belongs to the entire species but not to just one species. An example would be the having of two feet. Thus, every man is a biped, but not man only, because the dove is a biped, too, and so are others of the sort. Thirdly, that is said to be a property which is in the whole species and in it alone but not always. Such is the becoming gray-haired in man, because this is proper to every man and to man alone, yet not always, but only in old age. Fourthly, that is said to be a property which arises from the combination of the first three, namely, that which is in an entire species, is in that species only and always, and is convertible like laughter in man, neighing in the horse, and so on. For only man can laugh and every man can laugh and can always do so, even though he may not always exercise this power. (Thus, if something is a man, it most certainly can laugh; and if something can laugh, it is most certainly a man. And that is what is meant by being convertible. It is with this last meaning that the philosophers are concerned.[2]) Now, to describe it we say that a property

---

[3] *Ibid.*

[1] Porphyry, Isagoge IV.
[2] Lacking in the shorter recension

is that which belongs to a single species, to the whole species and always. This has a threefold division: being from the way a thing is formed, that is to say, the way it is shaped, as is the being broad-nailed and walking erect in man; being from the operation of the thing, as the being carried upward which is proper to fire; or being from the potentiality of the thing, as we say that the fire has a power of heating which exceeds the heat of other bodies. The property, moreover, is said to be added over and above the essence, or adventitious.

Chapter 15

Every *predicate*[1] is either more extensive than its subject or co-extensive with it, but it is never less extensive. It is more extensive when more general things are predicated of more particular ones. The more general, then, are the superior, whereas the more particular are the inferior. And the most general thing of all is the being, for which reason it is predicable of all things. For, substance is called a being, and so is accident called a being. But we cannot say that the being is substance, because not only is substance being, but so is accident. Genera, likewise, are predicable of their species, because they are more general; but the species are not predicable of their genera, because they are less general than their genera. Thus, substance is predicated of the animal, and the animal is predicated of man. This is because the animal is a substance and man is an animal. This is not, however, convertible, because, although every man is an animal, not every animal is a man—for the horse and the dog are animals, too. Moreover, not every substance is an animal, for stone and wood are substances which are not animals. Similarly, the species is predicable of the individuals

---

1 Cf. Aristotle, *Categories* III.

contained in it, that is to say, of the individual substances, because the species is more general. But the individual, that is to say, the individual substance, is not predicable of the species, because the individual substance is more particular than its species. Thus, Peter is a man and Paul is a man, but not every man is Peter or Paul, because there are other persons contained in the human species. The differences also are predicable of the species in which they inhere and of their individuals. This is because the differences are more general than the species. Thus, the rational is more general than the species of man, because, although every man is rational, not every rational being is a man. Although the angel also is rational, he is not a man. Such, then, is the predicate which is more extensive.

The predicate, on the other hand, is co-extensive with its subject, when it is convertible. Thus, properties are predicated of the species of which they are properties; and the species are predicated of their properties. For every man is capable of laughter and everything that is capable of laughter is a man. Even though a monkey may also be said to laugh, it does not laugh with its heart but only with its features, because it is an animal which is good at mimicking. And so, the predication of the genera of their species, that of the differences of their species and that of the species of their individuals, are said to be more extensive; while that of the properties is said to be co-extensive. Those which are co-extensive are convertible and are called reciprocal predicables.

Chapter 16

Predication is *univocal* when the subject admits of both the name and the definition of the name itself. For instance, the animal is predicated of man and admits of both the name and the definition of the animal, because an animal is an animate sentient substance and man admits of this definition. For man is an animate and sentient substance.

On the other hand, predication is *equivocal* when the subject admits indeed of the name, but not at all of the definition. For instance, the picture of a man admits of the name of the man, but it does not admit of the definition of man. For man is defined as a rational animal which is mortal and which is capable of understanding and knowing. The picture, however, is neither an animal (for it is not animate), nor is it rational or capable of understanding and knowing.

One should know that whatever is predicated of something as of a subject, predicated univocally, that is, will also be predicated of that which comes under it. For example, the animal is predicated of man as of a subject, that is to say, univocally. Man, in turn, is predicated of Peter, for Peter comes under man. Therefore, the animal is also predicated of Peter, because Peter is also an animal.

The term *subject* is taken in two ways: as subject of existence and as subject of predication. We have a subject of existence in such a case as that of substance, which is the subject of accidents, since these have existence in the substance, which is the subject of accidents, since these have existence in the substance but outside of it do not subsist. On the other hand, the subject of predication is the particular, for with predication the particular is subject to the more general, since the more general is predicated of the more particular—as the animal is predicated of man. Now, that which is universal is affirmed of a subject whereas that which is more particular is a subject of predication. And the accident is said to be in the substance as in a subject, whereas the substance is said to be a subject of existence.

Chapter 17

Predication of the essence of a thing is one thing, whereas that of its sort is another. Predication is of the essence of a thing when, being asked what a man is, we reply: 'an animal.' But it is of its sort when, being asked what sort of an animal, we answer: 'a rational mortal animal.' Thus, the genus and the species are predicated of the essence of a thing; whereas the difference, whether essential—that is to say, whether property or accident—is predicated of its sort. The individual substance neither signifies what the thing is nor of what sort it is, but it does signify *which one* it is. Thus, when we are asked who this man is, we reply that he is Peter. Then, when asked what sort of man he is, we reply that he is tall, let us say, or short.

Moreover, one should know that things which differ in nature are said to be one thing and another. Thus, we say that man is one thing and the horse another, and we mean *another* thing in nature, because the species of man is one thing and that of the horse is something else. Those things, however, which differ in number, that is to say, which are individual substances, are said to be one and another. Thus, we say that Peter is one and Paul another. However, we cannot say that Peter is one and Paul another, because, if we did, we should not be telling the truth. For in nature they are one thing, but numerically they are not.

And one should know that the substance is called *another thing,* and likewise the essential differences, while the accident is called *something of another sort.* This is because the essential differences are considered in connection with the species, that is to say, in connection with the nature which they go to make up. The accident is considered in connection with the individual, because the accidents are constituent of the individual substance. A man, then, is one thing and a horse another, but Peter is of one sort and one and Paul of another sort and another. Moreover, every difference, whether essential or not, makes for something else of a different sort (ἑτεροῖον), for ἑτεροῖον means both something else and a thing of a different sort. The nature, then, signifies what a thing is, whereas the individual substance specifies this certain person or thing and every difference shows of what sort something is.

Chapter 18

One must know that the five terms have this in common with each other, that they are all predicated of several things.[1] But they differ from one another for the following reason, namely, that: while genus is predicated of the essence of several things differing in species; species is predicated of the sort of several things differing in number; difference and accident are predicated of the sort of several things differing in species; and property is predicated of the sort of several things differing in number, that is, of one species and the individuals contained in it. Moreover, the difference differs from the accident in that, while the difference is essential, that is to say, is a part of the substance of the subject, the accident does not exist as a part of the substance but as a non-essential.

---

[1] Porphyry, *Isagoge* VI.

Chapter 19

Genus and difference[1] have this in common, that they both contain the species and that they are both predicated univocally of species and individuals. One should furthermore know that whatever is predicated of something as of a subject, that is, univocally, will also be predicated univocally of what comes under this. In the case of equivocal predication, however, that will by no means be true. The distinguishing peculiarities of the genus as compared with the difference are: that the genus is more extensive than the differences under it and than the three other terms; that the genus contains the differences virtually; that the genus is prior by nature to the differences; that the genus is predicated of the essence of a thing, whereas the difference is predicated of its sort; that the related genus is one, whereas the differences are several; and that the genus corresponds to matter, whereas the difference corresponds to form.

Chapter 20

Genus and species[1] have this in common: that they are predicated of the essence of several things; that by nature they are prior to those things that come under them; and that each is a whole something. Distinguishing peculiarities of genus and species are as follow, namely: that the genus is more general than the species; that the species is richer in differences than the genus; that the genus is predicated of the species univocally, whereas the species is not convertible; and that neither is the genus more specific, nor the

---
1 *Ibid.* VII.

---
1 *Ibid.* VIII.

species most general, nor can that which is most specific be a genus.

Chapter 21

Genus and property[1] have this in common, namely: that they both follow the species, that is to say, are predicated of them; that they are both predicated equally of the things of which they are predicated; and that they are predicated univocally. The differences between genus and property are: that the genus is prior by nature to the property; that the genus is predicated of several species, whereas the property is predicated of one; that the property is convertible with the species, but the genus never; and that the property exists in just one species, while the genus does not.

Chapter 22

Genus and accident[1] have this in common: that they are predicated of several things. Distinguishing peculiarities of genus and accident are: that the genus is prior to the species in which the accidents subsist, whereas the accidents are posterior to the species; that the participation of the genus is equal, but not that of the accidents; that the accident exists antecedently in the individuals and consequently in the species, whereas the contrary is true of the genus; and that the genera are predicated of the essence of a thing, whereas the accidents are predicated of its sort, or how the thing is.

---
[1] *Ibid.* IX.

---
[1] *Ibid.* X.

Chapter 23

Difference and species[1] have this in common: that they are participated in equally, and that they are always present in the things which participated in them. Distinguishing peculiarities of difference and species are these: that the difference is predicated of what sort something is, and the species of its difference; that the difference contains several species and their individuals, whereas the species contains only the individuals which come under itself; that the difference is prior by nature to the species; and that a difference may be combined with a difference, but a species with a species never.

Chapter 24

Difference and property[1] have this in common: that they are predicated equally of all the things that participate in them, and that they are always present in the whole species. Distinguishing peculiarities of difference and property are: that, whereas the difference contains several species, the property contains only one; and that the difference is not convertible with the species, whereas the property is.

Chapter 25

Difference and accident[1] have this in common: that they are both predicated of several things as to what sort they are, and that the difference and the inseparable accident

---
1 *Ibid.* XII.

---
1 *Ibid.* XIII.

---
1 *Ibid.* XIV.

are always present in the things of which they are predicated. One of the distinguishing peculiarities of difference and accident is that the differences contain and are not contained, while the accidents are contained. For, on the one hand, both contain the species, as being predicated of several species; but the difference is not contained, because the same species does not admit of contradictory differences. On the other hand, the accident is contained, for the reason that the same species and the same individual will admit of several accidents which may oftentimes even be contradictory. Other distinguishing peculiarities are: that the difference does not admit of more or less, whereas the accidents on the contrary do, and that contradictory differences may not be combined, whereas contradictory accidents may.

Chapter 26

Species and property[1] have this in common: that they are mutually predicable of each other, that is to say, that they are convertible; and that they are participated in equally because they do not communicate themselves to any one of the individuals participating in them more or less than to any other. Differences between species and property are: that the species is essential, whereas the property is superadded to the essence; that the species is always in act, whereas the property is always in potency and not always in act; and that those things which have different definitions are manifestly themselves different also.

---
1 *Ibid.* XV.

Chapter 27

Species and accident[1] have this in common: that they are predicated of several things. Differences between species and accident are: that the species is predicated of the essence of a thing, whereas the accident is predicated of its sort; that one may participate in just one species, whereas anyone may participate even in several accidents; that the species is by nature prior to the accidents; and that participation in the species is equal, whereas the accidents admit of more or less.

Chapter 28

Property and inseparable accident[1] have this in common: that without them those things in which they inhere cannot exist, and that both are always present. Distinguishing peculiarities of property and accident are: that the property belongs to one species, whereas the accident belongs to several; that whereas the property is convertible with the species, the accident never is; and that, whereas the accident admits of more or less, the property by no means does.

Chapter 29

The word *hypostasis* has two meanings. Thus, when used in the strict sense it means substance simply. However, the hypostasis subsisting in itself means the individual and the distinct person. *Enhypostaton,* or what has real existence, has two meanings also. Thus, it may mean being in the strict sense. In this sense we not only call substance in the

---

1 *Ibid.* XVI.

---

1 Cf. *Ibid.* XVII.

strict sense enhypostatic but the accident, also. And it also means the hypostasis in itself, that is to say, the individual. *Anhypostaton,* or what has not real existence, is also used in two senses. Thus, that which has absolutely no existence at all is called anhypostaton, and the accident is also so called, because it does not subsist in itself but in the substance.

Chapter 30

In this same way the pagan philosophers stated the difference between οὐσία, or substance, and φύσις, or nature, by saying that substance was being in the strict sense, whereas nature was substance which had been made specific by essential differences so as to have, in addition to *being in the strict sense, being in such a way,* whether rational or irrational, mortal or immortal. In other words, we may say that, according to them, nature is that unchangeable and immutable principle and cause and virtue which has been implanted by the Creator in each species for its activity—in the angels, for thinking and for communicating their thoughts to one another without the medium of speech; in men, for thinking, reasoning, and for communicating their innermost thoughts to one another through the medium of speech; in the brute beasts, for the vital, the sentient, and the respiratory operations; in the plants, for the power of assimilating nourishment, of growing, and reproducing; in the stones, the capacity for being heated or cooled and for being moved from place to place by another, that is to say, the inanimate capacity. This they called *nature,* or the most specific species—as, for example, angel, man, horse, dog, ox, and the like. For these are more general than the individual substances and contain them, and in each one of the individual substances contained by them they exist complete and in the same manner. And so, the more particular they called *hypostasis,* and the more general, which contained the hypostases, they called *nature,* but existence in the strict sense they called οὐσία, or substance.

The holy Fathers paid no attention to the many inane controversies, and that which is common to and affirmed of several things, that is to say, the most specific species, they called *substance,* and *nature,* and *form*—as, for example, angel, man, horse, dog, and the like. For, indeed, οὐσία, or substance, is so called from its εἶναι, or being; and φύσις, or nature, is so called from its πεφυκέναι, or being. But εἶναι and πεφυκέναι both mean the same thing. *Form,* also, and species mean the same thing as nature. However, the particular they called *individual,* and *person,* and *hypostasis* or individual substance—as, for example, would be Peter and Paul. Now, the hypostasis must have substance together with accidents, and it must subsist in itself and be found to be sensibly, that is, actually, existent. It is furthermore impossible for two hypostases not to differ from each other in their accidents and still to differ from each other numerically. And one should know that the *characteristic properties* are the accidents which distinguish the hypostasis.

Chapter 31

Those things are *equivocal*[1] which have a common name, but which differ in their definition or description. The term dog, for example, is an equivocal one, because it means both the land-dog and the sea-dog. The land-dog, however, has one definition, while the sea-dog has another, because one

---

1 Cf. Ammonius, *In Isagogen,* p. 84.

is one nature and the other is another. Now, equivocals are described as follows: those things are equivocal which have only their name in common, while the statement of the substances signified by the name is diverse. Take 'statement' here as meaning definition or description; and take 'by the name' as showing that the definitions of the name are diverse, for which reason the things are equivocal. Take, for example, the land-dog and the sea-dog. These are equivocal because of their name—dog. For, should anyone wish to give the definition of the land-dog and of the sea-dog, he will, in so far as each one of them is called a dog, give one definition of dog to the land one and another to the sea one. Nevertheless, it is possible for these to have a common definition as well as a common name. Thus, both are called animals and admit of the definition of the animal. In the name of animal, however, they are not equivocal, but univocal. Moreover, in the case of equivocal things one must ask three questions, namely: whether it is equivocal, in how many senses it is taken, and which meaning is in question.[2]

Although the ancients were of the opinion that *likeness* arose in four ways from quality alone, the more recent have thought that primarily and summarily it arises both from substance and quality. There is likeness in substance, as when we say that men are like angels, implying that they are equal to them, even though in their qualities men and angels do differ from each other very much. And in the same way we speak of horses, swans, and the like. However, since this likeness sometimes appears as without variance and sometimes with some variance, the heretics who

---

2 According to Lequien from here to the end of the chapter is an appendix which may or may not be the Damascene's. It may be the result of one of his revisions.

made the Son to be inferior would say that He was like the Father, and thus by the ambiguity of the term they would lead astray more simple folk. It is for this very reason that Basil the Great says: 'If the "without variance" be added, then I, too, accept it.'[3] So much, then, for likeness in substance. Likeness in quality is not just in this quality or that, but in every quality—that is to say, in shape, form, color, skill, virtue, and whatever else is included in the nature of quality.

Now, this likeness[4] has a fourfold division. Thus, it may be in one species and one quality, as when we say that things of the same species are like each other. For instance, we say that the Ethiopians are like each other in their being black, and again, that swans are alike in their being white. And so, these last are like each other in two ways, both in substance and appearance, that is to say, color. Or likeness may be in different species that have one and the same quality, as, for example, white and black pepper are like each other in quality. Or it will be in the same species with different qualities, as, for example, the pigeon is like the dove in its being white, and purple, and black, and in other things which they may have in common. But the quality of these last is different. A fourth kind of likeness is the appearance which is in the image and its original, as it would be with the picture of an animal and the live animal. In this way, too, they say that we are like God. Nevertheless, anyone who considers the matter carefully will discover how very great a difference there is. For the former have nothing else in common but their name and form, while man has that which is most important in him in common with God, namely, goodness, and wisdom, or even power. Yet, man

---

3 Basil, *Ep. IX (XLI), (PG* 32.269B-272A).
4 Written 'quality.'

is not absolutely like God, because God has these things by nature and we have them by adoption—each in a different way. And so, not only is the difference between God and man infinite, but also that between individual men proportionately. Likeness, therefore, is like the relation of things which are *derivative* and *relative*.

Chapter 32

All those things are *univocal*[1] which have in common both their name and the definition or description of their name. For example, the term animal signifies both man and the horse. And in this name, that is, in the name animal, they are univocal, because each of them admits both of the name and of the definition of the animal. Now, they describe univocal things as follows: those things are univocal which have a common name and the same definition for the substance signified by that name.

Chapter 33

All those things are *multinominal*[1] which have the same definition but differ in name. In other words, a thing is multinominal when this same thing is called by several names. Such, for example, would be sword, blade, broadsword, rapier, claymore. For all these names admit of one definition, namely, a double-edged piece of steel, that is, a piece of steel sharpened on both edges. Multinominals are described as follows: several names applied to one thing.

---
[1] Cf. Ammonius, *op. cit.*, p. 84, and *In Categorias*, p. 22.

[1] Cf. Ammonius, *In Categorias*, p. 16.

Chapter 34

Those things which differ in both, that is to say, in name and definition, may have one subject.[1] In such a case they are called *heteronymous,* as are ascent and descent, for they have one subject—the incline. Or they may not have one subject; in which case, they are called *different*. Such are substance and accident, because they both have different names and different descriptions and they do not have one subject. The description of both of these, the heteronymous and the different, is this: Those things of which the name and the definition are diverse.

Chapter 35

Midway between the equivocals and the univocals there are certain other things which both share and differ in their name and definition and which are called *conjugates*.[1] Such is 'grammarian,' which is derived from 'grammar.' These do share in their name, but they differ in the ending of the name, that is, in the last syllables. Furthermore, they both share and differ in their definition, because grammar is a knowledge, whereas the grammarian is the substance in which that knowledge is. Those things, then, are *conjugates* which get their appellation from something by inflective variation, that is to say, variation of the name of the thing.

Moreover, one must know that grammar and music and justice are not derivatives, but that the musician, the grammarian, and the just are. This is because grammarian is derived from grammar, musician from music, and just from justice.

---

[1] Cf. *ibid.*

[1] Cf. ibid., p. 22.

And one must know that the conjugates contain the things from which they are derived, as the grammarian contains the grammar and the just man justice. This, however, is by no means true in the case of things which are derivative. Thus, the medical instrument does not contain medicine.

Chapter 36

Some things which are affirmed are affirmed simply and without combination, as are substance, accident, and the like. Others, however, are affirmed in combination, as 'a horse runs' or 'Socrates philosophizes.' Of those things which are affirmed simply and without combination, one signifies *substance,* as, for example, man or horse; another, *quantity,* as, for example, two or three, two cubits long or three cubits long; another, *relation,* such as father or son; another, *quality,* such as white or black; another, *place,* such as in a temple or in a marketplace; another, *time,* such as last year, yesterday, or today; another, *position,* such as standing or sitting; another, *state,* such as being dressed or being shod; another, *action,* such as burning or cutting; another, *passion,* such as being burnt or being cut. In so far as these ten are affirmed of certain things, they are called *categories,* because to categorize is the same thing as to affirm.[1]

One should know, moreover, that each of the ten categories is a most general genus. Now, of these ten categories, which are also most general genera, one is substance, whereas the other nine are accidents. The ten are: (1) substance, (2) quantity, (3) relation, (4) quality, (5) time, (6) place, (7) position, (8) state, (9) action, and (10) passion.

---
1 Cf. Aristotle, *Categories* IV.

Chapter 37

All things that fall in the same category are generically the same (as man and horse).[1] Generically different are all those that fall in different categories (as animal and knowledge). They are different in genus. On the other hand, all things that come under the same species and thus have their substance in common, as Peter and Paul, are specifically the same. But those are specifically different which differ from one another in species, that is to say, by reason of their substance, as do man and the horse. All those things are numerically different which by the combination of their accidents have marked off for themselves the individuality of their own individual substance and have thus acquired individual existence, that is to say, those that are individuals, such as Peter and Paul and all other individual men.

The differences of all things that are generically different are also specifically different, as, for example, those of animal and knowledge—for the animal comes under substance, whereas knowledge comes under quality. Constituent differences of the animal are the animate and the sentient, whereas the rational, the irrational, the winged, the terrestrial, or the aquatic are dividing differences. On the other hand, constituent differences of knowledge are its inherence in animate rational beings and, besides this, its tendency to inalterability; whereas grammar and philosophy are dividing differences. For to that category to which the genus belongs the species also belongs, and so also do the differences of the species. And nothing prevents the same differences from belonging to the subaltern genera and species, but not all, because, for example, the living cannot make the non-living. Now, by differences here I mean those which constitute the genera and the species.

---

[1] This and the following parenthetical phrases are supplied by Combefis.

Moreover, one should know that the nine categories which are not substance, even though they are accidents, do each one have constituent and dividing differences. Each is a most general genus and each has subaltern species and genera and most specific species. For, without exception, where there is a genus, there there are species and dividing differences, since they are what divide the genera into species. And where there are species, there there are differences also, for they are what constitute the species.

The term 'one' is used in three ways. Either it will be one in genus, as, for example, we say that man and the horse are generically one and the same, because they belong to one genus, namely, the animal. Or it will be one in species, as we say that, since Socrates and Plato belong to one species, man, they are specifically one and the same. Or it will be one in number, as we say that Socrates is in himself one, being distinct from all other men.

Chapter 38

There are eleven ways of *being in something*:[1] (1) as genus in species, as the animal is in the definition of man; (2) as species in genus, as man is in the division of the animal; (3) in a place, as a priest in the temple; (4) in time, as Noe in the time of the flood; (4) in a receptacle, as wine is in a jar; (6) as a whole in parts, as Socrates in his own members, in his head, hands, and feet—although this is not being *in something* but, rather, *in some things*; (7) as the part in a whole, as the head or hand in Socrates; (8) as form in matter, as the form of the statue in the bronze; (9) as in the efficient cause, as all things are in God; (10) as in the final cause, as the bed is in man's rest, because

---

[1] Cf. Ammonius, *In Categorias*, p. 26.

it is for the purpose of man's resting that the bed is made; (11) as in a subject, as whiteness is in a body. One should know, moreover, that parts are said to belong to a whole, but a whole is never said to belong to parts but rather to be a whole in parts.

Chapter 39

Substance is a thing which subsists in itself and has no need of another for its existence. And again: substance is everything that subsists in itself and does not have its existence in another—that is to say, that which is not because of any other thing, nor has its existence in another, nor has need of another to subsist, but which is in itself and is that in which the accident has its existence. Thus, color was made because of the body, that it might color it, but the body was not made because of the color. And the color exists in the body, not the body in color. For this reason the color is said to belong to the body and the body not to belong to the color. Thus, for example, although the color may often be changed and altered, yet the substance, that is to say, the body, is not changed but remains the same. Now οὐσία, or substance, is so called from its εἶναι, or being (in the proper sense. On the other hand, συμβεβηκός, or accident, is so called from its συμβαίνειν, or happening, and sometimes being and sometimes not being, because it is possible for the same accident to exist in the same thing or not to exist, and not only that, but for its contrary to exist there).[1]

---

1 The material within the parenthesis has been added by some corrector.

Chapter 40

The nature of each being is the principle of its motion and repose. The earth, for example, is moved [i.e., ploughed] to make it produce, but, so far as concerns its being moved from place to place, it is at rest, because it is not moved from place to place. Now, the principles and cause of its motion and repose—or that according to which it is of its nature thus moved and rests substantially, that is to say, naturally and not accidentally—is called φύσις, or nature, from its πεφυκέναι, or naturally having being and existing in such a manner. This is nothing other than substance, because it is from its substance that it has such a potentiality, that is to say, that of motion and repose. The substance, then, is the cause of its motion and repose. Now, φύσις, or nature, is so called from its πεφυκέναι, or naturally having being.

Chapter 41

Form is the substance which has been, as it were, given form and made specific by the essential differences, and which signifies the most specific species. Thus, for example, the substance which has been given form and made specific by the animate and sentient body constitutes the animal. And again, when this last has taken on the rational and the mortal, it constitutes the species of man. It is precisely this most specific species which is called form, an informed substance, as it were.

And so the holy Fathers apply the terms *substance,* and *nature,* and *form* to the most specific species, and they say that substance and nature and form are the same thing, namely, the most specific species. And the individuals coming under the same most specific species they say to be of the same substance, of the same nature, of the same species, of the same genus, and of the same form. On the other hand, they say that the most specific species are of different substance, of different nature, of different species, of different genus, and of different form. This is because it is impossible for a species not to be of a different substance and of a different nature and of a different form from another species, or for a nature so not to differ from another nature, or for a substance so not to differ from another substance.

One should know that it is impossible for one compound nature to be made from two substances, that is to say, from two natures, because it is impossible for logically opposed constituent differences to exist in the same thing. It is possible, however, for one compound hypostasis to be made from diverse natures, which is how man is made up of body and soul. Now, even though men are said to have one nature, the individual man is not said to be of one nature. This is because, on the one hand, the one nature of man is said to be compound, since all the compound hypostases of men come under one species; whereas, on the other hand, the individual man is not said to be of one nature, since each human hypostasis is made up of two natures—soul and body, I mean—which it preserves unconfused in itself, to which fact the separation caused by death bears witness.

Chapter 42

The term *hypostasis* has two meanings. Sometimes it means simple existence. In this sense, substance and hypostasis are the same thing, which is why certain of the holy Fathers have said: 'the natures, that is to say, hypostases.'[1] At

---

1 Cyril of Alexandria, *Reply to Theodoret*, Anath. II (*PG* 76.401A).

other times, it means the existence of an individual substance in itself. In this sense, it signifies the individual, that which is numerically different, which is to say, Peter and Paul, or that certain horse.

Now, one should know that substance which is devoid of form does not subsist of itself, nor does an essential difference, nor a species, nor an accident. It is only the hypostases, the individuals, that is, that subsist of themselves, and in them are found both the substance and the essential differences, the species and the accidents. The simple substance, moreover, is found in the same manner in all hypostases: in inanimate and animate substances, in rational and irrational, in mortal and immortal. The essential differences, however, are one thing in inanimate substances and another in animate, one thing in rational and another in irrational, and, similarly, one thing in mortal and another in immortal. To put it simply, with the hypostases belonging to each most specific species, the same essential differences connect them one to another by reason of their substance, but they separate them from the hypostases of another species. In the same way, the accidents in these, that is, in the hypostases, are considered as separating each hypostasis from the other hypostases of the same species. For this reason the term hypostasis has been properly applied to the individual, since in the hypostasis the substance, to which the accidents have been added, actually subsists (ὑφίστασται).

Chapter 43

A *person* is one who by reason of his own operations and properties exhibits to us an appearance which is distinct and set off from those of the same nature as he. When Gabriel, for example, was conversing with the Mother of God,[1] while he was one of the angels, he alone was present there and speaking. Thus he was by his presence and conversation in that place made distinct from the angels of the same substance with him. And when Paul spoke to the people from the stairs,[2] while he was one of the number of men, by his properties and operations he was distinct from the rest of men.

One should know that the holy Fathers used the term *hypostasis* and *person* and *individual* for the same thing, namely, that which by its own subsistence subsists of itself from substance and accidents, is numerically different, and signifies a certain one, as, for example, Peter, and Paul, and this horse. *Hypostasis* has been so called from its ὑφεστάναι, or subsisting.

Chapter 44

The *enhypostaton,* too, sometimes means existence in the strict sense. In this sense, we call not only simple substance but also the accident an enhypostaton, although, properly speaking, the accident is not an enhypostaton but *heterohypostaton,* or something which subsists in another. Sometimes it means the self-subsistent hypostasis, that is to say, the individual, which, properly speaking, is not an enhypostaton but a *hypostasis* and is so called. In its proper sense, however, the enhypostaton is either that which does not subsist in itself but is considered in hypostases, just as the human species, or human nature, that is, is not considered in its own hypostasis but in Peter and Paul and the other human hypostases. Or it is that which is compound with another

---
1 Luke 1.28.
2 Acts 21.40.

thing differing in substance to make up one particular whole and constitute one compound hypostasis. Thus, man is made up of soul and body, while neither the soul alone nor the body alone is called a hypostasis, but both are called enhypostata. That which consists of both is the hypostasis of both, for in the proper sense hypostasis is that which subsists of itself by its own subsistence, and such this is called.

Again, that nature is called enhypostaton which has been assumed by another hypostasis and in this has its existence. Thus, the body of the Lord, since it never subsisted of itself, not even for an instant, is not a hypostasis, but an enhypostaton. And this is because it was assumed by the hypostasis of God the Word and this subsisted, and did and does have this for a hypostasis.

Chapter 45

The term *anhypostaton* is also used in two senses. Thus, it sometimes means that which has no existence whatsoever, that is to say, the non-existent. But it sometimes means that which does not have its being in itself but exists in another, that is to say, the accident.

Chapter 46

Being is divided[1] into substance and accident, not as genus into species, but as an equivocal term, or as those things which are derivative and relative.

---
1 Cf. Ammonius, *In Isagogen,* p.81.

Chapter 47

Substance is a most general genus. It is divided into *corporeal* and *incorporeal*.

The *corporeal* is divided into *animate* and *inanimate*.

The *animate* is divided into *sentient*, or *animal, zoophyte*, and *non-sentient*, or *plant*.

The *animal* is divided into *rational* and *irrational*.

The *rational* is divided into *mortal* and *immortal*.

The *mortal* is divided into man, ox, horse, dog, and the like.

Man is divided into Peter, Paul, and all other individual men. These are individuals, hypostases, and persons.

Substance, then, is a most general genus. The body is a species of substance, and genus of the animate. The animate is a species of body, and genus of the sentient. The sentient animal is a species of the animate, and genus of the rational. The rational is a species of the animal, and genus of the mortal. The mortal is a species of the rational, and genus of man. Man is a most specific species, for he is a species of the mortal and at the same time the species of Peter and of Paul, and this is just what the holy Fathers meant by nature and form and substance.

The things which stand between the most general genus, or substance, and the most specific species, or man, ox, and so on, are subaltern genera and species. These are called essential and natural differences and qualities. They divide from those higher and are constituent of those lower; they make for the most specific species, which they constitute; and they distinguish nature from nature. Nature, moreover, is classed as most specific. Now, it has already been explained what substance and nature and form are, and what hypostasis and individual person are, and enhypostaton and anhypostaton. It has also been explained what the difference is between substance and accidents and how substance is superior to the accidents, because in it the accidents have their existence. Division itself has also been explained, as well as how substance differs from essential differences, namely, in that the substance made specific by them constitutes a certain sort of species and becomes of such a sort. It has furthermore been explained what nature is, and what form is, and what hypostasis, and person, and individual, and what the pagan writers thought about these, and what the holy Fathers thought, they who, as disciples of the truth and of the real philosophy, were rightly teaching teachers. So come, let us now speak of the things which are proper to substance.

It is a property of the substance not to be in a subject. Rather, the substance is a subject for the existence of the accidents, but itself does not have existence in another. This is also a property of essential differences. For the being in a subject neither saves when present nor destroys when absent and hence, being entirely accidental, does not enter into the definition. Essential differences, however, are not accidents, since they do save when present and when absent they do destroy. Thus it is that they also enter into the definition.

Still another property of substance is that of being predicated univocally, that is to say, of communicating both its name and definition. Another property is that of not having any contrary. Thus, to the stone, that is to say, to the substance of the stone, there is nothing contrary. The not admitting of more or less is likewise a property, being also a property of essential differences. Thus, man is certainly no more a substance than the horse, nor is an animal either, nor is the horse more a substance than man. And there is the property of being capable of admitting contraries successively, not in itself but in its modifications. By contraries I mean those which are accidents, because the substance can by no means receive any contraries that are substantial. Thus, the rational does not admit of being irrational, but the body is heated and then by modification cooled. And a soul sometimes acquires virtue and at other times vice.

Chapter 48

Those things are generically the same which fall in the same category, as, for example, all things under substance—and in the same way with the other nine categories. One must know that in all there are ten categories, or most general genera, to which every absolute term is referred. They are as follows: (1) *substance,* as, for example, stone; (2) *quantity,* as, for example, two, three; (3) *relation,* as, for example, father, son; (4) *quality,* as, for example, white, black; (5) *place,* as, for example, in Damascus, and this is indicative of place; (6) *time,* as, for example, yesterday, tomorrow, and this is indicative of time; (7) *state,* as, for example, to be wearing a cloak; (8) *position,* as for example, to be standing, to be sitting; (9) *action,* as, for example, to burn; (10) *passion,* as, for example, to be burnt.

Those things are generically different which fall into different categories. Now, *man* and *horse* are generically the same, because they both belong to the category of substance; but *man* and *knowledge* are generically different, because *man* belongs to category of substance, while *knowledge* belongs to that of quality.

Those things are specifically the same which belong to the same species and agree in their essence. Peter, for instance, and Paul both belong to the same species, that of man. On the other hand, those things are specifically different which differ in species, that is, in their essence, as, for example, man and horse. The holy Fathers, however, use 'generically the same' and 'specifically the same' for the same things, namely, for things which are consubstantial, that is to say, are hypostases belonging to the same species.

Things are hypostatically the same when two natures are united in one hypostasis and have one compound hypostasis and one person, as in the case of soul and body. Those things are hypostatically and numerically different which, by the combination of their accidents, have set apart as distinct the peculiarity of their own hypostasis, or, in other words, those things which differ from one another in their accidents and have their existence individually. An example would be the individuals Peter and Paul, for the latter is one and the former another.

Chapter 49

Quantity[1] is an accumulation of units—for the unit is not called quantity. When one unit and one unit are combined, they become two. Thus quantity is not division, but an accumulation and addition of units. For, to divide two into separate units of one, this is division; but to say that one and one are two, this, rather, is addition.

One must know that *quantity* is the measure itself and the number—that which measures and that which numbers. *Quanta,* however, are subject to number and measure; in other words, they are the thing that are measured and numbered. Of the quanta, some are *discrete* and some are *continuous.* The quantum is continuous when one thing is measured, as when we have one piece of wood two or three cubits long, or a stone, or something of the sort. Being one, it is measured, and for this reason it is called continuous. Quanta, however, are discrete which are separated from each other, as in the case of ten stones or ten palm trees, for these are separated from each other. These, then, are

---

[1] Cf. Ammonius, *In Categorias,* pp. 54ff.; Aristotle, *Categories* VI.

said to be numbered, unless because of their small size and great number they are measured by the measure of something of the sort, as is grain and the like.

Those things are defined as *continuous* whose parts touch upon a certain common limit. Thus, since a two-cubit piece of wood, that is to say, a piece two cubits long, is one piece, then the end of one cubit and the beginning of the other are one. For they are joined together and connected, and they are not divided from each other. *Discrete* things are those whose parts do not touch upon a common limit, as in the case of ten stones. For, should you count off five and five, they will have no common limit connecting them. And should you put something in between this five and that five, then there will be eleven and not ten. The terms themselves, continuous and discrete, make this plain.

Now, among the discrete quanta come number and speech. By number we here mean things which are counted. And things which are counted are absolutely discrete, as has been shown. Speech, too, is discrete, for speech is counted in its words, and its parts do not have a common connecting limit. Thus, if the sentences has ten words and you separate them into groups of five, then they have no common limit connecting them. And so, should you add something in the middle, then there will be eleven and not ten. In the same way, the word is counted in its syllables, since it has no common limit connecting them together. Take the word Socrates, for example. Between the syllable *so* and the syllable *cra* there is no common limit to connect them.

There are five continuous quanta: solid, surface, line, space, and time. One should know that the point is quantityless. This is because, being dimensionless, it is neither measured nor counted. The line, however, has one dimension, for it is length without breadth. Consequently, it is reckoned a continuous quantum. Since it is one, it is measured and its parts do have a common limit connecting them, which is the point in between. Now, ἐπιφάνεια, or surface, which is the outer part of the solid, is derived from φαίνεσαι, to appear. It has two dimensions: length and breadth. Since it is one, it is measured and its parts do have a common limit connecting them, which is the line in between. Moreover, one should know that the flat and even surface is called a plane, whereas that which is uneven and warped is just called a surface. The solid has three dimensions: length, breadth, and depth or thickness. Since it is one, it is measured and its parts do have a common limit connecting them, which is the plane. Space is the surface of the air, for the space in which you are is a surface, that is to say, the terminating surface of the air containing you. As a surface, it is reckoned a continuous quantum. Time also is measured in the past and the future, and its parts have a common connecting limit, which is the present instant of time. The instant is quantityless. Notice, then, that there are three things which are quantityless: the unit, the point, and the instant. The following seven are properly called quanta: (1) number; (2) speech; (3) time; (4) space; (5) line; (6) surface; and (7) solid.

Those things which are considered in quanta, such as action, movement, color, and the like, we call *quanta per accidens*. For example, if the action and motion take place over a great length of time, we speak of much action and much motion; if over a short space of time, then we speak of a little. Similarly, if there is whiteness in an extensive body, we say much white; if in a small body, then we say little.

Furthermore, the quantum may be finite or infinite. That, then, which can be measured or counted is finite. On the other hand, that is infinite which by some degree of excessiveness exceeds all measure and number. And the term *great* and *very great* are used in the sense of *infinite,* as when we speak of 'the very great compassion of God' or the 'great mystery of the dispensation of God the Word.'

One should know that in the category of *relation* Aristotle places great and small, much and little, greater and smaller, less and more, double and half, and the like. Now, we say that under different aspects it is possible to place the same thing in different categories. Thus, when number and measure signify what has been explained above, they are put under *quantity*. On the other hand, when they have a mutual relation and are spoken of in relation to each other, then they are put under *relation*. Thus, 'great' is great in relation to 'small' and 'double' is double in relation to 'half, and so on with the rest. In so far as the solid is physical, it comes under *substance;* but, in so far as mathematical, that is to say, measurable, it comes under *quantity*. And again, size and numerical quantity belong to *quantity*. Thus, size is measured and numerical quantity counted. And the term 'how great' refers to size, whereas 'how many' refers to numerical quantity.

There are three properties of the quantum, and they are called *consequences*. The first is the property of its not having any contrary in itself. Thus, in itself the solid has no contrary. However, in so far as it may happen to be white, it will have some contrary, namely, the black. One must furthermore know that there is no other number which is contrary to the number two, for, if there is any, there will be many of them. This is because all the other numbers would be contrary, in which case nature would have been unjust in opposing several contraries of one thing. For it is impossible for there to be several contraries to one thing.

The second property is that of not admitting of more or less. Thus, two palm trees cannot be more than two palm trees, and neither can two men be more than two men.

That which has no contrary does not admit of more or less.

The third property is that to every quantum and to quantum alone there may be equal and inequal. Thus, a line may be equal to a line or not equal to it.

Chapter 50

Those things are *relative*[1] which, in what they themselves are, are said to belong to other things, or they are those which in any other way whatsoever are related to another thing. Now, they are said to belong to others, as a father to a son, for the father is necessarily said to be father of a son. On the other hand, they are related to another, as great is to little or much to little. For 'much' is not said to belong to 'little,' but to be 'much' in relation to 'little.'

One should know that, whenever a thing is considered in itself, it is not relative. When, however, it has a habitude to another thing, then it is said to be relative. Here, then, is the essence of relatives and here is their hypostasis; namely, in their being said to be relative to another, that is to say, in their having a habitude to another. For it is their mutual habitude which makes things relative.

Some relatives are called by the same name, as a friend is a friend of a friend and as an enemy is an enemy of an enemy. Others are called by different names, as a father is a father of a son and as a teacher is a teacher of a pupil.

And again, some things are relative by excess, as the greater is greater than the less. Others are relative according to the relation of the thing discerning to the thing discerned, as scientific knowledge is the knowledge of that which is scientifically knowable. For science discerns that which is scientifically knowable, or, in other words, cognition discerns that

---

1 Cf. Ammonius, *op. cit.*, pp. 66ff.; Aristotle, *op. cit.* VII.

which is knowable. And also, sensation is a feeling of the sensible object, placing is a placing of that which is placeable, standing is a standing of that which can stand, reclining is a reclining of that which can recline, and so on. Still others are relative according to potency and impotency. They are relative according to potency, as are the thing heating and the thing heated; according to impotency, or the privation of potency, as when we say that the eye does not have the power to see the sphere without stars. Others are relative according to the relation between the cause and the thing caused, as a father is a father of a son.

Proper to relatives is the fact that they may be affirmed convertibly. Thus, a friend is a friend of a friend, and the second is a friend of the first; a teacher is a teacher of a pupil, and a pupil is a pupil of a teacher. It is also proper to relatives that they go naturally together. Going naturally together means positing and being posited together, removing and being removed together. Thus, when there is a father there will definitely be a son; and when there is no father there will be no son. For, of whom would a son be, if there were no father? He who does not have a son will not be a father. And so the son is taken away when the father is; and the father is taken away when the son is. However, it is not his hypostasis which is taken away, but only the relation. Thus, even though he who was a son does remain, he does not remain as a son, because, if he does not have a father, then how will he be a son? Now, should we speak of a son of one deceased, either we should not be saying this in the proper sense but by a misuse of terms, or we should be saying it implying that the father, by reason of the immortality of his soul, had not died and become non-existent.

One should know that each category is a most general genus containing genera, subaltern species, differences which divide the genera and constitute the species, most specific species, and individuals. The constituent differences are not called essential except only in the category of substance, nor are the individuals called hypostases except only in the category of substance.

One should know that, in so far as substance itself is a genus and has habitude to another, it falls in the category of relatives. Thus, genus is genus of species and species are species of genus, and so they belong to the relatives.

Furthermore, things which are relative and convertible have their habitude either in things which are self-subsistent, or substances, or in things which are not, or accidents. Now, if the habitude is in self-subsistent things, then their relation will either be natural, like that of the father and son, or like that of slave and master, or artificial, like that of pupil and teacher, or by preference, like that of friend and friend or enemy and enemy. If, however, the habitude is not in self-subsistent things but in accidents, then the relation will either be natural, like that of double and half, or not not natural. If it is not natural it will be either fortuitous, like that of slave and master, or artificial, like that of pupil and teacher, or by preference, like that of friend and friend or enemy and enemy. If, however, the habitude is not in self-subsistent things but in accidents, then the relation will either be natural, like that of double and half, or not natural (like that of great and small, for this relation is rather accidental than natural. Fortuity, however, and preference have no place with things that are not self-subsistent, unless it be that some self-subsistent thing that is possibly being affirmed accidentally should somehow appear as referable to another).[2]

Now, relatives must first, as being considered in themselves, be put into one category. Then, as having a habitude to another, they must be put into the category of relatives. For

---
2 The material within the parenthesis has been added by Combefis.

a thing must first be without any relation, and then, afterwards, relation must be considered in it.

Habitude, which is the relation of one thing to another, is said to be a disposition, or affinity, of things which are predicated either of substance or of things connected with substance. Such may be either natural, or fortuitous, or artificial, or by preference.

Chapter 51

Quality[1] is that by which things are termed as being of such a sort. And again, quality is that from which those things which share it derive their names. Thus, from 'prudence' one who possesses prudence is said to be 'prudent,' and he who enjoys 'warmth' is said to be 'warm.'

One should know that τὸ ποιόν, or the *being of such a sort*, is more general than the quality. This is because the *being of such a sort* signifies both the quality and the thing which possesses it, that is, the quality, as 'the warm,' signifies that which has warmth. For, those who possess the quality are *of such a sort*, as, for example, those who have warmth are called 'warm.' And they who are warm are *of such sort*, but the warmth itself is a quality. Oftentimes, however, this quality is called *of such a sort*, and it is the same way with *quantum* and *quantity*.

Some of the qualities exist in animate and rational bodies, as various kinds of knowledge and virtues, sicknesses and health. And these are called *habits* and *dispositions*. Others exist in both animate and inanimate bodies, as heat and cold, form and shape, potency and impotency. Of these, some are potential and some actual. Now, if they are potential, they cause potency and impotency. If, on the other hand, they

---

1 Cf. Aristotle, *Categories* VIII.

are actual, then either they will pervade the whole—as heat pervades the whole fire and as whiteness pervades all the milk and all the snow, and produce a passion and a passive quality —or they will be superficial and produce shape and form. There are, then, four kinds of quality: (1) habit and disposition, (2) potency and impotency, (3) affection and passive quality, and (4) shape and form.

Moreover, habit differs from disposition, because the habit does not change easily and is more permanent. Take prudence, for example, for one does not quickly change from prudence to imprudence. Similarly, knowledge may be a habit, too, for, when a person attains a thorough scientific understanding of something, this knowledge becomes firmly fixed in him and is hard to change. And the same is true of manliness, and discretion, and justice. Dispositions, however, are the easily moved and quickly changed, as, for instance, heat, cold, sickness, health, and the like. Thus, man is subject to these and he changes rapidly from hot to cold and from sick to healthy. These same, however—sickness, for example, health, and the like—will be habits if they are lasting and hard to change. Moreover, the term disposition is more general, because, since man is somehow 'disposed' to them, they are both called 'dispositions.' On the contrary, that which is easily changed is called 'disposition' only.

A second kind of quality is that of potency and impotency. These are not in act, but they have a natural aptitude or power, or a natural inaptitude. Thus, we say that a boy is potentially musical because this boy, even though he does not actually possess the art of music, has an aptitude for its attainment. The brute beast, however, is unmusical, because it neither possesses the art of music nor is capable of attaining it. And that which is hard has the potentiality of not being speedily divided into parts.

A third kind of quality is the passive quality and the affection, such as heat, cold, whiteness, blackness, and the like. Now, the affection, like the disposition, is easily lost, as when one might blush for shame or turn pale from fear. The passive quality, on the other hand, is not easily altered or changed. Moreover, some of the passive qualities do not originate in an affection, that is to say, they do not come from anything extrinsic, but are intrinsic to the substance. It is in this way that the heat is present in the fire and the sweetness in the honey. For, neither is the heat extrinsic to the fire nor is the sweetness to the honey; and, since such things do not have prior existence, neither did they acquire heat and sweetness subsequently. Nevertheless, as far as our senses are concerned, they produce the same affection. Thus, because the fire is hot, it heats us; and because the honey is sweet, it tastes sweet to us. Other passive qualities, however, do originate in some affection, or temperament. These do at times produce an affection in our senses, but this is not the same affection and quality that they have. Such, for example, are colors. Thus, a whiteness arising from some affection and temperament will produce an affection in the eyes, that is to say, perception in the eyes, opening up of the eyes, and lighting up of the eyes, but it will not make us white. Now, the passive quality which is not extrinsic will either be inherent in the entire species, as is heat in all fire, or will not be, as blackness in the Ethiopians—for not all men are black. What is more, this third kind of quality is considered not only in connection with the body, but also in connection with the soul.

A fourth kind of quality is shape and form. Shape occurs in both animate and inanimate bodies, but form only in the animate. Thus, if one were to use the terms form or well-formed in regard to inanimate bodies, this would not be a proper use but an abuse of terms. Now, the term shape is the more general, because, whereas form is also called shape, the shape of inanimate things is not called their form. Moreover, straightness, or erectness, and crookedness, or distortion, belong to quality.

One should know that in most cases the things which *are of a sort* derive their names from the qualities, as 'hot' comes from 'heat.' Some of them, however, get their names by equivocation. Thus, μουσική, or music, is the knowledge of music, but μουσική, or musical, is what the woman who possesses this knowledge is. Still others, though rarely, have names which are entirely different. Thus, 'upright' comes from 'virtue' with a different name, for he who is virtuous is also called 'upright.'

One should know that the term *affection* is used in two ways. Thus, it may be said in respect to that which has already been affected, in which case it will come under the category of *quality,* as the garment which has already been made white is called white. Or it may be said in respect to that which is being affected now, in which case it will come under the category of *passion,* as with that which has not yet been made white but is being whitened now.

One should know that qualities are not corporeal but are incorporeal, for, if they were bodies, they would fall in the category of substance. All *accidents,* too, are incorporeal and in themselves have no existence, unless they are considered in the substance.

One should know that the essential qualities come under *substance,* for they are parts of substance and divide it, and they are included in the definitions of the species of substance. Now, under whatever category the whole comes, under that category all its parts will also come. Heaviness and lightness are either considered in masses, as with things which are being weighed, and come under *quantity*; or they are considered in a substance, as in the elements, say, of fire and earth, in which case they come under *substance,* because they are essential differences. It is the same with density and rarity, or tenuousness, for either they will belong to the essence of the elements and come under *substance,* or they will be non-essential and come under the category of *position,* as in garments, for in such a case they are positions.

Quality has three properties or attributes. The first is that it admits of contrariety. Thus, heat is contrary to cold and white to black. The second is that they admit of more and less, for, where there is contrariety, there will also be more and less. The *more* is an increase in intensity, and the *less* a decrease. Therefore, it is possible to say that this species is more white and less cold than this other species. The third attribute and that which is most proper is that of like and unlike. Nevertheless, one must know that shape has no contrary.

(One should know that not all privations are expressed negatively. On the contrary, they may also be expressed positively, as blindness and deafness. And again, not every species is termed positively, for some may also be termed negatively. For example, although 'intemperance' is a species, it has been given not a positive name but a negative one. Declaration is called an affirmation, as would be 'he is noble.' Denial, however, is a negation, as would be 'he is not noble.' But, when we say 'lawless,' the *less* implies negation just as much as does the particle *not.*)[2]

Moreover, if this particular whiteness is said to be equal to this other, it is not as a *quality* that it is said to be equal, but as a *quantity.* And, since similarity and dissimilarity are considered in *place,* too, the equality of this surface to this other does not lie in its quantity but in its sharing quality.

Chapter 52

One should know that *action* and *passion,* or the active

---

[2] This paragraph is out of context and probably belongs to Chapter 58.

and passive potencies, come under *quality,* but that which acts and which is acted upon is some *substance* acting in a certain way. To act, then, is to have within oneself a cause of action, whereas to be acted upon is to have in oneself and in another the cause of being acted upon, as with the creator and the creature. Thus, the creator has in himself the cause of creation, whereas on the other hand, the creature has in the creator the principle of creation and in its own self the suitability of being acted upon. By *creator* we here mean the artisan, such, for example, as the carpenter. And by *creature* we mean the matter subjected to the artisan, such, for example, as wood, for this last is subjected to the carpenter.

Of the things which come under *action* and *passion* some are said simply to *make* and to *be made,* as in the case of the practical arts, such as wood-working, metal-working, and the like. With these the thing made endures even after the maker has ceased making. Thus, when the builder has finished building, that which has been built by him endures. Other things one is said to *do,* in which case that which is done does not last after the doer has ceased doing. Thus, when the flute-player has stopped playing, the flute-playing does not keep on, but stops entirely. In the case of other things one is said to *consider,* as in the practice of astronomy and geometry, and in thinking, and the like. Then, again, there are those other kinds which are observed in such inanimate beings as fire, stone, wood, and so forth. The first of all these concern rational beings, whereas the very last kind concerns the inanimate and irrational beings. For the inanimate being does not act as the animate beings do, but as a body approaching a body.

This category has two properties. The first is that it admits of contrariety, for to heat is the contrary of to cool. The second is that it admits of more and less, for it is possible to heat more and to cool less; similarly, with being heated and being cooled.

Activity and *passivity*, then, are observed in all the categories: in *substance*, begetting and being begotten; in *quantity*, counting and being counted; in *relation*, doubling and being doubled; in *quality*, whitening and being whitened; in *position*, seating and being seated; in *state*, carrying and being carried; in *place*, containing and being contained; in *time*, containing and being contained in present, past, and future time.

Chapter 53

Position is the having of a certain position in respect to another position, as, for example, the body which is in a certain position in relation to such another position, whether this last be lying, sitting, or standing. *Position* has three species, which are standing, sitting, and lying prone. Being erect constitutes standing. Partly lying and partly standing constitute sitting. And lying completely down constitutes lying prone. *Position* does not indicate either the thing in position or the place, but it does show the position itself of the thing in relation to the place.

Some of the things that have position have it naturally, as do the elements in their proper places—earth, for example; water, air, fire, and the like. Others have their position from being placed that way according to the rules of art, as a statue, a column, and the like. A further classification is that which says that some of the things having position are stationary, as the earth, while others are in motion, as the heavenly bodies. Still again, some of them are in position potentially, as, for example, things which are capable of moving to another place; while others are actually so, as those which are located somewhere.

Chapter 54

The category of *place* indicates place. Thus, upon being asked where so-and-so is, we reply that he is in the house or in the city, and that indicates place. The species of the category of place correspond to the differences of places, which are: up, down, right, left, before, and behind.

Chapter 55

The category of *time* shows time. Thus, when we are asked when this happened, we reply that it happened last year, or the year before last, both of which indicate time. There are as many species of the category of time as there are differences of time. These last are three: present, past, and future.

Chapter 56

Having[1] is a substance around a substance. It means containing or being contained without being any part of the other thing. Now, a tunic contains, and so does armor and the like, but a ring is contained, as well as any other small object of the sort. Both the thing containing and the thing contained must be substances, because, if the one were a substance and the other an accident, as would be knowledge and the knower, it would no longer fall into the category of having or state. The differences of having correspond to those of beings. Thus, there is either animate or inanimate, and we are said to have either an animate thing like a boy, a horse, and so forth, or an inanimate thing like a

---

[1] τὸ ἔχειν, or *having*, is the Aristotelean category commonly called *state* or *habit*.

ring, a sandal, and the so forth. The word *to have* is used equivocally in several other meanings which we shall discuss later on.[2]

Chapter 57

Every *opposite*[1] is opposite either as a thing or as an assertion. If it is opposite as an assertion to an assertion, then it makes for affirmation and negation. Now, affirmation is the stating of what belongs to something, as, for example, 'he is noble.' Negation, on the other hand, is the stating of what does not belong to something, as, for example, 'he is not noble.' Both of these are called statements. If, however, the opposites are opposed as things, then either they are stated as of convertibles and constitute relatives which mutually induce and cancel each other, or they are not stated as of convertibles and do not have any relation. These last either change into each other, both being equally natural, and constitute such contraries as heat and cold; or the one changes into the other, whereas the other does not change. The former is natural, but the latter is unnatural and constitutes opposites by privation and habit, such as are sight and blindness. For sight is a habit, as from having, but blindness is a privation of the habit—the sight, that is.

Some contraries have no intermediate, whereas others have. Those which have no intermediate are those of which one or the other, that is to say, one of them, must necessarily be in their subject, or, in other words, in those things of which they are predicated. An example would be sickness and health in the subject body of an animal, for it is absolutely necessary for that body to have either sickness or health.

---
2 Chapter 62, below.

---
1 Cf. Ammonius, *In Categorias*, p. 93.

By sickness we mean every disorder of the nature. Now, those which have an intermediate are those of which one or the other must not necessarily be in the subject, or in the things of which they are predicated. An example is that of white and black, for these are contraries, yet it is not at all necessary for one of them to be in the body, because it is not necessary for every body to be either white or black—there are gray bodies and tawny ones. There is indeed an exception to this in the case of opposites belonging by definition to some nature, as heat does to fire and cold to snow. Now, in the case of those contraries which have intermediates, some of the intermediates have names, as the mean between white and black is called gray. Others, however, have no names, as the mean between just and unjust has no name. In such a case the mean is made known by the negation of both of the opposites, as, for example, 'neither just nor unjust.'

The contraries have certain accompanying peculiarities. The first is that evil is necessarily contrary to good, while to evil sometimes good is contrary and sometimes another evil. Thus, to moderation (immoderation is contrary, but to immoderation sometimes moderation[2]) is contrary and sometimes stolidity. Stolidity is that state in which the affections are neither moved nor aroused. Thus, immoderation is a defect of moderation, while stolidity is an excess. And the excess is contrary to the defect. The second peculiarity is that it is impossible for contraries to be in the same individuals simultaneously, for it is impossible for Socrates to be well and sick at the same time, or for the same one of his members to be simultaneously hot and cold. The third peculiarity is that the contraries will be in the same subject, whether this be the same in genus, in species, or in number.

---

2 The material within the parenthesis has been supplied by Migne.

They are in a subject which is the same in genus, as white and black in a simple body; the same in species, as health and sickness in an animal body; and the same in number, as is obvious—since the same body can be susceptible to contraries through a change of itself. The fourth is that contraries either come under the same genus, as white and black under color; or under contrary genera, as justice and injustice come under good and evil, which are contrary genera; or the contraries themselves are genera, as good and evil are contrary genera.

Chapter 58

The act of the one had and of the one having, as that of the arms and the armed or that of the wearer and the worn, is called a *habit*.[1] In the second place, habits are adventitious acts which are stable, whether physical or spiritual. Such would be physical, as heat in heated things, or spiritual, as knowledge. Thirdly, habit is that which one does not yet have, but for having which one does have a suitability. And this is the first meaning of being *in potency*. Fourthly, there is the natural quality or habit, as the heat of the fire and the dream of the sleeper. And this is the second meaning of being *in potency* and the first meaning of being *in act*, for the fire *can* burn but *actually* does not. Fifthly, habit is the perfect act, as with the sight which is now seeing and the heat which is now heating.

Privation is the absence of the habit. Thus, the privation of arms or clothing is opposed to the first meaning of habit. To the second meaning of habit is opposed the absence of extrinsic habits, as when the object which has been heated

---

1 Cf. Aristotle, *Categories* X.

becomes cold. Opposed to the third meaning is the absence of that which the genus definitely does not have naturally, as we say that, while the child has a suitability for music, the fig tree definitely has not. Thus, the fig tree suffers a privation, because the genus of plants does not have any suitability for music. However, some one of the species may not have the suitability which the genus has. Thus, the animal has the suitability for seeing, but the mole, which is a species of animal, does not. Opposed to the fourth meaning of habit is the absence of habitual potency. And to the fifth is opposed the absence of the perfect act, or of the power, whether active or passive, and this is what we spoke of above as the opposition of opposites by privation and habit. This last has the three following characteristics: that what it is natural to have is not had at all, but is completely absent; that it is not had, when it is natural to have it; and that it is not had, where it is natural to have it. For example, we do not say that the stone is blind, for it is not of its nature to have the habit of sight. Neither do we say that the newly born puppy is blind, nor the new born child toothless, because is not of their nature to have these at this particular time. Neither do we say that the foot is blind, because it is not of the nature of the animal to have the habit of sight in its foot. So, when it is natural for one to have in these three ways, yet one does not, then this is called *privation*.

Chapter 59

There are four distinct meanings of the term *prior*.[1] Of these, the most proper is the *prior in time*. In the case of animate beings, this is properly called 'elder' and with inani-

---
1 Cf. *ibid*. XII.

mate beings 'older,' but these terms are also used interchangeably, although improperly.

The second meaning is that of *prior in nature*. A thing having this kind of priority is implied in the positing of that to which it is prior, but its positing does not imply the other; when it is removed, the other is removed with it, but the removal of the other does not imply its removal. For example, the animal is prior to man. For, when there is an animal, although man is an animal, there will not necessarily be a man. But, if there is no man, there may still be an animal, because the horse and the dog are also animals. And if there is a man, there will necessarily be an animal, because man is an animal. If, however, there is no animal, then there will be no man at all, nor horse either, nor dog, nor anything else of the sort, because these are animals. (Thus far what concerns the second meaning.[2])

The third is that of *prior in order*, as for example, when we say that *a* comes first and *b* second, and that then come the syllables and then the whole phrases.

The fourth is that of *prior in dignity*, as when we say that the bishop comes first and then the priest. Some, however, reject this sense, because it is possible for the first in order to be posterior in dignity.

The fifth is as when we speak of *the cause* and *the caused*. Thus Socrates is prior to the picture of himself, because he is causative of his own picture. The father, too, is prior to and greater than the son, because the father is causative of the son, in so far as the son is begotten of the father. It is for this reason that the blessed Gregory took in this sense what was said by our Lord in the Gospels, namely, 'the Father is greater than I.'[3]

---

[2] The sentence in parenthesis is not in most manuscripts.
[3] John 14.28; Gregory of Nazianzus, *Sermon XXX.7 (PG* 36.113A).

Others add a priority *in purpose,* as, for example, the wall is prior to its foundations. However, this reduces to the fourth sense, which is that of priority in dignity. For, in this case, what is prior in intention is actually posterior. There are, moreover, as many kinds of *posterior* as there are of *prior.* Prior and posterior, and more and less, do not belong to the equivocal terms, but to those which are derivative.

Chapter 60

Simultaneous[1] is properly said of things whose beginnings of being were at the same time, as, for instance, when two individuals have been born at the same instant. This mode is opposed to the first meaning of *prior.* According to a second meaning, those things are simultaneous which exist together mutually without one being the cause of the other or caused by the other. Such are the double and the half, for these simultaneously exist together and simultaneously introduce each other. This mode is opposed to the second and fifth mode of prior. This is because in the second the things do not mutually introduce and remove each other, while in the fifth they are the cause and the caused. According to the third meaning, things which are logically divided are simultaneous. Logically divided species are those which result from the same division, as, for example, the rational and the irrational, which result from the division of animal. This mode is opposed to the first and the second modes of prior, and, to some extent, to the other three.

---

1 Cf. Aristotle, *Categories* XIII.

Chapter 61

Motion[1] is the actualization of potency as such. For example, the bronze is potentially a statue, because it can take on the form of the statue. Thus, the melting down, the molding, and the finishing, which are all motions, are an actualization of the metal which is potentially a statue. Consequently, motion will be considered in all the categories in which potency is considered. And in those in which potency is not considered, motion will not be considered either. Thus motion is considered in the categories of substance, quantity, quality, and place. In *substance* there is generation and destruction; in *quantity* there is increase and decrease; in *quality,* alteration; and in *place,* motion in a circle, which is called 'circular,' and motion in straight line, which is called 'direct.' There are, moreover, six kinds of direct motion: upward, downward, inward, outward, motion to the right, and motion to the left. And so with circular motion there are seven kinds of motion with respect to place.

Now, everything that is changed is changed either in itself, or in something within itself, or in something around itself. If this is in the thing itself, it will constitute generation and destruction. If, however, it is in something in the thing itself, this will either be in quantity, in which case it will constitute increase and decrease, or it will be in quality, in which case it will constitute alteration. And if it is in something around the thing, then it will constitute change in place, because place is neither the thing itself which is moved, nor is it anything in it; rather, it accompanies the things moved and is round about them.

Generation differs from destruction. This is because gen-

---

1 Cf. *ibid.* XIV

eration is the passing from non-being to being, for that comes into being, or is generated, which was not before. But with destruction it is just the reverse, for destruction is the change from being to non-being. And increase differs from decrease, because increase is the motion to a greater quantity, whereas decrease is that to a lesser. And again, there are opposite passions in alteration, as heat is opposed to cold and black to white. Thus, while destruction is opposed to generation, and increase to decrease, to alteration are opposed the corresponding opposite and rest. For cooling is opposed to heating and so is rest, because, when the object being heated attains its highest temperature and reaches a limit, then it rests and ceases being heated. In the same way, both the contrary motion and rest are opposed to change in place. For here, while there are contraries, such as upward and downward, there is also rest. Thus, should one throw a lump of earth up into the air, it will not start its downward motion before it first comes to rest. There is, however, no contrary motion to that of the heavens.

Moreover, it seems that alteration accompanies the other kinds of motion. This is because the thing which is being generated and that which is being destroyed, the thing which is increasing and that which is decreasing, and that which is being moved with respect to place are all definitely being altered. Although with the natural motions we do find the motion of alteration accompanying the others, nevertheless it is possible for a thing to be altered without, however, its being moved with any other motion. A stone, for example, may be heated and cooled, but it will neither increase nor cease to be. And in the same way with the rest. So, even if alteration does accompany the other motions, it is possible for it to be considered in itself, and for that reason the distinction between it and the others has been conceded.

Now, Aristotle does not call change a motion. Thus in Book 5 of his *Physics* he has demonstrated that generation and destruction are changes, but not motions, because motion takes place while the thing moved remains intact. However, although we said that there were two contraries to alteration and to change in place, namely the opposite motion and rest, one should know that it is not impossible for two things to be contrary to one thing in different respects. Thus, rest is like habit and privation, whereas the opposite motion is contrary in the proper sense as cooling is to heating.

Chapter 62

The term *to have*[1] is used in eight senses. Thus, either it will be as with a habit and disposition, or with some other quality, for we are said to have knowledge and virtue. Or it will be as with a quantity, for a piece of wood is said to have a length of three cubits. Or it will be as with a substance around a substance, which is a most general genus, and which may be around the whole body like a tunic or around some part thereof like a ring on the finger. Or it will be as with a part in a whole, for we are said to have a hand. Or as with something in a receptacle, as we say that the jar has wine in it. Or as with possessions, for we are said to have a house or a field. Moreover, we are also said to have a wife, and the wife is said to have a husband, but this kind of things seems to be different from having, because it is convertible. Thus, it no more means the husband having a wife than a wife having a husband, because, both being equal and without difference, neither prevails over the other. And even though the owner

---
1 *Ibid.* XV.

has possessions and the possessions have an owner, this is not the same as in the case of a man having a wife and a wife having a husband. This is because the owner is absolute possessor and controller of his possessions. For this reason, it is more properly said that the owner has his possessions, whereas the possessions are had.

It is clear that having is one of the equivocal terms. There are, furthermore, some who say that there are as many differences of having as there are of action and passion. Thus, just as the things which act and are acted upon will either be animate or inanimate, so is it in this case—that which has and that which is had will either be animate or inanimate. How, then, will diverse genera have the same differences? Well, one can reply that having is either around the whole object or around a part thereof, and, again, this: that it is either a means of defense or an ornament.

Chapter 63

One should know that the *affirmation* and the *negation*[1] are called *statements*. An affirmation is that statement which signifies what belongs to someone, or what someone is, for example: Socrates is wise, Socrates walks. A negation, on the other hand, is that which shows what does not belong to someone, or what someone is not, for example: So-and-so is not wise, so-and-so does not walk. Since a negation is opposed to every affirmation and an affirmation to every negation, the negation opposed to the affirmation and the affirmation opposed to the negation are called *contradictions*. One of these, moreover, must necessarily be false and one true.

---
1 Cf. Aristotle, *On Interpretation* VI.

Chapter 64

One should know that the purpose of the logical process is to make a clear statement of proof. The proof is a *syllogism,* and this syllogism is made up of two true *premises* and the conclusion. For example, if I want to prove that the soul is immortal, I say: 'Everything that is perpetually in motion is immortal.' This is a premise. Then I state a second premise: 'The soul is perpetually in motion.' Then the conclusion: 'Therefore, the soul is immortal.' Each part of the premise is called a *term*. A term is that into which every premise is resolved. For example, the premise goes: 'Everything that is perpetually in motion is immortal.' The part 'everything,' in so far as it is a part of the premise, is called a term. The 'that is perpetually in motion' is likewise called a term, as is the 'immortal,' and also the 'is.'

One should know that all the premises must be true and that the conclusion must follow from the premises. For, if one of the premises were found to be false, or the conclusion, then it would not be a syllogism, but a paralogism. Furthermore, there is the simple word, the noun, the verbal phrase, the statement, and the term. In respect to their subject, these five do not differ from one another. Their difference is only relative. 'Man,' for example, as a simple significant term, is called a simple word; as subject, it is called a noun; as fulfilling the functions of a predicate, it is called a verbal phrase; as part of an affirmation and negation, it is called statement; and as part of a premise and of a syllogism, it is called a term.

One should know that in the premise, that is, in the affirmation and negation, the subject is called a noun, whereas the predicate is called a verbal phrase. For example, 'the man walks' is an affirmation. 'The man' is the subject, and is called noun. 'Walks' fulfills the function of a predicate, and is called a verbal phrase. In 'Socrates is noble' the subject is 'Socrates' and it is called a noun. The phrase 'is noble' fulfills the function of a predicate, and, as a part of the affirmation, is called a verbal phrase. Even though grammarians call 'noble' a complementary word, yet, to put it simply, whatever accompanies the 'is' is a verbal phrase.

It should be known that there is no difference between the following five terms: statement, premise, question, objection, and conclusion. Thus, when I simply state that 'the soul is immortal,' this is called a *statement*. But when it is taken as a part of a syllogism, then to say that 'the soul is immortal' is to state a *premise*. And when someone objects to the premise by saying: 'How is it evident that the soul is immortal?'—then such is termed an *objection*. Again, when we proffer it as an inquiry: 'Now, is the soul immortal?'—this is called a *question*. When, finally, it has been deduced from the premises, it is called a *conclusion*. Take, for example, 'the soul is perpetually in motion' and 'that which is perpetually in motion is immortal.' From these premises it is deduced that 'therefore the soul is immortal,' and that is a conclusion.

Chapter 65

A *premise* is either a sentence denying something of something—which is a negation, as, for example, 'Socrates does not laugh'; or it is a sentence affirming something of something—which is affirmation, as 'Socrates does laugh.' A *term* is that into which the premise is resolved. A *syllogism* is a discourse in which, when two things have been laid down, or acknowledged as true, a third necessarily follows from the things laid down, and follows because of them. Thus, because of the premises laid down, the conclusion is made without any need of external support. A *question* is an examination directed to acceptance or rejection, that is to say, denial or approval, with respect to knowledge and speculation. An *interrogation* is an inquiry requiring a detailed, or full answer. Now, the *inquiry* differs from the *interrogation* in that the answer to it is short, that is to say, is given in a few words, whereas the answer to the *interrogation* is long and requires many words. That which is in the form of question and answer is said to be in *dialogue form*. An *objection* is that which from the very beginning upsets the assertion, while *antiparastasis* accepts the assertion as true but shows how it has no bearing on the matter at hand. A *lemma* is that which has been taken for granted for the purpose of proving something. A *heresy* is a persuasion, or opinion, held by several persons in agreement with each other but at variance with others. A *common opinion* is one acknowledged by everyone, as, for example, that the sun exists. A *thesis* is an unusual assumption made by some person who is distinguished for his wisdom, or, in other words, it is an extraordinary theory like that of Parmenides, who held that being is one, or that of Heraclitus, who held that all things are in motion.

That is *common* which is observed in several or is predicated of several. There are four ways in which a thing is said to be common: (1) either as that which is divisible into parts, as land is parcelled out; (2) or as that which is indivisible but is used in common, as one slave or one horse belonging to two masters and now carrying out the orders of one and now those of the other; (3) or as that which becomes private by reservation but reverts again to the common use, as a seat at the theatre or a place at the baths; (4) or, finally, as to that which is indivisible, yet proposed to the same common consideration, as the voice of the herald. It is in this last sense that the expression 'having a common name' is to be understood with respect to equivocal and univocal terms. That is *of itself* which does not belong accidentally to something, but primarily and essentially, as does the rational to man. And that is *universal* which signifies several individual things, as do the terms *man, animal,* and *substance.* That is *accidental* which may or may not exist in something, as sickness or health in a man. The term *to make* is used in connection with the creative arts, where the thing done endures—as in the case of carpentry and the like. Thus, after the process of making the couch remains. On the other hand, the term *to do* is used in cases where the work does not endure, that is to say, where the result of the work does not endure, as in the case of fluteplaying and dancing. *Speculation* is that which we call thinking, the practice of astronomy and geometry, and so on.

Correct speech exhibits two kinds of *excogitation* (ἐπίνοια). Thus there is that which is, as it were, a certain extra thinking out and consideration by which the general concept and unanalyzed knowledge of things are unfolded and made fully clear. Such is the case when that which to the senses appears simple is by careful investigation discovered to be manifold and varied. Man, for example, appears to be simple, but by excogitation he is discovered to be twofold—made up of a body and a soul. The other kind is that which, through a combination of the sensitive and imaginative faculties, from things which exist makes up and imagines things which do not and produces a figment of thought. Such is the concoction of fabulous centaurs, sirens, and tragelaphs. For this kind has taken parts of wholes and, quite freely and arbitrarily composing something else from these parts, has in thought and speech given form to things never seen in reality and substance. Then, by taking on material form, also, it has produced idols. And this is called *simple excogitation.*

(When one predicates the things contained in something

of the thing contained, we have *redundance*. For example, both the animal and the biped are included in man, and in Socrates both the cultivated and the white. If, then, one should predicate these of man or Socrates and say that man is a two-footed animal or that Socrates is something white and cultivated, he would be talking redundantly by saying the same thing several times over. This is *redundance*, because these things are contained in man and in Socrates, so that by mentioning the latter one also reveals the former.

Nearness is a *relation*, and so is fondness, that is to say, friendship, and so is possession, and participation, and connection. Furthermore, we call *relation* that connection, habitude, and disposition to which and such a thing which is expressed by 'whither,' 'whence,' and 'where.' It must still further be known that among four men there are six *relations*: that of the first to the other three, which makes three *relations*; that of the second to the last two, which makes five; and that of the third to the last one. Thus, it turns out that the four have six *relations*. And among five men there are ten *relations*.)[1]

A *union* is brought about in various ways. Thus, it may be by mixture, as in the case of several kinds of flour being put together and mixed. Or it may be by welding, as with copper and lead; or by joining, as with stones and wood; or by fusion, as with molten materials like wax, pitch, and the like, and as with molten metals like gold and silver and such; or by mingling, as with liquids such as wine and water, or wine and honey. It may be by coalescence, as in the case of things which have been separated and then put back together again—for example, a brand taken from a fire and then put back.

Union by *composition* is the mutual association together

---

[1] The preceding two paragraphs are added by Combefis, although in only one manuscript.

of the parts without detriment to any of them, as in the case of the soul and the body. This is what some have called a blending together, that is to say, a knitting together. One must know, however, that while some of the Fathers did not accept the term *blending* in connection with the Mystery of Christ, *union by composition* was acceptable to them all. This union which is by composition is the *hypostatic* union. That thing which subsists of two natures is one *hypostatically*. And again, that is one hypostatically which is perceived to be of two things but in one person. Still again, the union is hypostatic when the nature joins with another hypostasis.

Blending is an opposition of bodies and a mutual combination of qualities. And again, blending is an intimate union of bodies with an intermingling of their qualities. Blending is the concurrence of substances of different sorts accompanied by the interpenetration of the qualities associated with them.

That which is by apposition is also a *union,* and it is like that which is by joining.

Again, a union is *apparent* when one assumes the appearance of another and in his stead proffers the statements of this other about himself. A union may also be *relative,* as is that of a friend to a friend. And Nestorius thought up still other kinds of union—such, I mean, as those according to dignity, and equality in honor, and identity of will, and good pleasure, and the bearing of the same name.

It must further be known that in the hypostatic union the spiritual things are united to those things which can receive them, as are those which are corruptible. Once united, they remain unconfused, incorruptible, and unchangeable like things in juxtaposition. For such is the nature of spiritual things.

Chapter 66

One should know that the *hypostatic union* produces one compound hypostasis of the thing united and that this preserves unconfused and unaltered in itself both the uniting natures and their difference as well as their natural properties. Moreover, this has no hypostatic difference with itself, because those characteristic differences of the things uniting, by which each of them is distinguished from others of the same species, become its own. Thus it is with the hypostasis in the case of the soul and the body, for here one hypostasis is made of both—the compound hypostasis of Peter, let us say, or of Paul. This keeps in itself the two perfect natures—that of the soul and that of the body— and it preserves their difference distinct and their properties unconfused. And in itself it has the characteristic differences of each, those of the soul, which distinguish it from all other souls, and those of the body, which distinguish it from all other bodies. These, however, in no wise separate the soul from the body, but they unite and bind them together, at the same time marking off the one hypostasis composed of them from all other hypostases of the same species. Moreover, once the natures become hypostatically united, they remain absolutely indivisible. And this is so because, even though the soul is separated from the body in death, the hypostasis of both remains one and the same. For the constitution in itself of each thing at its beginning of being is a hypostasis. Therefore, the body remains, as does the soul; both always having the one principle of their being and subsistence, even though they are separated.

It is further necessary to know that it is possible for natures to be united to each other hypostatically, as in the case of man, and that it is also possible for the hypostasis to assume an additional nature. Both of these are to be observed in Christ, because in Him the divine and human natures were united, while His animate body subsisted in the pre-existent hypostasis of God the Word and had this for a hypostasis. It is, however, quite impossible for one compound nature to be made from two natures or for one hypostasis to be made from two, because it is impossible for contrary essential differences to exist together in one nature. This is because it is of the very nature of these to distinguish from each other the natures in which they exist. And again, it is impossible for things that have once begun to subsist in themselves to have another principle of subsistence, for the hypostasis is subsistence in self. It must further be known that in the Holy Trinity a hypostasis is the timeless mode of each external existence.

One should know, moreover, that whenever a compound nature is produced, the parts must be coincident and a new thing made from other things. This new thing will not preserve the thing of which it has been composed as such, but will change and alter them. Thus, when the body has been made up from the four elements, a new thing has been made out of other things, and this new thing is neither pure fire nor any of the other elements, nor is it so called. It is the same with the mule, which is bred from a horse and an ass, for it is neither a horse nor an ass, nor it is so called. On the contrary, it is a new thing produced from others and which does not preserve unconfused and unchanged either one of those things of which it is composed.

Chapter 67

Philosophy[1] is knowledge of things which are in so far as they are; that is to say, a knowledge of their nature. Philo-

---
[1] See above, Chapter 3. This belongs to the shorter recension.

sophy is a knowledge of divine and human things. Philosophy is a study of death, both that which is deliberate and that which is natural. Philosophy is a becoming like God, in so far as this is possible for man. Now, it is in justice, sanctity, and goodness that we become like God. And justice is that which is distributive of equity; it is not wronging and not being wronged, not prejudicing a person, but rendering to each his due in accordance with his works. Sanctity, on the other hand, is that which is over and above justice; that is to say, it is the good, the patience of the one wronged, the forgiving of them that do wrong, and, more than that, the doing of good to them. Philosophy is the art of arts and the science of sciences, for, since through philosophy every art is discovered, it is the principle underlying every art. Philosophy is love of wisdom. But, the true wisdom is God. Therefore, the love of God—this is the true philosophy.

Philosophy is divided into *speculative* and *practical*. Speculative philosophy is divided into theology, mathematics, and natural science. Mathematics is divided into arithmetic, geometry, and astronomy. Practical philosophy is divided into ethics, domestic economy, and political economy. Speculative philosophy, then, is the consideration of things that are incorporeal and immaterial, that is to say, it is the consideration of God, who primarily and properly is incorporeal and immaterial. But it also treats of angels, demons, and souls, which themselves are termed immaterial in comparison with the body, although in comparison with that which is immaterial in the true sense, namely, the divine, they are material. This, then, is theology. But consider the nature of material things, that is to say, of animals and plants, of stones and the like, that is what natural science is. And to consider those things which stand midway between these, which are now considered in matter and now outside of matter, and which stand midway between the immaterial and the material, this is mathematics. Thus, the number in itself is immaterial, but it is also found in matter, in grain, say, or wine, for we do speak of ten measures of grain and of ten pints of wine. This is also true of the other branches of mathematics. Practical philosophy governs manners and teaches how one must live in society. If it regards the guidance of the individual man, it is called ethics; if of the whole household, it is called domestic economy; and if of the entire state, political economy.

Chapter 68

One must know that there are four *dialectical or logical methods*.[1] That is by *division* which divides the genus into species by means of the intermediate specific differences. That is by the *definition* which defines the subject by the genus and the specific differences divided out by the method of division. That is by *analysis* which resolves the more composite thing into its simpler elements. Thus, the body is resolved into the humors; the humors, into the fruits; the fruits into four elements; the elements, into matter and form. That is by *demonstration* which proves the matter at hand by means of something intermediary. For instance, I have to prove that the soul is immortal, so I take an intermediary, namely, the *being ever in motion,* and I reason as follows: The soul is ever in motion. But, that which is ever in motion is immortal. Therefore, the soul is immortal.

It must further be known that syllogisms belong to the method by demonstration. And one must know that the analytical method is of three kinds. Thus, it may be *natural,* as in the example cited above. We also have *logical* analysis when we resolve the proposed syllogism into its proper form;

---

1 Cf. Ammonius, *In Isagogen,* pp. 34ff.

and we have *mathematical* when we take the thing asked for granted and thence arrive at something which is acknowledged to be true and from which the proposition is proved. For example, let the question be: Is the soul immortal? I take for granted that which has been asked and I say: Since the soul is immortal, there is a reward for its bad and good actions. Now, if there is such a reward, then there is that which is passed judgment upon and that which passes judgment. But, if there is that which is judged and that which judges, then there is a provider and a providence. And so we have arrived at providence, which is acknowledged by everyone. From this point on I put things together and say: Since there is a providence and a dispenser of justice, there are also rewards. And since there are rewards, there is that which is judged. But, if there is that which is judged, then the soul is immortal.

Explanation of Expressions[1]

Necessity is a cause of violence. In general, an *element* is that first thing from which something is made and to which it is ultimately reducible. In particular, however, an element is that of which a body is made and to which it is reducible—and such are fire, water, air, and earth. *Fire* is a body which is very rare, hot, and dry. *Earth* is a body which is very dry and heavy. *Water* is a body which is wet and very cold. *Air* is a body which is very wet and soft. *Origination* is a substantial motion from non-being to being. (*Destruction* and *corruption* is a motion from being to non-being.[2]) *Increase* is a motion in quantity by enlargement. *Decrease* is a motion in quantity by diminution. *Alteration* is a motion in quality by change. *Motion* is a motion from place to place. *Rotation* is a motion in the same place.

---
1 This heading is missing in some manuscripts.

Self-motion is the motion of the soul and it is also to be found in animals. *Time* is a measure of motion and a number of the prior and posterior in motion. *Day* is the passage of the sun over the earth, or the period of time during which the sun passes over the earth. *Night* is the shadow of the mass of the earth, or the time during which the sun is passing under the earth. A *space of a night and a day* is a revolution of the universe. A *month* is the space of time between one conjunction of the moon with the sun and the next conjunction. A *year* is the time it takes for the sun to pass through the cycle of the zodiac. A *seasonable time* is a time when things may be done successfully. *Unseasonableness* is the absence of a seasonable time for the successful prosecution of the thing required. An *hour* is either the fourth part of a year, or the twelfth part of the day, or the zenith of the spirit, or the prime of the body. *Spring* is the time during which wetness prevails. *Summer* is the time during which heat prevails. *Autumn* is the time during which dryness prevails. *Winter* is the time during which cold prevails. A *barbed star* is a starlike mass of fire having rays in front. A *comet* is a fiery mass of stars sending out rays round about like a long head of hair. A *meteor* is a starry shaft, that is to say, a beam sending rays upward. A *fireball* is an incandescent mass of fire. An *iris* is a majestic reflection of the sun in a hollow moist cloud. It appears circular like a ring, giving the impression of a star reflected in a mirror and it is caused by condensation of the air. A *parhelion* is a dense circular cloud resembling the sun, or it is a reflection of the sun in a dense and smooth cloud. A *thunderbolt* is a spiral blast which makes a fiery motion and is borne down from above in a flame of fire setting fire all around. A *typhoon* is a spiral movement of dark air drawn down to the earth from above. A *waterspout* is a spiral movement of radiant

---

2 A printer's omission from the Migne text; cf. Lequien, *Opera* I 73.

air borne down from above. A *bolt of lightning* is a thunderbolt apart from clouds. *Hail* is completely frozen water which has been frozen up above the earth. *Ice* is water which has been frozen on the earth. *Snow* is half-frozen water that comes down through the clouds onto the earth. *Frost* is entirely frozen water which has been frozen on the earth through the agency of another wet material. A *rainstorm* is a continuous fall of water excreted by clouds. A *shower* is a quantity of dew. *Dew* is moisture gathered into drops. *Mist* is the density which precedes the cloud. *Vapor* is a quantity of emanations on the earth. A *lake* is a large body of fresh water formed in hollows and low places. A *sea* is salty bitter water filling the cavities of the gulfs of the lowest part of the earth. A *fountain* is the gushing source of a spring, or outflowing water produced by a disturbance in the earth. An *earthquake* is a violent motion of wind entering in under the earth and forcing it to shake. A *volcanic crater* is an aperture, or vent, out of which flows subterranean fire. A *lyre* is a frame fitted with strings.

With the help of God, the philosophies of the most holy John of Damascus have been brought to completion.

ON HERESIES

THE PARENTS AND ARCHETYPES of all heresies are four in number, namely: (1) Barbarism; (2) Scythism; (3) Hellenism; (4) Judaism. Out of these came all the rest.

1. *Barbarism* is that which prevailed from the days of Adam down through ten generations to the time of Noe. It is called barbarism because of the fact that in those times men had no ruling authority or mutual accord, but every man was independent and a law unto himself after the dictates of his own will.

2. *Scythism* prevailed from the days of Noe down to the building of the Tower of Babel and for a few years after the Tower period, that is to say, until the time of Phaleg and Ragau.[1] These last migrated to the regions of Europe and, from the time of Thare[2]—from whom the Thracians sprung —and on, have been associated with the country and peoples of Scythia.

3. *Hellenism* arose from idolatry in the time of Sarug.[3] Since in those times everyone was given to superstition, when the races of men had begun to turn to a much more civil way of life, they turned also to idolatrous rites and usages,

---
1 Phaleg, the father of Ragau (Reu), who was the great great grandfather of Abraham (Gen. 11; Luke 3).
2 The father of Abraham.
3 The great-grandfather of Abraham.

and they began to deify men who had once walked among
them. At first, they painted with colors and made pictures of
those whom they had once held in esteem, whether tyrants
or sorcerers or men who in their lifetime had done something
deemed worthy of note in the line of courage or bodily
strength. Then, after idolatry had been introduced, beginning
with the times of Thare, the father of Abraham, they first
put the potter's skill to use for the making of figures of their
dead. And then they applied every art to their portrayal—
the builders sculpturing in stone, the gold and silversmiths
fashioning out of their own materials, and similarly the
woodworkers, and so on. The Egyptians, however, together
with the Babylonians and Phrygians and Phoenicians, were
the first to introduce this kind of cult with its statues and
mysteries. From them it passed to the Greeks, first in the
time of Cecrops,[4] and from then on. Then, considerably
later, the cults of Chronos, Ares, Zeus, Apollo, and the rest of
the gods were introduced. Now the Greeks are called *Hellenes*
after a certain Helenus, who was one of those who had
come to settle in Greece. However, according to others, they
are so called from the *elaea*, or olive tree, which sprung up
at Athens. Their progenitors were the Ionians, who, by accurate report, descend from Javan.[5] He was one of those
engaged in the building of the Tower, when the tongues of
all were confounded, which is the reason for their all being
also called Meropes, that is to say, 'men of divided voice,'
because of the division of the tongues. Later on, as time
went by, Hellenism split up into such sects as those of the
Pythagoreans, Stoics, Platonists, and Epicureans. Besides,
there was an ingrained religious sense which, along with the
force of the natural law, had existed distinct from these
nations and midway between Barbarism and Hellenism from

---

4 The mythical first king of Athens.
5 Joel 3.6 (Septuagint) has 'children of the Greeks' for the Hebrew 'sons of Javan.'

the foundation of the world down until such time as it converged with the religion of Abraham.

4. *Judaism* had from the time of Abraham received the seal of circumcision. By Moses, who was seventh after Abraham, it was committed to writing in the Law given by God. From Juda, the fourth son of Jacob, surnamed Israel, through David, who was the first of the tribe of Juda to rule, it acquired the definitive name of Judaism. It is apparent that the Apostle was summarizing these four heresies when he said: 'In Christ Jesus there is neither Barbarian, nor Scythian, nor Greek, nor Jew: but a new creature.'[6]

The Divisions of the Greeks.

5. *The Pythagoreans or Peripatetics.* Pythagoras held the monad and providence. He also held that it was forbidden to sacrifice, that is to say, to sacrifice to the gods. He furthermore forbade the eating of animals and enjoined abstinence from wine. He made a distinction between things from the moon on up, which he said were immortal, and those below, which he said were mortal. He also held the transmigration of souls from body to body, even in the case of animals and reptiles. He taught that silence should be kept for a period of five years, and finally he called himself God.

6. *The Platonists* held God and matter and form, and that the universe was created and subject to destruction, whereas the soul was uncreated, immortal, and divine. They held that this last had three parts: the rational, the irascible, and the appetitive. They also held that women should be the common property of all and that no one should have his own wife, but that those who wished might have intercourse with them that were agreeable. They likewise held the transmigration of souls into bodies, even into those of reptiles. And they also held that there were several gods produced from the One.

---

[6] Col. 3.11; Gal. 6.15.

7. *The Stoics* hold that the universe is a body and they think that this sensible world is God. Certain of them have declared that it has its nature from the substance of fire. They also define God as a mind which is at the time the soul of the entire mass of heaven and earth. His body is, as I have said, the universe and His eyes the luminaries. Moreover, they hold that the flesh is completely destroyed and that the souls of all things pass from body to body.

8. *The Epicureans* supposed the beginning of all things to be in indivisible bodies with no parts, homogeneous, and infinite in number. And they held the end to be the enjoyment of pleasure, and that neither God nor providence governs things.

9. *Samaritanism* and the *Samaritans* of this sect. This originated with the Jews before the appearance of heresies among the Greeks and before their teachings took definite form but after they had received their religion. It stands between Judaism and Hellenism and took occasion to arise in the time of Nabuchodonosor and the Jewish captivity. These were Assyrian colonists who had settled in Judea and had received the Pentateuch of Moses which the king had sent them from Babylon at the hands of the priest called Esdras. They hold everything that the Jews do, except that they hold the Gentiles in abomination, avoid contact with certain things, deny the resurrection of the dead, and reject the post-Mosaic prophecies.

The Four Classes of Samaritans.

10. *The Gorthenes* celebrate their feasts at other times than Sebyaeans.

11. *The Sebyaeans* differ from the Gorthenes by reason of their feasts.

12. *The Essenes* are opposed to neither, but celebrate their feasts indifferently with whomsoever they chance to be.

13. *The Dosthenes* follow the same customs as do the

Samaritans, practicing circurmcision and other things and using the Pentateuch. Like the others, but more so, they abstain from animal food and pass their lives in continuous fasting. Some of them also practice virginity and other asceticism. Some also believe in the resurrection of the dead, which belief is foreign to the Samaritans.

The Seven Heresies of the Jews.

14. *The Scribes,* who were certain lawyers and expounders of the traditions, come down to them from their forebears, very superstitiously observed customs which they had not learned from the Law, but had devised for themselves as rites and ceremonies over and above the prescriptions of the Law.

15. *The Pharisees,* which is interpreted as meaning 'those who are set apart,' followed the most perfect form of life and were, as they pretended, more to be esteemed than other people. They also held the resurrection of the dead, which the Scribes held too. As regards angels and the Holy Ghost, they agreed that such exist. They followed a special way of life, practicing asceticism and virginity for a period of time and fasting twice a week.[7] They performed the purifications of pots and plates and cups,[8] as did the Scribes, the paying of tithes, the offering of first-fruits, and the recitation of interminable prayers. They wore superstitious styles of clothing, such as the shawl, the tunics, or colobia, the wide phylacteries, that is, amulets made of purple stuff, the fringes,[9] and the tassels on the ends of their shawls—all of which served as signs of their periodic asceticism. They also introduced the horoscope and fate.

16. *The Sadduccees,* which is interpreted as meaning 'the most just,' were from the Samaritan race and from a priest

---
7 Luke 18.12.
8 Mark 7.4.
9 Matt. 23.5.

named Sadoc.[10] They denied the resurrection of the dead and acknowledged neither the angels nor the Spirit, but in other things were like the Jews.

17. *The Hemerobaptists*[11] were Jews in everything. However, they did say that no one would attain to eternal life unless he bathe himself every day.

18. *The Ossenes,*[12] which is interpreted as meaning 'the most reckless,' carried out everything according to the Law. However, while they use some of the Scriptures coming after the Law, they rejected most of the later Prophets.

19. *The Nasaraeans,* which is interpreted as meaning 'the rebellious,' forbid all eating of flesh meat and do not eat any animal food at all. Up to Moses and Josue the son of Nave, they accept and believe in the holy names of the patriarchs in the Pentateuch—Abraham, I mean, and Isaac, and Jacob, and their predecessors, and Moses himself, and Aaron, and Josue. They claim that Moses is not the author of the books of the Pentateuch, but they stoutly defend other books different from these.

20. *The Herodians* were Jews in everything. They looked for Christ in Herod and to him they imputed the dignity and the name of Christ.

Thus far the first part, which contains all these twenty heresies, and in which there is also something of the coming of Christ.[13]

21. *The Simonians* stem from Simon Magus, who lived in the time of the Apostle Peter and was a native of the village of Gitta in Samaria. This man was of Samaritan

---

10 3 Kings 1.34; 1 Paral. 29.22.
11 'Daily bathers.'
12 The only mention of this is by Epiphanius. They are probably mistakenly distinguished from the Essaeans, or Essenes.
13 This refers to the first part of the first book of the *Panarion* of Epiphanius. The descriptions of these first twenty heresies is taken verbatim from Epiphanius' summary of the first part of Book 1 (*PG* 41.165-172).

origin and became a Christian in name only. He taught a filthy obscenity of prosmicuous bodily intercourse. He rejected the resurrection and affirmed that the universe was not created by God. He furthermore gave his disciples for adoration a likeness of himself as Zeus and of the harlot named Helen, who was his companion, as Athena. To the Samaritans he said that he was the Father, while to the Jews he said he was Christ.

22. *The Menandrianists* came from Simon through a certain Menander,[14] but in certain things they differed from the Simonians. They said that the universe was created by angels.

23. *The Saturnilians* were to be found throughout Syria. They followed the obscene doctrine of the Simonians, but they professed other things far more extraordinary. They originated with Saturnilus.[15] With Menander they held the universe to have been created by angels, but, in accordance with the opinion of their founder, by seven only.

24. *The Basilidians* follow the same obscene doctrine. They originate with Basilides, who with Saturnilus, was a disciple both of the Simonians and of the Menandrianists. He held similar opinions, although he differs in some things. Thus, he says that there are 365 heavens and to these he assigns angelic names. It is for this reason that the year has this same number of days, and the name *Abrasax*, which is 365,[16] is a holy name.

25. *The Nicolaitans* stem from Nicolas, who was ordained to serve by the Apostles.[17] Because of jealousy for his own wife, he was motivated to teach his disciples the practice of im-

---

14 An early second-century Samaritan magician and disciple of Simon Magus; cf. Irenaeus, *Against Heresies* I xxiii 5 (*PG* 7.670-673).
15 Or Saturninus, an early Syrian Gnostic; cf. Irenaeus, *op. cit.*, I xxiv 1 (*PG* 7.673ff.)
16 That is, the sum of the numerical values of the Greek letters of the name.
17 Acts 6.5. The Nicolaites are mentioned in Apoc. 2.6,15.

morality with others. He also introduced to the world the doctrine of Caulacau, Prunicus, and other barbaric names.

26. *The Gnostics* succeeded to the foregoing heresies, but were more insanely given to the practice of immorality than all these others. In Egypt they are called Stratiotics and Phibionites, while in the upper regions they are called Socratites, and in still other places Zanchaeans. Some others call them Coddians, while still others call them Borborites. These make much of Barbelo and Bero.[18]

27. *The Carpocratians* originated with a certain Carpocrates, who was an Asiatic. He taught the practice of every sort of immorality and the cultivation of every kind of sin. Unless, he said, one pass through everything and do the will of all the demons and angels, he cannot attain the highest heaven or pass beyond the Principalities and the Powers. He furthermore said that Jesus had assumed an intellectual soul and, when He had come to know the things above, then He proclaimed them. And he said that should one do such things as Jesus had done, then one would be the same as He. Like the heresies originating with Simon and the others thus far treated, he repudiated both the Law and the resurrection of the dead. The Marcellina who was at Rome became a disciple of his. He furthermore secretly used to make images of Jesus, Paul, Homer, and Pythagoras, and to burn incense before them and worship them.

28. *The Cerinthians,* who are also called *Merinthians,* originated with Cerinthus and Merinthus.[19] They were certain Jews who made much of the circumcision and who said that the universe was created by the angels and that Jesus attained to the name of Christ by degrees.

---

18 Variations of the name of Barbero, one of the aeons of some Gnostic systems, a sort of female principle. Epiphanius has the proper form, *Panarion,* I.2 epitome *sub* vi (*PG* 41.284A).

19 Merinthus is mentioned only by Epiphanius and is probably the same as Cerinthus.

29. *The Nazarenes* confess Jesus Christ to be the Son of God, but live in all things according to the Law.

30. *The Ebionites* closely resemble the aforementioned Cerinthians and Nazarenes. In some respects the heresy of our Sampsaeans and Helcesaeans approaches theirs. They assert that Christ and the Holy Ghost were created in heaven and that Christ came to dwell in Adam, then for a time put him off, and finally put him on again. They say that He did this in His coming in the flesh. Although they are Jews, they use the Gospels. The eating of meat they hold in abomination. They hold water to be in the place of God. They furthermore hold, as I have said, that Christ put on man in His coming in the flesh. They bathe in water constantly, both summer and winter, reputedly for the sake of purification, as do the Samaritans.

31. *The Valentinians*[20] reject the resurrection of the flesh. They furthermore set the Old Testament aside, although they do accept the Prophets and whatsover else is susceptible of an allegorical interpretation resembling their own heresy. They introduce certain strange myths, saying that there are thirty names of aeons and that these, whom they consider to be both gods and aeons, were begotten bisexual by the father of the universe. And they say that Christ brought His body from heaven and passed through Mary as through a channel.

32. *The Secundians*, who were joined by Epiphanes and Isidore, being like-minded with Valentinus, have the same syzygies.[21] To some extent, however, they detail other things which the Valentinians do not. They also forbid the use of flesh meat.

---
20 Valentinus, a second-century Alexandrian heretic, was one of the most important of the Gnostic leaders.
21 The male-female pairs of aeons in the Valentinian Gnostic system.

33. *The Ptolemaeans,* with whom Flora[22] is associated, are also disciples of Valentinus. In regard to the syzygies, they hold the same as do the Valentinians and Secundians, but they differ from these last in some respects.

Thus far the summary of the thirteen heresies contained in the second part of Book 1.[23]

The following belong to this third part, in which thirteen heresies are contained.[24]

34. *The Marcosaeans.* There was a certain Mark who was a fellow pupil with Colarbasus. He introduced two principles and rejected the resurrection of the dead. He furthermore used to perform certain tricks with drinking cups by changing the color of their contents to a dark purple by means of incantations; then he would initiate the women whom he had thus deluded. Like Valentinus, he pretended that all things were made up of the twenty-four elements.

35. *The Colarbasaeans.* This Colarbasus also taught the same things. In some respects, however, he differed from the other heresies, that is, from those of Mark and Valentinus, because he taught the emissions and the ogdoads in a different way.

36. *The Heracleonites* also seem to accept the mythology of the ogdoads, but differently from Mark, Ptolemy, Valentinus, and the rest. Like Mark, however, they redeem their dying at the hour of death with oil of opobalsam and water, at the same time reciting certain invocations couched in Hebrew words over the one supposedly being redeemed.

---

22 Flora is only known from the *Letter to Flora* composed by the Gnostic Ptolemaeus and preserved in *Panarion,* Heresy 33.3-7 (*PG* 41.557-568).

23 This refers to the second part of Book 1 of the *Panarion.* The description of the preceding thirteen heresies is taken verbatim from Epiphanius' epitome of Book I.2 (*PG* 41.281-286).

24 This refers to the third part of Book 1 of the *Panarion.* The description of the following thirteen heresies is Epiphanius' epitome of this part (*PG* 41.577-581).

37. *The Ophites* hold the serpent in honor and claim that it is Christ. And they keep a real serpent, the snake, in some sort of a basket.

38. *The Cainites* hold the same things as do those heresies which repudiate the Law and Him who spoke in the Law. While they deny the resurrection of the body, they hold Cain in honor and attribute to him extraordinary power. They likewise deify Judas, together with them that were with Core, Dathan, and Abiron, and together with the Sodomites.

39. *The Sethians* in turn, hold Seth in honor and claim that he was born of the supernatural mother after she had repented of giving birth to Cain and his. They say that, after she had given birth to Cain and Cain killed Abel, she had commerce with the supernal Father and produced the pure seed, which was Seth, from whom thereafter the entire human race was descended. These hold the doctrine of Principalities and Powers, and of a number of other things.

40. *The Archontics,* in turn, attribute the universe to a number of archons and claim that all things that have been made have been made by them. They are also guilty of certain immoral practices. They deny the resurrection of the flesh and reject the Old Testament. But they use both the Old and the New Testaments, distorting the meaning of every word to conform with their own way of thinking.

41. *The Cerdonians* are from Cerdon, who succeeded to the error of Heracleon and then added to the deceit. He came from Syria to Rome and, afterwards, in the time of Bishop Hyginus, expounded his teachings. He teaches that there are two principles which are opposed to each other and that Christ was not born. He likewise rejects the resurrection of the dead and the Old Testament.

42. *The Marcionites.* Marcion was a native of Pontus and the son of a bishop. But he violated a virgin and, having

on that account been excommunicated from the Church by his own father, he took to flight. He came to Rome, where he requested those who were ruling the Church at that time to receive him to penance; when he failed to obtain this, he became stirred up against the faith and gave out that there were three principles—the good, the just, and the evil—and that the New Testament was foreign to the Old Testament and to Him who spoke therein. Both he and his followers, the Marcionites, reject the resurrection of the body, but they do confer baptism—not only once, but even a second and third time after lapses into sin. And they even have others baptized for the catechumens who have died. They furthermore, without the least constraint, permit women to confer baptism.

43. *The Lucianists.* A certain Lucian—not he who lived in the time of Constantine, but an older one—held everything as Marcion did. They are, however, reputed to hold certain other things that were not taught by Marcion.

44. *The Apellians.* This Apelles also holds doctrines similar to those of Marcion and Lucian. He vilifies all creation and the Creator. He did not teach three principles, as did the others, but one God, who is supreme and nameless. And he taught that this God made another one. This last, he says, who was begotten, turned out to be evil and by his own wickedness created the world.

45. *The Severians.* A certain Severus, in turn, going still further than Apelles, rejects wine on the basis of a legend that the vine was bred of the commerce that Satan in the form of a serpent had with the earth. Woman, moreover, he deprecates, declaring that she has her existence from a sinister power. He furthermore introduces certain appellations of archons, and certain apocryphal books. Like the rest, he rejects the resurrection of the body and the Old Testament.

46. *The Tatianists.* This Tatian flourished contemporaneously with the most holy martyr and philosopher Justin. But after the death of St. Justin he unfortunately came under the influence of the teachings of Marcion and taught the same things as he, with some additions. He was said to have been a native of Mesopotamia.

Thus far the thirteen heresies contained in the first part of Book 2.[25]

The following are contained in the third part of the Book 2, totaling eighteen heresies.[26]

47. *The Encratites,* who happen to be a branch of the Tatianists, also reject marriage, which they declare to be of Satan. And they forbid all eating of animal food.

48. *The Cataphrygians,* or *Montanists,* or *Ascodrugites*[27] accept the Old and New Testaments, but they also introduce other prophets of whom they make much—a certain Montanus and a Priscilla.

49. *The Pepuzians,* who are also called *Quintillians,* and with whom the *Artotyrites*[28] are connected, constitute a distinct heresy. Although they belong to the Cataphrygians, they hold other things which these last do not. Pepuza, which is a certain town lying between Galàtia and Cappadocia and Phrygia, they hold sacred. In fact, they claim that it is Jerusalem. There is, however, still another Pepuza. Furthermore, they permit women to hold authority and to officiate as priests. And they celebrate certain mysteries during

---

25 Obviously erroneous; see note 24.
26 Actually, this refers to the first part of Book 2 of the *Panarion.* The description of the following eighteen heresies is Epiphanius' epitome of this part (*PG* 41.845-850).
27 The correct form is *Tascodrugite.* According to Epiphanius, it is a name of Phrygian origin meaning 'nose-pegger,' from their custom of putting the forefinger to the nose while praying (*Panarion,* Heresy 48.14, *PG* 41.877B).
28 'Bread and cheese eaters.'

the course of which they pierce a new-born child with bronze needles, as is the custom of the Cataphrygians. Then, having mixed flour with its blood, they bake a host of which they partake as communion. They also tell a mythical tale of Christ revealing Himself there in Pepuza to Quintilla or Priscilla, in female form. They use both the Old and New Testaments, altering them in conformance with their own ideas.

50. *The Quartodecimans* celebrate Easter on a fixed day of the year. On that day which coincides with the fourteenth of the moon, whether it be a Saturday or Sunday, they fast and celebrate the vigil and the feast simultaneously.

51. *The Alogians*,[29] as we call them, repect the Gospel according to John and his Apocalypse, because they do not accept the divine Word as proceeding from the Father and existing eternally.

52. *The Adamians*, who get their name from a certain contemporary Adam, have a doctrine which is more absurdity than truth. They do something of this sort. Both men and women meet together, as naked as when they were born, and in this state they have their lections and prayers and whatever else they do. Leading a solitary life, as they pretend, and practicing continence, they do not accept marriage and they consider their own church to be paradise.

53. *The Sampsaeans*, or *Elkesaites*, up to the present time inhabit that part of Arabia which lies on the further side of the Dead Sea. They were led into error by Elxas, a certain false prophet, whose kinfolk, the women Marthus and Marthina, have survived to the present day and are worshiped as goddesses by the sect. They hold everything very much as do the Ebionites.

54. *The Theodotians* are named from Theodotus the shoemaker of Byzance. This man had had an excellent Greek

---
29 'Deniers of the Word.'

education. However, having been arrested with some others during the days of the then persecution, he alone recanted, while all the rest suffered martyrdom for the sake of God. And so, when he had fled and was reproached for this, in order to avoid the accusation of having denied God he invented the doctrine that Christ was a mere man.

55. *The Melchisedechians* venerate Melchisedech, claiming him to be some sort of a power and not just a man. They have also undertaken to reduce all things to his name.

56. *The Bardesanites.* This Bardesanes was a native of Mesopotamia. At first he held the true faith and excelled in philosophy, but he fell away from the truth and came to hold nearly the same as did Valentinus, with the exception of some things in which he differed from Valentinus.

57. *The Noetians.* This Noetus was from Smyrna in Asia. Together with some others he was carried away by vanity[30] and said that Christ was a son-father. He maintained that the Father and the Son and the Holy Ghost were the same. He furthermore said that he himself was Moses and that his brother was Aaron.

58. *The Valesians,* as we have come to understand, are they who dwell in Bacathus, which is the chief town of Philadelphia of the Arabs. They make eunuchs of visitors and of chance comers among them. And among themselves, too, the greater number have been castrated and are eunuchs. They teach certain other things which are redolent of heresy and they refuse to follow the Law and the Prophets. They have also introduced certain other obscene practices.

59. *The Cathari* were connected with Novatus of Rome. They absolutely reject those who have married a second time and they do not accept penance.[31]

---

30 The text has ἐφ' ἅρματι ('on a chariot'), but the original reading is without any doubt ἐπάρματι ('by vanity'); cf. Oehler, *Corpus Haereseologicum* II-2, p. 4, n. 7.

31 That is, forgiveness of sins after baptism.

60. *The Angelici* have entirely disappeared. They either claimed to belong to an angelic order, or [they got their name] from their practice of invoking the angels.

61. *The Apostolici,* who are also called *Apotactici,* or 'Renuntiants,' appear only in Pisidia. They accept only those who give up their property. They resemble the Encratites, but have some other ideas which these last do not have.

62. *The Sabellians* hold opinions like those of Noetus, except they do not say that the Father suffered, while they do say that the Word was uttered and then again returned.

63. *The Origenians,*[32] who come from a certain Origen, are practicers of immorality. They practice unspeakable obscenities and give over their own bodies to corruption.

64. Still other *Origenians* are from Origen Adamantius the composer. They reject the resurrection of the dead. What is more, they teach that Christ and the Holy Ghost are creatures, and they explain paradise, the heavens, and everything else in an allegorical sense. They talk such nonsense as that the kingdom of Christ has sometime ceased and that the angels, too, will come to an end. They have the strange idea that Christ will rule together with the Devil and that He was crucified for the demons.

Thus far for the eighteen heresies of the fourth part of Book 2.[33]

The following five heresies are contained in the fifth part of Book 2.[34]

65. *The Paulianists* come from Paul of Samosata. This Paul comes very close to affirming that Christ does not exist, for he has made Him out to be a spoken word that began

---

[32] Epiphanius is the only source for the existence of this sect. They are probably the same as the Origenists of the following heresy.
[33] See above, note 26.
[34] This refers to the second part of Book 2 of the *Panarion.* The description of the following five heresies is Epiphanius' epitome of this part (*PG* 42.9-12).

to exist from Mary. Those things said about Him in sacred Scripture as existing were spoken prophetically at a time when He did not exist. On the contrary, He began to exist from Mary from that time when He became present in the flesh.

66. *The Manichaeans,* who are also called *Aconites,*[35] are disciples of Manes the Persian. While they say that Christ is some sort of apparition, they worship the sun and moon and pray to the stars and powers and demons. They introduce two eternally existing principles, the one good and the other evil, and they hold that Christ only apparently came and suffered. They speak impiously of the Old Testament and of the God who spoke in it. They state that the whole world was not made by God, but only a part of it.

67. *The Hieracites* come from Hierax, who was a casuist from Leontopolis in Egypt. They deny the resurrection of the flesh, but use both the Old and New Testaments. Absolutely forbidding marriage, they receive anchorets, virgins, celibates, and widows. They say that children who have not as yet come of age have no share in the kingdom, because they have not been engaged in the struggle.

68. *The Meletians* in Egypt are not heretics, but schismatics. They do not hold communion with those who lapsed during the persecutions. Now they have joined with the Arians.

69. *The Arians,* who are also called *Ariomanites* and *Diatomites,*[36] are they who say that the Son of God is a creature and that the Holy Ghost is the creature of a creature. They assert that Christ did not receive His soul from Mary, but only His body.

Thus far the five heresies of the fifth part of Book 2.[37]

---

35 The correct form is *Acuanite,* from Acuas, the name of a third-century Manichaean teacher from Mesopotamia (*Panarion,* Heresy 66.1, PG 42.29A).

36 'Separaters.'

37 See above, note 34.

The following seven heresies are contained in the first part of Book 3.[38]

70. *The Audians* form a schism and faction, but not, however, a heresy. They pursue a well-ordered way of life and profess a faith which is in every respect like that of the Catholic Church. The greater part of them live in monasteries and they do not hold communion with all. They are also much addicted to the use of the apocryphal scriptures. They overly censure such of our bishops as are wealthy, and other of our bishops for other reasons. They are peculiar in that they celebrate Easter with the Jews. They also hold something peculiar and contentious in that they give a most harsh interpretation to the expression 'after the image.'[39]

71. *The Photinians.* This Photinus[40] was a native of Sirmium and had ideas similar to those of Paul of Samosata, but he differed from him in some things. He, too, asserts that Christ had his beginning from Mary.

72. *The Marcellians* come from Marcellus of Ancyra in Galatia.[41] This man was originally reputed to think very much like Sabellius, yet, although he oftentimes defended himself even in writing, he was accused by some of continuing to adhere to the Sabellians. It is possible, however, that he changed his mind and may have set himself straight, or that his disciples may have done so, because some of the moderate orthodox came to the defense of his statements.

73. *The Semiarians,* while they on the one hand confess

---

38 This refers to the first part of Book 3 of the *Panarion.* The description of the following seven heresies is Epiphanius' epitome of this part (*PG* 42.336-337).
39 Namely, that the 'after the image' of Gen. 1.27 refers to the body of Adam. Epiphanius, *Panarion,* Heresy 70.2 (*PG* 42.341AB).
40 Bishop of Sirmium (d. 375), a disciple of Marcellus of Ancyra. There is doubt as to the nature of his heresy and he has been accused of both Sabellianism and Arianism.
41 One of the first victims of the Arian reaction after the Council of Nicea. A strong defender of the Nicean faith, he was condemned and deposed by the arianizing party, possibly not unjustifiably, for Sabellianism.

Christ to be a creature, on the other hand captiously declare that He is not a creature like other creatures. 'But,' they say, 'we do call him Son—yet we say that He is created, lest we attribute suffering to the Father because of His having begotten Him.' In the same way they also definitely postulate a creature in the case of the Holy Ghost. They reject the 'identity in substance' of the Son and prefer to say 'similarity in substance.' Some of them, however, have rejected the similarity in substance as well.[42]

74. *The Pneumatochi*,[43] while they speak very well concerning Christ, blaspheme the Holy Ghost by making Him a creature and not of the Godhead. Rather, by a misuse of words, they say that He was produced through an operation and is nothing more than a sanctifying force.

75. *The Aerians*. This Aerius was a native of Pontus and, being still alive, he continues to be a source of annoyance. He became a priest of the Bishop Eustathius,[44] who has been accused of being an Arian. Since Aerius had not been appointed bishop, he gave out may things against the Church. While absolutely Arian in his faith, he has gone to even greater excess by holding that it is unnecessary to offer Mass for the deceased. He forbids fasting on Wednesdays and Fridays and during Lent, and also forbids the celebration of Easter. He preaches the renunciation of all worldly goods. He indulges without restraint in every sort of meat and food. Should any one of his followers wish to fast, he tells him not to do so on the stated days, but whenever he wishes—

---

42 The 'identity in substance' is the *homooúsion*, or 'consubstantial,' of Nicea. The 'similarity in substance' is the *homoioúsion* of the conservative Semiarians to which was added 'in all things.' The Semiarians who are here stated to have rejected the 'similarity' are those who supported the formula of the Council of Rimini (359) which contained the 'similarity' but had the 'in all things' deleted.

43 The Pneumatomachi, or 'Fighters against the Spirit'; otherwise known as Macedonians.

44 Bishop of Sebaste (in Armenia Minor), who was excommunicated as an Arian by the Semiarian Council of Seleucia in 359.

'For,' says he, 'you are not under any law.' He furthermore claims that there is no differences between bishop and priests.

76. *The Aetians* come from Aetius, a Cilician who was ordained deacon by the Arian bishop of Alexandria, George. They are also called *Anomoeans*[45] and, by some, *Eunomians* after a certain Eunomius who was a disciple of Aetius. Eudoxius also was one of them, but it would seem that he dissociated himself out of fear of Emperor Constantine, so that only Aetius was banished. At any rate, Eudoxius continued to be Arian-minded—although not, indeed, after the fashion of Aetius. These Anomoeans, or Aetians, completely separate Christ and the Holy Ghost from God the Father. They aver that Christ is a creature, and say that He has not even a similarity to the Father. By means of Aristotelian syllogisms and geometric proofs they attempt to explain the nature of God and in the same way try to show that Christ cannot, as they pretend, be from God. The Eunomians, who stem from them, rebaptize all those who come to them— not only [non-Arians] but even those that come from the Arians. As a strong rumor has it, they put the feet of those being baptized up in the air and baptize them on the head. They say that it is nothing serious to have erred in any way, whether by fornication or some other sin, since God requires nothing else save that one adhere to this faith which they hold.

Thus far similarly the seven heresies of the first part of Book 3.[46]

In the second part of Book 3 there are four heresies.[47]

---
45 'Those who reject any likeness'; extreme Arians of the post-Nicean period.
46 See above, note 38.
47 This refers to the second part of Book 3 of the *Panarion*. The description of the following four heresies in Epiphanius' epitome of this part (*PG* 42.640).

77. *The Dimoerites*,[48] who are also called *Apollinarists*,[49] confess that Christ's coming, that is to say, His Incarnation, is not perfect. Some of them have been so bold as to say that His body is consubstantial with the Godhead, while others have denied that He assumed a soul. Still others, basing their opinion upon the expression 'the Word was made flesh,' denied that He took His body from a created body, that is to say, from Mary; they stubbornly held that the Word only was made flesh. Later on, however, with what in mind I can not say, they declared that He did not assume a mind.

78. *The Antidicomarianites*,[50] say that, after having given birth to the Saviour, the blessed Mary, the ever-virgin, had marital relations with Joseph.

79. *The Collyridians*, on a certain day of the year appointed for that purpose, offer up certain *collyrida*, or cakes, in honor of this same Mary; this is the reason we have given them the name of Collyridians.

80. *The Massalians*, have a name which is interpreted as meaning *Euchites*, or 'praying people.' Also connected with these are the so-called *Euphemites, Martyrians*, and *Satanians*, who all follow the heresies practiced by the Greeks.

Thus far the recapitulation of the seventh part.[51]

Chapters of the impious doctrine of the Massalians, taken from their book.[52]

---

48 'Two-Parters,' for their claiming that the Word assumed only two parts of the humanity, that is, body and animal soul, instead of three: body, animal and spiritual soul.
49 From their founder, Apollinaris, Bishop of Laodicea in the latter half of the fourth centruy.
50 'Opponents of Mary.'
51 See above, note 47.
52 Evidently, these are chapter headings from some book of the Massalians, possibly the *Asceticus*. They are not given by Epiphanius. Timothy of Constantinople in his *The Reception of Heretics* (PG 86.48-52) gives nineteen points of the Massalian doctrine which appear

(1) That Satan dwells personally with man and dominates him in all things.

(2) That Satan and the demons possess the minds of men, and that human nature is held in common with the spirits of evil.

(3) That Satan and the Holy Ghost dwell together in man, and that not even the Apostles were free of the demoniac power.

(4) That not even baptism makes man perfect, nor does the communion of the Sacred Mysteries purify the soul but only that prayer which is so zealously cultivated by themselves.

(5) That even after baptism man is permeated with sin.

(6) That the faithful man receives the incorruptible godly garment not through baptism, but through prayer.

(7) That one must also attain to impassibility and that there must be a participation of the Holy Ghost experienced sensibly and with certainty.

(8) That it is necessary for the soul to feel such communion with the heavenly bridegroom as the wife feels while having relations with her husband.

(9) That spiritual men perceive both sin possessing and grace operating from within and without.

(10) That revelation is that which is given as a decree sensibly and by a divine person.

(11) That fire is a creator.

(12) That the soul which does not possess Christ sensibly and in every operation is an abode of serpents and venomous monsters, that is to say, of every adverse power.

(13) That evil is natural.

(14) That even before the fall Adam had relations with Eve impassionately.

---

to be taken from some book of theirs, but, although the doctrine is the same, the eighteen points given by the Damascene show no dependence upon them.

(15) That seed and the Word fell into Mary.

(16) They say that a man must have two souls: the one common to men and the other heavenly.

(17) They say that it is possible for man sensibly to receive the person of the Holy Ghost with all certainty and in every operation.

(18) That to them who pray it is possible for the Saviour to appear in light; and that once a man was found standing by the altar and three loaves soaked in oil were offered to him.[53]

What is more, they also avoid manual labor as not befitting Christians. And they are especially inhuman in their treatment of the poor, declaring that it is not proper that they who have renounced all worldly goods or who are entirely devoted to the doing of good should help public beggars, or abandoned widows, or those in straightened circumstances, or the mutilated, or the diseased, or those suffering from harsh creditors or from the incursions of thieves or barbarians, or such as have met with any misfortune of the sort. Rather, they say that they themselves should be furnished with everything, because they are the truly poor in spirit.

To all this they have added a contempt for churches and altars, alleging that ascetics have no need to frequent church services, since their prayers in their own oratories are quite sufficient. For such, they were accustomed to say, was the power of prayer as to make the Holy Ghost sensibly manifest to themselves and their disciples. They have this strange idea that those who would be saved must, without engaging in any other occupation whatsoever, pray until such time as they feel the sin being perceptibly driven out by the force of their prayers like some sort of smoke, or fire, or serpent, or other such beast; and until they sensibly experience the

---

[53] The next three paragraphs are based upon some unknown source which is independent of Epiphanius, Timothy of Constantinople, and Theodoret.

return of the Holy Ghost and have in their soul a manifest perception of His entrance.⁵⁴ And this, they say, is the true communion of Christians. For those who have been baptized do by no means all participate in the Holy Ghost through the baptism of the Church or by the ordinations of clerics, unless they most assiduously have communion by their own prayers and, apart from baptism, receive the communion of the Holy Ghost, and unless they be willing to remain with them and be instructed in their doctrines. Thus, when certain priests said to them that 'we confess that we possess the Holy Ghost in faith but not sensibly,' they promised them that they, too, by praying with them should receive a share of the sensation of the Spirit. Such is the absurdity of their humbug that those of them who have supposedly participated in the sensation of the Spirit are held to be blessed, as being perfect, free of all sin, and superior. These they treat with great respect and venerate as being no longer subject to the dangers of sin. And besides all this they are indulged and exempted in the matter of food and they are shown every sort of attention, honor, and luxury. Yet, many of them, after so great a recognition of their perfection on the part of their own, have, when among outsiders, whom they do not even consider worthy to be called Christians, been observed committing various disgraceful actions, thefts of money, and fornication.

In addition to the things already recounted, they have many other strange ideas, such as that of dissolving legitimate marriages for no cause whatsoever. Those who have thus withdrawn from the married state they receive as ascetics and hold as blessed. They persuade fathers and mothers to neglect the rearing of their children. They are constantly repeating that everything should be offered to them. And

---

54 Cf. Timothy of Constantinople, *The Reception of Heretics* (The Marcianists) 3 (*PG* 86.48BC).

they furthermore receive with alacrity slaves running away from their masters, and sinners coming to them without any absolution, without priestly sanction, and without having passed through any of the penitential degrees established by the canons of the Church, and they engage to cleanse them speedily of all sin—provided only that they practice that much-vaunted prayer of theirs and become zealous initiates in their charlatanry. They go so far as to present certain of these for ordination as clerics before they have been absolved of sin, fraudulently persuading the bishops to impose hands by misleading them with the testimony of those of their number who are reputed to be ascetics. They are eager to do this, not because they have any esteem for clerical orders—indeed, they show contempt for the bishops themselves, whenever they have a mind to—but because they are anxious to work up a degree of power and authority for themselves. Some of them, moreover, say that they do not partake of the Mysteries unless they feel the Spirit becoming sensibly present to them at that hour. And some of them permit those who wish to cut off their own genitals. They have little regard even for excommunications. Furthermore, they take oaths and perjure themselves without any hesitation, and they will deceitfully pretend to anathematize their own heresy.

Further on the aforementioned heresy of the Massalians, who are for the most part to be found in monasteries, which is taken from the History of Theodoret.[55]

The heresy of the Massalians made its appearance in the time of Valentinian and Valens. Those who translate this name into Greek call them *Euchites,* or 'praying people.' They also have another name which is based upon fact, for, from their receiving into themselves the operation of some

---
55 Theodoret, *Ecclesiastical History* 4.10 (*PG* 82.1141-1145).

demon, which operation they take to be that of the Holy Ghost, they are called *Enthusiasts,* or 'possessed ones.' Those who are afflicted with this madness to the last degree shun manual labor as evil and indulge excessively in sleep, calling the impressions received in their dreams 'enthusiasm,' or divine possession. The authors of this heresy were Dadoes, Sabas, Adelphius, Hermas, and Simeon, and some others in addition to these. They withdrew from the Church's communion, declaring that there is neither profit nor harm in that divine Food of which Christ says: 'He that eateth my flesh and drinketh my blood hath everlasting life.'[56] Nevertheless, when they are put to the test, they without any shame publicly repudiate those who have these same opinions which they themselves hold in their own hearts. There was, however, a certain Litoius,[57] who ruled the Church of Melitene and was gifted with great zeal. This man, when he beheld a number of monasteries—dens of thieves, rather—infected with this plague, burned them down and drove the wolves away from the flock. And it was the same with the most praiseworthy Amphilochius, to whom was entrusted the metropolitan see of Lycaonia and who ruled over a whole nation. When he learned that this filthiness had invaded those parts, he routed it out again and freed the flocks committed to his care from that outrage.

And Flavian, the famed Bishop of Antioch,[58] having learned that they were active in Edessa and letting loose their poison to fill up whomsoever came near them, sent a band of monks and had them brought to Antioch. Then, when they absolutely denied the madness, he exposed them in the following manner. First he said that the accusers were false informers and that the witnesses were lying; then, with

---
56 John 6.55.
57 Letoius, Bishop of Melitene, to whom was addressed the *Canonical Epistle* (c. 390) of Gregory of Nyssa.
58 Bishop of Antioch (381-404).

great kindness, he invited Adelphius, who was by far the eldest, to sit down by him. 'Old man,' he said, 'we have lived life longer and have come better to know human nature and we are acquainted with the wickedness of our adversaries the demons; we have also learned through experience of the abundance of grace. But these, who are young and have no exact knowledge of these things, are unable to bear talk of a more spiritual nature. So, tell me, how do you say that it is that the hostile spirit withdraws and the grace of the Holy Ghost enters in?' Softened by these words, that old man vomited out all the hidden poison and told how baptism brings no help to its recipients and how only earnest prayers will expel the indwelling demon. He said that, just as every one born inherits his nature from his first parents, so also does he inherit a state of servitude to the demons. But, when these demons are driven out by earnest prayer, then the all-holy Spirit enters in, revealing its own presence in a sensible and visible manner, freeing the body from the movement of the passions, and entirely releasing the soul from its evil inclinations. Thus, nothing else is needed—whether it be that fasting which oppresses the body, or that discipline which restricts and teaches to walk rightly. And he who has attained this state is not only freed from the impulses of the body, but clearly foresees the future and with his eyes contemplates the Holy Trinity. The divine Flavian, having thus made the foul well-spring erupt and having contrived to lay bare the thoughts of the impious old man, then said to him: 'O inveterate of evil days, it is not I but thy mouth that hath condemned thee; thy lips have born witness against thee.' And now that this disease had been brought into the open, they were driven out of Syria. But they migrated to Pamphylia and filled that country with their infection.

Thus far the heresies up to the time of Marcian.[59]

---
59 Emperor of the East (450-457).

From Marcian on for a short time, and under Leo,[60] *the following heresies made their appearance.*

81. *The Nestorians*[61] hold that God the Word exists by Himself and separately, and that His humanity exists by itself. And the more humble of the Lord's actions during His sojourn among us they attribute to His humanity alone, whereas the more noble and those befitting the divinity they ascribe to God the Word alone. But they do not attribute the both to the same Person.

82. *The Eutychians,* who get their name from the heresy of Eutyches,[62] say that our Lord Jesus Christ did not take His flesh from the blessed Virgin Mary, but contend that He became incarnate in a more divine manner. For they could not conceive how God the Word could unite to Himself from the Virgin Mary this man, who was subject to the sin of his first father Adam, to the effect that 'despoiling the principalities and powers, he hath exposed them confidently in open shew,' as has been written, 'triumphing on the cross'[63] over those very things which He had put on because of the fall of the first man.

83. *The Egyptians,* who are also called *Schematics* and *Monophysites,*[64] separated from the orthodox Church on the pretext of that document [approved] at Chalcedon [and known as] the *Tome.* They have been called *Egyptians* because of the fact that during the reign[65] of Emperors Marcian and Valentian the Egyptians were the first authors of this particular kind of heresy. Because of their strong

---

60 Leo I, the Thracian, Emperor of the East (457-474).
61 From Nestorius, Archbishop of Constantinople (428-431).
62 Archimandrite from Constantinople, originator of Monophysism in its extreme form, but certainly not responsible for the errors here described.
63 Col. 2.15.
64 Monophysite means 'holder of one nature' (i.e., in Christ). Various explanations of Schematic have been proposed, of which the most probable is that it is a misreading of Schismatic.
65 From 450 to 455.

attachment to Dioscorus of Alexandria, who was deposed by the Council of Chalcedon for defending the teachings of Eutyches, they opposed this council and to the limit of their ability fabricated innumerable charges against it, which charges we have already taken up in this book and sufficiently refuted by showing them to be clumsy and stupid. Their leaders were Theodosius of Alexandria,[66] from whom come the Theodosians, and James of Syria,[67] from whom come the Jacobites. Privy to these as champions and strong defenders were Severus,[68] the seducer from Antioch, and John the Tritheite,[69] who expended his efforts on vain things. Both of these last denied the mystery of salvation. They wrote many things against the inspired council of the 630 Fathers of Chalcedon, and they set many snares, so to speak, and 'laid stumbling blocks by the wayside'[70] for those who are lost in their pernicious heresy. Although they hold individual substances, they destroy the mystery of the Incarnation. We have considered it necessary to discuss their impiety in brief and to add short explanations in refutation of their godless and most abominable heresy. Hence, I shall present the teachings, or ravings, rather, of their champion John, in which they take so much pride.

---

66 Monophysite patriarch of Alexandria (536-538), exiled to Constantinople where he carried on his Monophysite activities until his death in 566.
67 James Baradaeus ('the ragged'), founder of the Monophysite Jacobite hierarchy of Syria and Egypt, clandestinely consecrated by Theodosius in 543.
68 Monophysite patriarch of Antioch (512-518) the great theologian and saint of the Monophysites, from whom they are called Severians.
69 John Philoponus, the Grammarian, a sixth-century philosopher of Alexandria and one of the leaders of the division of the Monophysites called Tritheites. These held that for each hypostasis there was one nature, and, consequently, that Christ had one nature, while the three hypostases of the Trinity had three, and hence the name of Tritheites, or 'those who hold three Gods.' Some claim that the Damascene depended much upon Philoponus for the matter of the *Dialectica*.
70 Ps. 139.6.

On nature and hypostasis according to the teachings of the Severians, and how they teach individual substances: by John the Grammarian and Tritheite, called Philoponus, and taken from the fourth discourse of his work entitled The Arbiter.[71]

Although the common and universal basis of man's nature is in itself one, nevertheless, since it is realized in several subjects, it is multiplied and exists not partially but wholly in each of these subjects. It is just as that which makes a shipbuilder a shipbuilder, while it is one, is yet multiplied by existing in many subjects. In the same way, while the theory in the teacher is by its own nature one, yet, when it is reproduced in the pupils, it is multiplied with them and exists entirely in each of them. And again, the seal of the signet ring, which is one, is reproduced in its entirety in each of the several impressions and thus becomes many and is so said to be. Thus, the several ships, the several men, the several seals, and the several concepts in the several pupils all result as several in number in the individual subjects and they are distinct and not united. But, by their common species, many men are one, and many ships are one, and concepts, too, and the impressions have their unity in the identity of the common seal. Thus, these are all in one respect several and distinct, whereas in another respect they are united.

Now, although we often attribute number to objects having extension—as, for example, when we say that this piece of wood is two cubits—we mean that the one object is potentially two, but not actually so, because actually it is one and not two. However, we do say that it is two, because it can become two by being cut up.

---

71 *The Arbiter*, the most important of the works of John Philoponus. The following two fragments are from Books 4 and 7 respectively and represent all that is extant of the original Greek text, although there is a Syriac translation of the entire work.

Chapter 7 from The Arbiter.

In this seventh discourse the real truth will be confirmed from the principles laid down by them that hold the contrary. Thus, while they maintain that Christ has two natures, they hold that He has only one hypostasis, that is to say, person. They likewise disclaim both those who hold that there is one nature in Christ and those who hold that He has two hypostases. But before we undertake to refute this supposition, I think that it is wise first to define just what the teaching of the Church intends to be meant by the term *nature,* and what by that of *person* and *hypostasis.* Now, *nature* is considered to be the common basis of those things which share the same essence. Thus, common to every man is his being a rational mortal animal with the ability to understand and know, for in these things no man differs from any other. And so his essense and his nature amount to the same thing. But *hypostasis,* that is to say, *person,* is the very individual real existence of each nature, and, so to speak, an individuality made up of certain peculiarities, by which they who share in the same nature differ from each other. To put it briefly, it is that which the Peripatetics like to call atoms, or *indivisibles,* in which the division of the common genera and species terminates.

These are what the teachers of the Church called *hypostases,* or, at times, *persons.* Thus, when the animal is divided into the rational and the irrational, and then the rational into man, angel, and devil, they call those things into which each of these ultimate species is split up *individuals.* For example, man is split up into Peter and Paul, while angel is split up into Gabriel, say, and Michael, and each one of the other angels. This is because it is impossible further to divide any one of these into still other things which will continue to preserve the one same nature after the division. Thus, the division of man into soul and body brings about the destruction of the complete animal. And so, they like to call these *individuals*. In the language of the Church, however, they are called *hypostases*, because in them the genera and the species get their existence. For, although there is a particular essence for animal, let us say, and for man, of which the former is the genus and the latter the species, yet it is in the individuals that these have their existence—as in Peter and Paul, for example—and apart from the individuals they do not subsist. And so we have explained what *hypostasis* and *nature* are according to the Church's way of explanation.

Now, this common human nature, in which no one man differs from any other, when it comes to exist in any one of the individuals, then becomes particular to that one and no other, as we set forth in Chapter 4. Thus that rational mortal animal which is in me is common to no other living thing. Certainly the individuals of the same species are not necessarily affected when a particular man, or ox, or horse is affected. It is also quite possible that when Paul died no other men did. And when Peter is born and brought into existence, those who are to come after him are not yet in existence. Consequently, each nature may be taken as an essence not in one way alone, but in two. Thus, it is taken in one way when the common basis of a nature is considered in itself as not existing in any one of the individuals, as, for example, the nature of man, of that of the horse. But it is taken in the other way when we take this same common nature as it exists in the individuals and in each of them takes on their individual existence fitting that one individual alone and no other. Thus, the rational mortal animal which is in me is not common to any other man. Neither would the animal nature which is in this particular horse be in any other, as we have just shown. That the teaching of the Church conceives of natures and hypostases in these ways is evident from the fact that, while we confess one nature of the Father and of the Son and of the Holy Ghost, we hold that these have three hypostases, that is to say, persons, by which each one is distinguished from the rest in some peculiar property. For, what might the one nature of the Godhead be but the common basis of the divine nature as considered in itself and conceived as distinct from the peculiar property of each hypostasis? Furthermore, from the fact that we hold a union of two natures in Christ—the divine I mean, and the human—from this fact it is evident that when we consider the common basis of the nature in each one of the individuals, that is to say, in each one of the hypostases, as being particular and thus not common to any of the others referable to the common species, then we acknowledge the term nature to be more particular. For we certainly do not say that the nature of the Godhead which is understood as being common to the Holy Trinity was incarnate, for in such a case we would be declaring the incarnation of the Holy Ghost. And neither do we hold the common essence of human nature to have been united to God the Word. For thus in the same way the Word of God could rightly be said to have been united both with the men living before His sojourn on earth and with those to come after. However, it is evident that we hereupon declare that nature of the common Godhead which is in the hypostasis of the Word to be a nature of the Godhead. Whence, also, we confess 'one nature incarnate of God the Word,'[72] in which by the addition of the 'of God the Word' we clearly distinguish that nature from both the Father and the Holy Ghost. And so by our having already conceived of the common essence of the divine nature as proper to the divine Word we here again declare the nature of God the Word

---

72 Cyril of Alexandria is responsible for this expression, which, although perfectly orthodox in the sense intended by St. Cyril, was taken in an heretical sense by the Monophysites and used by them as a watchword.

to have been incarnate. And again, we say that a human nature was united to the Word, which was that most particular existence which alone out of all the rest the Word assumed. And so, if we were to take nature in this sense, nature and hypostasis would be nearly the same thing, except for the fact that the term hypostasis includes properties which must be taken into consideration. These are they which are added to the common nature of each individual and make them distinct from one another. For this reason many of us may be found to have different ways of saying that the union was 'of natures, which is to say, of hypostases.' For the hypostasis, as we have shown, signifies the particular and individual existence of each, and so they oftentimes use these terms equivalently, since it is evident that they intend by these to signify to us the very particular nature. And this also since, both in the present discourse and in the usage of those who have treated of such things, it is the universally accepted custom to refer to the common basis of the nature as *man*—as when one says that man is a species of animal, even though no individual man is a species under the genus, nor is so called. Furthermore, we also say that man differs from the horse, quite obviously taking them as universal natures. And again, we say that Peter is a man, and Paul, and John, and that a man has been born and a man died, quite obviously taking him as an individual, even though the common basis of human nature is expressed by the same term. Now, it is only fair to state this: that with us the terms person and hypostasis often have the same meaning, just as if one were to call the same object both a sword and a blade. Thus it is that we speak indifferently of three persons or three hypostases in the Holy Trinity, treating both terms as equivalent and by either one of them meaning the same thing. Frequently, however, the person is distinguished from the hypostasis, the person being taken to mean the mutual relation between certain individuals. This meaning of person is recognized by common usage. Thus, we say: 'such a one took on my person' and 'such a one brought action against this man's person.' We also say that the prefect represents the person of the emperor. Whence it is that the followers of Nestorius' teaching refuse to affirm either one nature in Christ or one hypostasis, since they hold there to be no union of the hypostases in themselves but suppose Him who was of Mary to be a mere man who contained within Himself the entire divine illumination. And it is by this that He differs from the rest of men, since in each one of these the divine illumination is only partially realized. Nevertheless, they confidently assert that the person of Christ is one, explaining that the relation of God the Word to the man born of Mary is one person, because He worked the entire divine dispensation in the person of the divinity of God the Word. In this sense the bad treatment accorded the man is rightly referred back to God, because both the honor and the ill treatment accorded the prefect by the subjects of the emperor is referred back to the emperor himself. In any event they declare that the appellation of *Christ* is indicative of this relation. Thus, they do not hesitate to call Christ one, because, as has been said, the relation is one, even though there may be several participating in it. So, I think that it should be clear to them that revere the Incarnation of the Saviour that we say that the Person of Christ is one, although not in the sense employed by the friends of Nestorius, that is, not in the mere relation of God to man. And it should be clear that we use the term *person* in such a sense as to declare the Person of Christ to be one hypostasis of a man like, let us say, that of Peter or of Paul.

Along with the other things, let us furthermore bear in mind this, too: that there was absolutely no lapse of time during which the humanity of Christ subsisted disunited from the Word, but that its very beginning to be was simultaneous with its union with the Word. But we do not say that that nature is enhypostatic whose existence is independent and self-contained in respect to all other men as being distinguished from the common nature of all the rest by certain peculiar properties. For we have already shown that this is the meaning of the term hypostasis. Therefore, as in the divinity of Christ we confess both its nature and its hypostasis, so naturally we must confess this particular hypostasis as well as a nature, so that we may not be obliged to say that nature is non-subsistent, as I have said. For, one thing is clear, namely, that the humanity of the Saviour was one of the individuals participating in the common nature.

Now that these things have been accurately and clearly explained, and, I presume, have been agreed to by all, let them who suppose there to be two natures and one hypostasis in Christ tell us this: Do they confess the union to have been as well of the natures of the hypostases, since each of the parts united necessarily had a nature as well as a hypostasis, as reason has demonstrated, or do they rather think that the hypostases were united, since there was one hypostasis made of both, but that the natures were not, so that they remained two after the union?

And after some more, in which he treats of how the essence does not admit of more or less, he continues:

Now I think that it is clear that all individuals have one nature which can be realized in several hypostases. Thus, then, while we confess the nature of the Divinity to be one, we declare that It has three hypostases. Furthermore, men also have one nature, while the hypostases coming under this nature are almost infinitely multiplied. And it is the same way with other things. It is impossible for two natures to constitute one hypostasis and to preserve their duality in number. And this is confirmed not only by the process of induction from particular examples (for how would stone or wood, or the ox or the horse, have one hypostasis or constitute one individual?), but also by the very force of reason. Thus, if each nature receives its existence in the hypostases (which is the same thing as to say 'in the individual'), then it is absolutely necessary that where there are two natures there be also at least two hypostases in which these natures will have received their existence. For it is impossible for the nature to subsist in itself without being considered as in some individual. And we have already shown that the individual is the same thing as the hypostasis. Consequently, they who affirm that not only the hypostasis was made one by the union, but the nature, also, are plainly consistent both with themselves and with the truth. On the other hand, those that affirm one hypostasis and two natures are plainly inconsistent both with themselves and with the truth. 'But,' they say, 'since the humanity of Christ had its hypostasis in the Word and did not exist before the union with the Word, for this reason we say that the hypostasis of Christ is one.' Then we ourselves might reply by asking: 'Do you or do you not think that *nature* and *hypostasis* mean the same thing, as just being different terms with the same meaning like *sword* and *blade,* or *other* and *another?*' If they are the same, then, if there is one hypostasis, there must necessarily be one nature, too—as, when there is one blade, then there must necessarily be one sword. But, if there are two natures, then the hypostases will of necessity also be two. If, however, the term nature means one thing, while that of hypostasis means something else, and if they consider a reason of Christ's hypostasis being one to be the fact that the human hypostasis, that is to say, person, did not exist prior to the union with the Word—then would not the fact of Christ's having two natures also be a reason for the human nature's having existed prior to the union with the Word? If, however, the particular nature which was united to the Word did exist beforehand, then it is absolutely necessary for its hypostasis to have existed beforehand, too. Now, it is impossible for either of these to exist if the other one does not—I refer to the particular nature without its own hypostasis. For in their subject the both are one, even though they are oftentimes used synonymously, as we have shown a short while before. If, then, like the hypostasis, the nature that was united to the Word did not exist prior to its union with the Word—for precisely which reason they hold one hypostasis in Christ—then let them also hold that His nature is one, for as long as they do not differ in the union, then neither should they differ in this respect.

84. *The Aphthartodocetae*,[73] who come from Julian of Halicarnassus and Gaianus of Alexandria, are also called *Gaianites*. They agree with the Severians[74] in all things, with this one exception, that, while the Severians seem to hold a difference[75] in the union of Christ, they hold that the body of the Lord was incorruptible from the first instant of its formation. They also confess that the Lord endured suffering—hunger, I mean, and thirst, and fatigue—but they say that He did not suffer these in the same way that we do. For they say that we suffer these by physical necessity, while the Christ suffered them voluntarily and was not subject to the laws of nature.[76]

85. *The Agnoetae*, who are also called *Themistians*, im-

---

73 'Holders of incorruptibility.
74 See above, note 68.
75 That is, a distinction between the body of Christ and the Word, which would seem to contradict the Monophysite doctrine of one nature. Here the Ms. reading of διαφθοράν (corruptibility) has been changed to διαφοράν (difference) by Lequien on the basis of the Damascene's source, Leontius of Byzance (*Chapters Against Severus* 23, *PG* 86. 1909A).
76 Leontius of Byzance, *On Sects* 10 (*PG* 86.1260C).

piously declare that Christ does not know the day of judgment,[77] and they attribute fear to Him. They are a sect of the Theodosians, for Themestius,[78] the author of their heresy, held one composite nature in Christ.

86. *The Barsanouphites,* who are also called *Semidalites,* agree with the Gaianites and the Theodosians, but they have something in addition. Thus, they add fine flour[79] to the elements which Dioscorus is supposed to have consecrated, and, touching this with the tip of their finger, they taste the flour and receive it instead of the Mysteries, without making any oblation at all. Having thus eked out the elements consecrated by Dioscorus, as has been related, they keep adding the fine flour as these become gradually consumed, and for them this is considered to take the place of consecrated elements.

87. *The Hicetae*[80] are ascetics and in everything orthodox, with this exception, that they congregate with women in monasteries and offer to God hymns accompanied by music and dancing in imitation, as it were, of the dance organized in Moses' time on the occasion of the destruction of the Egyptians which took place in the Red Sea.[81]

88. *The Gnosimachi*[82] are opposed to all Christian knowledge, asserting that those who search the sacred Scriptures for some higher knowledge are doing something useless, because God requires of the Christian nothing more than good deeds. Consequently, it is better to take a more simple course and not to be curious after any doctrine arrived at by learned research.

89. *The Heliotropites* say that those plants called heliotropes which turn about with the rays of the sun have a

---

77 From a misinterpretation of Mark 13.32.
78 A seventh-century deacon of Alexandria.
79 σεμίδαλις; hence, the name Semidalite.
80 Lequien suggest that these might be the Euchites (or Massalians, cf. Heresy 80). The Damascene is the only source for this sect.
81 Exod. 15.20,21.
82 'Enemies of knowledge.'

certain virtue which causes such rotations in them. For this reason they are anxious to venerate them, not understanding that the movement observed in them is a natural one.

90. *The Thnetopsychites*[83] introduce the doctrine that the human soul is similar to that of beasts and that it perishes with the body.

91. *The Agonyclites* will not kneel during any of the times of prayer, but rather always pray standing up.

92. *The Theocatagnostae*,[84] who are also called *Blasphemers*, try to find fault with [the Lord] for certain words and actions, as well as with the holy persons associated with Him, and with the sacred Scriptures. They are foolhardy and blasphemous people.

93. *The Christolytae*[85] say that after His resurrection from the dead our Lord Jesus Christ left His animate body here below and ascended into heaven with His divinity alone.

94. *The Ethnophrones*,[86] while they follow some practices of pagans, are Christians in all other respects. They bring in nativity and fortune and fate, and they admit every kind of astronomy and astrology as well as every sort of divination and augury. They have recourse to auspices, the averting of evil by sacrifice, omens, interpretations of signs, spells, and similar superstitions of impious people, together with all the rest of the pagan practices. They also observe certain Greek feasts, and they furthermore keep days, and months, and seasons, and years.

95. *The Donatists* originated in Africa with a certain Donatus,[87] who handed down to them a certain bone which

---

[83] 'Holders of the mortality of the soul.'
[84] 'Condemners of God.'
[85] 'Dissolvers of Christ.'
[86] 'Pagan-minded.'
[87] Schismatic bishop of Carthage during first half of the fourth century. The custom here referred to may well have been followed by the Donatists. At least, it was the practice of the lady Lucilla, one of the founders of the schism.

they hold in their hand and kiss before partaking of the consecrated species, whenever these are to be offered.

96. *The Ethicoproscoptae*[88] offend in the matter of morals, that is to say, in conduct; while they reject some of the most praiseworthy moral teachings, certain blameworthy ones they condone as useful.

97. *The Parermeneutae*[89] misinterpret certain passages of the Sacred Scriptures, both of the Old and of the New Testaments, and manipulate them to serve their own purpose. They are stubbornly opposed to most of the interpretations which are exact and above reproach. They suffer from a certain lack of education and judgment, whence it is that they do not know how to defend themselves and some of their heretical teachings.

98. *The Lampetians* are so called after a certain Lampetius.[90] They allow each individual to follow whatever state of life he may wish and deem fit, whether it be to live in common and lead the cenobitic life or to assume the monastic habit of his choosing. For, they say, the Christian does nothing under compulsion, because it is written: 'I will freely sacrifice to thee,'[91] and again, 'With my will I will give praise to Him.'[92] And, as some say, they permit the endurance of physical sufferings without resistance, on the ground that this is nature's due. They are also said to hold other things which very much resemble those held by those who are called Aerians.[93] (One of their number was a certain Eustathius, from whom come the *Eustathians*.)[94]

---

88 'Offenders against morals.'
89 'Misinterpreters.'
90 A prominent Cappadocian leader of the Euchites, or Massalians, during the last half of the fifth century.
91 Ps. 53.8.
92 Ps. 27.7.
93 For the Aerians and their founder, Aerius, see Heresy 75.
94 A later interpolation. The Euchites were sometimes called Eustathians, probably from Eustathius of Edessa, one of those condemned by Flavian of Antioch (see Heresy 80). Later, this Eustathius was confused with Eustathius of Sebaste (see note 44), who had been closely associated with Aerius.

Thus far the heresies up to the time of Heraclius.[95]

From Heraclius to the present time the following have appeared.

99. *The Monothelites* originated with Cyrus of Alexandria, but received their definite establishment from Sergius of Constantinople.[96] They proclaim two natures and one hypostasis in Christ, but they hold one will and one operation, thus destroying the duality of the natures and coming very close to the teachings of Apollinaris.

(100. *The Autoproscoptae*,[97] while they are orthodox in every respect, boldly cut themselves off from the communion of the Catholic Church. Although they pretend to require the observance of canonical ordinances, yet, being neither bishops nor presidents of the common herd, they themselves offend in the very things of which they accuse others. Thus, they openly cohabit with women and maintain them privately in their homes. They are addicted to business and profit-making and other worldly affairs. They live unreasonably and neglect in deed those things which in word they profess to maintain, so that by the judgment of the Apostle they are transgressors.[98] For, although they are monks and organized under a clergy, they honor God in word but in deed dishonor Him. Those that follow them are exalted, as it were, and walking in their own simplicity. On the contrary, the sane members of the Church respect the sacred canons, and refer matters pertaining to these to bishops and presidents, thus showing by their deeds a great respect for those whom they esteem for the sake of the good order.)

---

95 Greek emperor (610-641).
96 Cyrus, Patriarch of Alexandria (630-643); Sergius, Patriarch of Constantinople (610-638).
97 'Offenders against themselves.' This heresy is not found in some manuscripts.
98 Rom. 2.3.

101. There is also the superstition of the *Ishmaelites* which to this day prevails and keeps people in error, being a forerunner of the Antichrist. They are descended from Ishmael, was was born to Abraham of Agar, and for this reason they are called both *Agarenes* and *Ishmaelites*. They are also called *Saracens,* which is derived from Σάρρας κενοί, or *destitute of Sara,* because of what Agar said to the angel: 'Sara hath sent me away destitute.'[99] These used to be idolaters and worshiped the morning star and Aphrodite, whom in their own language they called Khabár, which means *great*.[100] And so down to the time of Heraclius they were very great idolaters. From that time to the present a false prophet named Mohammed has appeared in their midst. This man, after having chanced upon the Old and New Testaments and likewise, it seems, having conversed with an Arian monk,[101] devised his own heresy. Then, having insinuated himself into the good graces of the people by a show of seeming piety, he gave out that a certain book had been sent down to him from heaven. He had set down some ridiculous compositions in this book of his and he gave it to them as an object of veneration.

He says that there is one God, creator of all things, who has neither been begotten nor has begotten.[102] He says that the Christ is the Word of God and His Spirit, but a creature and a servant, and that He was begotten, without seed, of Mary the sister of Moses and Aaron.[103] For, he says, the

---

99 Cf. Gen. 16.8. Sozomen also says that they were descended from Agar, but called themselves descendants of Sara to hide their servile origin (*Ecclesiastical History* 6.38, PG 67.1412AB).
100 The Arabic *kabirun* means 'great,' whether in size or in dignity. Herodotus mentions the Arabian cult of the 'Heavenly Aphrodite' but says that the Arabs called her Alilat (Herodotus 1.131).
101 This may be the Nestorian monk Bahira (George or Sergius) who met the boy Mohammed at Bostra in Syria and claimed to recognize in him the sign of a prophet.
102 Koran, Sura 112.
103 Sura 19; 4.169.

Word and God and the Spirit entered into Mary and she brought forth Jesus, who was a prophet and servant of God. And he says that the Jews wanted to crucify Him in violation of the law, and that they seized His shadow and crucified this. But the Christ Himself was not crucified, he says, nor did He die, for God out of His love for Him took Him to Himself into heaven.[104] And he says this, that when the Christ had ascended into heaven God asked Him: 'O Jesus, didst thou say: "I am the Son of God and God"?' And Jesus, he says, answered: 'Be merciful to me, Lord. Thou knowest that I did not say this and that I did not scorn to be thy servant. But sinful men have written that I made this statement, and they have lied about me and have fallen into error.' And God answered and said to Him: 'I know that thou didst not say this word.'[105] There are many other extraordinary and quite ridiculous things in this book which he boasts was sent down to him from God. But when we ask: 'And who is there to testify that God gave him the book? And which of the prophets foretold that such a prophet would rise up?'—they are at a loss. And we remark that Moses received the Law on Mount Sinai, with God appearing in the sight of all the people in cloud, and fire, and darkness, and storm. And we say that all the Prophets from Moses on down foretold the coming of Christ and how Christ God (and incarnate Son of God) was to come and to be crucified and die and rise again, and how He was to be the judge of the living and dead. Then, when we say: 'How is it that this prophet of yours did not come in the same way, with others bearing witness to him? And how is it that God did not in your presence present this man with the book to which you refer, even as He gave the Law to Moses, with the people looking on and the mountain smoking,

---

104 Sura 4.156.
105 Sura 5.116ff.

so that you, too, might have certainty?'—they answer that God does as He pleases. 'This,' we say, 'We know, but we are asking how the book came down to your prophet.' Then they reply that the book came down to him while he was asleep. Then we jokingly say to them that, as long as *he* received the book in his sleep and did not actually sense the operation, then the popular adage applies to him (which runs: You're spinning me dreams.)[106]

When we ask again: 'How is it that when he enjoined us in this book of yours not to do anything or receive anything without witnesses, you did not ask him: "First do you show us by witnesses that you are a prophet and that you have come from God, and show us just what Scriptures there are that testify about you" '—they are ashamed and remain silent. [Then we continue:] 'Although you may not marry a wife without witnesses, or buy, or acquire property; although you neither receive an ass nor possess a beast of burden unwitnessed; and although you do possess both wives and property and asses and so on through witnesses, yet it is only your faith and your scriptures that you hold unsubstantiated by witnesses. For he who handed this down to you has no warranty from any source, nor is there anyone known who testified about him before he came. On the contrary, he received it while he was asleep.'

Moreover, they call us *Hetaeriasts,* or *Associators,* because, they say, we introduce an associate with God by declaring Christ to the Son of God and God. We say to them in rejoinder: 'The Prophets and the Scriptures have delivered this to us, and you, as you persistently maintain, accept the Prophets. So, if we wrongly declare Christ to be the Son of God, it is they who taught this and handed it on to us.' But some of them say that it is by misinterpretation that we have

---
106 The manuscripts do not have the adage, but Lequien suggests this one from Plato.

represented the Prophets as saying such things, while others say that the Hebrews hated us and deceived us by writing in the name of the Prophets so that we might be lost. And again we say to them: 'As long as you say that Christ is the Word of God and Spirit, why do you accuse us of being Hetaeriasts? For the word, and the spirit, is inseparable from that in which it naturally has existence. Therefore, if the Word of God is in God, then it is obvious that He is God. If, however, He is outside of God, then, according to you, God is without word and without spirit. Consequently, by avoiding the introduction of an associate with God you have mutilated Him. It would be far better for you to say that He has an associate than to mutilate Him, as if you were dealing with a stone or a piece of wood or some other inanimate object. Thus, you speak untruly when you call us Hetaeriasts; we retort by calling you Mutilators of God.'

They furthermore accuse us of being idolaters, because we venerate the cross, which they abominate. And we answer them: 'How is it, then, that you rub yourselves against a stone in your Ka'ba[107] and kiss and embrace it?' Then some of them say that Abraham had relations with Agar upon it, but others say that he tied the camel to it, when he was going to sacrifice Isaac. And we answer them: 'Since Scripture says that the mountain was wooded and had trees from which Abraham cut wood for the holocaust and laid it upon Isaac,[108] and then he left the asses behind with the two young men, why talk nonsense? For in that place neither is it thick with trees nor is there passage for asses.' And they are embarrassed, but they still assert that the stone is Abraham's. Then we

---

[107] The Ka'ba, called 'The House of God,' is supposed to have been built by Abraham with the help of Ismael. It occupies the most sacred spot in the Mosque of Mecca. Incorporated in its wall is the stone here referred to, the famous Black Stone, which is obviously a relic of the idolatry of the pre-Islam Arabs.
[108] Gen. 22.6.

say: 'Let it be Abraham's, as you so foolishly say. Then, just because Abraham had relations with a woman on it or tied a camel to it, you are not ashamed to kiss it, yet you blame us for venerating the cross of Christ by which the power of the demons and the deceit of the Devil was destroyed.' This stone that they talk about is a head of that Aphrodite whom they used to worship and whom they called Khabár. Even to the present day, traces of the carving are visible on it to careful observers.

As has been related, this Mohammed wrote many ridiculous books, to each one of which he set a title. For example, there is the book *On Woman*,[109] in which he plainly makes legal provision for taking four wives and, if it be possible, a thousand concubines—as many as one can maintain, besides the four wives. He also made it legal to put away whichever wife one might wish, and, should one so wish, to take to oneself another in the same way. Mohammed had a friend named Zeid. This man had a beautiful wife with whom Mohammed fell in love. Once, when they were sitting together, Mohammed said: 'Oh, by the way, God has commanded me to take your wife.' The other answered: 'You are an apostle. Do as God has told you and take my wife.' Rather—to tell the story over from the beginning—he said to him: 'God has given me the command that you put away your wife.' And he put her away. Then several days later: 'Now,' he said, 'God has commanded me to take her.' Then, after he had taken her and committed adultery with her, he made this law: 'Let him who will put away his wife. And if, after having put her away, he should return to her, let another marry her. For it is not lawful to take her unless she have been married by another. Furthermore, if a brother puts away his wife, let his brother marry her, should he so wish.'[110]

---
109 Koran, Sura 4.
110 Cf. Sura 2.225ff.

In the same book he gives such precepts as this: 'Work the land which God hath given thee and beautify it. And do this, and do it in such a manner'[111]—not to repeat all the obscene things that he did.

Then there is the book of *The Camel of God*.[112] About this camel he says that there was a camel from God and that she drank the whole river and could not pass through two mountains, because there was not room enough. There were people in that place, he says, and they used to drink the water on one day, while the camel would drink it on the next. Moreover, by drinking the water she furnished them with nourishment, because she supplied them with milk instead of water. Then, because these men were evil, they rose up, he says, and killed the camel. However, she had an offspring, a little camel, which, he says, when the mother had been done away with, called upon God and God took it to Himself. Then we say to them: 'Where did that camel come from?' And they say that it was from God. Then we say: 'Was there another camel coupled with this one?' And they say: 'No.' 'Then how,' we say, 'was it begotten? For we see that your camel is without father and without mother and without genealogy, and that the one that begot it suffered evil. Neither is it evident who bred her. And also, this little camel was taken up. So why did not your prophet, with whom, according to what you say, God spoke, find out about the camel—where it grazed, and who got milk by milking it? Or did she possibly, like her mother, meet with evil people and get destroyed? Or did she enter into paradise before you, so that you might have the river of milk that you so foolishly talk about? For you say that you have three rivers flowing in paradise—one of water, one of wine, and one of milk. If your forerunner the camel is outside of paradise,

---
111 Sura 2.223.
112 Not in the Koran.

it is obvious that she has dried up from hunger and thirst, or that others have the benefit of her milk—and so your prophet is boasting idly of having conversed with God, because God did not reveal to him the mystery of the camel. But if she is in paradise, she is drinking water still, and you for lack of water will dry up in the midst of the paradise of delight. And if, there being no water, because the camel will have drunk it all up, you thirst for wine from the river of wine that is flowing by, you will become intoxicated from drinking pure wine and collapse under the influence of the strong drink and fall asleep. Then, suffering from a heavy head after sleeping and being sick from the wine, you will miss the pleasures of paradise. How, then, did it not enter into the mind of your prophet that this might happen to you in the paradise of delight? He never had any idea of what the camel is leading to now, yet you did not even ask him, when he held forth to you with his dreams on the subject of the three rivers. We plainly assure you that this wonderful camel of yours has preceded you into the souls of asses, where you, too, like beasts are destined to go. And there there is the exterior darkness and everlasting punishment, roaring fire, sleepless worms, and hellish demons.'

Again, in the book of *The Table,* Mohammed says that the Christ asked God for a table and that it was given Him. For God, he says, said to Him: 'I have given to thee and thine an incorruptible table.'[113]

And again, in the book of *The Heifer*,[114] he says some other stupid and ridiculous things, which, because of their great number, I think must be passed over. He made it a law that they be circumcised and the women, too, and he ordered them not to keep the Sabbath and not to be baptized. And, while he ordered them to eat some of the things forbidden

---
113 Sura 5.114,115.
114 Sura 2.

by the Law, he ordered them to abstain from others. He furthermore absolutely forbade the drinking of wine.

102. The *Christianocategori,* or *Accusers of Christians,* are such and are so called, because those Christians who worship one living and true God praised in Trinity they accused of worshiping as gods, after the manner of the Greeks, the venerable images of our Lord Jesus Christ, of our immaculate lady, the holy Mother of God, of the holy angels, and of His saints. They are furthermore called *Iconoclasts,* because they have shown deliberate dishonor to all these same holy and venerable images and have consigned them to be broken up and burnt. Likewise, some of those painted on walls they have scraped off, while others they have obliterated with whitewash and black paint. They are also called *Thymoleontes,* or *Lion-hearted,* because, taking advantage of their authority, they have with great heart given strength to their heresy and with torment and torture visited vengeance upon those who approve of the images. This last name they have also received from their heresiarch.[115]

103. The one-hundred-and-third heresy is that of the *Aposchistae,* who are also called *Doxarii.*[116] These seek after their own glory and submit neither to the law of God nor to His priests. They are thoroughly acquainted with the heresy of the Autoproscoptae.[117] Like them, they require the observance of canonical ordinances and, although they are neither bishops nor presidents of the people, but only members of the common herd, they separate themselves from the Catholic Church. Rivaling the Euchites,[118] that is to say, the Massalians, they tell the ascetics not to frequent church services, but to be satisfied with the prayers in their own

---

115 Leo III, the Isaurian, Greek emperor (717-741).
116 'Makers of schism' and 'Gloriers.' These may have been connected with the Massalians or they may have been Paulicians.
117 Heresy 100.
118 Heresy 80.

monasteries. They differ among themselves and are in a state of utter confusion, because their falsehood is split into many factions. They have separated from the communion of the Church and pretend to a great severity of discipline, with each one vying to prove himself better than the next. Some of them do not admit holy baptism and do not receive Holy Communion, whereas others will kiss neither a newly made figure of the venerable cross nor a holy image. What is worst of all, since they consider themselves to be superior to all men they will accept absolutely no priest, but 'speaking lies in hypocrisy and having their conscience seared'[119] they contend in words of no profit and lay up for themselves wood, hay, and stubble[120] as most inflammable fuel for the eternal fire. May we be delivered both from the frenzy of the Iconoclasts and from the madness of the Aposchistae, which, although they are diametrically opposed evils, are equal in their impiety.

These heresies detailed above have been described in brief, because, although they amount to but a hundred altogether, all the rest come from them. The Catholic Church has kept itself away from all these, as from so many pitfalls, and, instructed by the Holy Trinity, it teaches rightly and religiously and cries out: We believe in Father and Son and Holy Ghost; one Godhead in three hypostases; one will, one operation, alike in three persons; wisdom incorporeal, uncreated, immortal, incomprehensible, without beginning, unmoved, unaffected, without quantity, without quality, ineffable, immutable, unchangeable, uncontained, equal in glory, equal in power, equal in majesty, equal in might, equal in nature, exceedingly substantial, exceedingly good, thrice radiant, thrice bright, thrice brilliant. Light is the Father, Light the

---
119 1 Tim. 4.2.
120 2 Tim. 2.14; 1 Cor. 3.12.

Son, Light the Holy Ghost; Wisdom the Father, Wisdom the Son, Wisdom the Holy Ghost; one God and not three Gods; one Lord the Holy Trinity discovered in three hypostases. Father is the Father, and unbegotten; Son is the Son, begotten and not unbegotten, for He is from the Father; Holy Ghost, not begotten but proceeding, for He is from the Father. There is nothing created, nothing of the first and second order, nothing of lord and servant; but there is unity and trinity—there was, there is, and there shall be forever—which is perceived and adored by faith—by faith, not by inquiry, nor by searching out, nor by visible manifestation: for the more He is sought out, the more He is unknown, and the more He is investigated, the more He is hidden. And so, let the faithful adore God with a mind that is not overcurious. And believe that He is God in three hypostases, although the manner in which He is so is beyond manner, for God is incomprehensible. Do not ask how the Trinity is Trinity, for the Trinity is inscrutable. But, if you are curious about God, first tell me of yourself and the things that pertain to you. How does your soul have existence? How is your mind set in motion? How do you produce your mental concepts? How is it that you are both mortal and immortal? But, if you are ignorant of these things which are within you, then why do you not shudder at the thought of investigating the sublime things of heaven? Think of the Father as a spring of life begetting the Son like a river and the Holy Ghost like a sea, for the spring and the river and the sea are all one nature. Think of the Father as a root, and of the Son as a branch, and of the Spirit as a fruit, for the substance in these three is one. The Father is a sun with the Son as rays and the Holy Ghost as heat. The Holy Trinity transcends by far every similitude and figure. So, when you hear of an offspring of the Father, do not think of a corporeal offspring. And when you hear that there is a Word, do not suppose Him to be a corporeal word. And when you hear of the Spirit of God, do not think of wind and breath. Rather, hold your persuasion with a simple faith alone. For the concept of the Creator is arrived at by analogy from His creatures. Be persuaded, moreover, that the incarnate dispensation of the Son of God was begotten ineffably and without seed of the blessed Virgin, believing Him to be without confusion and without change both God and man, who for your sake worked all the dispensation. And to Him by good works give worship and adoration, and venerate and revere the most holy Mother of God and ever-virgin Mary as true Mother of God, and all the saints as His attendants. Doing thus, you will be a right worshiper of the holy and undivided Trinity, Father and Son and Holy Ghost, of the one Godhead, to whom be glory and honor and adoration forever and ever. Amen.

AN EXPOSITION
OF THE ORTHODOX FAITH

BOOK I

Chapter 1

NO MAN HATH SEEN GOD at any time: the only-begotten Son who is in the bosom of the Father, he hath declared him.'¹ The God-head, then, is ineffable and incomprehensible. For 'no one knoweth the Father, but the Son: neither doth any one know the Son, but the Father.'² Furthermore, the Holy Spirit knows the things of God, just as the spirit of man knows what is in man.³ After the first blessed state of nature, no one has ever known God unless God Himself revealed it to him—not only no man, but not even any of the supramundane powers: the very Cherubim and Seraphim, I mean.

Nevertheless, God has not gone so far as to leave us in

---

1 John 1.18.
2 Matt. 11.27.
3 Cf. 1 Cor. 2.11.

complete ignorance, for through nature the knowledge of the existence of God has been revealed by Him to all men. The very creation of its harmony and ordering proclaims the majesty of the divine nature.[4] Indeed, He has given us knowledge of Himself in accordance with our capacity, at first through the Law and the Prophets and then afterwards through His only-begotten Son, our Lord and God and Saviour, Jesus Christ. Accordingly, we accept all those things that have been handed down by the Law and the Prophets and the Apostles and the Evangelists, and we know and revere them, and over and above these things we seek nothing else. For, since God is good, He is the author of all good and is not subject to malice or to any affection. For malice is far removed from the divine nature, which is the unaffected and only good. Since, therefore, He knows all things and provides for each in accordance with his needs, He has revealed to us what it was expedient for us to know, whereas that which we were unable to bear He has withheld. With these things let us be content and in them let us abide and let us not step over the ancient bounds[5] or pass beyond the divine tradition.

Chapter 2

Now, one who would speak or hear about God should know beyond any doubt that in what concerns theology and the Dispensation[1] not all things are inexpressible and not all are capable of expression, and neither are all things unknowable nor are they all knowable. That which can be known is one thing, whereas that which can be said is

---

4 Cf. Wisd. 13.5; Rom. 1.20.
5 Cf. Prov. 22.28.

1 οἰκονομία, or Dispensation, is the term commonly used for the Incarnation by the Greek Fathers.

another, just as it is one thing to speak and another to know. Furthermore, many of those things about God which are not clearly perceived cannot be fittingly described, so that we are obliged to express in human terms things which transcend the human order. Thus, for example, in speaking about God we attribute to Him sleep, anger, indifference, hands and feet, and the alike.

Now, we both know and confess that God is without beginning and without end, everlasting and eternal, uncreated, unchangeable, inalterable, simple, uncompounded, incorporeal, invisible, impalpable, uncircumscribed, unlimited, incomprehensible, uncontained, unfathomable, good, just, the maker of all created things, all-powerful, all-ruling, all-seeing, the provider, the sovereign, and the judge of all. We furthermore know and confess that God is one, that is to say, one substance, and that He is both understood to be and is in three Persons—I mean the Father and the Son and the Holy Ghost—and that the Father and the Son and the Holy Ghost are one in all things save in the being unbegotten, the being begotten, and the procession. We also know and confess that for our salvation the Word of God through the bowels of His mercy, by the good pleasure of the Father and with the co-operation of the All-Holy Spirit, was conceived without seed and chastely begotten of the holy Virgin and Mother of God, Mary, by the Holy Ghost and of her became perfect man; and that He is perfect God and at the same time perfect man, being of two natures, the divinity and the humanity, and in two intellectual natures endowed with will and operation and liberty—or, to put it simply, perfect in accordance with the definition and principle befitting each, the divinity, I mean, and the humanity, but with one compound hypostasis. And we know and confess that He hungered and thirsted and was weary, and that He was crucified, and that for three days He suffered death and the tomb, and that He returned into heaven whence He had come to us and whence He will come back to us at a later time. To all this holy Scripture and all the company of the saints bear witness.

But what the substance of God is, or how it is in all things, or how the only-begotten Son, who was God, emptied Himself out and became man from a virgin's blood, being formed by another law that transcended nature, or how He walked dry-shod upon the waters, we neither understand nor can say.[2] And so it is impossible either to say or fully to understand anything about God beyond what has been divinely proclaimed to us, whether told or revealed, by the sacred declarations of the Old and New Testaments.

Chapter 3

Now, the fact that God exists is not doubted by those who accept the sacred Scriptures—both the Old and New Testaments, I mean—nor by the majority of the Greeks, for, as we have said, the knowledge of God's existence has been revealed to us through nature. However, since the wickedness of the Evil One has so prevailed over men's nature as even to drag some of them down to the most unspeakable and extremely wicked abyss of perdition and to make them say that there is no God (of whose folly the Prophet David said: 'The fool hath said in his heart: There is no God'[1]), then the Lord's disciples and Apostles, made wise by the All-Holy Spirit, did by His power and grace show signs from God and draw up those people alive in the net of their miracles from the depths of the ignorance of God to the light of his knowledge. Similarly, the shepherds and teachers who succeeded to their grace of the Spirit and by the power of their miracles and the word of their grace enlightened those who were in darkness and converted those who were

---

2 Cf. Pseudo-Dionysius, *The Divine Names* 2.9 (*PG* 3.648A).

---

1 Ps. 13.1.

in error. Now, let us who have not received the gifts of miracles and teaching, because by our being given to material pleasures we have made ourselves unworthy, let us invoke the aid of the Father and of the Son and of the Holy Ghost, and discuss some few of the things which the expounders of grace have handed down to us.

All things are either created or uncreated. Now, if they are created, then they are also definitely changeable, for things whose being originated with a change are definitely subject to change, whether it be by corruption or by voluntary alteration. If, on the other hand, they are uncreated, then it logically follows that they are definitely unchangeable. For, of those things whose being is contrary, the manner of being, which is to say, properties, is also contrary. Who, then, will not agree that all beings that fall within our experience, including even the angels, are subject to change and alteration and to being moved in various ways? The intellectual beings—by which I mean angels and souls and demons—change by free choice, progressing in good or receding, exerting themselves or slackening; whereas the rest change by generation or corruption, increase or decrease, change in quality or change in position. Consequently, things which are changeable must definitely be created. Created beings have certainly been created by something. But the creator must be uncreated, for, if he has been created, then he has certainly been created by some one else—and so on until we arrive at something which has not been created. Therefore, the creator is an uncreated and entirely unchangeable being. And what else would that be but God?

What is more, the very harmony of creation, its preservation and governing, teach us that there is a God who has put all this together and keeps it together, ever maintaining it and providing for it. For how could such contrary natures as fire and water, earth and air, combine with one another to form one world and remain undissolved, unless there were some all-powerful force to bring them together and always keep them that way?[2]

What is it that has ordered the things of heaven and those of earth, the things which move through the air and those which move in the water—nay, rather, the things which preceded them: heaven and earth and the natures of fire and water? What is it that combined and arranged them? What is it that set them in motion and put them on their unceasing and unhindered courses? Or is it that they had no architect to set a principle in them all by which the whole universe be moved and controlled? But who is the architect of these things? Or did not he who made them also bring them into being? We shall certainly not attribute such power to spontaneity. Even grant that they came into being spontaneously; then, whence came their arrangement? Let us grant this, also, if you wish. Then, what maintains and keeps the principles by which they subsisted in the first place? It is most certainly some other thing than mere chance. What else is this, if it is not God?[3]

Chapter 4

Thus, it is clear that God exists, but what He is in essence and nature is unknown and beyond all understanding. That He is without a body is obvious, for how could a body contain that which is limitless, boundless, formless, impalpable, invisible, simple, and uncompounded? How could it be immutable, if it were circumscribed and subject to change? And how could that which is composed of elements and reducible to them be not subject to change? Composition is the cause of conflict, conflict the cause of separation, and separation

---

2 Cf. Athanasius, *Against the Pagans* 35-36 (*PG* 25.69C-73A).
3 Cf. Gregory Nazianzen, *Sermon* 28.16 (*PG* 36.45D-48B).

the cause of dissolution—but dissolution is altogether foreign to God.[1]

And again, how can the principle be maintained that God permeates and fills all things, as Scripture says: 'Do not I fill heaven and earth, saith the Lord'?[2] For it is impossible for one body to permeate others without dividing and being divided, without being blended and contrasted, just as when a number of liquids are mixed together and blended.[3]

Now, should some people speak of an immaterial body, the so-called fifth body of the Greek philosophers, which is impossible, then this will be subject to motion just like the heavens, which they call a fifth body. But, since everything that is moved is moved by another, then who is it that moves this? And who is it that moves that? And so we go on endlessly in this way until such time as we arrive at something that is immoveable.[4] For the first mover is unmoved, and it is just this that is the Divinity. Furthermore, how can that which is not locally contained be moved? Therefore, only the Divinity is unmoved, and by His immovability He moves all things. Consequently, one can only answer that the Divinity is without body.

All this, however, is by no means indicative of His essence—no more than is the fact of His being unbegotten, without beginning, immutable, and incorruptible, or any of those other things which are affirmed of God or about Him. These do not show what He is, but, rather, what He is not.[5] One who would declare the essence of something must explain what it is, but not what it is not. However, as regards what God is, it is impossible to say what He is in His essence, so it is better to discuss Him by abstraction from all things

---

1 Cf. *ibid.* 7 (*PG* 36.33).
2 Jer. 23.24.
3 Cf. Gregory Nazianzen, *Sermon* 28.8 (*PG* 36.36A).
4 Cf. *ibid.* (*PG* 36.36AB).
5 Cf. *ibid.* (*PG* 36.36C-37B).

whatsoever. For He does not belong to the number of beings, not because He does not exist, but because He transcends all beings and being itself. And, if knowledge respects beings, then that which transcends knowledge will certainly transcend essence, and, conversely, what transcends essence will transcend knowledge.[6]

The Divinity, then, is limitless and incomprehensible, and this His limitlessness and incomprehensibility is all that can be understood about Him. All that we state affirmatively about God does not show His nature, but only what relates to His nature. And, if you should ever speak of good, or justice, or wisdom, or something else of the sort, you will not be describing the nature of God, but only things relating to His nature. There are, moreover, things that are stated affirmatively of God, but which have the force of extreme negation. For example, when we speak of darkness in God we do not really mean darkness.[7] What we mean is that He is not light, because He transcends light. In the same way, when we speak of light we mean that it is not darkness.

Chapter 5

It has been sufficiently demonstrated that God exists and that His essence is incomprehensible. Furthermore, those who believe in sacred Scripture have no doubt that He is one and not several. For the Lord says at the beginning of His lawgiving: 'I am the Lord thy God, who brought thee out of the land of Egypt. Thou shalt not have strange gods before me.'[1] And again: 'Hear, O Israel: the Lord thy God is one Lord.'[2] And through the mouth of the Prophet Isaias: 'I am,' He says, 'the first God and I am the last and there is no God

---

6 Cf. Pseudo-Dionysius, *Mystical Theology* 2 (*PG* 3.1000AB).
7 Cf. *ibid.* 1 (*PG* 3.1000A).

1 Exod. 20.2,3.
2 Deut. 6.4.

besides me. Before me there was no God and after me there shall be none, and beside me there is none.'³ And the Lord speaks thus to His Father in the holy Gospels: 'This is eternal life: that they may know thee, the only true God.'⁴ With those who do not believe in sacred Scripture we shall reason as follows.

The Divinity is perfect and without deficiency in goodness or wisdom or power. He is without beginning, without end, eternal, uncircumscribed; to put it simply, He is perfect in all things. Now, if we say that there are several gods, there must be some difference to be found among them. For it there is no difference at all among them, then there is one God rather than several. But, if there is some difference, then where is the perfection? For, if one should come short of perfection in goodness, or power, or wisdom, or time, or place, then he would not be God. The identity of God in all things shows Him to be one and not several.⁵

And again, if there are several gods, how can one support the fact of God's being uncircumscribed? For where there is one there cannot be another.

And, since there is bound to be conflict among several governing, how can the world be governed by several gods without being broken up and utterly destroyed? Now, should any one say that each one rules over a part, then what was it that arranged for this and made the distribution among them? This last being would more likely be God. God, then, is one, perfect, uncirumscribed, the maker of the universe, the maintainer of order and governor, preceding and transcending all perfection.

Besides all this, it is naturally necessary that the originating principle of duality be unity.⁶

---

3 Isa. 43.10.
4 John 17.3.
5 Cf. Gregory of Nyssa, *Cathetical Discourse,* Prologue (*PG* 45.12AD).
6 Cf. Pseudo-Dionysius, *Divine Names* 13.3 (*PG* 3.980-981).

Chapter 6

Now, this one sole God is not without a Word. And, if He has a Word, this Word will not be non-subsistent (ἀνυπόστατον), nor will it have any beginning or end of being. For there never was a time when God the Word was not. God always has His Word begotten of Himself—not like our speech, which is non-subsistent and dissipated in the air, but distinctly subsistent (ἐνυπόστατον), living and perfect, not passing out from Him but always existing within Him.[1] For where will He be if He is outside of God? Because our nature is mortal and subject to dissolution, for this reason our speech is non-subsistent. But, since God is existing always and is perfect, His Word must be always existing, living, perfect, distinctly subsistent, and having all things that His Begetter has. Now, our speech in proceeding from our mind is not entirely distinct from it. For, in so far as it comes from the mind, it is something distinct from it; whereas, in so far as it reveals the mind itself, it is not entirely distinct from it. Actually, it is identical with it in nature while distinct from it in its subject. Similarly, the Word of God, in so far as He subsists in Himself, is distinct from Him from whom He has His subsistence. But, since He exhibits in Himself those same things which are discerned in God, then in His nature He is identical with God. For, just as perfection in all things is to be found in the Father, so is it also to be found in the Word begotten of Him.

Chapter 7

It is further necessary that the Word have a Spirit. Thus, even our own speech is not devoid of breath, although in our case the breath is not of our substance. It is an inhaling and exhaling of the air which is breathed in and out for the

---
[1] Cf. Gregory of Nyssa, *op. cit.* 2 (PG 45.17BC).

sustainment of the body. It is this which on the occasion of articulation becomes the vocal expression of speech and evidences in itself the power of speech.[1] Now, in the simple and uncompounded divine nature the existence of a Spirit of God is piously to be confessed, for the Word of God is no more deficient than our own word. It would be impious to reckon the Spirit as something foreign to God and later introduced from outside, as is the case with us who are compounded. On the contrary, it is as when we heard there was a Word of God and did not conceive of this as not being distinctly subsistent, or as accruing from learning, or as being expressed vocally and being diffused in the air and lost. Rather, we conceived of Him as substantially subsisting, endowed with will and operation, and all-powerful. In the same way, too, having learned that there is a Spirit of God, we conceive of Him as associated with the Word and making the operation of the Word manifest. We do not conceive of Him as an impersonal breath of air, for the majesty of the divine nature would be reduced to low estate if its Spirit were likened to our own breath. Rather, we conceive of Him as a substantial power found in its own individuating personality, proceeding from the Father, coming to rest in the Word and declaring Him, not separated from God in essence or from the Word with whom it is associated, having might, not dissipated away into non-existence, but distinctly subsistent like the Word—living, endowed with will, self-moving, active, at all times willing good, exercising His power for the prosecution of every design in accordance with His will, without beginning and without end. For the Word fell short of the Father in nothing, and the Spirit did not fall short of the Word in anything.

Thus, on the one hand, the unity in nature exposes the polytheistic error of the Greeks; on the other hand, the doctrine of the Word and the Spirit demolishes the teaching of the Jews. At the same time, the good in both of these

---

1 Cf. *ibid.* 2 (*PG* 45.17A).

heresies remain: from the Jewish opinion the unity of nature; and from Hellenism the unique distinction according to persons.[2]

Should the Jew gainsay the doctrine of the Word and the Spirit, then let sacred Scripture refute him and reduce him to silence. Thus the divine David says concerning the Word: 'For ever, O Lord, thy word standeth firm in heaven.' And again: 'He sent his word and healed them.' But a spoken word is not sent and neither does it stand firm forever. Concerning the Spirit the same David says: 'Thou shalt send forth thy spirit, and they shall be created.' And again: 'By the word of the Lord the heavens were established and all the power of them by the spirit of his mouth.'[3] Job likewise says: 'The spirit of God made me: and the breath of the Almighty maintaineth me.'[4] Now a spirit which is sent, and acts, and strengthens, and maintains is not breath which is dissipated any more than the mouth of God is a bodily member. Both in fact are to be understood as appropriately referring to God.[5]

Chapter 8

Therefore, we believe in one God: one principle, without beginning, uncreated, unbegotten, indestructible and immortal, eternal, unlimited, uncircumscribed, unbounded, infinite in power, simple, uncompounded, incorporeal, unchanging, unaffected, unchangeable, inalterate, invisible, source of goodness and justice, light intellectual and inaccessible; power which no measure can give any idea of but which is measured only by His own will, for He can do all things whatsoever He pleases;[1] maker of all things both visible and invisible,

---

2 Cf. *ibid.* 3 (*PG* 45.17D-20A).
3 Ps. 118.89; 106.20; 32.6.
4 Job 33.4.
5 Cf. Basil, *The Holy Ghost* 18.46 (*PG* 32.152B).

1 Ps. 134.6.

holding together all things and conserving them, provider for all, governing and dominating and ruling over all in unending and immortal reign; without contradiction, filling all things, contained by nothing, but Himself containing all things, being their conserver and first possessor; pervading all substances without being defiled, removed far beyond all things and every substance as being supersubstantial and surpassing all, supereminently divine and good and replete; appointing all the principalities and orders, set above every principality and order, above essence and life and speech and concept; light itself and goodness and being in so far as having neither being nor anything else that is from any other; the very source of being for all things that are, of life to the living, of speech to the articulate, and the cause of all good things for all; knowing all things before they begin to be; one substance, one godhead, one virtue, one will, one operation, one principality, one power, one domination, one kingdom; known in three perfect Persons and adored with one adoration, believed in and worshiped by every rational creature, united without confusion and distinct without separation, which is beyond understanding. We believe in Father and Son and Holy Ghost in whom we have been baptized. For it is thus that the Lord enjoined the Apostles: 'Baptizing them in the name of the Father and of the Son and of the Holy Ghost.'[2]

We believe in one Father, the principle and cause of all things, begotten of no one, who alone is uncaused and unbegotten, the maker of all things and by nature Father of His one and only-begotten Son, our Lord and God and Saviour, Jesus Christ, and Emitter[3] of the All-Holy Spirit. We also believe in one Son of God, the only-begotten, our Lord Jesus Christ, who was begotten of the Father before all the ages, light from light, true God from true God, begotten not made, consubstantial with the Father, by whom all

---

2 Matt. 28.19.
3 προβολεύς, Gregory Nazianzen, *Sermon* 29.2 (*PG* 36.76B).

things were made; in regard to whom, when we say that He is before all ages, we mean that His begetting is outside of time and without beginning, for the Son of God was not brought from nothing into being; who is the brightness of the glory and the figure of the substance of the Father, His living power and wisdom, the subsistent Word, the substantial and perfect and living image of the invisible God.[4] Actually, He was always with the Father, being begotten of Him eternally and without beginning. For the Father never was when the Son was not, but the Father and the Son begotten of Him exist together simultaneously, because the Father could not be so called without a Son. Now, if He was not Father when He did not have the Son, and then later became Father without having been Father before, then He was changed from not being Father to being Father, which is the worst of all blasphemies. For it is impossible to speak of God as naturally lacking the power of begetting. And the power of begetting is the power to beget of oneself, that is, of one's own substance, offspring similar to oneself in nature.

Accordingly, it is impious to say that time intervened in the begetting of the Son and that the Son came into existence after the Father.[5] For we say that the begetting of the Son is of the Father, that is to say, of His nature; and if we do not grant that the Son begotten of the Father exists together with Him from the beginning, then we are introducing a change into the substance of the Father: namely, that He once was not Father, but became Father later. Now, creation, even if it was made at a later time, was not of the substance of God, but was brought from nothing into being by His will and power and does not involve any change in the nature of God. Begetting means producing of the substance of the begetter an offspring similar in substance to the begetter. Creation, on the other hand—making—is the bringing into being, from the outside and not from

---
4 Heb. 1.3; 1 Cor. 1.24; Col. 1.15.
5 Cf. Gregory Nazianzen, *Sermon* 20.7 (*PG* 35.1073B).

the substance of the creator, of something created and made entirely dissimilar [in substance].

Therefore, neither the act of begetting nor that of creation has any effect on the one, unaffected, unvarying, unchanging, and ever-the-same God. For, being simple and uncompounded and, consequently, by nature unaffected and unchanging, He is by nature not subject to passion or change, whether from begetting or from creating, nor does He stand in need of any co-operation. On the contrary, because the begetting is an action belonging to His nature and proceeding from His substance, it is without beginning and eternal, so that the Begetter undergoes no change and so that He is not a first God and a later God, but receives no addition. But, since with God creation is a work of His will, it is not co-eternal with Him—which is because it is not of the nature of that which is produced from nothing to be co-eternal with that which is without beginning and always existing. Indeed, God and man do not make in the same way.[6] Thus, man does not bring anything from non-being into being. What man makes he makes from already existing material, not by just willing but by thinking it out beforehand and getting an idea of what he is to make and then working with his hands, toiling and troubling and oftentimes failing because the object of his endeavor does not turn out as he wished. God, on the other hand, has brought all things from nothing into being by a mere act of His will. Hence, God and man do not beget in the same way. For, since God is without time and without beginning, unaffected, unchanging, incorporeal, unique, and without end,[7] He begets without time and without beginning, unaffectedly, unchangingly, and without copulation. Neither does His unfathomable begetting have beginning or end. It is without beginning, because He is immutable; it is unchanging, because He is unaffected and incorporeal; it is without copulation, also because He

---

6 Cf. *ibid.* (*PG* 35.1076CD).
7 Cf. Cyril of Alexandria, *Thesaurus,* Assert. 5 (*PG* 75.60CD).

is incorporeal and because He is the only one God and without need of any other; it is unending and unceasing, because He is without time and without end and ever the same—for that which is without beginning is without end, although that which is without end by a gift of grace is by no means without beginning, as is the case with the angels.

Accordingly, the ever-existing God begets without beginning and without end His own Word as a perfect being, lest God, whose nature and existence are outside of time, should beget in time. Now, it is obvious that man begets in quite another manner, since he is subject to birth and death and flux and increase, and since he is clothed with a body and has the male and female in his nature—for the male has need of the female's help. May He be propitious to us who is beyond all things and surpasses all understanding and comprehension.

Therefore, the holy Catholic and apostolic Church teaches that the Father exists simultaneously with His only-begotten Son, who is begotten of Him without time or change or passion and in a manner beyond understanding, as only the God of all knows. They exist simultaneously, as does the fire with its light—without the fire being first and the light afterwards, but both simultaneously. And just as the light is ever being begotten of the fire, is always in it, and is in no way separated from it, so also is the Son begotten of the Father without in any way being separated from Him, but always existing in Him. However, the light, which is inseparably begotten of the fire and always remains in it, does not have any individual existence apart from the fire, because it is a natural quality of the fire. On the other hand, the only-begotten Son of God, who was inseparably and indivisibly begotten of the Father and abides in Him always, does have His own individual existence apart from that of the Father.

Now the Word is also called 'Brightness'[8] because He was begotten of the Father without copulation, without passion,

---

[8] Heb. 1.3.

without time, without change, and without separation. He is also called 'Son' and 'Figure of the substance of the Father'[9] because He is perfect and distinctly subsistent and in all things like the Father except in the Father's being unbegotten. And He is called 'Only-begotten' because He alone was begotten alone of the only Father. For neither is there any other begetting like that of the Son of God, nor is there any other Son of God. Thus, although the Holy Ghost does proceed from the Father, this is not by begetting but by procession. This is another manner of existence and is just as incomprehensible and unknowable as is the begetting of the Son. Hence, the Son has all things whatsoever the Father has, except the Father's being unbegotten, which does not imply any difference in substance, nor any quality, but, rather, a manner of existence.[10] Thus, in the same way, Adam is unbegotten, because he was formed by God, while Seth is begotten, because he is the son of Adam; Eve, too, was not begotten, because she was produced from the rib of Adam. Yet, they do not differ in nature, because they are all human beings; they only differ in the manner of their existence.[11]

Now, one ought to know that ἀγένητον written with one ν means that which has not been created, or, in other words, that which is unoriginated; while ἀγέννητον written with two ν's means that which has not been begotten. Therefore, the first meaning implies a difference in essence, for it means that one essence is uncreated, or ἀγένητος with one ν, while some other is created, or originated. On the other hand, the second meaning does not imply any difference in essence, because the first individual substance of every species of living being is unbegotten but not unoriginated. For they were created by the Creator, being brought into existence by His Word. But they were certainly not begotten,

---
9 Cf. Gregory Nanzianzen, *Sermon* 30.20 (*PG* 36.128B-129B).
10 Cf. Basil, *Against Eunomius* 4 (*PG* 29.680D-681A).
11 Cf. *ibid.* (*PG* 29.681B); Gregory Nazianzen, *Sermon* 31.11 (*PG* 36.144D-145A).

because there was no other like substance pre-existing from which they might have been begotten.

Thus, the first meaning applies to all three of the super-divine Persons of the sacred Godhead, for they are uncreated and of the same substance.[12] On the other hand, the second meaning definitely does not apply to all three, because the Father alone is unbegotten in so far as He does not have His being from another person. And only the Son is begotten, for He is begotten of the substance of the Father without beginning and independently of time. And only the Holy Ghost proceeds: not begotten, but proceeding from the substance of the Father. Such is the teaching of sacred Scripture, but as to the manner of the begetting and the procession, this is beyond understanding.

This also should be known, that the terms 'paternity,' 'sonship,' and 'procession' as applied to the blessed Godhead did not originate with us, but, on the contrary, were handed down to us from Scripture, as the divine Apostle says: 'For this cause I bow my knee to the Father, of whom all paternity in heaven and earth is named.'[13]

And if we say that the Father is the principle of the Son and greater than the Son, we are not giving to understand that He comes before the Son either in time or in nature, for 'by him he made the world,'[14] nor in any other thing save causality. That is to say, we mean that the Son is begotten of the Father, and not the Father of the Son, and that the Father is naturally the cause of the Son. Similarly, we do not say that the fire comes from the light, but that the light comes from the fire. So, when we hear that the Father is the principle of the Son and greater than He, let us understand this as being by reason of His being the cause. And just as we do not say that the fire is of one substance and the light of another, neither is it proper to say that the

---
12 Cf. Cyril of Alexandria, *Thesaurus,* Assert. 7 (*PG* 75.24AC).
13 Eph. 3.14,15.
14 Heb. 1.2.

Father is of one substance and the Son of another; on the contrary, they are of one and the same substance. What is more, just as we say that the fire is made visible by the light coming from it, yet do not make the fire's light a subsidiary organ of the fire but, rather, a natural power; in the same way, we say that the Father does all things whatsoever through His only-begotten Son, not as through a subsidiary organ, but as through a natural and distinctly subsistent force. And just as we say that the fire gives light, and, again, that the fire's light gives light, so: 'What things soever the Father doth, these the Son also doth in like manner.'[15] But the light was not created an individual substance apart from the fire, whereas the Son is a perfect individual substance inseparable from that of the Father, as we have set forth above. For it is impossible to find in creation any image which exactly portrays the manner of the Holy Trinity in Itself. For that which is created is also compounded, variable, changeable, circumscribed, having shape, and corruptible; so, how shall it show with any clarity the supersubstantial divine essence which is far removed from all such? It is evident that all creation is subject to these several conditions and that it is of its own nature subject to corruption.

We likewise believe in the Holy Ghost, the Lord and Giver of life, who proceeds from the Father and abides in the Son; who is adored and glorified together with the Father and the Son as consubstantial and co-eternal with Them; who is the true and authoritative Spirit of God and the source of wisdom and life and sanctification; who is God together with the Father and the Son and is so proclaimed; who is uncreated, complete, creative, almighty, all-working, all-powerful, infinite in power; who dominates all creation but is not dominated; who deifies but is not deified; who fills but is not filled; who is shared in but does not share; who sanctifies but is not sanctified; who,

---
15 John 5.19.

as receiving the intercessions of all, is the Intercessor; who is like the Father and the Son in all things; who proceeds from the Father and is communicated through the Son and is participated in by all creation; who through Himself creates and gives substance to all things and sanctifies and preserves them; who is distinctly subsistent and exists in His own Person indivisible and inseparable from the Father and the Son; who has all things whatsoever the Father and the Son have except the being unbegotten and the being begotten. For the Father is uncaused and unbegotten, because He is not from anything, but has His being from Himself and does not have from any other anything whatsover that He has. Rather, He Himself is the principle and cause by which all things naturally exist as they do. And the Son is begotten of the Father, while the Holy Ghost is Himself also of the Father—although not by begetting, but by procession. Now, we have learned that there is a difference between begetting and procession, but what the manner of this difference is we have not learned at all. However, the begetting of the Son and the procession of the Holy Ghost from the Father are simultaneous.

Accordingly, all things whatsoever the Son has from the Father the Spirit also has, including His very being. And if the Father does not exist, then neither does the Son or the Spirit; and if the Father does not have something, then neither has the Son or the Spirit. Furthermore, because of the Father, that is, because of the fact that the Father is, the Son and the Spirit are; and because of the Father, the Son and the Spirit have everything that they have, that is to say, because of the fact that the Father has them, excepting the being unbegotten, the begetting, and the procession. For it is only in these personal properties that the three divine Persons differ from one another, being indivisibly divided by the distinctive note of each individual Person.

We say that each of the three has perfect distinct subsistence; not, however, in such a way as to understand one perfect nature compounded of three imperfect natures, but one simple essence, eminently and antecedently perfect, in three Persons.[16] For, anything that is made up of imperfect things is most definitely compounded, and it is impossible for there to be a compound of perfect individual substances. Hence, we do not say that the species is of the Persons, but in the Persons. Those things which do not retain the species of the thing made of them we call imperfect. Thus, stone, wood, and iron are each perfect in themselves according to their individual natures; but in relation to a house built of them they are all imperfect, because no one of them by itself is a house.

And so we speak of perfect individual substances to avoid giving any idea of composition in the divine nature. For composition is the cause of disintegration. And again, we say that the three Persons are in one another, so as not to introduce a whole swarm of gods.[17] By the three Persons we understand that God is uncompounded and without confusion; by the consubstantiality of the Persons and their existence in one another and by the indivisibility of the identity of will, operation, virtue, power, and, so to speak, motion we understand that God is one. For God and His Word and His Spirit are really one God.

[*On the Distinction of the Three Persons; and on Actuality and Reason and Thought.*][18]

One should know that it is one thing actually to observe something and another to see it through reason and thought. Thus, in all creatures there is an actual distinction to be seen between the individual substances. Peter is seen to be actually distinct from Paul. But, that which is held in common, the connection, and the unity is seen by reason and thought.

---
16 Cf. *Basil, Against the Sabellians, Arians, and Eumomians* 4 (PG 31.605BC).
17 Cf. *ibid.* (PG 31.605C); Gregory Nazianzen, *Sermon* 38.8 (PG 36.320B).
18 This is a marginal addition to the manuscript.

Thus, in our mind we see that Peter and Paul are of the same nature and have one common nature, for each is a rational mortal animal and each is a body animated by a rational and understanding soul. Hence, this common nature is perceived by the reason. Now, individual persons do not exist in one another at all, but each one is separate and by itself, that is to say, is distinct and considered in itself, since it has a great many things to distinguish it from the other. For, truly, they are separated in place and they differ in time, judgment, strength, form—or shape, habit, temperament, dignity, manner of life, and all the other distinctive properties—but most of all they differ by the fact that they do not exist in each other but separately. Hence, we speak of two, or three, or several men.

The aforesaid is true of all creation, but it is quite the contrary in the case of the holy, supersubstantial, all-transcendent, and incomprehensible Trinity. For, here, that which is common and one is considered in actuality by reason of the co-eternity and identity of substance, operation, and will, and by reason of the agreement in judgment and the identity of power, virtue, and goodness—I did not say *similarity*, but *identity*—and by reason of the one surge of motion. For there is one essence, one goodness, one virtue, one intent, one operation, one power—one and the same, not three similar one to another, but one and the same motion of the three Persons. And the oneness of each is not less with the others than it is with itself, that is to say, the Father and the Son and the Holy Ghost are one in all things except the being unbegotten, the being begotten, and the procession. It is by thought that the distinction is perceived. For we know one God and Him in the properties of fatherhood, and sonship, and procession only. The difference we conceive of according to cause and effect and the perfection of the Person, that is to say, His manner of existing.[19] For

---

19 Cf. Gregory of Nyssa, *That There Are Not Three Gods* (PG 45.-133BC).

with the uncircumscribed Godhead we cannot speak of any difference in place, as we do with ourselves, because the Persons exist in one another, not so as to be confused, but so as to adhere closely together as expressed in the words of the Lord when He said: 'I in the Father and the Father in me.'[20] Neither can we speak of a difference in will, or judgment, or operation, or virtue, or any other whatsoever of those things which in us give rise to a definite real distinction. For that reason, we do not call the Father and the Son and the Holy Ghost three Gods, but one God, the Holy Trinity, in whom the Son and the Holy Ghost are related to one Cause without any composition or blending such as is the coalescence of Sabellius. For they are united, as we said, so as not to be confused, but to adhere closely together, and they have their circumincession one in the other without any blending or mingling and without change or division in substance such as is the division held by Arius.[21] Thus, must one put it concisely, the Godhead is undivided in things divided, just as in three suns joined together without any intervening interval there is one blending and the union of the light.[22] So, when we contemplate the Godhead, and the First Cause, and the Monarchy, and the unity and identity, so to speak, of the motion and will of the Godhead, and the identity of substance, virtue, operation, and dominion, then that which appears to us is One. But, when we contemplate the things in which the Godhead exists, or, to put it more accurately, those things which are the Godhead and which come from the First Cause independently of time, with equal glory, and inseparably—that is, the Persons of the Son and the Spirit—then we adore Three. One Father, the Father without beginning, that is to say, uncaused, for He is from no one. One Son,

---

20 John 14.11.
21 Cf. Gregory Nazianzen, *Sermon* 20.6 (*PG* 35.1072B); Pseudo-Dionysius, *Divine Names* 2.4 (*PG* 3.641AB).
22 Cf. Gregory Nazianzen, *Sermon* 31.14 (*PG* 36.149A).

the Son who is not without beginning, that is to say, not uncaused, for He is from the Father; but, should you take the beginning as being in time, then He is without beginning, because He is the maker of the ages and not subject to time. One Spirit, the Holy Ghost coming forth from the Father, not by filiation but by procession. And, as the Father does not cease to be unbegotten because He has begotten, nor the Son cease to be begotten because He is begotten of the Unbegotten—for how could He?—so neither does the Spirit change into the Father or the Son, because He proceeds and is God. The property is unchangeable, since how would it otherwise remain a property should it be changed and transformed? Thus, if the Son is the Father, then He is not properly the Father, because there is only one who is properly the Father; and, if the Father is the Son, He is not properly the Son, because there is only one who is properly the Son, and only one who is properly the Holy Ghost.

One should know that we do not say that the Father is of anyone, but that we do say that He is the Father of the Son. We do not say that the Son is a cause or a father, but we do say that He is from the Father and is the Son of the Father. And we do say that the Holy Ghost is of the Father and we call Him the Spirit of the Father. Neither do we say that the Spirit is from the Son, but we call Him the Spirit of the Son—'Now if any man have not the Spirit of Christ,' says the divine Apostle, 'he is none of his.'[23] We also confess that He was manifested and communicated to us through the Son, for 'He breathed,' it says, 'and he said to his disciples: Receive ye the Holy Ghost.'[24] It is just like the rays and brightness coming from the sun, for the sun is the source of its rays and brightness and the brightness is communicated to us through the rays, and that it is which lights us and is enjoyed by us. Neither do we say that the Son is of the Spirit, nor, most certainly, from the Spirit.

---
23 Rom. 8.9.
24 John. 20.22.

Chapter 9

The Divinity is simple and uncompounded. But, that which is composed of several different things is compounded. Consequently, should we say that the increate, unoriginate, incorporeal, immortal, eternal, good, creative, and the like are essential differences in God, then, since He is composed of so many things, He will not be simple but compounded, which is impious to the last degree. Therefore, one should not suppose that any one of these things which are affirmed of God is indicative of what He is in essence. Rather, they show either what He is not, or some relation to some one of those things that are contrasted with Him, or something of those things which are consequential to His nature or operation.

Now, it seems that of all the names given to God the more proper is that of HE WHO IS, as when in conversing with Moses on the mountain He says: 'Say to the children of Israel: HE WHO IS hath sent me.'[1] For, like some limitless and boundless sea of essence, He contains all being in Himself.[2] But then, as St. Dionysius says, He is 'The Good,' for in God one may not say that the being comes first and then the good afterwards.[3]

A second name is Θεός which derives from θέειν, to run, because of His running through all things and having care for them. Or it is from αἴθω, that is, to burn, because God is a fire consuming all evil.[4] Or it is from His θεᾶσθαι,[5] or seeing all things, because nothing escapes Him and He watches over all, and because He saw all things before they came to pass.[6] For He conceived of them independently

---
1 Exod. 3.14.
2 Cf. Gregory Nazianzen, *Sermon* 38.7 (*PG* 36.317B).
3 Pseudo-Dionysius, *Divine Names* 2.1 (*PG* 3.636-637).
4 Cf. Gregory Nazianzen, *Sermon* 30.18 (*PG* 36.128A); Deut. 4.24.
5 Cf. Gregory of Nyssa, *In Cant. Hom.* 5 (*PG* 44.861B), and *That There Are Not Three Gods* (*PG* 45.121D).
6 Cf. 2 Mach. 9.5; Dan. 13.42.

of time and each one comes to pass at the foreordained time in accordance with the predetermination and image and exemplar contained in His timeless will and design.

The former name, then, is expressive of His existence and His essence, while the latter is expressive of His operation. But the names 'Without beginning,' 'Incorruptible,' 'Unoriginate' or 'Uncreated,' 'Incorporeal,' 'Invisible,' and the like all show that He had no beginning of being, that He is not corruptible, is not created, is not a body, and is not visible. The names 'Good,' 'Just,' 'Holy,' and the like are consequential to His nature and are not indicative of the essence itself. Those of 'Lord,' 'King,' and the like are indicative of a relation to things that are contrasted with Him. Thus, of those that are lorded over He is called Lord, of those that are ruled over He is called King, of those that are created He is called Creator, and of those that are shepherded He is called Shepherd.

Chapter 10

All the aforesaid names are to be taken as applying in common, in the same manner, simply, indivisibly, and unitedly to the whole Godhead.[1] But the names 'Father' and 'Son' and 'Spirit,' 'Uncaused' and 'Caused,' 'Unbegotten' and 'Begotten' and 'Proceeding' are to be taken as applying in a different way, because they declare not the essence, but the mutual relationship and manner of existence [of the Persons].

Even when we have perceived these things and have been guided by them to the Divine Essence, we still do not grasp the essence itself, but only things relating to it. Just as, although we may know that the soul is without body, without quantity, and without shape, even then we have not grasped its essence. And in the same way, if we happen

---

[1] Cf. Pseudo-Dionysius, *Divine Names* 2.3 (PG 3.640B).

to know that the body is white or black, we have not comprehended the essence of the body, but only something related to it. True reason teaches us that the Divinity is simple and has one simple operation which is good and which effects all things, like the rays of the sun which warm all things and exercise their force in each in accordance with the natural capacity of each, having received such power of operation from God who created them.

On the other hand, everything that pertains to the divine and benevolent incarnation of the Word of God has a distinct application. For, in these, neither the being Father nor the being Spirit is in any way communicated save by good pleasure and the ineffable wondrous operation which God the Word worked, when, while being God unchangeable and the Son of God, He became a man like us.[2]

Chapter 11

Since in sacred Scripture we find many things said symbolically of God as if He had a body, one should know that since we are men clothed in this gross flesh, we are unable to think or speak of the divine, lofty, and immaterial operations of the Godhead unless we have recourse to images, types, and symbols that correspond to our own nature.[1] Consequently, everything that is said of God as if He had a body is said symbolically and has a loftier meaning. Thus, by the eyes and eyelids and sight of God let us understand His power of penetrating all things and His unescapable knowledge, by analogy with our own acquisition of more complete knowledge and certainty through this particular sense. By His ears and hearing let us understand His gracious acceptance of our supplications, for by this sense we, too,

---

[2] Cf. *ibid.* 2.6 (*PG* 3.644C); Gregory Nazianzen, *Sermon* 34.10 (*PG* 36.252A).

---

[1] Cf. Pseudo-Dionysius, *op. cit.* 1.8 (*PG* 3.597AB).

become well disposed toward them that petition us and more favorably incline our ear to them. By His mouth and speech let us understand the expression of His will, by analogy with our own expression of our innermost thoughts by mouth and speech. By His food and drink let us understand our concurrence with His will, for by the sense of taste we, too, satisfy the necessary appetite of our nature. By His smelling let us understand His acceptance of our good will toward Him and our thoughts, by analogy with our own perception of fragrance through this sense. By His face let us understand His being declared and revealed through His works, inasmuch as we ourselves are discovered by our faces. By His hands let us understand the prosecution of His operation, for it is by means of our hands that we successfully perform necessary and most worthy works. By His right hand let us understand His aid in advantageous things, by analogy with our own use of our right hand in the performance of the more noble and worthy actions and those which require our full strength. By His touching let us understand His most accurate discernment and exaction of exceedingly minute and hidden things, because those whom we feel all over are unable to conceal anything upon their persons. By His feet and walking let us understand His coming to the aid of the needy, or to work vengeance on enemies, or to do some other thing, by analogy with our accomplishing our own coming through the use of our feet. By His swearing let us understand the immutability of His will, because it is by oaths that we make conventions with one another. By His wrath and indignation let us understand His aversion to evil and His hatred of it, for we, too, hate things which are against our wishes and we are angry at them.[1] By His forgetfulness and His sleep and His drowsiness let us understand His putting off vengeance on His enemies and His delaying aid for His own. Thus, to put it simply, all these things which are affirmed of God as if He had a body con-

---

1 Cf. Gregory Nazianzen, *Sermon* 31.22 (*PG* 36.157B).

tain some hidden meaning which, through things corresponding to our nature, teaches us things which exceed our nature—except it be something said respecting the presence of the Word of God in the flesh. For, for our salvation He took on the whole man, both the intellectual soul and the body, and the peculiar properties of human nature as well as the natural but not blameworthy passions.

Chapter 12

In these things, then, have we been instructed by the sacred sayings, as the divine Dionysius the Areopagite has said,[1] namely, that God is the Cause and Principle of all things, the Essence of things that are, the Life or the living, the Reason of the rational, the Understanding of them that have understanding, the Revival and the raising up of them that fall away from Him, the Remaking and Reforming of them that are by nature corruptible, the holy Support of them that are tossed on an unholy sea, the sure Support of them that stand, and the Way and the outstretched guiding Hand to them that are drawn to Him. Moreover, I shall add that He is the Father of them that have been made by Him. For our God, who has brought us from nothing into being, is more properly our Father than they who have begotten us, but who have received from Him both their being and their power to beget. He is the Shepherd of them that follow after Him and are led by Him. He is the Illumination of the enlightened. He is the Initiation of the initiate. He is the Godliness of the godly. He is the Reconciliation of them that are at variance. He is the Simplicity of them that are become simple. He is the Unity of them that seek unity. As Principle of Principles He is the transcendent Principle of every principle. He is the good Communication of His hidden things, that is, of His knowledge, in so far as is allowable and meets with the capacity of each individual.

---

1 Pseudo-Dionysius, *op. cit.* 1.1 (*PG* 3.585B).

[More on the Names of God and More Precisely][2]

Since the Divinity is incomprehensible, He must remain absolutely nameless. Accordingly, since we do not know His essence, let us not look for a name for His essence, for names are indicative of what things are. However, although God is good and has brought us from nothing into being to share His goodness and has given us knowledge, yet, since He did not communicate His essence to us, so neither did He communicate the knowledge of His essence. It is impossible for a nature to know a nature of a higher order perfectly; but, if knowledge is of things that are, then how will that which is superessential be known? So, in His ineffable goodness He sees fit to be named from things which are on the level of our nature, that we may not be entirely bereft of knowledge of Him but may have at least some dim understanding. Therefore, in so far as He is incomprehensible, He is also unnameable. But, since He is the cause of all things and possesses beforehand in Himself the reasons and causes of all, so He can be named after all things—even after things which are opposites, such as light and darkness, water and fire—so that we may know that He is not these things in essence, but is superessential and unnameable. Thus, since He is the cause of all beings, He is named after all things that are caused.

Wherefore, some of the divine names are said by negation and show His superessentiality, as when He is called 'Insubstantial,' 'Timeless,' 'Without beginning,' 'Invisible'—not because He is inferior to anything or lacking in anything, for all things are His and from Him and by Him were made and in Him consist,[3] but because He is pre-eminently set apart from all beings. The names that are given by negation are predicated of Him as being the cause of all things. For, in so far as He is the cause of all beings and of every essence,

---

[2] This additional chapter is found only in some of the later codices, but the Byzantines have always considered it to be genuine.
[3] Col. 1.17.

He is called 'Being' and 'Essence.' As the cause of all reason and wisdom, and as that of the reasoning and the wise, He is called 'Wisdom' and 'Wise.' In the same way, He is called 'Mind' and 'Understanding,' 'Life' and 'Living,' 'Might' and 'Mighty,' and so on with all the rest. But especially may He be named after those more noble things which approach Him more closely. Immaterial things are more noble than material, the pure more so than the sordid, the sacred more so than the profane, and they approach Him more closely because they participate in Him more. Consequently, He may be called sun and light much more suitably than darkness, day more suitably than night, life more suitably than death, and fire, air, and water (since these are life-giving) more suitably than earth. And, above all, He may be called goodness rather than evil, which is the same thing as to say being rather than non-being, because good is existence and the cause of existence. These are all negations and affirmations, but the most satisfactory is the combination of both, as, for example, the 'superessential Essence,' the 'superdivine Godhead,' the 'Principle beyond all principles,' and so on. There are also some things which are affirmed of God positively, but which have the force of extreme negation, as, for example, darkness—not because God is darkness, but because He is light and more than light.

And so, God is called 'Mind,' and 'Reason,' and Spirit,' and 'Wisdom,' because He is the cause of these, and because He is immaterial, and because He is all-working and all-powerful.[4] And these names, both those given by negation and those given by affirmation, are applied jointly to the whole Godhead. They also apply in the same way, identically, and without exception, to each one of the Persons of the Holy Trinity. Thus, when I think of one of the Persons, I know that He is perfect God, a perfect substance, but

---

4 Cf. Pseudo-Dionysius, *op. cit.* 7 (*PG* 3.865ff.).

when I put them together and combine them, I know one perfect God. For the Godhead is not compounded, but is one perfect, indivisible, and uncompounded being in three perfect beings. However, whenever I think of the negation of the Persons to one another, I know that the Father is a supersubstantial sun, a well-spring of goodness, an abyss of essence, reason, wisdom, power, light, and divinity, a begetting and emitting well-spring of the good hidden in Himself. Thus, He is 'Mind,' 'Abyss of reason,' 'Begetter of the Word,' and, through the Word, 'Emitter' of the revealing Spirit. And, not to speak at too great length, the Father has no reason, wisdom, power, or will other than the Son, who is the only power of the Father and the primordial force of the creation of all things. As a perfect hypostasis begotten of a perfect hypostasis, in a manner which He alone knows, is He who is the Son and is so called. Then there is the Holy Ghost, a power of the Father revealing the hidden things of the Godhead and proceeding from the Father through the Son, not by begetting, but in a manner which He alone knows. Wherefore the Holy Ghost is also perfecter of the creation of all things. Consequently, whatsoever pertains to the Father as cause, well-spring, and begetter must be attributed to the Father alone. Whatsoever pertains to the Son as caused, begotten son, word, primordial force, will, and wisdom must be attributed to the Son alone. And whatsoever pertains to the caused, proceeding, revealing, and perfecting power must be attributed to the Holy Ghost. The Father is well-spring and cause of Son and Holy Ghost—He is Father of the only Son and Emitter of the Holy Ghost. The Son is son, word, wisdom, power, image, radiance, and type of the Father, and He is from the Father. And the Holy Ghost is not a son of the Father, but He is the Spirit of the Father as proceeding from the Father. For, without the Spirit, there is no impulsion. And He is the Spirit of the Son, not as being from Him, but as proceeding through Him from the Father—for the Father alone is Cause.

Chapter 13

Place is physical, being the limits of the thing containing within which the thing contained is contained. The air, for example, contains and the body is contained, but not all of the containing air is the place of the contained body, but only those limits of the containing air which are adjacent to the contained body. And this is necessarily so, because the thing containing is not in the thing contained.

However, there is also an intellectual place where the intellectual and incorporeal nature is thought of as being and where it actually is. There it is present and acts; and it is not physically contained, but spiritually, because it has no form to permit it to be physically contained. Now, God, being immaterial and uncircumscribed, is not in a place. For He, who fills all things and is over all things and Himself encompasses all things, is His own place.[1] However, God is also said to be in a place; and this place where God is said to be is there where His operation is plainly visible. Now, He does pervade all things without becoming mixed with them, and to all things He communicates His operation in accordance with the fitness and receptivity of each—in accordance with their purity of nature and will, I mean to say. For the immaterial things are purer than the material and the virtuous more pure than such as are partisan to evil. Thus, the place where God is said to be is that which experiences His operation and grace to a greater extent. For this reason, heaven is His Throne,[2] because it is in heaven that the angels are who do His will and glorify Him unceasingly. For heaven is His resting place and the earth his footstool, because on the earth He conversed in the flesh with men.[3] And the sacred flesh of God has been called His foot. The Church, too, is called the place of God, because we have set it apart

---
1 Cf. Gregory Nazianzen, *Sermon* 28.8-10 (*PG* 36.33-40).
2 Cf. Isa. 66.1.
3 *Ibid.;* Baruch 3.38.

for His glorification as a sort of hallowed spot in which we also make our intercessions to Him. In the same way, those places in which His operation is plainly visible to us, whether it is realized in the flesh or out of the flesh, are called places of God.

Moreover, one must know that the Divinity is without parts and that He is wholly everywhere in His entirety, not being physically distributed part for part, but wholly in all things and wholly over the universe.

[*On the Place of an Angel and of the Soul, and on the Uncircumscribed*][4]

Although the angel is not contained physically in a place so as to assume form and shape, he is said to be in a place because of his being spiritually present there and acting according to his nature, and because of his being nowhere else but remaining spiritually circumscribed there where he acts. For he cannot act in different places at the same time, because only God can act everywhere at the same time. For the angel acts in different places by virtue of a natural swiftness and his ability to pass without delay, that is, swiftly, from place to place; but the Divinity being everywhere and beyond all at the same time acts in different places by one simple operation.

The soul is united with the body, the entire soul with the entire body and not part for part. And it is not contained by the body, but rather contains it, just as heat does iron, and, although it is in the body, carries on its own proper activities.

Now, to be circumscribed means to be determined by place, time, or comprehension, while to be contained by none of these is to be uncircumscribed. So the Divinity alone is uncircumscribed, who is without beginning and without end, who embraces all things and is grasped by no comprehension

---

4 This is a marginal addition to the manuscript.

at all. For He alone is incomprehensible, undefinable, and known by no one; and He alone has a clear vision of Himself. The angel, however, is circumscribed by time, because he had a beginning of being; and by place, even though it be spiritually, as we have said before; and by comprehension, because their natures are to some extent known to each other and because they are completely defined by the Creator. Bodies also are circumscribed by beginning, end, physical place, and comprehension.

[*A Miscellany on God, and the Father, and the Son, and the Holy Ghost; and on the Word and the Spirit*][5]

The Divinity, therefore, is absolutely unchangeable and inalterable. For, all things which are not in our power He predetermined by His foreknowledge, each one in its own proper time and place. It is in this sense that it is said: 'Neither does the Father judge any man: but hath given all judgment to the Son.'[6] For, of course, the Father has judged, and so has the Son of God, and so has the Holy Ghost. But, as man, the Son Himself will come down in His body and sit upon the throne of glory—for both the coming down and the sitting will be of His circumscribed body—and He will judge the whole world in equity.'[7]

All things are far from God: not in place, but in nature. With us, prudence and wisdom and counsel come and go like habits, but that is certainly not the case with God. With Him, nothing comes into being or ceases to be, and one must not speak of accidents, because He is inalterable and unchangeable. The good is concomitant to His essence. He sees God who always longs for Him, for all things that are are dependent upon Him who is, so that it is impossible for anything to be, unless it have its being in Him who is. Indeed,

---
5 *Ibid.*
6 John 5.22.
7 Acts 17.31.

in so far as He sustains their nature, God is mixed in with all things. God the Word, however, was united to His sacred body hypostatically and was combined with our nature without being mingled with it.

No one sees the Father, except the Son and the Spirit.[8]

The Son is the counsel, the wisdom, and the power of the Father. For we must not speak of quality in God, lest we say that He is composed of substance and quality.

The Son is from the Father, and whatsoever He has He has from Him. For that reason, He can do nothing of Himself.[9] Thus, He has no operation that it is distinct from the Father.[10]

That God, although invisibile by nature, becomes visible through His operations we know from the arrangement of the world and from its governing.[11]

The Son is image of the Father, and image of the Son is the Spirit, through whom the Christ dwelling in man gives it to him to be to the image of God.

The Holy Ghost is God. He is the median of the Unbegotten and the Begotten and He is joined with the Father through the Son. He is called Spirit of God, Spirit of Christ, Mind of Christ, Spirit of the Lord, True Lord, Spirit of adoption, freedom, and wisdom—for He is the cause of all these.[12] He fills all things with His essence and sustains all things. In His essence He fills the world, but in His power the world does not contain Him.

God is substance eternal, unchangeable, creative of the things that are, and to be adored with devout consideration.

The Father is also God. It is He who is ever-unbegotten, because He was never begotten of anyone, but He has begotten a co-eternal Son. The Son is also God. It is He who is

---

8 Cf. John 6.46.
9 Cf. John 5.30.
10 Cf. Gregory Nazianzen, *Sermon* 30.11 (*PG* 36.116C).
11 Cf. Rom. 1.20.
12 Cf. Gregory Nazianzen, *Sermon* 31.29 (*PG* 36.165BC).

ever with the Father, having been begotten of Him timelessly, eternally, without change, without passion, and without cease. The Holy Ghost is also God. He is a sanctifying force that is subsistent, that proceeds unceasingly from the Father and abides in the Son, and that is of the same substance as the Father and the Son.

The Word is He who is ever present with the Father substantially. In another sense, a word is the natural movement of the mind, by which the mind moves and thinks and reasons, as if it were the light and radiance of the mind. And again, a word is that internal thought which is spoken in the heart. Still again, there is the spoken word which is a messenger of the mind. Now, God the Word is both substantial and subsistent, while the other three kinds of word are faculties of the soul and are not found to exist in their own hypostases. The first of these is a product of the mind, ever springing naturally from the mind. The second is called internal, and the third called spoken.

The term 'spirit' is understood in several ways. There is the Holy Spirit. And the powers of this Holy Spirit are also called spirits. The good angel is likewise a spirit, and so is the demon and the soul. There are times when even the mind is called spirit. The wind is also a spirit, and so is the air.

Chapter 14

The uncreate, the unoriginate, the immortal, the boundless, the eternal, the immaterial, the good, the creative, the just, the enlightening, the unchangeable, the passionless, the uncircumscribed, the uncontained, the unlimited, the indefinable, the invisible, the inconceivable, the wanting nothing, the having absolute power and authority, the life-giving, the almighty, the infinitely powerful, the sanctifying and communicating, the containing and sustaining all things, and the providing for all—all these and the like He possesses by His nature. They are not received from any other source;

on the contrary, it is His nature that communicates all good to His own creatures in accordance with the capacity of each.

The abiding and resting of the Persons in one another is not in such a manner that they coalesce or become confused, but, rather, so that they adhere to one another, for they are without interval between them and inseparable and their mutual indwelling is without confusion. For the Son is in the Father and the Spirit, and the Spirit is in the Father and the Son, and the Father is in the Son and the Spirit, and there is no merging or blending or confusion. And there is one surge and one movement of the three Persons. It is impossible for this to be found in any created nature.

Then there is the fact that the divine irradiation and operation is one, simple, and undivided; and that, while it is apparently diversely manifested in divisible things, dispensing to all of them the components of their proper nature, it remains simple. Indivisibly, it is multiplied in divisible things, and, gathering them together, it reverts them to its own simplicity.[1] For, toward Him all things tend, and in Him they have their existence, and to all things He communicates their being in accordance with the nature of each. He is the being of things that are, the life of the living, the reason of the rational, and the intelligence of intelligent beings. He surpasses intelligence, reason, life, and essence.

And then again, there is His pervading of all things without Himself being contaminated, whereas nothing pervades Him. And yet again, there is His knowing of all things by a simple act of knowing. And there is His distinctly seeing with His divine, all-seeing, and immaterial eye all things at once, both present and past and future, before they come to pass.[2] And there is His sinlessness, His forgiving of sins and saving. And, finally, there is the fact that all that He wills He can do, even though He does not will all the things that He can do—for He can destroy the world, but He does not will to do so.

---

[1] Cf. Pseudo-Dionysius, *Divine Names* 2 (*PG* 3.636ff.).
[2] Cf. Dan. 13.42.

BOOK TWO

Chapter 1

HE MADE THE AGES who exists before the ages, of whom the divine David says: 'From eternity and to eternity thou art;'[1] and the divine Apostle: 'By whom also he made the ages.'[2]

Now, one should note that the term *age* has several meanings, because it signifies a great many things. Thus, the span of life of every man is called an age. Again, a period of one thousand years is called an age. Still again, this whole present life is called an age, and so is the age without end to come after the resurrection.[3] And again, that is called an age which is neither time nor any division of time measured by the course and motion of the sun—that is to say, made up of days and nights—but which is co-extensive with eternal things after the fashion of some sort of temporal period and interval. This kind of age is to eternal things exactly what time is to temporal things.[4]

---

1 Ps. 89.2.
2 Heb. 1.2.
3 Cf. Matt. 12.32.
4 The *aevum* of the Scholastics. Cf. Gregory Nazianzen, *Sermon* 29.3 (PG 36.77AB).

Now, this world is said to have seven ages, that is to say, from the creation of heaven and earth until the general consummation and resurrection of men. For, while there is a particular consummation, which is the death of each individual, there is also a general and final consummation which will come when the general resurrection of men takes place. The eighth age is that which is to come.

Before the framing of the world, when there was no sun to separate day from night, there was no measurable age, but only an age co-extensive with eternal things after the fashion of some sort of temporal period and interval. In this sense, there is one age in respect to which God is said to be of the ages, and, indeed, before the ages, for He made the very ages—since He alone is God without beginning and Himself creator both of the ages and of the things that are. When I speak of God, however, it is obvious that I mean the Father and His only-begotten Son, our Lord Jesus Christ, and His All-Holy Spirit—our one God.

We also speak of the ages of ages, inasmuch as the seven ages of the present world contain many ages, that is to say, generations of men, whereas there is one age containing all ages and which is called the age of ages—both present and future. Furthermore, the expressions 'age-enduring life' and 'age-enduring chastisement' show the eternity of the age to come. For, after the resurrection, time will not be numbered by days and nights at all; rather, there will be one day without evening, with the Sun of Justice shining brightly upon the just and a deep and endless night reserved for the sinners. How, then, will the time of Origen's millenium be measured? God, therefore, is the one maker of the ages—He who also created all things and who exists before the ages.

Chapter 2

Now, because the good and transcendentally good God was not content to contemplate Himself, but by a superabundance of goodness saw fit that there should be some things to benefit by and participate in His goodness, He brings all things from nothing into being and creates them, both visible and invisible, and man, who is made up of both. By thinking He creates, and, with the Word fulfilling and the Spirit perfecting, the object of His thought subsists.[1]

Chapter 3

He is the maker and creator of the *angels*. He brought them from nothing into being and made them after His own image into a bodiless nature, some sort of spirit, as it were, and immaterial fire—as the divine David says: 'Who maketh his angels spirits: and his ministers a burning fire.'[1] And He determined their lightness, fieriness, heat, extreme acuity, their keenness in their desire for God and His service, and their being raised up and removed from every material consideration.

So, an angel is an intellectual substance, ever in motion, free, incorporeal, ministering to God, with the gift of immortality in its nature. And the form and the definition of this substance only the Creator understands. Now, compared with us, the angel is said to be incorporeal and immaterial, although in comparison with God, who alone is incomparable, everything proves to be gross and material—for only the Divinity is truly immaterial and incorporeal.

So, the angel is of a nature which is rational, intelligent, free, and variable in judgment, that is, subject to voluntary

---

1 Cf. Gregory Nazianzen, *Sermon* 38.9 (*PG* 36.320).

1 Ps. 103.4.

change. It is only the Uncreated which is unchangeable. Also, every rational being is free. The angelic nature, then, in so far as it is rational and intelligent, is free; while, in so far as it is created, it is changeable and has the power to persevere and progress in good or to turn to evil.

Although man, by reason of the infirmity of his body, is capable of repentance, the angel, because of his incorporeality, is not.

The angel is immortal, not by nature, but by grace; for, naturally, everything that has beginning has an end, too. Only God is always existing—rather, transcends always, because He who made the times is not subject to time but transcends it.

The angels are secondary spiritual lights, who receive their brightness from that first Light which is without beginning. They have no need of tongue and hearing; rather, they communicate their individual thoughts and designs to one another without having recourse to the spoken word.

Now, all the angels were created by the Word and perfected by the sanctification of the Holy Ghost, and in accordance with their dignity and rank they enjoy brightness and grace.[2]

The angels are circumscribed, because when they are in heaven they are not on earth, and when they are sent to earth by God they do not remain in heaven. However, they are not confined by walls or doors or bars or seals, because they are unbounded. I say that they are unbounded, because they do not appear exactly as they are to the just and to them that God wills them to appear to. On the contrary, they appear under such a different form as can be seen by those who behold them. Of course, only the Uncreated is by nature unbounded, for all creation is bounded by God who created it.

The angels do not receive their sanctification by the Spirit as something due their essence. It is by the grace of God that they prophesy. They have no need of marriage, precisely because they are not mortal.

---

2 Cf. Gregory Nazianzen, *loc. cit.*

Since they are intellects, they are in places intellectually and are not corporeally circumscribed. For by nature they do not have bodily shape and they are not extended in three dimensions; rather, they are present and act in space intellectually in whatsoever place they are commanded to do so, and they are not able to be present and act in different places at the same time.

Whether the angels are equal in essence or whether they differ from one another we do not know. Only God knows, who made them and knows all things. They do, however, differ from one another in brightness and station, either having their station in accordance with their brightness or enjoying their brightness in accordance with their station. They illuminate one another by the excellence of their rank or nature. Moreover, it is evident that the more excellent communicate their brightness and their knowledge to them that are inferior.[3]

They are vigorous and prompt in the execution of the divine will and by a natural quickness they appear immediately in whatever place the divine pleasure may command. They watch over the parts of the earth and are set over nations and places in accordance with their disposition by the Creator. They direct our affairs and help us. Moreover, they are ever round about God for the very reason that in accordance with the divine will and command they are above us.[4]

They are with difficulty moved towards evil, but they can be so moved.[5] However, they cannot be moved toward evil—not because of their nature, but by grace and their diligent pursuit of the only Good.

They see God to such an extent as is possible for them, and this is their food.[6]

Although, because they are incorporeal, they are superior

---
[3] Cf. Pseudo-Dionysius. *Celestial Hierarchy* 3 (PG 3.164ff.).
[4] Cf. *ibid.* 9 (PG 3.257ff.).
[5] Gregory Nazianzen, *op. cit.* (PG 36.321A).
[6] Cf. Tobias 12.19 (Vulgate).

to us and free of all bodily passion, they are certainly not passionless, because only the Divinity is passionless.

They take whatever form the Lord may command, and thus they appear to men and reveal the divine mysteries to them.

They live in heaven and have as their one work to sing the praises of God and minister to His sacred will.

As the most holy and sacred Dionysius the Areopagite, who is very well versed in theology, says,[7] all theology, that is to say, sacred Scripture, has given the heavenly substances as nine in number. The divine initiator divides these into three orders of three. He says that the first of these is ever round about God and that to it has it been given to be united directly and immediately to Him. This is the order of the six-winged Seraphim and the many-eyed Cherubim and the most holy Thrones. The second order is that of the Dominations and the Virtues and the Powers. The third is that of the Principalities and the Archangels and the Angels.

Now, some say that the angels were made before all creation, as Gregory the Theologian says: 'First He conceived the angelic and heavenly powers, and His conception was an accomplished work.'[8] But there are others who say that they were made after the creation of the first heaven. However, they all agree that it was before the formation of man. For my part, I agree with the Theologian, because it was fitting for the spiritual substance to be created first and then the sensible and then finally man himself from both.

Moreover, if there is anyone who says that there is any kind of substance whatsoever that the angels can create, he is the mouthpiece of his father, the Devil. For, since they are creatures, they are not creators. He who made all things, provides for all, and sustains them is God, who alone is uncreated, who is praised and glorified in the Father and the Son and the Holy Ghost.

---

[7] Pseudo-Dionysius, *op. cit.* 6.2 (*PG* 3.200D-201A).
[8] Gregory Nazianzen, *op. cit.* (*PG* 36.320C).

Chapter 4

One of these angelic powers was chief of the terrestrial order and had been entrusted by God with the custody of the earth. Although he was not evil by nature, but good, and although he had been made for good and had in himself not the slightest trace of evil from the Creator, he did not keep the brightness and dignity which the Creator had bestowed upon him. By his free choice he turned from what was according to nature to what was against it. Having become stirred up against the God who created him and having willed to rebel against Him, he was the first to abandon good and become evil. For evil is no more than the privation of good, just as darkness is the absence of light. And good is spiritual light, while in the same way evil is spiritual darkness. Now, light was made by the Creator and it was good, for 'God saw all the things which he had made, and they were very good,'[1] but darkness came by free will. And together with him a numberless horde of the angels that he had marshaled were torn away, and followed after him and fell. Hence, although they were of the same nature as the angels, they have become bad by freely turning from good to evil.[2]

They have no power or strength against anyone, unless this be permitted them by the dispensation of God, as in the case of Job and as has been written in the Gospel about the swine.[3] If God does give them permission, they have strength and change and transform themselves into whatever apparent form they may desire.

Neither the angels of God nor the evil spirits know the future. Nevertheless, they foretell it. The angels do so when God reveals the future to them and orders them to foretell it, for which reason whatever they say happens. On the

---
1 Gen. 1.31.
2 Cf. *Questions to Antiochus* 7 (PG 28.604A).
3 Cf. Job. 1.12, 2.6; Mark 5.13.

other hand, the evil spirits foretell the future, sometimes by seeing the things that are to happen far ahead, and sometimes by guessing at them. For this reason one must not believe them, even though they may often speak the truth by the manner of which we have spoken. Moreover, they also know the Scriptures.

And so, all evil and the impure passions have been conceived by them and they have been permitted to visit attacks upon man. But they are unable to force anyone, for it is in our power either to accept the visitation or not. Wherefore, the unquenchable fire and everlasting torment have been prepared for the Devil and his evil spirits and for them who follow him.[4]

One should note that the fall is to the angels just what death is to men. For, just as there is no repentance for men after their death, so is there none for the angels after their fall.[5]

Chapter 5

Our God, who is glorified in trinity and unity, Himself 'made heaven and earth, and all things that are in them.'[1] He brought all things from nothing into being: some, such as heaven, earth, air, fire, and water, from no pre-existing matter; and others, such as animals, plants and seeds, He made from those things which had their existence directly from Him. For, by the command of the Creator these last were made from earth, water, air, and fire.

Chapter 6

The *heavens* are the outer shell which contains both visible

---
4 Cf. Matt. 25.41.
5 Cf. Nemesius, *On the Nature of Man* 1 (PG 40.524A).

1 Ps. 145.6.

and invisible created things. For, enclosed and contained within them are the spiritual powers, which are the angels, and all sensible things. Only the Divinity is uncircumscribed, filling, containing, and surrounding all things, because He transcends all things and it is He who has created all.

Now, since Scripture speaks of 'heaven,' the 'heaven of heaven,' and the 'heavens of heavens,' and says that the blessed Paul was caught up to the *'third heaven,'*[2] we say that in the creation of the universe we consider as heavens that which the pagan philosophers, making the teachings of Moses their own, call a starless sphere. And again, God called heaven the 'firmament,'[3] which He ordered to be made in the midst of the water and so arranged that it was separated from the midst of the water above the firmament and from the midst of that which is below the firmament. Instructed by sacred Scripture, the divine Basil says[4] that its substance is subtle—like smoke, as it were. Others say that it is watery, because it was made in the midst of the waters. And others say that it is made from the four elements. Still others say that it is a fifth body and distinct from the four elements.[5]

Furthermore, some have surmised that the heavens surround the universe and have the form of a sphere which is everywhere the highest point, while the center of the space enclosed by it is the lowest point; and that the airier and lighter bodies have been assigned by the Creator to the higher positions, while the heavy and unbuoyant have been consigned to the lower, which is the center. Now, the lightest and the most buoyant of the elements is fire, so they say that it comes directly below the heavens. They call it ether. Just below the ether comes the air. Earth and water, since they are heavier and less buoyant, are said to be hung in the midmost position, so that by contrast they are below. The water, however, is lighter than the earth—whence its greater mobility. Everywhere above this, like a blanket, lies

---

2 Ps. 113.16, 148.4; 2 Cor. 12.2.
3 Gen. 1.8.
4 Cf. Isa. 40.22; Basil *Homily 1 on the Six Days* 8, (PG 29.20C-21A).
5 Cf. Basil, *op. cit.* 11 (PG 29.25B).

the encircling air; everywhere around the air is the ether; and on the outside encircling them all are the heavens.

Furthermore, they say that the heavens revolve and that they so bind together the things contained within that they stay firmly together and do not fall apart.

They say that the heavens have seven spheres, one above the other.[6] They further say that the substance of the heavens is very subtile, like smoke, and that in each one of the spheres is one of the planets. For they have said that there are seven planets: the Sun, the Moon, Jupiter, Mercury, Mars, Venus, and Saturn. Venus, they say, is sometimes the morning star and sometimes the evening star. They called them planets, or wanderers, because their motion is contrariwise to that of the heavens. For, while the heavens and the rest of the stars move from east to west, these alone have their motion from west to east. This we may know from the example of the moon, which moves back a little every evening.

Now, those who held that the heavens were spherical say that they are removed from the earth by an equal distance above, on the sides, and below. By 'below' and 'on the sides' I mean in so far as is apparent to our senses, because it logically follows that the heavens occupy the highest position at all points and the earth the lowest. They also say that the heavens surround the earth like a sphere and by their very rapid movement carry the sun, moon, and stars around with them. And they say that, when the sun is over the earth, then it is day here, while when it is under the earth, it is night; but when the sun goes down under the earth, then it is night here and day there.

Others, however, have imagined the heavens to have the form of a hemisphere, because the inspired David says: 'Who stretchest out the heaven like a pavilion,' which means a tent; and the blessed Isaias: 'He that establisheth the

---

6 Cf. Basil, *Homily 3 on the Six Days* 3 (PG 29.57B).

heavens like a vault';⁷ and because the sun, the moon, and the stars, when they set, go round the earth from west to north and thence return again to the east. However, whichever way it may be, all things have been made and established by the command of God and have their foundation in the divine will and desire. 'For he spoke, and they were made: he commanded and they were created. He hath established them for ever, and for ages of ages: he hath made a decree and it shall not pass away.'⁸

So there is a heaven of heaven, which is the first heaven and is above the firmament. But now, because God also called the firmament 'heaven,'⁹ there are two heavens. However, it is customary for sacred Scripture to call the air heaven, too, because of its being seen above, as it says: 'O all ye fowls of the heaven, bless the Lord,'¹⁰ meaning the air, although the air is not heaven but a medium of passage for the fowls. Here we have the three heavens of which the divine Apostle spoke.¹¹ Then, if you want to take the seven spheres as seven heavens, there will still be nothing contrary to the Word of Truth. It is also customary in the Hebrew tongue to speak of heaven in the plural as 'heavens.' So, when Scripture meant to say 'heaven of heaven,' it said 'heavens of heavens,' which would mean precisely 'heaven of heaven'—that which is over the firmament and the waters which are above the heavens, whether over the air and the firmament or over the seven spheres of the firmament, or over the firmament expressed in the plural as 'heavens' according to the Hebraic usage.

Now, all things which have a beginning are subject to corruption as a logical consequence of their nature, and the heavens are no exception. It is by the grace of God that they

---

7 Ps. 103.2; Isa. 40.22 (Septuagint).
8 Ps. 148.5,6.
9 Gen. 1.8.
10 Dan. 3.80.
11 Cf. 2 Cor. 12.2.

are held together and sustained.[12] Only the Divinity is by nature without beginning and without end. For this reason was it said that: 'They shall perish but thou remainest.' However, the heavens will not entirely disappear: 'For they shall perish, and they shall be changed as a vesture, and there will be a new heaven and a new earth.'[13]

In size the heavens are much greater than the earth. Nevertheless, one must not inquire into the substance of the heavens, because we can know nothing about it.

Furthermore, let no one maintain that the heavens or the heavenly bodies are animate, for they are inanimate and without feeling. So, even though sacred Scripture says: 'Let the heavens rejoice, and let the earth be glad,'[14] it is really calling upon the angels in heaven and the men on earth to rejoice. Of course, Scripture can personify inanimate things and talk about them as if they were alive, as for example: 'The sea saw and fled: Jordan was turned back,' and: 'What ailed thee, O thou sea, that thou didst flee? and thou, O Jordan, that thou was turned back?' and again: mountains and hills are asked the reason for their skipping.[15] In just the same way it is customary for us to say that 'the city was gathered together, not intending to mean the houses, but the occupants of the houses. Still again, 'the heavens shew forth the glory of God'[16] not by speaking in voice audible to sensible ears, but by manifesting to us through their own greatness the power of the Creator, and when we remark their beauty, we give glory to their Maker as the best of all artificers.[17]

---

12 Cf. Basil, *Homily 1 on the Six Days* 9 (*PG* 29.24B).
13 Ps. 101.27; Heb. 1.11,12; Apoc. 21.1.
14 Ps. 95.11.
15 Ps. 113.3,5,6.
16 Ps. 18.2.
17 Cf. Basil, *Homily 1 on the Six Days* 11 (*PG* 29.28A).

Chapter 7

Fire is one of the four elements. It is light and more buoyant than the others, and it both burns and gives light. It was made by the Creator on the first day, for sacred Scripture says: 'And God said: Be light made. And light was made.' According to what some say, fire is the same thing as *light*. Others speak of the cosmic fire above the air and they call it ether. 'In the beginning,' then, which is to say, on the first day, God made the light to adorn and enhance all visible creation. For, remove the light and everything will be in darkness and will be indistinguishable and incapable of displaying its inherent comeliness. 'And God called the light day, and the darkness night.'[1] Darkness, moreover, is not a substance, but an accident, because it is the absence of light. For light is no part of the substance of the air.[2] Hence, it was just the absence of light in the air that God called darkness; and darkness is not the substance of the air but the absence of light—which indicates an accident rather than a substance. Furthermore, it was not night that was called first, but day, so that day is first and night last. Accordingly, the night follows the day, and we have a period of a day and a night from the beginning of one day to that of the next—for Scripture says: 'And there was evening and morning one day.'[3]

And so, during those three days, day was made by the alternate diffusion and shutting out of the light at the divine command. On the fourth day God made the great luminary, the sun that is, to terminate and control the day. Thus it is that the day is determined by the sun, for, when the sun is above the earth it is day; and the duration of the day is that of the sun's course over the earth from east to west. He made a lesser luminary, too—that is, the moon—and the

---

1 Gen. 1.3,1,5.
2 Cf. Basil, *Homily 2 on the Six Days* 5 (PG 29.40C).
3 Gen. 1.5.

stars to determine and control the night and give it light. Now, it is night when the sun is below the earth, and the duration of the night is that of the sun's course underneath the earth from west to east. Thus, the moon and the stars have been set to light the night—but this does not mean that they are always under the earth during the daytime, for even in the daytime there are stars in the heavens over the earth. However, when the sun is shining at the same time as the stars and the moon, it dims them by its brighter radiance and keeps them from showing.

It was into these luminaries that the Creator put the primordial light, not that He was in want of any other light, but that that particular light might not remain idle. For the luminary is not the light itself, but its container.[4]

They hold the seven planets to be of the number of these luminaries and they say that their motion is opposite to that of the heavens, for which reason they have been called planets, or wanderers. For it is said that the heavens move from east to west, whereas the planets move from west to east. And the heavens bear the seven planets around with themselves by their own more rapid motion, as it were. The names of the seven planets are as follows: Moon, Mercury, Venus, Sun, Mars, Jupiter, and Saturn. Furthermore, it is said that there is one planet for each of the celestial spheres:

In the first, that is to say, the highest, Saturn.
In the second, Jupiter.
In the third, Mars.
In the fourth, the Sun.
In the fifth, Venus.
In the sixth, Mercury.
In the seventh and lowest, the Moon.

They follow the unceasing course set for them by the Creator according as He founded them, as the divine David says: 'The moon and the stars which thou hast founded.'[5]

---

4 Cf. Basil, *Homily 6 on the Six Days* 2-3 (*PG* 29.120-121)
5 Ps. 8.4.

By saying 'founded' he meant the stability and immutability of the order and succession given them by God. For He arranged them 'for signs, and for seasons, and for days and years.'[6] It is by the Sun that the four solstices are determined. The first of these is the spring solstice, for it was at the spring solstice that God made all things, which is evident from the fact that even down to the present time the budding of the flowers takes place then. It is also called an equinoctial solstice, because both the day and the night are twelve hours long. It is determined by the mean rising of the sun. The spring is mild and promotes the growth of the blood, and it is warm and wet. It stands midway between winter and summer, being warmer and drier than winter and cooler and wetter than summer. This season extends from March [21] to June 24. Then, as the sun rises farther and farther to the north, the summer solstice follows. Summer stands midway between spring and autumn. From spring it has warmth and from autumn dryness, for it is hot and dry. It also promotes the growth of the yellow bile. The summer solstice has the longest day, fifteen hours long, while its night is very short indeed, being nine hours long. Summer extends from June 24 to September 25. Then, the sun comes back again to its mean rising, summer is succeeded by autumn, which has a sort of medium coolness and warmth, dryness and wetness. It stands midway between summer and winter and has its dryness from summer and its cold from winter, for it is by its nature cold and dry. It also promotes the growth of the black bile. This solstice is also equinoctial, both its day and its night being twelve hours long. Autumn extends from September 25 to December 25. Then, as the sun's course becomes shorter and lower, that is to say, southerly, the winter solstice follows. Winter is cold and wet. It stands midway between autumn and spring and has its cold from autumn and its wetness from spring. The winter solstice has the shortest day, nine hours long, and the longest

---

6 Gen. 1.14.

night, fifteen hours long. Moreover, winter promotes the growth of the phlegm, and extends from December 25 to March 21. Thus, the Creator made wise provision against our contracting serious sicknesses from passing from the extremes of cold, heat, wetness, or dryness to the opposite extremes—for reason tells us that sudden changes are dangerous.

In this way, then, the sun produces the seasonal changes and, through them, the year. It also causes the days and nights: the former by rising and being over the earth, the latter by going down underneath the earth. By withdrawing, it causes the other luminaries to shine: the moon, that is, and the stars.

Now, they say that there are also twelve signs of the zodiac, made up of the stars in the heavens and having a motion contrary to that of the sun, the moon, and the five other planets, and that the seven pass through these twelve signs. Thus, the sun completes one month for each sign of the zodiac and in twelve months passes through the twelve signs. The following are the names of the twelve signs of the zodiac, and their months:

The sun enters *Aries* on March 21, *Taurus* on April 23, *Gemini* on May 24, *Cancer* on June 24, *Leo* on July 25, *Virgo* on August 25, *Libra* on September 25, *Scorpio* on October 25, *Sagittarius* on November 25, *Capricorn* on December 25, *Aquarius* on January 25, *Pisces* on February 24.

The moon passes through the twelve signs of the zodiac every month, because it is lower and travels through them more rapidly. For, if you put one orbit within another, the inside one will be found to be smaller. Thus, because it is lower, the course of the moon is shorter and more quickly completed.

Now, the Greeks say that all our affairs are governed by the rising, setting, and conjunction of these stars and of the sun and moon. With such things is astrology concerned. But we say that, while they do give indications of rain and drought, cold and heat, wetness and dryness, winds, and the like, they give absolutely no indication of our actions.[7] For we have been made free by the Creator and we control our own actions. But, if everything that we do is governed by the movement of the stars, then whatever we do we do by necessity.[8] Now, what is done by necessity is neither virtue nor vice, and, if we have neither virtue nor vice, we deserve neither reward nor punishment. Hence, God will prove to be unjust when He gives good things to some and tribulations to others. What is more, if all things are driven and moved by necessity, then God will not be exercising either control over His creatures or providence for them. Reason also will be useless to us, for, if we have no control over any of our actions, then it is useless for us to make our own resolves. But reason has been given to us so that we may deliberate, which is why every being that is rational is also free.

We say that the stars do not cause anything to happen, whether it be the production of things that are made, or events, or the destruction of things that are destroyed. Rather, they are signs of rains and atmospheric change. One might possibly say, however, that, although they do not cause wars either, they are signs of them; and that the condition of the atmosphere, which is determined by the sun, moon and stars, in various ways favors various temperaments, habits, and dispositions. Nevertheless, habits are something under our own control, for, in so far as they are subject to the reason, they may be controlled and cultivated by it.

And there are comets, too, which oftentimes appear as portents of the death of kings. They are not of the number of the stars which have existed from the beginning, but by the divine command they take form at just the right time and then are dissolved again. And neither was the star that was seen by the Magi at the time of the Lord's gracious and saving birth according to the flesh for us one of those that

---
[7] Cf. Basil, *op. cit.* 5 (*PG* 29.128-129).
[8] Cf. Nemesius, *On the Nature of Man* 35 (*PG* 40.741).

were made at the beginning. This is also evident from the fact that they make their course now from east to west, and now from north to south, and that they now disappear and now appear. For this is not in accord with the regularity and the nature of the stars.[9]

One should note that the moon is lit by the sun. This is not because God was unable to give it its own light, but rather, that harmony and order might be imposed upon creation, with one ruling and another being ruled, and that we might be taught to have things in common with others, to share with them, and to be subject to them—first of all to the Maker and Creator, God and Lord, and then to them whom He has appointed to rule. Nor is it for me to inquire why this particular one rules; rather, I should thankfully and willingly accept all things that come from God.

The fact that the sun and moon suffer eclipse utterly refutes the folly of those who worship the creature rather than the Creator,[10] and it shows that they are subject to change and variation. Now, anything that is subject to change is not God, for by its very nature it is subject to corruption and change.

The sun suffers eclipse when the mass of the moon, becoming like a sort of partition wall, casts a shadow and does not permit the light to get through to us. The extent of the eclipse, then, is proportionate to the amount of the mass of the moon concealing the sun. Now, even though the mass of the moon be smaller, do not be surprised, because, although it is maintained by some that the sun is many times larger than the earth, and by the holy Fathers that it is equal to the earth in size, it oftentimes is hidden by a small cloud, or even by a hillock or a wall.

The eclipse of the moon is brought about by the earth's shadow, when the moon is fifteen days old and directly opposite at its highest point, the sun being below the earth

---

9 Cf. Basil, *On the Nativity of Christ* (PG 31.1469-1472).
10 Cf. Rom. 1.25.

and the moon above the earth. For the earth casts a shadow and the sunlight is unable to light the moon, so that it is eclipsed.

Moreover, one should know that the Creator made the moon as full—in other words, as it is fifteen days old—for it was fitting that it should be created in its most perfect state.[11] However, as we said, the sun was created on the fourth day. Therefore, the moon was eleven days ahead of the sun, for from the fourth to the fifteenth there are eleven days. For this reason, the twelve lunar months have eleven days less than the twelve solar months every year. For the twelve solar months have 365 and a quarter days, whence the quarter accumulating through four years makes one full day, which is called *bissextile*—and that year has 366 days. On the other hand, the lunar years have 354 days, because from the time of its nascency, or renewal, the moon waxes until it is fourteen and three quarters days old, and then it begins to wane and wanes until it is twenty-nine and a half days old and becomes entirely dark. Then, having again made contact with the sun, it is reborn, or renewed, thus giving a reminder of our own resurrection. Consequently, the moon is eleven days behind the sun every year. Therefore, the Hebrews have an intercalary month every third year, and that year has thirteen months by reason of the accumulation of the eleven days.

Moreover, it is evident that the sun, moon, and stars are composite, and by their very nature subject to corruption. However, we do not know their nature. Thus, some say that when fire is apart from any matter it is invisible, whereas others say that when it is quenched it is changed into air.

The belt of the zodiac moves obliquely and is divided into twelve sections which are called signs of the zodiac. The sign of the zodiac has three decans, which is thirty degrees. The degree has sixty minutes. Therefore, the heavens

---

11 Cf. Severus Gabal., *Homily 3 on the Creation of the World 2* (*PG* 56.449).

have 360 degrees, the hemisphere over the earth having 180 and that under the earth 180.

The *house* of Mars is Aries and Scorpio; that of Venus is Taurus and Libra; that of Mercury is Gemini and Virgo; that of the Moon is Cancer; that of the Sun is Leo; that of Jupiter is Sagittarius and Pisces; and that of Saturn is Capricorn and Aquarius.

Aries is the *ascension* of the Sun, Taurus that of the Moon, Cancer that of Jupiter, Virgo that of Mars, Libra that of Saturn, Capricorn that of Mercury, and Pisces that of Venus.

The moon is in *conjunction* when it is in the same degree as the sun. It is *nascent* when it is fifteen degrees distant from the sun. It is twice *rising* when it is sixty degrees distant and appears in the form of a crescent. It is twice *half full* when it is ninety degrees distant. It is twice *near full* and nearly fully lighted when it is 150 degrees distant. It is *full* when it is 180 degrees distant. It is twice *gibbous* when it is 120 degrees distant. And when we say that the moon is in a phase twice, we mean once when waxing and once when waning. It takes the moon two and one half days to pass through each sign of the zodiac.

Chapter 8

Air is a very subtle element and is both wet and warm. It is heavier than fire, but lighter than earth and water. It is the cause of breath and voice. It is colorless, that is to say it has no color by nature. It is clear and transparent, for it is receptive of light. It also serves three of our senses, since by it we see, hear, and smell. It can be heated or cooled, dried or made wet. All of its movements are local—motion upward, downward, inward, outward, to the right, to the left, and in a circle.

It does not have light from itself but gets it from the sun, the moon, the stars, and fire. This is what Scripture meant when it said that 'darkness was upon the face of the deep,'[1] intending to show that the air does not have light from itself, but that the substance of light is something else.

Wind is a movement of the air. Or again, wind is a current of air which takes various names after the various places from which it flows.[2]

Air has its place, too. For the place of any body is its containing boundary. And what contains bodies, unless it be the air? There are, moreover, various places from which the movement of the air comes and after which the winds take their names. These are twelve altogether. And they say that the air is quenched fire, or that it is vapor from hot water. At any rate, air is of its own nature warm. It is, however, cooled by proximity to water and the earth, so that its lower portions are cool, while its upper portions are warm.[3]

The wind blows as follows: from the northeast, Caecias, which is also called Meses; from the east, Apeliotes; from the southeast, Eurus; from the southwest, Lips; from the west, Zephyr; from the northwest, Argestes or Olympias, which is also called Japyx; then Notus, the south wind, and Aparctias, the north wind, blow in directions opposite to each other; and midway between Aparctias and Caecias is Boreas; midway between Eurus and Notus is Phoenix, which is called Euronotus; midway between Notus and Lips is Libonotus, which is also called Leuconotus; and midway between Arpactias and Argestes is Thrascias, or Cercius, as it is called by the local inhabitants.

(The races that inhabit the extreme confines are: to the east, the Bactrians; to the southeast, the Indians; to the south-southeast lie the Red Sea and Ethiopia; to the south-southwest, the Garamantes, who dwell beyond Syria; to the southwest, the Ethiopians and the West Moors; to the west

---

[1] Gen. 1.2.
[2] Cf. Severus Gabal., *Homily 1 on the Creation of the World* 5 (*PG* 56.436).
[3] Cf. Nemesius, *op. cit.* 5 (*PG* 40.617B-620A).

lie the Pillars of Hercules and the confines of Lybia and Europe; to the northwest, Iberia, which is now called Spain; to the north-northwest, the Celts and bordering nations; to the north, the Scythians, who dwell beyond Thrace; to the north-northeast, Pontus, Maeotia, and the Sarmatians; to the northeast, the Caspian Sea and the Sacae.)[4]

Chapter 9

Water is also one of the four elements and a most admirable creation of God. Water is a wet and cold element which is heavy and unbouyant and which is fluid. Sacred Scripture refers to it when it says: 'And darkness was upon the face of the deep. And the spirit of God moved over the waters,'[1] for the deep is nothing else but a great quantity of water. In the beginning, then, water covered the whole earth. And first God made the firmament that 'divided the waters that were above the firmament, from those that were under the firmament,'[2] for in the midst of the abyss of waters it was made firm by the Lord's command. Thus, God said for a firmament also to be made, and it was made. Why did God put water over the firmament? Because of the burning heat of the sun and the ether. For the ether is spread immediately under the firmament, and the sun and moon and stars are in the firmament; if water did not lie over it, the firmament would be burnt up by the heat.[3]

Then God ordered the waters to be gathered together into one place. Now, the fact that Scripture speaks of one gathering does not mean that they were gathered together into one place, for notice that after this it says: 'And the

---

4 This passage is not found in most codices.

1 Gen. 1.2.
2 Gen. 1.7.
3 Cf. Basil, *Homily 3 on the Six Days* 7 (PG 29.68ff.).

gathering together of the waters he called seas.'[4] Actually, the account meant that the waters were segregated by themselves apart from the earth. And so the waters were brought together into their gathering places and the dry land appeared. Thence came the two seas which surround Egypt, for Egypt lies between two seas. Various seas are gathered together, having mountains, islands, capes, and harbors, and bordering upon various bays, beaches and headlands. The sandy shore is called a beach, but the rocky and precipitous shore that extends directly into deep water is called a headland. Thence, also, in the same way were gathered together that sea to the east which is called the Indian, and that to the north called the Caspian, and the lakes.

Then there is the ocean which encircles the entire earth like a sort of river and to which it seems to me that Scripture referred when it said that 'a river went out of the place of pleasure.'[5] It has a sweet potable water and supplies the seas, but because the water remains stagnant in the seas for a long time it becomes brackish. The sun and the waterspouts are constantly drawing up the less dense water and from this the clouds are formed and the rains come, the water becoming sweet by filtration.

This ocean is divided into four heads, or four rivers. The name of the first is Phison; this is the Ganges of India. The name of the second is Gehon; this is the Nile which comes down from Ethiopia into Egypt. The name of the third is Tigris, and of the fourth, Euphrates. There are also a great many other very large rivers, of which some empty into the sea, while others are absorbed into the earth. This is why the whole earth is porous and undermined, as if it had some sort of veins through which it receives water from the sea and sends it up in springs. The quality of the water of the springs corresponds with that of the earth, for, although the sea water is strained and filtered through the earth and thus is made sweet, yet, if the place from which the spring gushes

---
4 Gen. 1.9,10.
5 Gen. 2.10.

happens to be bitter or salty, the water will come up like the earth.⁶ Moreover, the water is oftentimes compressed and then bursts forth violently and becomes heated. This is the cause of the natural hot springs.

And so, by the divine command hollow places were made in the earth. Thus it was that the waters were brought together into their gathering places, and this is the cause of the mountains being made. Then God commanded the first-made water to bring forth life, because it was His intention to renew man by water and by that Holy Spirit which was borne over the waters in the beginning, which is what the divine Basil said.⁷ And it brought forth living things both small and great—whales, dragons, fish swimming in the waters, and winged fowl. Now, it is through the winged fowl that the water, earth, and air meet, for they were made from the water, they busy themselves upon the earth, and they fly in the air.⁸ Water is a most admirable element and has many uses, and it cleanses from filth, not only the bodily kind but the spiritual as well, provided the grace of the Spirit is added to it.

(The Aegean Sea empties into the Hellespont, which ends at Abydus and Sestus. Then comes the Propontis, which ends at Chalcedon and Byzantium. There the straits are which lead into the Black Sea, beyond which is Lake Maeotis. And again, at the confines of Europe and Lybia there is the Iberian Sea, which extends from the Pillars of Hercules to the Pyrenees. Then comes the Ligurian Sea, which extends as far as the limits of Etruria; then the Sardinian Sea extending from above Sardinia down toward Libya; and the Tyrrhenian Sea beginning at the limits of Liguria and ending at Sicily; then the Sea of Libya, then that of Crete, and that of Sicily, and the Ionian Sea, and the Adriatic, which flows out of the Sea of Sicily and which is called the Gulf of Corinth

---

6 Cf. Basil, *Homily 4 on the Six Days* 6 (PG 29.92C).
7 Gen. 1.2; Cf. Basil, *Homily 2 on the Six Days* 6 (PG 29.44B).
8 Cf. Basil, *Homily 8 on the Six Days* 2 (PG 29.168C-169A).

or the Alcyonian Sea. That between Sunium and Scyllaeum is the Saronic Sea. Then comes the Sea of Myrtos, and the Icarian Sea, in which are the Cyclades; then the Carpathian, the Pamphylian, and the Egyptian Seas. And beyond the Icarian Sea the Aegean extends on. The coastline of Europe from the mouth of the Tanais River[9] to the Pillars of Hercules is 69,709 stades long. That of Libya from Tingis[10] to the Canobic mouth of the Nile is 29,252 stades long. And that of Asia from Canobus to the Tanais River is 40,111 stades long, including the bays. Altogether the seaboard of our inhabited world, including the bays, is 139,072 stades long.[11])[12]

Chapter 10

Earth is one of the four elements. It is dry and cold, heavy and inert, and it was brought from nothing into being by God on the first day. For 'in the beginning,' it says, 'God created heaven and earth.'[1] What its seat and foundation is no man has been able to tell. Some say that it was set upon the waters and made fast, because the divine David says: 'Who established the earth above the waters.'[2] Others say upon the air. Still another says: 'He hangeth the earth upon nothing.'[3] And again the prophet David, speaking[4] as in the person of the Creator, says: 'I have

---

9 The Don River.
10 Tangier.
11 The figures given by Lequien and reproduced by Migne are obviously erroneous; they neither add up correctly nor do they correspond at all with the estimates of the early geographers. The figures here given seem to be those originally intended, for they both agree with the Greek, allowing for some error in the copying of the numerical accents, and with the geographical estimates of the geographers (for which, cf. Strabo). They also add correctly.
12 This appendix is not found in all manuscripts.

1 Gen. 1.1.
2 Ps. 135.6.
3 Job 26.7.
4 Ps. 74.4, 23.2.

established the pillars thereof,' calling His sustaining power pillars. However, the assertion that 'he hath founded it upon the seas' makes it plain that the substance of water was poured round the earth on every side. But, whether we hold the earth to have been set upon itself, or upon air, or upon water, or upon nothing, we must not depart from the principles of religion and we must confess that all things are sustained and held together by the power of the Creator.

In the beginning, then, as sacred Scripture says,[5] the earth was covered by the waters and was empty, that is to say, unadorned. But at God's command the receptacles for the waters were made. Then the mountains came into being and by the divine command the earth assumed its natural beauty and was adorned with every sort of verdure and plant. In these last the divine command implanted the power to grow, to absorb nourishment, and to seed, that is, to reproduce their kind. Then at the Creator's command there came forth every sort of animal: creeping things, and wild beasts, and cattle. Everything was for the suitable use of man. Of the animals, some were for food, such as deer, sheep, gazelles, and the like; some for work, such as camels, oxen, horses, asses, and the like; still others for diversion, such as monkeys and such birds as magpies, parrots, and the like. Of the plants and herbs, some were fruit-bearing and some edible, and some, such as the rose and the like, were fragrant and flowering and were given us for our enjoyment; and still others were given us for the curing of diseases. For there is no animal or plant in which the Creator has not put some virtue that is of use for the needs of man. He knew all things before they were made and He saw that man in his freedom would fall and be given over to corruption; yet for man's suitable use He made all the things that are in the sky and on the earth and in the water.

Before the fall, all things were subject to the control of man, because God had made him ruler over all the things

---

5 Gen. 1.2.

on the earth and in the water. And the serpent was on intimate terms with man, associating with him more than all the rest and conversing agreeably with him. For that reason it was through it that the Devil, who is the source of evil, made that most evil suggestion to our first parents.[6] At that time the earth brought forth of itself fruits for the use of the animals that were subject to man, and there were neither violent rains upon the earth nor wintry storms. But, after the fall, 'when he was compared to senseless beasts, and was become like to them,'[7] and when he had caused the unreasoning desire within himself to prevail over his rational intellect and had become disobedient to the commandment of the Lord, then the creation subject to him rose up against this ruler appointed by the Creator, and he was ordered to work in the sweat of his face the earth from which he had been taken.[8]

Nevertheless, the usefulness of the wild beasts is not even now past, because by exciting fear they bring man to recognize the God who made them and to call upon Him for help. Furthermore, after the fall, thorns grew out of the earth, as the Lord had declared.[9] Later, the thorn was joined to the sweetness of the rose to remind us of that fall on account of which the earth had been condemned to bring forth thorns and thistles for us.[10]

Indeed, that such is the case is credible from the fact that their continuance is being assured down to the present time by those words spoken by the Lord when He said: 'Increase and multiply and fill the earth.'[11]

Some say that the earth is spherical in form; others, that it is conical. It is lower than the heavens, and much smaller, being hung like a small point at their center. And it will

---

6 Cf. Gen. 3.1.
7 Ps. 48.13.
8 Cf. Gen. 3.19.
9 Cf. Gen. 3.18.
10 Cf. Basil, *Sermon on Paradise* 4 (*PG* 30.65A).
11 Gen. 1.28.

pass away and be changed.¹² Blessed is he who inherits the earth of the meek, for the earth which is to receive the saints is unending.¹³ Who, then, could sufficiently admire the boundless and incomprehensible wisdom of the Creator? Or who could adequately thank the Giver of good things?

(There are, furthermore, the known provinces of the earth, or satrapies, of which Europe has thirty-four, and the great continent of Asia forty-eight, and twelve canons.¹⁴)¹⁵

Chapter 11

Since God intended to fashion man after His own image and likeness from the visible and invisible creation to be a sort of king and ruler over the whole earth and the things in it, He prepared a sort of kingdom for him, in which he might dwell and lead a blessed and blissful life.¹ And this divine paradise prepared in *Eden* by the hands of God was a treasure house of every joy and pleasure. For 'Eden' is interpreted as meaning 'delight.' It was situated in the east and was higher than all the rest of the earth. It was temperate in climate and bright with the softest and purest of air. It was luxuriant with ever-blooming plants, filled with fragrance, flooded with light, and surpassing all conception of sensible fairness and beauty. In truth, it was a divine place and a worthy habitation for God in His image. And in it no brute beasts dwelt, but only man, the handiwork of God.²

---

12 Cf. Apoc. 21.1.
13 Cf. Matt. 5.4.
14 *District,* a rare use of the word *canon.* Here it probably refers to the dioceses of the Roman Empire, the principal function of which came to be the collection and transmission of the 'canon' or regular taxes.
15 This paragraph is missing in most codices.

---

1 Cf. Gregory of Nyssa, *On the Making of Man* 2 (PG 44.132-133).
2 Cf. Basil, *Sermon on Paradise* 2 (PG 30.64).

In its midst God planted a tree of life and a tree of knowledge.³ He planted the tree of knowledge as a sort of trial, test, and exercise of man's obedience and disobedience. It is either for this reason that it has been called the tree of knowledge of good and evil, or because it gave to them that partook of it the power to know their own nature—which, while it is good for the perfect, is bad for them that are less perfect and more given to their desires, as strong meat is to them that are tender and still in need of milk.⁴ For God who created us did not want us to be 'careful and troubled about many things,'⁵ nor to be anxious and concerned for our own life—which is just what happened to Adam. Thus, after he had eaten, he became aware of the fact that he was naked and put an apron around himself. For he took fig leaves and girded himself, although before they had eaten 'they were both naked, to wit, Adam and Eve, and they were not ashamed.'⁶ God wanted us to be dispassionate like that, for that is passionlessness to the highest degree. And He also wanted us to be free from care and to have but one task, that of the angels, which is unceasingly and unremittingly to sing the praises of the Creator and to rejoice in contemplating Him. He also wanted us to cast our cares upon Him, which is just what He told us through the Prophet David, saying: 'Cast thy care upon the Lord, and he shall sustain thee.'⁷ In the Gospels, too, when teaching His own disciples, He says:⁸ 'Be not solicitous for your life, what you shall eat, nor for your body, what you shall put on'; and again: 'Seek ye the kingdom of God and his justice, and all these things shall be added unto you'; and to Martha: 'Martha, Martha, thou art careful and troubled about many things: but one thing is necessary. Mary hath chosen the

---

3 Cf. Gen. 2.9.
4 Heb. 5.12; Gregory Nazianzen, *Sermon* 38.12 (*PG* 36.324BC), and *Sermon* 45.8 (*PG* 36.632-633).
5 Luke 10.41.
6 Gen. 2.25.
7 Ps. 54.23.
8 Matt. 6.25,33; Luke 10.41,42.

best part, which shall not be taken away from her,' namely, to sit at His feet and hear His words.

The tree of life was either a tree possessing a life-giving force or a tree that was to be eaten of only by such as were worthy of life and not subject to death. Some have imagined paradise to have been material, while others have imagined it to have been spiritual. However, it seems to me that, just as man was created both sensitive and intellectual, so did this most sacred domain of his have the twofold aspect of being perceptible both to the senses and to the mind. For, while in his body he dwelt in this most sacred and superbly beautiful place, as we have related, spiritually he resided in a loftier and far more beautiful place. There he had the indwelling God as a dwelling place and wore Him as a glorious garment. He was wrapped about with His grace, and, like some one of the angels, he rejoiced in the enjoyment of that one most sweet fruit which is the contemplation of God, and by this he was nourished. Now, this is indeed what is fittingly called the tree of life, for the sweetness of divine contemplation communicates a life uninterrupted by death to them that partake of it. It is just this that God meant by 'every tree' when He said: 'Of every tree of paradise thou shalt eat.'[9] For He is the all, in whom and by whom the universe endures.

The tree of knowledge of good and evil is the power of discernment by multiple vision, and this is the complete knowing of one's own nature. Of itself it manifests the magnificence of the Creator and it is good for them that are fullgrown and have walked in the contemplation of God—for them that have no fear of changing, because in the course of time they have acquired a certain habit of such contemplation. It is not good, however, for such as are still young and are more greedy in their appetites, who, because of the uncertainty of their perseverance in the true good and because of their not yet being solidly established in their

---

9 Gen. 2.16.

application to the only good, are naturally inclined to be drawn away and distracted by their solicitude for their own bodies.[10]

It is in such a way that I think that the divine paradise was of a twofold nature, and the inspired Fathers taught rightly, both those who taught the one aspect and those who taught the other. Moreover, it is possible to take 'every tree' as meaning the knowledge of the divine power which comes from the things that have been created, as the divine Apostle says: 'For the invisible things of him from the creation of the world are clearly seen, being understood by the things that are made.'[11] Of all these thoughts and considerations, the loftiest are those which concern ourselves—which concern our constitution, I mean, as the divine David says: 'Thy knowledge from myself is become wonderful,'[12] that is to say, 'from my own make-up.' In the newly made Adam, however, this was dangerous—for the reasons we have stated.

Again, the tree of life may be taken as the greater understanding of God that comes from all material things, and the process of induction leading from these to the productive and creative cause of them all. And it is just this that is called 'every tree,' the whole and undivided tree that brings the only participation in the Good. And by the tree of knowledge of good and evil may be understood that material and enjoyable food which, while seeming to be sweet, actually makes the partaker to be a partaker of evil. For God says:[13] 'Of every tree of paradise thou shalt eat,' meaning, I think: By means of all created things be thou drawn up to Me, their Creator, and from them reap the one fruit which is Myself, who am the true life; let all things be fruitful life to thee and make participation in Me to be the substance of thy own existence; for thus thou shalt be immortal.

---
10 Cf. Gregory Nazianzen, *loc. cit.*
11 Rom. 1.20.
12 Ps. 138.6 (Septuagint).
13 Gen. 2.16,17.

'But of the tree of knowledge of good and evil, thou shalt not eat. For in what day soever thou shalt eat of it, thou shall die the death.' For it is of the nature of material food to replace that which has been consumed, and it is voided into the privy and so to corruption. And it is impossible for him who partakes of material food to remain incorruptible.

Chapter 12

Thus, then, God created the intellectual substance. By that I mean angels and all the heavenly orders, for these quite plainly have an intellectual and incorporeal nature. When I say incorporeal, I mean incorporeal in comparison with the grossness of matter, for only the Divinity is really immaterial and incorporeal. Besides this, He also created the material substance, that is to say, the heavens and the earth and the things that lie between them. The former of these substances is akin to Him, for the rational nature which can only be grasped by the intellect is akin to God; while the latter, in so far as it is manifestly perceptible to the senses, is very very far removed from Him. 'But, as a mark of greater wisdom and of His munificence toward created natures, it was also necessary that a combination of both substances should be made,' as the inspired Gregory says, 'as a sort of bond between the visible and invisible natures.'[1] The phrase 'it was necessary,' I say, implies the intention of the Creator, for this intention is a most fit law and ordinance. Thus, no one will ask the molder: 'Why did you make me like this?'—for the potter has the power to make different vessels from the same lump of clay[2] in accordance with the dictates of his own wisdom.

Since this was the case, with His own hands He created *man* after His own image and likeness from the visible and

---
1 Gregory Nazianzen, *Sermon* 38.11 (*PG* 36.321D).
2 Cf. Rom. 9.21.

invisible natures. From the earth He formed his body and by His own inbreathing gave him a rational and understanding soul, which last we say is the divine image—for the 'according to His image' means the intellect and free will, while the 'according to His likeness' means such likeness in virtue as is possible.

The body and the soul were formed at the same time—not one before and the other afterwards, as the ravings of Origen would have it.

And so God made man innocent, straightforward, virtuous, free from pain, free from care, ornamented with every virtue, and adorned with all good qualities. He made him a sort of miniature world within the larger one, another adoring angel, a compound, an eye-witness of the visible creation, an initiate of the invisible creation, lord of the things of earth, lorded over from on high, earthly and heavenly, passing and immortal, visible and spiritual, halfway between greatness and lowliness, at once spirit and flesh—spirit by grace and flesh by pride, the first that he might endure and give glory to his Benefactor, and the second that he might suffer and by suffering be reminded and instructed not to glory in his greatness. He made him a living being to be governed here according to this present life, and then to be removed elsewhere, that is, to the world to come, and so to complete the mystery by becoming divine through reversion to God—this, however, not by being transformed into the divine substance, but by participation in the divine illumination.[3]

He moreover made him sinless and endowed with freedom of will. By being sinless I do not mean being incapable of sinning, for only the Divinity is incapable of sinning, but having the tendency to sin not in his nature but, rather, in his power of choice—that is to say, having the power to persevere and progress in good with the help of divine grace, as well as having the power to turn from virtue and fall into vice, God

---

3 Cf. Gregory Nazianzen, *op. cit.* 11 (*PG* 36.324A).

permitting because of the freedom of the will. For, that which is done by force is not an act of virtue.

Now, a soul is a living substance, simple and incorporeal, of its own nature invisible to bodily eyes, activating an organic body in which it is able to cause life, growth, sensation, and reproduction. It does not have the mind as something distinct from itself, but as its purest part, for, as the eye is to the body, so is the mind to the soul. It is free, endowed with will and the power to act, and subject to change, that is, subject to change of will, because it is also created. And this it has received according to nature, through that grace of the Creator by which it has also received both its existence and its being naturally as it is.

[*In how many ways a thing may be said to be incorporeal.*[4]]

Things that are incorporeal, invisible and without shape we conceive of in two ways. Some are so by essense and some by grace; some are so by nature and some by comparison with the grossness of matter. Thus, God is said to be incorporeal by nature, but the angels, evil spirits, and souls are said to be so by grace and by comparison with the grossness of matter.

A body is three-dimensional, that is, having height, breadth, and depth or thickness. Every body is composed of the four elements, but the bodies of living things are composed of the four humors.

One should note that the four elements are: earth, which is dry and cold; water, which is cold and wet; air, which is wet and warm; and fire, which is warm and dry. Likewise, there are also four humors corresponding to the four elements: black bile, which corresponds to the earth, because it is dry and cold; phlegm, which corresponds to the water, because it is cold and wet; blood, which corresponds to the air, because it is wet and warm; yellow bile, which corresponds

---

4 A marginal addition.

to fire, because it is warm and dry. Now, while fruits are made from the elements, the humors are made from the fruits, and the bodies of living things are made from the humors and are reducible to the elements, for every compound is reducible to them.

[*That man has something in common with the inanimate, the irrational, and the rational beings.*[5]]

One should note that man has something in common with inanimate things, that he shares life with the rational living beings, and that he shares understanding with the rational. In common with inanimate things, he has his body and its composition from the four elements. In common with the plants, he has these same things plus the power of assimilating nourishment, of growing and of semination of generation. In common with the brute beasts, he has all these plus appetite—that is to say, anger and desire—sensation, and spontaneous movement.

Now, the senses are five; namely, sight, hearing, smell, taste, and touch. Belonging to spontaneous movement are the power of moving from place to place, that of moving the entire body, and that of speech and breathing—for in us we have the power either to do these things or not to do them.

Through his power of reason man is akin to the incorporeal and intellectual natures, reasoning, thinking, judging each thing, and pursuing the virtues, particularly the acme of the virtues which is religion. For this reason, man is also a microcosm.

One should note that section, flux, and change are proper to the body alone.[6] *Change* is that which is in quality, such as being heated, cooled, and so forth. *Flux* is an emptying out, for solids, liquids, and the breath are voided and then

---
5 *Ibid.*
6 Cf. Nemesius, *On the Nature of Man* 1 (PG 40.516C).

need to be replaced. Consequently, hunger and thirst are natural sensations. *Section* is the separation of the humors from one another and the division into matter and form.

Proper to the soul are religion and understanding. Although the virtues are referred to the soul, yet, in so far as the soul utilizes the body, they are common to both.

One should note that the rational part of the soul governs the irrational part. Indeed, the faculties of the soul are divided into those belonging to its rational part and those belonging to its irrational part. There are two groups belonging to the irrational part, of which one is deaf to reason, that is to say, does not obey the reason, whereas the other listens to the reason and complies with it. Now, deaf and disobedient to reason are the vital principle, which is also called pulsating, the seminal or generative principle, and the vegetable principle, which is also called nutritive and to which also belongs the principle of growth that builds up the body. For these are governed not by reason but by nature. The group listening to reason and complying with it is divided into anger and desire. Moreover, the irrational part of the soul is commonly called emotional and appetitive. And one should know that the faculty of spontaneous movement is one of those which are obedient to reason.

To those which are not obedient to reason belong the nutritive, the generative, and the pulsating principles. The growing, nutritive, and generative principles are called vegetable; the pulsating is called vital.

The nutritive principle has four faculties: the attractive, which attracts the food; the retentive, which retains the food and does not permit it to be excreted immediately; the transformative, which changes the food into the humors; and the excretive, which separates the superfluity and expels it through the rectum.[7]

One should note that some of the faculties in the living being are animal, some vegetable, and some vital. The

---

7 Cf. *ibid.* 23 (*PG* 40.693A).

animal faculties are those which depends upon choice; namely, spontaneous movement and sense. To spontaneous movement belong moving from place to place, moving the entire body, speaking, and breathing, for it is in our power either to do them or not. Vegetable and vital faculties are those which do not depend upon choice. The nutritive, growing, and generative faculties are vegetable, while the pulsating faculty is vital. These all operate regardless of whether we want them to or not.

Furthermore, one must note that some things are good and others evil. Now, when a good thing is expected, it gives rise to desire, but when it is present it causes pleasure. Similarly, when a bad thing is expected, it gives rise to fear, but when it is present it causes pain. One must also understand that, when we say 'good' here, we mean both that which is really good and that which is apparently so, and similarly, when we say 'bad.'

Chapter 13

Some *pleasures*[1] are of the soul, while others are of the body. Of the soul are all those which belong to the soul alone as distinct from the body, such as those coming from learning and contemplation. Bodily pleasures are those which are shared by the soul and the body. For this reason, all those coming from eating, sexual intercourse, and the like, are called bodily. However, one would not find any pleasures belonging to the body alone.

Again, some pleasures are true, whereas others are false. Some pleasures, also, which come from knowledge and contemplation, are purely intellectual; others, arising from sensation, are shared by the body. Of the pleasures shared by the body, some are both natural and necessary. Without these it would be impossible to live; such are food eaten to supply a deficiency, and necessary clothes. Still others are natural

---

[1] Cf. *ibid.* 18 (*PG* 40.677ff.).

but not necessary, such as natural and legitimate sexual relations. For, although these last do assure the permanency of the entire race, it is nevertheless possible to live in virginity without them. Still others are neither necessary nor natural, such as intoxicating liquors, lewdness, and surfeits that exceed our needs. These do nothing for the maintenance of our life or for perpetuation of the race; on the contrary, they do harm. Hence, he who lives according to God must seek those pleasures which are both necessary and natural, while those which are natural but not necessary he must relegate to second place and only indulge in them as permitted by the suitability of time, manner, and moderation. The others, however, must be absolutely rejected.

Such pleasures may be considered to be good as do not involve pain, cause remorse, do any damage, exceed the limits of moderation, distract us for long from good works, or enslave us.

Chapter 14

There are four kinds of *pain*;[1] namely, grief, distress, envy, and compassion. *Grief* is a pain which makes one speechless; *distress* is one which oppresses; envy is one arising from another's good fortune; and *compassion* is one arising from another's misfortune.

Chapter 15

Fear[1] also has its divisions, which are six; namely, apprehension, diffidence, shame, terror, consternation, and anxiety. *Apprehension* is fear of something which is going to happen. *Diffidence* is a fear due to an expected reproach, and this is an excellent affection. *Shame* is a fear due to the perpetra-

---

1 Cf. *ibid.* 19 (PG 40.688).

1 Cf. *ibid.* 20 (PG 40.688ff.).

tion of a shameful act, nor is this beyond hope of salvation. *Terror* is a fear arising from a strong mental impression. *Consternation* is a fear arising from an unaccustomed mental impression. *Anxiety* is a fear of failure, that is to say, of misfortune—for when we are afraid that our undertaking will turn out badly, we are anxious.

Chapter 16

Anger[1] is a seething of the blood about the heart caused by the fuming up or thickening of the bile. For this reason, it is also called bile or spleen. There is also a kind of anger which is a desire for revenge, for when we are wronged or think that we have been wronged, we are pained and there arises in us that combined feeling of desire and anger.

There are three kinds of anger; namely, wrath (which is called bile and spleen), rancor, and vindictiveness. When anger arises and starts to move, it is called *wrath, bile,* and *spleen. Rancor* is an enduring wrath, or bearing malice. It is called μῆνις from its μένειν, or remaining, and being impressed upon the memory. *Vindictiveness* is wrath on the watch for an opportunity for revenge. It is called κότος from κεῖσθαι, or being laid down.

Anger is the spearman of the reason and the avenger of desire. Thus, when we desire a thing and are thwarted by someone, our reason decides that for such as would maintain their own natural position this occurrence is worthy of vexation, and we get angry at him over our having been wronged.

Chapter 17

The *imagination*[1] is the faculty belonging to the irrational part of the soul. It acts through the sense organs and is

---
1 Cf. *ibid.* 21 (*PG* 40.692).

1 Cf. *ibid.* 6 (*PG* 40.632-633).

called a sensation. Moreover, that which comes within the province of the imagination and the senses is the imaginative and the sensible, just as the visible—say, a stone or something of the sort—comes within the province of sight, which is the power of vision. An *imagination,* or fantasy, is an affection of the irrational part of the soul arising from some imagineable object. But an *imagining,* or phantasm, is an empty affection arising in the irrational parts of the soul from no imagineable object at all. The organ of the imagination is the anterior ventricle of the brain.

Chapter 18

Sense is a faculty of the soul by which material things are perceived, or distinguished. The sense organs are the organs or members by means of which we perceive. *Sensible* things are those which come within the province of the senses. The animal endowed with sense is *sensitive.* There are five senses and, likewise, five sense organs.

The first sense is that of *sight.*[1] The sense organs or media of sight are the nerves leading from the brain and the eyes. Fundamentally, it is the visual impression of color that is received, but along with the color the sight distinguishes the colored body, also: its size and shape, the place where it is and the intervening distance, its number, its motion or motionlessness, its roughness or smoothness, its evenness or unevenness, sharpness or bluntness, and whether it has the consistency of water or that of earth; in other words, whether it is liquid or solid.

The second sense is that of *hearing.*[2] This is capable of discerning voices and sounds, of which it distinguishes the high or low pitch, the degree of smoothness, and the volume. Its organs are the soft nerves leading from the brain and the

---
1 Cf. *ibid.* 7 (*PG* 40.637ff.).
2 Cf. *ibid.* 10 (*PG* 40.657).

apparatus of the ears. Moreover, only man and the monkey do not move their ears.

The third sense is that of *smell*,[3] which originates with the nose sending the odors up to the brain and is terminated at the extremities of the anterior ventricles of the brain. The sense of smell is capable of discerning and perceiving odors. The most general division of odors is into sweet-smelling and foul-smelling and that which stands midway between these and is neither the one nor the other. Thus, a sweet smell arises when the juices in bodies have been cooked to a nicety. When they have been cooked middling well, the result is middling. But when they have been very poorly or incompletely cooked, then there is a foul smell.

The fourth sense is that of *taste*.[4] This sense is capable of perceiving or discerning flavors. Its organs are the tongue—especially its tip—and the palate, which some call the roof [of the mouth]. The nerves leading from the brain have been broadened out in these and report back to the authoritative part of the soul the impression or sensation received. The so-called taste qualities or flavors are as follows: sweetness, bitterness, acidity, sourness, tartness, pungency, saltiness, greasiness, and stickiness. For it is these that the sense of taste can distinguish. Water, however, in so far as these qualities are concerned, is tasteless, because it has none of them. Sourness is an intense and excessive tartness.

The fifth sense is that of *touch*,[5] which is common to all animals. It comes from the nerves leading out from the brain into the entire body, for which reason both the entire body and the other sense organs, too, possess the sense of touch. Subject to touch are heat and cold, softness and hardness, stickiness and friability, and heaviness and lightness, because these things are recognized only by the sense of touch. Common to both the sense of touch and that of sight

---

3 Cf. *ibid.* 11 (*PG* 40.657-658).
4 Cf. *ibid.* 9 (*PG* 40.656-657).
5 Cf. *ibid.* 8 (*PG* 40.649ff.).

are: roughness and smoothness; dryness and wetness; thickness and thinness; up and down; place; size, whenever it is such as can be determined with one application of the sense of touch; compactness and looseness, or density; roundness, if on a small scale, and various other shapes. Similarly, with the aid of the memory and the understanding, it can also perceive the approach of a body, as well as number, too, up to two or three, provided the objects be small and easily grasped. Sight, however, is more perceptive of these than is touch.

One should note that the Creator constructed each one of the sense organs in pairs,[6] so that, should one be harmed, the other might fulfill the function. Thus, there are two eyes, two ears, two nostrils, and two tongues. These last, however, while they are separate in some animals, such as snakes, in others, such as man, are joined together. On the other hand, the sense of touch is in the entire body, with the exception of the bones, nerves, nails and horns, hair, sinews, and certain other parts of the same sort.

One should note that sight sees along straight lines, but that smell and hearing get their impressions not only along straight lines, but from all directions. Touch and taste, however, get their impressions neither along straight lines nor along any line, but only when their proper organs are in contact with their objects.

Chapter 19

To the *thinking faculty*[1] belong judgments, assents, inclinations and disinclinations to act, and avoidances of action. In particular, concepts of intellectual things, the virtues and sciences, the principles of the arts, and the deliberative and

---

6 Cf. *ibid.* (*PG* 40.649A).

1 Cf. *ibid.* 12 (*PG* 40.660).

elective powers belong to the thinking faculty. It is also this faculty which foretells the future to us through dreams, which the Pythagoreans, following in the steps of the Hebrews, claim to be the only true divination. The organ of this faculty is the middle ventricle of the brain and the vital spirit residing therein.

Chapter 20

The faculty of *memory*[1] is both the cause and the repository of memory and recollection. Memory is an image which has been left behind by some sensory or mental impression that has actually been received. In other words, it is the retention of sensation and thought. Thus, on the one hand, the soul apprehends or senses sensible objects through the organs of sense, and a mental impression is formed; on the other hand, it apprehends intellectual objects through the mind and a conjecture is formed. Hence, when it retains the forms of things of which it has received impressions, or of things of which it has thought, then it is said to remember.

One must note that the apprehension of intellectual things comes only through learning, or the natural process of thinking. It does not come from sensation, because sensible things are remembered in themselves, whereas intellectual things we do remember, provided we have learned something of them, but of their substance we have no memory.

Recollection is the recovery of memory that has been lost by forgetting, and forgetting is the loss of memory. When the imaginative faculty has apprehended material things by means of the senses, it communicates [the impression] to the thinking faculty, or reasoning faculty—for both of these are the same thing. When this faculty has received the impression and formed a judgment of it, it passes it on to the faculty of memory. The organ of the faculty of memory is the posterior ventricle of the brain, which is also called the cerebellum, and the vital spirit residing therein.

---

1 Cf. *ibid.* 13 (*PG* 40.660ff.).

Chapter 21

The speaking (or rational) part of the soul is again divided into *mental and spoken speech*.[1] Mental speech is a movement of the soul made in its reasoning faculty without any vocal expression. Thus, we oftentimes go silently through an entire discourse in detail, and we converse in our dreams. In this respect we are all speaking (or rational) in the most proper sense. For, certainly, those who have been born dumb or who have lost their voice through some illness or accident are by no means less rational. Spoken speech acts through the voice and language, that is to say, it is the speech which is spoken by means of the tongue and mouth. For this reason it is said to be spoken. It is, moreover, the messenger of thought. In respect to this faculty we are also said to be talking.

Chapter 22

The term *passion* is equivocal, because, while it may refer to the body, as in the case of sickness and sores, it may also refer to the soul, as with desire or anger. In its common and general sense, however, it means an animal passion such as is followed by pleasure or pain. Now, pain does follow passion, but pain is not the passion itself, because insensible things, when they suffer, do not feel pain. Thus, then, pain is not passion but the feeling of passion. This passion, moreover, must be considerable, that is to say, so intense as to come within the province of sensation.

The definition of the passions of the soul is as follows: passion is a movement of the appetitive faculty which is felt as a result of a sensory impression of good or evil.[1] It may also be defined in another way: passion is an irrational move-

---
1 Cf. *ibid.* 14 (*PG* 40.665ff.).

---
1 Cf. *ibid.* 16 (*PG* 40.673B).

ment of the soul due to an impression of good or evil. Thus, the impression of good arouses the desire, whereas that of evil arouses the anger. Passion in the general or common sense is defined thus: passion is a movement in one thing caused by another. But *action* is an active movement, that being called *active* which moves of itself. Hence, when one is driven violently into action by anger, this anger is, on the one hand, an action of the irascible part of the soul; on the other, it is a *passion* of both parts, and of the entire body as well. For [in this last case] the movement in one thing has been caused by another, which is precisely what is called passion.

In still another way, action is called passion. For, while action is a movement according to nature, passion is a movement against nature. So, for this reason, action is called passion when one is not moved according to nature, whether by himself or by another. Thus, the pulsating movement of the heart is action, because it is natural; but its palpitating movement, because it is immoderate and not according to nature, is passion and not action.

Not every movement of the passible part of the soul is called a passion, but only the more violent ones which come within the range of sensation, because the little imperceptible ones are not passions at all. The passion must also have a considerable intensity. Consequently, a perceptible movement comes under the definition of passion, but the little movements which elude sensation do not make for passion.

One should note that our soul possesses two kinds of faculties: the *cognitive* and the *vital*. The cognitive faculties are mind, thought, opinion, imagination, and sensation. Will and choice, on the other hand, are vital, or appetitive, faculties. To make what has just been said more clear, let us discuss these things in detail. First of all, let us speak about the cognitive faculties.

Imagination and sensation have already been sufficiently discussed in what has been said before. Thus, through *sensa-*

tion a passion is caused in the soul and this is called *imagination*. From imagination there arises an *opinion*. Then, when the thinking faculty has examined the opinion as to whether it is true or false, it decides what is true. For this reason, this faculty is called *thought* from its thinking and discerning. That which has been judged and set down as true is called *mind*.

Or, to put it in another way—one should note that the first movement of the mind is called *intelligence*. Intelligence being excercised about something is called *thinking*. When this has continued a while and has impressed the soul with the thing thought about, it is called *consideration*. And when the consideration has continued in the same subject and has thoroughly examined itself and interrogated the soul in regard to the thing thought about, then it is called *prudence* [or practical wisdom]. Then prudence extends on and produces *reasoning*, which is termed mental speech, and which they define as a most complete movement of the soul arising in its reasoning part without any vocal expression. It is from this that they say that the spoken word expressed by the tongue proceeds. And so, now that we have spoken about the cognitive faculties, let us speak of the vital, or appetitive faculties.

One should note that in the soul there is an innate force appetitive of what is natural to the soul and embracing all those things which pertain to its nature essentially. This is called *will* (θέλησις). The substance [of the soul] tends to exist and live, to think and feel; and it desires its own natural and complete actuality. This is why the natural will is defined as follows: Will is a rational and vital appetite attached solely to natural things.[2] Hence, the will is the same natural, vital, and rational appetite for everything that goes to make up the nature; it is a simple faculty. The appetite of brute animals is not called a will, because it is not rational.

Wishing (βούλησις) is a sort of natural willing, that is

---

2 Cf. Maximus, *Opuscula theologica ad Marinum* (PG 91.12C).

to say, a natural and rational appetite for some thing. For, inherent in the human soul, there is a faculty for rationally desiring. And so, when this rational appetite is moved toward some thing, it is called volition, for wishing is a rational appetition and desiring for something.

We speak of wishing both in respect to things which are in our power and in respect to things which are not; in other words, in respect to possible and impossible things. Thus, oftentimes we may wish to fornicate, or to excercise self-control, or to sleep, or some other such thing. These things are in our power and are possible. On the other hand, we may also wish to be a king, and that is not in our power. Then, possibly, we may wish never to die, and that is an impossible thing.

Wishing concerns the end, and not the means to the end. Now, the end is the thing desired, such as to be king or to enjoy good health, whereas the means to the end is the thing deliberated, or the way in which we may become healthy or get to be king.[3] Immediately after wishing come inquiry and consideration. Then, after these, provided the thing is within our power, comes deliberation, or counsel. *Deliberation* is an inquisitive appetite arising in respect to such things which are to be done as are in our power. Thus, one deliberates as to whether or not he should pursue the object. Then he decides which is the better course, and this is called *judgment*. Then he becomes disposed to the thing decided as a result of the deliberation and prefers it, and this is called *opinion*. For, should one judge and not become disposed to the thing judged, that is to say, not prefer it, then it is not called opinion. Then, after this disposition, there comes *choice* or selection. Choice is the choosing and picking out of this one rather than the other of two things proposed. Then one moves to act, and this is called *impulse*. Then one enjoys, and this is called *use*. Then, after the use, the appetite ceases.

---

3 Cf. *ibid.* (*PG* 91.13C-16A).

Now, in the case of the brute animals, when an appetite for something arises it is immediately followed by an impulse to act. This is because the appetite of brute animals is irrational and because they are led by their natural appetite. For this reason the appetite of brute animals is said to be neither a will nor a volition. Will is a rational and free natural appetite and with men, who are rational, the natural appetite is led rather than leads. Thus, man is moved freely with the aid of reason, since in him the cognitive and vital faculties are joined together. Hence, he freely desires and freely wills, freely lives and inquires, freely deliberates, freely judges, freely disposes himself, freely chooses, freely moves to act, and freely acts in respect to those things which are in accord with his nature.

One should note that, while we speak of wishing in God, in the strict sense we do not speak of choice. For God does not deliberate, because deliberation is due to ignorance. No one deliberates about what he knows. But, if deliberation is due to ignorance, then choice, too, is most certainly so. Hence, since God knows all things absolutely, He does not deliberate.

Neither do we speak of deliberation or choice in the soul of the Lord, because He did not suffer from ignorance.[4] Even though He did have such a nature as was ignorant of future events, nevertheless, in so far as this nature was hypostatically united to God the Word, it did have knowledge of all things—not by grace, but, as has been said, by virtue of the hypostatic union. Thus, He was Himself both God and man, and therefore did not have a will based upon opinion. He did have a will that was natural and simple and such as is to be found in all human persons, but His sacred soul held no opinion, that is to say, willed nothing contrary to His divine will, nor did it have a will in opposition to His divine will. Now, opinion varies with the persons except in the case of the sacred, simple, uncompounded, and undivided

---

4 Cf. Maximus, *Disputatio cum Pyrrho* (*PG* 91.308-309).

Godhead. For, since the Persons there are by no means divided and set at variance, neither is the object of their will divided. And since there is but one nature there, there is, likewise, only one natural will. Moreover, since, again, the Persons are not at variance, there is one thing willed and one movement of the three Persons. But with men, while there is one nature and, consequently, one natural will, yet, since the persons are separate and varying from one another in time and place, in their disposition toward things, and in very many other ways, for this reason their wills and opinions differ. Now, since in the case of our Lord Jesus Christ the natures are different, so also are the natural wills of His divinity and humanity different, that is to say, the willing faculties. Since, however, there is but one Person and but one who wills, then the thing willed, or the will based on opinion, must also be one—with His human will, of course, following His divine will and willing those things which the divine will has willed it to will.

One should note that will is one thing and wishing another, and that the thing willed is one thing, the principle willing another, and the one willing still another. Whereas will is the simple faculty itself of willing, wishing is the will in regard to something, and the thing willed is the object of the will, or that which we will. For instance, the appetite tends to food. In this case, the simple acting appetite is a rational will, while the willing principle is that which possesses the faculty of willing, such as a man, and the one willing is he who uses the will.

One must bear in mind that when will means the will, or willing faculty, it is said to be a natural will; but that when it means the thing willed, then it is said to be will based on opinion.

Chapter 23

One should note that all the faculties heretofore discussed are called *acts*, whether they be the cognitive, the vital, the natural, or the technical. Act is the natural force and movement of any substance. Again, *natural act* is the innate movement of every substance. Whence it is clear that those things that have the same substance have also the same act, whereas those that have different natures have different acts. For it is inconceivable that a substance should be devoid of natural act.[1]

Again, that force which is indicative of any substance is natural act. Still again, the first ever-moving force of the intellectual soul, that is to say, the ever-moving reason perpetually springing naturally from it, is natural act. Still again, the force and movement of any substance, which only non-being does not have, is natural act.

Moreover, such actions as talking, walking, eating, drinking, and the like are also called acts. And the natural passions, too, such as hunger, thirst, and the like are frequently called acts. And, finally, the actuation of potency is called act.

There are, moreover, two ways in which a thing is said to be: in potency and in act. Thus, we say that a suckling child is potentially lettered, because it has the capacity to become so through instruction. Again, we say that a lettered person is both potentially and actually so. He is actually so, because he has the knowledge of letters; but he is potentially so, if, although he can expound, he actually is not doing so. Again, we say that he is lettered actually when he is acting, that is to say, expounding. Consequently, one should note that this second way of being is common to both potency and act, but that the second belongs rather to potency, whereas the first belongs to act.

A first, only, and true natural act is that independent, or

---

[1] Cf. Gregory of Nyssa, *The Guide* (PG 89.65B); Maximus, *Disputatio cum Pyrrho* (PG 91.337A).

rational, and free life which constitutes our species. When some people deprive our Lord of this, I do not understand how they say that He who is God became man.

Act is an active movement of nature. And that is called active which is moved of itself.

Chapter 24

Since it is in some action that the *voluntary* consists,[1] and also in some action that the involuntary in the commonly accepted sense of the term consists, there are many who put the involuntary in the absolute sense not only under passion but also under action. However, one must bear in mind that an action is a rational act. Actions incur praise or blame. The performance of some is accompanied by pleasure; of others, by pain. Some of them are desirable to the doer, whereas others are distasteful. Moreover, some of those which are desirable are always so, whereas others are so only at certain times. And it is the same with those which are distasteful. Then again, some actions are worthy of mercy and forgiveness, while others are detestable and to be punished. Therefore, concomitant with the absolutely voluntary are praise or blame, its performance with pleasure, and the fact that the actions are desirable to them that perform them, whether at all times or only at the particular time when they are performed. On the other hand, concomitant with the involuntary are the facts of the actions being worthy of forgiveness or mercy, or their being performed with pain, and of their not being desirable to the doer, whether because of his not doing them of his own accord or because of his being forced.

Now, the *involuntary*[2] is due either to compulsion or to

---
1 Cf. Nemesius, *op. cit.* 29 (*PG* 40.717-718).
2 Cf. *ibid.* 30 (*PG* 40.720ff.).

ignorance. It is due to compulsion when the efficient principle, or cause, is extrinsic—in other words, when we are compelled by another without our full agreement, without the concurrence of our own impulse, and without our co-operating or doing of our own accord the thing that we have been compelled to do. In defining it we say that that is involuntary of which the principle is extrinsic and in which the one compelled does not concur with his own impulse. By *principle* we mean the efficient cause. On the other hand, the involuntary is due to ignorance when we ourselves do not furnish the cause of the ignorance, and the thing just happens by chance. Thus, should someone commit murder while drunk, he would be doing it unwittingly, but certainly not involuntarily, because he himself has supplied the cause of the ignorance, that is to say, the drunkenness. If, however, someone has been shooting arrows in an accustomed place and has killed his father who had chanced by, he is said to have done this involuntarily through ignorance.[3]

And so, since there are two kinds of involuntary, that due to compulsion and that due to ignorance, the voluntary is opposed to both.[4] Thus, that is voluntary which is brought about by neither compulsion nor ignorance. Now, that is voluntary of which the principle, or cause, is in the doer himself as thoroughly understanding all the circumstances because of which and under which the action was performed. *Circumstances* are what the grammarians call 'circumstantial parts of speech.' For example: we have *who*, or the person who acted; *whom*, or the person acted upon; *what*, or the very thing that was done, as, for example, murder; *with what*, or the instrument; *where*, or in what place; *when*, or at what time; *how*, or the manner of action; and *because of what*, or for what cause.

It should be borne in mind that there are some things which come between what is voluntary and what is involuntary

---

3 Cf. *ibid.* 31 (*PG* 40.724-725).
4 Cf. *ibid.* 32 (*PG* 40.728).

and which, although they may be unpleasant and painful, we permit in order to avoid a greater evil—as, for example, when we jettison a ship's cargo to avoid shipwreck.[5]

It should be borne in mind that, while children and brute beasts act voluntarily, they certainly do not do so through deliberate choice, and that all that we do in anger without previous consideration we do voluntarily, but certainly not through deliberate choice. Likewise, when a friend drops in on us unexpectedly, we accept his visit voluntarily but certainly not through deliberate choice. In the same way, one who has unexpectedly happened upon a treasure has indeed happened upon it willingly, but certainly not through deliberate choice. All these things are indeed voluntary because of the pleasure connected with them, but certainly not because of their having been chosen deliberately, since they did not happen as a result of deliberation. Choice must definitely be preceded by deliberation, as has been said.

Chapter 25

In treating of *free will*,[1] that is to say, of what depends upon us, the first consideration is as to whether there is anything that does depend upon us, because there are a number of people who deny it. A second consideration is as to what things depend upon us and over what things we do have control. A third consideration is how to explain the reason for which the God who made us made us free. And so, let us take up the first question and at the very outset prove from things accepted as true by our adversaries that there are some things that depend upon us. And let us proceed as follows.

They say that everything that happens is caused either by

---

5 Cf. *ibid.* 30 (*PG* 40.720B).

1 Cf. *ibid.* 39 (*PG* 40.761ff.).

God, or necessity, or fate, or nature, or chance, or spontaneity. But essence and providence are the work of God, while the movement of things which are always the same belongs to necessity. And to fate belongs the necessary fulfillment of what it has decreed, for fate also implies necessity. Generation, growth, corruption, plants, and animals belong to nature. The unusual and unexpected belong to chance. For chance is defined as the accidental concurrence of two causes originating in deliberate choice but resulting in something other than was intended, as in the case of someone digging a grave and finding a treasure. In this case, the one who put the treasure there did not do so in order that it might be found by another, and neither did the one who found it dig for the purpose of finding a treasure. On the contrary, the first put it there in order that he might get it whenever he should so choose, whereas the second dug in order to make a grave; but something else resulted, quite different from what was intended by either. Finally, to spontaneity belongs what befalls inanimate things or brute beasts without the intervention of nature or art. All this they themselves maintain. Now, if man is not an effective principle of action, to which of these causes are we to attribute human actions? It is definitely wrong ever to ascribe immoral and unjust actions to God; neither can they be ascribed to necessity, for they are not the actions of things which are always the same; nor can they be ascribed to fate, for they declare that the things decreed by fate are not contingent but necessary; nor to nature, for the works of nature are animals and plants; nor to chance, for human actions are not unusual and unexpected; nor yet to spontaneity, for they say that that is spontaneous which befalls inanimate things or brute beasts. Indeed, nothing remains but the fact that man himself as acting and doing is the principle of his own works and is free.

What is more, if man is not a principle of action, then his power of deliberation is superfluous, for to what use would he put his deliberation if he were not master of any action at all? All deliberation is on account of action, and it would furthermore be absurd were the most excellent and noble of the faculties in man to prove useless. Besides, when a man deliberates, he does so on account of action, because all deliberation is on account of and for the sake of action.

Chapter 26

Some *things done*[1] depend upon us, while others do not. Those things depend upon us which we are free either to do or not to do, that is to say, everything which we do voluntarily —for a thing would not be said to be done voluntarily if the action did not depend upon us. To put it simply: those things depend upon us which incur blame or praise and in respect to which one may be urged or bound by law. Properly speaking, all those things depend upon us which pertain to the soul and about which we deliberate. And it is about contingents that deliberation is exercised. A *contingent* is that which we can do itself, and of which we can also do the opposite. Our mind makes this choice of itself, and this is the beginning of action. Those things, then, depend upon us which are contingent—as, for example, to move or not to move, to start or not to start, to desire things that are not absolutely necessary or not to desire them, to lie or not to lie, to give or not to give, to rejoice when one should and, similarly, not to when one should not, and all such things as imply virtue or vice—for in these things we are free. The arts also belong to the number of the contingents, because it is in our power to cultivate them, if we so wish, or not to cultivate them.

One should note that the choice of things to be done always rests with us, but that their doing is oftentimes prevented by some disposition of Divine Providence.[2]

---

1 Cf. *ibid.* 40 *(PG* 40.765ff.).
2 Cf. *ibid.* 37 *(PG* 40.749ff.).

Chapter 27

We maintain, then, that the freedom of the will is directly connected with the reason.[1] We also maintain that transformation and change are inherent in created beings. For everything that is created is also changeable, because whatever has originated in a change must needs be subject to change. Being brought from non-being to being is change, and so is being made into something else from an existing material. Now, inanimate things and brute beasts are changed by the corporeal alterations which have already been spoken of, whereas rational beings are changed by deliberate choice. This last is because of the fact that to the reason belong both the contemplative and active faculties. The contemplative faculty is that which examines the state of things, whereas the active faculty is the power of deliberation which applies right reason to such things as may be done. The contemplative faculty is also called *mind*, and the active faculty *reason*. Still again, the contemplative faculty is called *wisdom,* and the active faculty *prudence*. Thus, everyone who deliberates, as having in himself the power to choose such things as may be done, deliberates so that he may choose what has been selected through deliberation, and so that, having chosen it, he may act. But, if this is so, then freedom of will is necessarily connected by nature with the reason. Thus, a being may be irrational or rational; but, if it is rational, it will be the master of its actions and free. Whence it follows that the irrational beings are not free, since, instead of leading nature, they are led by it. And so it is that they do not deny their natural appetite, but, just as soon as they feel an appetite for something, they move to act. Man, however, since he is rational, leads his nature rather than is led by it. And so, when he feels an appetite, he has the power to resist it, should he so wish, or to obey it. This is why irrational beings are neither

---
[1] Cf. *ibid.* 41 (*PG* 40.773ff.).

to be praised nor blamed, while man is to be praised or blamed.

One should note that, since the angels are rational, they are free, and that, since they are created, they are subject to change. And a proof of this is the Devil, who, although he had been created good by the Creator, of his own free will became the discoverer of evil; and so also are the powers that rebelled with him, that is to say, the evil spirits, while the rest of the angelic orders persevered in the good.

Chapter 28

Some of those things which do not depend upon us have their origin, or cause, in things which do depend upon us. Such are the recompenses for our deeds, which we receive both in the present world and in that to come. All the rest, however, depend upon the divine will. The creation of all things is due to God, but corruption came in afterwards due to our own wickedness and as a punishment and a help. 'For God made not death: neither hath he pleasure in the destruction of the living';[1] rather, it was through man, that is to say, Adam's transgression, that death came with the other punishments. All the rest, however, are to be attributed to God. Thus, our creation is due to His creative power, our permanence to His providential power, and to His goodness the eternal enjoyment of the good things reserved for them that keep the law of nature—for which reason we were made. However, since there are some who deny His providence, let us go on to say a few things about providence.

---
[1] Wisd. 1.13.

Chapter 29

Providence, then, is the solicitude which God has for existing things. And again, providence is that will of God by which all existing things receive suitable guidance through to their end.[1] But, if providence is God's will, then, according to right reason, everything that has come about through providence has quite necessarily come about in the best manner and that most befitting God, so that it could not have happened in a better way. Now, the Maker of existing things must be the same as their Provider, for it is neither fitting nor logical that one should be their creator and another their provider, because in such a case they would both be definitely wanting—the one in the matter of creating and the other in that of providing.[2] Hence, God is both Creator and Provider, and is power of creating, sustaining, and providing is His good will. For 'whatsoever the Lord pleased he hath done, in heaven, and in earth,'[3] and none resisted His will.[4] He willed all things to be made and they were made; He wills the world to endure and it does endure; and all things whatsoever He wills are done.

Moreover, that He provides and provides well anyone might most correctly learn from the following consideration. God alone is by nature good and wise. Consequently, in so far as He is good He provides, because one who does not provide is not good. Even men and brute beasts naturally provide for their own offspring, and the one that does not will incur blame. Then, in so far as He is wise He provides for existing things in the very best way.[5]

And so, bearing these things in mind we should admire, praise, and unconditionally accept all the works of providence. And should these appear to a number of people to be unjust,

---

1 Cf. Nemesius, *op. cit.* 43 (*PG* 40.792-793).
2 Cf. *ibid.* 42 (*PG* 40.788-789).
3 Ps. 134.6.
4 Cf. Rom. 9.19.
5 Cf. Nemesius, *op. cit.* 44 (*PG* 40.813).

it is because of the fact that God's providence is beyond knowledge and beyond comprehension, and because to Him alone are our thoughts and actions and the events of the future known. However, when I say 'all,' I am referring to those things which do not depend upon us, because those which do depend upon us do not belong to providence, but to our own free will.

Some of the things that are due to providence are by approval, whereas others are by permission. All those that are undeniably good are by approval, whereas of those that are by permission [there are many kinds].[6] Thus, He often permits even the just man to meet with misfortunes so that the virtue hidden in him may be made known to others, as in the case of Job.[7] At other times, He permits something iniquitous to be done so that through this apparently iniquitous action some great and excellent thing may be brought about, as was the salvation of men by the Cross. In still another way, He permits the devout man to suffer evil either so that he may not depart from his right conscience or so that he may not fall into presumption from the strength and grace that have been given him, as in the case of Paul.[8]

Someone may be abandoned for a while for the correction of others so that by observing his state they may be instructed, as in the case of Lazarus and the rich man.[9] For we are naturally humbled when we see the sufferings of others. Someone may also be abandoned not because of his own sins or his parents' but for the glory of another, as was the man born blind for the glory of the Son of Man.[10] Again, someone may be permitted to suffer as an object of emulation for others so that because of the greatness of the glory of the one that suffered they may without hesitation accept suffering in hope of future glory and with a desire for the good things

---
6 Supplied from *ibid.* (*PG* 40.812A).
7 Cf. Job. 1.12; cf. Nemesius, *loc. cit.*
8 Cf. 2 Cor. 12.7.
9 Cf. Luke 16.19ff.; Nemesius, *loc. cit.*
10 Cf. John 9.3; Nemesius, *loc. cit.*

to come, as in the case of the martyrs. A person may even be allowed at times to fall into a immoral action for the correction of another and worse affliction. For example, a certain person is conceited about his virtues and righteousness, and God permits him to fall into fornication so that by his fall he may become conscious of his own weakness, be humbled, and, drawing nigh, confess to the Lord.

One should, moreover, note that, while the choice of things that may be done rests with us, the accomplishment of the good ones is due to the co-operation of God, who in accordance with His foreknowledge justly co-operates with those who in right conscience choose the good. The accomplishment of the bad things, however, is due to abandonment by God, who, again in accordance with His foreknowledge, justly abandons us.

Now, there are two kinds of abandonment, for there is one by dispensation which is for our instruction and there is another which is absolute rejection. That abandonment is by dispensation and for our instruction which happens for the correction, salvation, and glory of the one who experiences it, or which happens either to give others an object for emulation and imitation, or even for the glory of God. On the other hand, there is absolute abandonment, when God has done everything for a man's salvation, yet the man of his own accord remains obdurate and uncured, or rather, incorrigible, and is then given over to absolute perdition, like Judas. May God spare and deliver us from this sort of abandonment.

One should furthermore bear in mind that the ways of God's providence are many, and that they can neither be explained in words nor grasped by the mind.

One must note that for those who accept them with thanksgiving the attacks of adversity redound to salvation and definitely become instruments of aid.

One should also bear in mind that God antecedently wills all to be saved and to attain to His kingdom.[11] For He did

---

11 Cf. 1 Tim. 2.4.

not form us to be chastised, but, because He is good, that we might share in His goodness. Yet, because He is just, He does wish to punish sinners. So, the first is called *antecedent will* and *approval,* and it has Him as its cause; the second is called *consequent will* and *permission,* and it has ourselves as its cause. This last is twofold: that which is by dispensation and for our instruction and salvation, and that which is abandonment to absolute chastisement, as we have said. These, however, belong to those things which do not depend upon us.

As to the things which do depend upon us, the good ones He wills antecedently and approves, whereas the evil, which are essentially bad, He neither wills antecedently nor consequently, but permits them to the free will. Now, that which is done under compulsion is not rational; neither can it be a virtuous act. God provides for all creation, and through all creation He does good and instructs, oftentimes using even the demons themselves for this purpose, as in the case of Job and in that of the swine.[12]

Chapter 30

One should note that God foreknows all things but that He does not predestine them all.[1] Thus, He foreknows the things that depend upon us, but He does not predestine them—because neither does He will evil to be done nor does He force virtue. And so, predestination is the result of the divine command made with foreknowledge. Those things which do not depend upon us, however, He predestines in accordance with His foreknowledge.[2] For, through His fore-

---

12 Cf. Job 1.12; Mark 5.13.

1 Cf. John Chrysostom, *Homily 1 on the Obscurity of the Prophecies* 4 (*PG* 56.171).
2 Cf. *Acts of St. Maximus* (*PG* 90.137).

knowledge, He has already decided all things beforehand in accordance with His goodness and justice.

One should furthermore note that our nature has been endowed by God with virtue, and that He is the source and author of all good, without whose co-operation and assistance we are powerless either to will good or to do it. Moreover, it depends upon ourselves whether we are to persevere in virtue and be guided by God who invites us to practice it; or whether we are to abandon virtue, which is to become attached to vice and be guided by the Devil, who, without forcing us, is inviting us to practice vice. For evil is nothing else but the absence of good, precisely as darkness is the absence of light. Consequently, when we persevere in what is according to nature, we are in a state of virtue; but, when we abandon what is according to nature, that is to say, virtue, we come to what is contrary to nature and become attached to vice.

Repentance is a return through discipline and toil from that which is against nature to that which is according to it, from the Devil to God.

Now, the Creator fashioned this man as a male and imparted His own divine grace to him, thus putting him in communion with Himself. And thus it was that man, like a prophet and lord, gave names to the animals which had been given him as slaves. For, since he had been made in the image of God rational, understanding, and free, it was reasonable that he should be entrusted by the common Creator and Lord of all with the government over the things on earth.

However, since God knew the future and foresaw that man was to fall and be subject to death, He made from him a female as a helpmate for him of his own kind to aid him in the establishment of the race after the fall by succession through the process of begetting. Now, the first forming is called 'creation,' not 'begetting.' Creation is the first forming by God, whereas begetting is the succession of one from another made necessary by the sentence of death resulting from the fall.

This man He set in the paradise which was both of the mind and of the senses. Thus, while in his body he lived on earth in the world of sense, in his spirit he dwelt among the angels, cultivating thoughts of God and being nurtured on these. He was naked because of his innocence and his simplicity of life, and through creatures he was drawn up to their only Creator, in whose contemplation he rejoiced and took delight.

Since God had endowed man's nature with a free will, He made it a law for him not to taste of that tree of knowledge of which we have spoken sufficiently and to the best of our ability in the chapter on paradise. This command He gave to man with the promise that should he let reason prevail, recognizing his Creator and observing his Creator's ordinance, and thus preserve the dignity of his soul, then he would become stronger than death and would live forever in the enjoyment of everlasting bliss. On the other hand, should he shake off the yoke of his Maker and disregard His divine ordinance, thus subordinating soul to body and preferring the pleasures of the flesh, 'not understanding his own honor and compared to senseless beasts,'[3] then he would be subject to death and corruption and would be obliged to drag out his miserable existence in toil. For it was not profitable for him to attain incorruptibility while yet untried and untested, 'lest he fall into pride and the judgment of the devil.'[4] For it was by reason of his incorruptibility that, after his fall by deliberate choice, the Devil became unrepentingly and immoveably rooted in evil. In the same way again, after their deliberate election of virtue, the angels were immutably founded in good by grace.

And so it was necessary first for man to be tested, since one who is untried and untested deserves no credit.[5] Then,

---

3 Ps. 48.13.
4 1 Tim. 3.6.
5 Cf. Eccli. 34.11.

when trial had made him perfect through his keeping of the commandment, he should thus win incorruptibility, the reward of virtue. For, since he had been created half way between God and matter, should he be freed from his natural relationship to creatures and united to God by keeping the commandment, then he was to be permanently united to God and immutably rooted in good. Should he, on the other hand through his disobedience turn his mind away from his Author—I mean God—and tend rather toward matter, then he was to be associated with corruption, to become passible rather than impassible, and mortal rather than immortal. He was to stand in need of carnal copulation and seminal generation, and because of his attachment to life was not only to cling to these pleasures as if they were necessary to sustain this life, but also to hate without limit such as would think of depriving him of them. And while he was to transfer his attachment from God to matter, he was also to transfer his anger from the real enemy of his salvation to his own kind. And so it was that man was overcome by the envy of the Devil. For that envious and hateful demon, having himself been brought low by his conceit, would not suffer us to attain the higher things. So the liar tempted that wretched man with the very hope of divinity, and, having raised him up to his own heights of conceit, dragged him down to the same abyss of ruin.

BOOK THREE

Chapter 1

AND SO, MAN SUCCUMBED to the assault of the demon, the author of evil; he failed to keep the Creator's commandment and was stripped of grace and deprived of that familiarity which he had enjoyed with God; he was clothed with the roughness of his wretched life—for this is what the fig leaves signify—and put on death, that is to say, the mortality and grossness of the flesh—for this is what the garment of skins signifies;[1] he was excluded from paradise by the just judgment of God; and was condemned to death and made subject to corruption. Even then the Compassionate One, who had given him his being and had favored him with a blessed existence, did not disregard him. On the contrary, He first schooled him and exhorted him to conversion in many ways—by groaning and trembling, by a flood of waters and the near destruction of the entire race, by the confusion and division of tongues, by the tutelage of angels, by the destruction of cities by fire, by prefigurative divine appearances, by war, victories and defeats, by signs and portents, by diverse influences, by the Law and the Prophets[2], all of which were directed to the destruction of that sin which had abounded under many forms and had enslaved man and heaped every sort of evil into his life,

---

[1] Cf. Gen. 3.7,21.
[2] Cf. Gen. 6.13; 11.7; 18.1ff; 19.1ff; cf. Gregory Nazianzen, *Sermon* 38.13 (*PG* 36.325A).

and to his return to the blessed existence. Since it was by sin that death had come into the world like some wild and savage beast to destroy the life of man, it was necessary for the one who was to effect a redemption to be sinless and not liable to the death which is due to sin. And it was further necessary for human nature to be strengthened and renewed, to be taught by experience, and to learn the way of virtue which turns back from destruction and leads to eternal life. Finally, the great sea of His benevolence toward man was made manifest, for the Creator and Lord Himself took up the struggle in behalf of His own creation and became a teacher in deed. And, since the enemy had caught man with the bait of the hope of divinity, he himself was taken with the bait of the barrier of the flesh; and at the same time the goodness and wisdom and justice and power of God were made manifest. His goodness, because He did not despise the weakness of His own handiwork, but, when he fell, had compassion on him and stretched out His hand to him. His justice, because, when man had suffered defeat, He did not have another conquer the tyrant nor did He snatch man away from death by force, but He, the Good and Just, made him victor against whom death had once enslaved through sin; and like He rescued by like, which was most difficult to do. And His wisdom, because He found the most fitting solution for this most difficult problem.[3] For by the good pleasure of God the Father the only-begotten Son and Word of God and God, who is in the bosom of God the Father, consubstantial with the Father and with the Holy Ghost, existing before the ages, without beginning, who was in the beginning and was with God the Father and was God,[4] He, being in the form of God,[5] bowed down the heavens and descended—that is, without lowering it, He brought down His exalted sublimity and condescended

---

3 Cf. Gregory of Nyssa, *Catechetical Discourse* 24 (PG 45.65).
4 Cf. John 1.1,18.
5 Cf. Phil. 2.6.

to His servants with an ineffable and incomprehensible condescension, for such is the meaning of the term condescension. And He, while being perfect God, became perfect man and accomplished the newest of all new things, the only new thing under the sun, by which the infinite power of God was clearly shown. For what is greater than for God to become man? So, without suffering change, the Word was made flesh of the Holy Ghost and the holy and ever-virgin Mary, Mother of God. And He stands as mediator between God and men. He, the only loving One, was conceived in the immaculate womb of the Virgin not by the will of man, nor by concupiscence, nor by the intervention of a husband, nor by pleasurable generation, but of the Holy Ghost and the first offspring of Adam. And He became obedient to the Father by healing our disobedience with that which is like to us and which was taken from us, and by becoming to us a model of that obedience without which it is impossible to attain salvation.

Chapter 2

Now, an angel of the Lord was sent to the holy Virgin, who was descended from the tribe of David, 'for it is evident that our Lord sprung out of Juda: of which tribe no one attended on the altar,'[1] as the divine Apostle said and concerning which we shall speak more fully later on. Bringing the good tidings to her, he said: 'Hail, full of grace, the Lord is with thee.' And she was troubled at his saying, and the angel said to her: 'Fear not, Mary, for thou hast found grace with God, and thou shalt bring forth a son and thou shalt call his name Jesus; for he shall save his people from their sins.' It is for this reason that the name Jesus is interpreted as meaning saviour. And she was troubled and said: 'How shall this be done to me, because I know

---

1 Heb. 7.13,14.

not man?' Again the angel spoke to her: 'The Holy Ghost shall come upon thee and the power of the Most High shall overshadow thee. And therefore also the Holy which shall be born to thee shall be called the Son of God.' Then she said to him: 'Behold the handmaid of the Lord: be it done to me according to thy word.'[2]

And so, after the holy Virgin had given her assent, the Holy Ghost came upon her according to the Lord's word, which the angel had spoken, and purified her and gave her the power both to receive the divinity of the Word and to beget.[3] Then the subsistent Wisdom and Power of the Most High, the Son of God, the Consubstantial with the Father, overshadowed her like a divine seed and from her most chaste and pure blood compacted for Himself a body animated by a rational and intellectual soul as first-fruits of our clay. This was not by seed, but by creation through the Holy Ghost, with the form not being put together bit by bit, but being completed all at once with the Word of God Himself serving as the person to the flesh. For the divine Word was not united to an already self-subsistent flesh,[4] but, without being circumscribed, came in His own person to dwell in the womb of the holy Virgin and from the chaste blood of the ever-virgin made flesh subsist animated by a rational and intellectual soul. Taking to Himself the first-fruits of the human clay, the very Word became person to the body. Thus, there was a body which was at once the body of God the Word and an animate, rational, intellectual body. Therefore, we do not say that man became God, but that God became man. For, while He was by nature perfect God, the same became by nature perfect man. He did not change His nature and neither did He just appear to become man. On the contrary, without confusion or alteration or division He became hypostatically united to the rationally and intel-

---
2 Luke 1.28-38.
3 Cf. Gregory Nazianzen, *Sermon* 38.13 (*PG* 36.325B).
4 Cf. Proclus of Constantinople, *Epistle* 2.5 (*PG* 65.860-861).

lectually animated flesh which He had from the holy Virgin and which had its existence in Him. He did not transform the nature of his divinity into the substance of His flesh, nor the substance of His flesh into the nature of His divinity, and neither did He effect one compound nature out of His divine nature and the human nature which He had assumed.

Chapter 3

The natures were united to each other without change and without alteration. The divine nature did not give up its proper simplicity, and the human nature was certainly not changed into the nature of the divinity, nor did it become non-existent. Neither was there one compound nature made from the two natures. For the compounded nature can in no wise be consubstantial with either one of the natures from which it has been compounded, since from diverse natures it has been made into something else. For example, the body, which is made up of the four elements, is not said to be consubstantial with fire, nor is it called fire, nor is it called water or earth or air either, nor is it consubstantial with any one of these. Accordingly, if Christ had one compound nature after the union,[1] having changed from one simple nature to a compound one, as the heretics say, then He is neither consubstantial with His Father, who has a simple nature, nor with His Mother, because she was not composed of divinity and humanity. Nor, indeed, will He belong to divinity or humanity, nor can He be called God or man, but just Christ alone, and, according to them, 'Christ' will not be the name of the person but the name of the one nature. We, however, declare that Christ has a compound nature, not in the sense of something new made from different things, as man is made up of body and soul or as the body

---

1 Cf. Maximus, *Epistle 12* (PG 91.488-489); Leontius, *Against the Arguments of Severus* (PG 86.1928A).

is composed of the four elements, but in the sense of being made up of different things which remain the same. For we confess that from divinity and humanity there is the same perfect God and that He both is and is said to be of two natures and in two natures. We say that the term 'Christ' is the name of the person and that it is not used in a restricted sense, but as signifying what is of the two natures. Thus, He anointed Himself—as God, anointing His body with His divinity, but as man, being anointed, because He is both the one and the other. Moreover, the anointing of the humanity is the divinity. Now, if Christ, who is consubstantial with the Father, has one compounded nature, then the Father, too, will certainly be compounded and consequently consubstantial with the flesh, which is absurd and redolent of every blasphemy.

What is more, how can one nature comprise different substances that are contradictory? How is it possible for the same nature to be at once created and uncreated, mortal and immortal, circumscribed and uncircumscribed?

Now, were they to say that Christ had one nature and that this was simple, then either they would be confessing Him to be pure God and would be introducing a mere appearance that would not be incarnation, or they would be confessing Him to be mere man after the manner of Nestorius. Then, where is the perfection in divinity and the perfection in humanity? How can they ever say that Christ has two natures, while they are asserting that after the union He has one compound nature? For it is obvious to anyone that, before the union, Christ had one nature.

However, the reason for the herectics' error is their saying that nature and hypostasis are the same thing.[2] Now, when we say that men have one nature, it must be understood that we do not say this with the body and soul in mind, because it is impossible to say that the soul and the body as compared to each other have one nature. Nevertheless,

---

2 Cf. Anastasius Sinaite, *The Guide* 9 (PG 89.140ff.).

when we take a number of human hypostases, all of these are found to admit of the same basis of their nature. All are made up of a soul and a body, all share the nature of the soul and possess the substance of the body, and all have a common species. Thus, we say that several different persons have one nature, because each person has two natures and is complete in these two natures, that is to say, the natures of the soul and of the body.

In the case of our Lord Jesus Christ, however, it is impossible to have a common species, for there never was, nor is, nor ever will be another Christ of divinity and humanity, in divinity and humanity, the same being perfect God and perfect man. Hence, in the case of our Lord Jesus Christ, one cannot speak of one nature made up of divinity and humanity as one can in the case of the individual made up of soul and body. In this last case we have an individual, but Christ is not an individual, because He does not have a predicated species of Christness. It is precisely for this reason that we say that it was of two perfect natures, the divine and the human, that the union was made. It was not made by mixing, or mingling, or blending, or compounding as was asserted by the fatal Dioscorus, by Eutyches, too, and Severus, and their accursed associates; neither was it apparent (προσωπική) nor relative, nor by dignity or harmony of will or equality in honor or identity of name or complaisance as was asserted by that enemy of God, Nestorius, and by Diodorus, too, and Theodore of Mopsuestia, and their hellish band. Rather, it was by composition—hypostatically, that is to say—without change or mingling or alteration or division or separation. And we confess one Person of the Son of God incarnate[3] in two natures that remain perfect, and we declare that the Person of His divinity and of His humanity is the same and confess that the two natures are preserved intact in Him after the union. We do not set each nature apart by itself, but hold them to be united to each

---

3 Cf. Maximus, *Epistle 12* (*PG* 91.501BC).

other in one composite Person. For we say that the union is substantial; that is to say, true and not imaginary. We do not, however, define the substantial union as meaning that the two natures go to make up one compound nature, but as meaning that they are truly united to each other into one composite Person of the Son of God, each with its essential difference maintained intact. Thus, that which was created remained created, and that which was uncreated, uncreated; the mortal remained mortal and the immortal immortal; the circumscribed remained circumscribed and the uncircumscribed, uncircumscribed; the visible remained visible and the invisible, invisible. 'The one glows with miracles, while the other has succumbed to insults.'[4]

Moreover, the Word makes human things His own, because what is proper to His sacred flesh belongs to Him; and the things which are His own He communicates to His flesh. This is after the manner of exchange on account of the mutual immanence of the parts and the hypostatic union and because He who 'with each form co-operating with the other performed'[5] both divine and human acts was one and the same. Wherefore, the Lord of Glory is even said to have been crucified,[6] although His divine nature did not suffer; and the Son of Man is confessed to have been in heaven before His passion, as the Lord Himself has said.[7] For one and the same was the Lord of Glory and He who was naturally and truly Son of Man, that is, He who became man. And we recognize both the miracles and the sufferings as His, even though it was in one nature that He worked miracles and in another that He endured suffering. For we know that His one Person thus preserves for itself the essential difference of the natures. How, indeed, would the difference be preserved, were not those things preserved

---

4 Leo, *Epistle* 28.4 (*PL* 54.768B).
5 *Ibid.* (*PL* 54.772A).
6 Cf. 1 Cor. 2.8.
7 Cf. John 3.13.

in which they differ from each other? For difference is that by which things that are different differ. Therefore, we say that Christ is joined to the extremes by the fact of His natures differing from each other, that is, by the fact of His essence. On the one hand, He is joined to the Father and the Spirit by His divinity, while on the other He is joined by His humanity to His Mother and to all men. However, because of the fact that His natures are united, we say that He differs both from the Father and the Spirit and from His Mother and other men. For His natures are united in His Person and have one composite Person, and in this He differs both from the Father and the Spirit and from His Mother and us.

Chapter 4

We have repeatedly said that *substance* is one thing and *person* another, and that *substance* means the common species including the persons that belong to the same species —as, for example, God, man—while *person* indicates an individual, as Father, Son, Holy Ghost, Peter, Paul. One must furthermore know that the terms *divinity* and *humanity* are indicative of the substances or natures, but that the terms *God* and *man* are used in reference to the nature, as when we say: 'God is an incomprehensible substance' and 'God is one.' But these are also taken as referring to the persons, with the more particular receiving the name of the more general, as when Scripture says: 'Therefore God, thy God, hath anointed thee,'[1] for in this case it means the Father and the Son. And again, when it says: 'There was a man in the land of Hus,'[2] for it means Job only.

Since, then, in our Lord Jesus Christ we recognize two natures and one composite Person for both, when we are considering the natures, we call them divinity and humanity.

---
1 Ps. 44.8.
2 Job 1.1.

But, when we consider the composite Person of the two natures, we sometimes call Christ both God and Man and God incarnate, naming Him from both; and sometimes we name Him from one of the two and call Him just God and Son of God, or just Man and Son of Man. And also, we sometimes name Him from just the sublime attributes and sometimes from just the more humble ones. For He is one who is alike both the one and the other—the one existing uncaused and eternally from the Father; the other come into being at a later time because of love for men.[3]

Therefore, when we speak of the divinity, we do not attribute the properties of the humanity to it. Thus, we never speak of a passible or created divinity. Neither do we predicate the divine properties of the flesh, for we never speak of uncreated flesh or humanity. In the case of the person, however, whether we name it from both of the parts or from one of them, we attribute the properties of both the natures to it. And thus, Christ—which name covers both together— is called both God and man, created and uncreated, passible and impassible. And whenever He is named Son of God and God from one of the parts, He receives the properties of the co-existent nature, of the flesh, that is to say, and can be called passible God and crucified Lord of Glory[4]—not as being God, but in so far as the same one is also man. When, again, He is named Man and the Son of Man, He is given the properties and splendors of the divine nature. He is called Child before the Ages and Man without beginning, not as a child or a man, but as God, who is before the ages and became a child in latter times. Such, then, is the manner of this exchange by which each nature communicates its own properties to the other through the identity of their person and their mutual immanence. This is how we can say of Christ: 'This is our God, who was seen upon earth

---

[3] Cf. Gregory Nazianzen, *Sermon* 29.19 (PG 36.100A).
[4] Cf. 1 Cor. 2.8.

and conversed with men,'[5] and: 'This man is uncreated, impassible, and uncircumscribed.'

Chapter 5

In the Divinity we confess one nature, while we hold three really existing Persons.[1] And we hold everything belonging to the nature and the essence to be simple, while we recognize the difference of the Persons as residing only in the three properties of being uncaused and Father, of being caused and Son, and of being caused and proceeding. And we understand them to be inseparable and without interval between them, and united to one another and mutually immanent without confusion. And we understand them, while being separated without interval, to be united without confusion, for they are three, even though they are united. For, although each is subsistent in itself, that is to say, is a perfect Person and has its own property or distinct manner of existence, they are united in their essence and natural properties and by their not being separated or removed from the Person of the Father, and they are one God and are so called. In the same way, when it comes to that divine and ineffable Incarnation of one of the Holy Trinity, God the Word and our Lord Jesus Christ, which surpasses all understanding and comprehension, while we confess two natures, a divine and a human, conjoined with each other and hypostatically united, we also confess one composite Person made of those natures. We furthermore hold that, even after the union, the two natures are preserved intact in the one composite person, that is to say, in the one Christ, and that they and their natural properties have real existence, being nevertheless united without con-

---

5 Bar. 3.36,38.

1 Cf. Leontius, *Against the Arguments of Severus* (PG 86.1920-1921).

fusion, differing without separation, and numbered. Now, just as the three Persons of the Holy Trinity are united without confusion and are distinct without separation and have number without the number causing division, or separation, or estrangement, or severance among them—for we recognize that the Father and the Son and the Holy Ghost are one God—so in the same way the natures of Christ, although united, are united without confusion, and, although mutually immanent, do not suffer any change or transformation of one into the other. For each one keeps its own distinctiveness unchanged. Thus, too, they are numbered, yet the number does not introduce division. For Christ is one and He is perfect both in divinity and humanity. And number is not by nature a cause of division or union, but is, rather, a sign of the quantity of the things numbered, whether they be united or divided. Thus, as an example of things that are united, this wall contains fifty stones; or, as an example of things that are divided, there are fifty stones lying in this field. Or again, as an example of things that are united, there are two natures in a coal—that of fire, I mean, and that of wood; or these may be divided, because the nature of fire is one thing and that of wood another. And these are not united or divided by their number but in some other manner. And so, just as it is impossible to say that the three Persons are one Person, even though they are united, without bringing about confusion or suppression of the difference, so it is impossible to say that the two hypostatically united natures of Christ are one nature without our bringing about suppression, confusion, or annihilation of their difference.

Chapter 6

Things that are common and universal are predicated of particulars subordinate to them. Now, the substance as a species is a common thing, while the person is a particular.

A thing is a particular not in that it possesses a part of the nature, because it does not have such a part, but in that it is particular in number, as an individual. Thus, persons are said to differ in number but not in nature. The substance, moreover, is predicated of the person, because the substance is complete in each of the persons of the same species. For that reason, persons do not differ from one another in substance, but rather in the accidents, which are their characteristic properties—characteristic, however, of the person and not of the nature. And this is because the person is defined as a substance plus accidents. Thus, the person has that which is common plus that which is individuating, and, besides this, existence in itself. Substance does not subsist in itself, but is to be found in persons. Accordingly, when one of the persons suffers, then, since the whole nature in which the person has suffered is affected, this whole nature is said to have suffered in one of its persons. This, however, does not necessitate all the persons of the same species suffering together with the one that does suffer.

Thus, then, we confess that the nature of the divinity is entirely and completely in each one of its Persons—all in the Father, all in the Son, all in the Holy Ghost. For this reason, the Father is perfect God, the Son is perfect God, and the Holy Ghost is perfect God. In the same way, we say that in the Incarnation of one of the Holy Trinity, the Word of God, the entire and complete nature of the divinity was united in one of its Persons to the entire human nature, and not a part of one to a part of the other. And so the divine Apostle say that 'in Him dwelleth the fullness of the Godhead corporeally,'[1] that is to say, in His flesh. And his inspired disciple Dionysius, who was most learned in matters divine, says that the Divinity in its entirety has community with us in one of its Persons.[2] But, certainly, let us not be constrained to say that all the Persons of the sacred Godhead,

---
1 Col. 2.9.
2 Cf. Pseudo-Dionysius, *Divine Names* 2.6 (*PG* 3.644BD).

the Three, that is, were hypostatically united to all the persons of humanity. For in no wise did the Father and the Holy Ghost participate in the incarnation of the Word of God except by Their good pleasure and will. We do say that the entire substance of the Divinity was united to the entire human nature, because God the Word lacked none of those things which He implanted in our nature when He formed us in the beginning; He assumed them all—a body and a rational, intellectual soul, together with the properties of both, for the animal which lacks one of these is not a man. He in His entirety assumed me in my entirety and was wholly united to the whole, so that He might bestow the grace of salvation upon the whole. For that which has not been assumed cannot be healed.[3]

And so, the Word of God is united to the flesh by the intermediary of mind which stands midway between the purity of God and the grossness of the flesh.[4] Now, the mind has authority over both soul and body, but, whereas mind is the purest part of the soul, God is the purest part of mind. And when the mind of Christ is permitted by the stronger, then it displays its own authority. However, it is under the control of the stronger and follows it, doing those things which the divine will desires.

Moreover, the mind became the seat of the Divinity which had been hypostatically united to it, just as, of course, the flesh did—but not an associate, as the accursed opinion of the heretics falsely teaches, when, judging immaterial things in a material way, they say that one measure will not hold two. But, how shall Christ have been said to be perfect God and perfect man and consubstantial both with the Father and with us, if a part of the divine nature is united in Him to a part of the human nature?

Furthermore, when we say that our nature rose from the

---

[3] Cf. Gregory Nazianzen, *Epistle* 101 (*PG* 37.181C).
[4] Cf. *ibid., Sermon* 38.10 (*PG* 36.321AC).

dead and ascended and sat at the right hand of the Father, we do not imply that all human persons arose and sat at the right hand of the Father, but that our entire nature did so in the Person of Christ. Certainly, the divine Apostle says: 'He hath raised us up together and hath made us sit together in Christ.'[5]

And we also say this: that the union was made of common substances. For every substance is common to the persons included under it. And it is not possible to find a partial and individuating nature of substance, since it would then be necessary to say that the same persons were of the same substance and of different substances, and that the Holy Trinity was in its divinity both of the same substance and of different substances. Consequently, the same nature is found in each one of the Persons. And when, following the blessed Athanasius and Cyril, we say that the nature of the Word became incarnate, we are declaring that the Divinity was united to the flesh. For this reason, we may by no means say: 'The nature of the Word suffered,' because the Divinity did not suffer in Him. But we do say that human nature suffered in Christ without any implication that all human persons did; confessing that Christ suffered in His human nature. Thus, when we say 'the nature of the Word,' we mean the Word Himself. And the Word possesses the community of substance and the individuality of person.

Chapter 7

We say, then, that the divine Person of God the Word exists before all things timelessly and eternally, simple and uncompounded, uncreated, incorporeal, invisible, intangible, and uncircumscribed. And we say that it has all things that the Father has, since it is consubstantial with Him, and that it differs from the Person of the Father by the manner

---
5 Eph. 2.6.

of its begetting and by relation, that it is perfect and never leaves the Person of the Father. But, at the same time, we say that in latter times, without leaving the bosom of the Father, the Word came to dwell uncircumscribed in the womb of the holy Virgin, without seed and without being contained, but after a manner known to Him, and in the very same Person as exists before the ages He made flesh subsist for Himself from the holy Virgin.

Thus, He was in all things and above all things, and at the same time He was existing in the womb of the holy Mother of God, but He was there by the operation of the Incarnation. And so, He was made flesh and took from her the first-fruits of our clay, a body animated by a rational and intellectual soul, so that the very Person of God the Word was accounted to the flesh. And the Person of the Word which formerly had been simple was made composite.[1] Moreover, it was a composite from two perfect natures, divinity and humanity. And it had that characteristic and distinctive property of sonship by which God the Word is distinct from the Father and the Spirit, and also had those characteristic and distintive properties of the flesh by which He is distinct both from His Mother and from the rest of men. It further had those properties of the divine nature in which He is one with the Father and the Spirit, and also had those features of human nature in which He is one with His Mother and with us. Moreover, He differs from the Father and the Spirit and from His Mother and us in yet another way, by His being at once both God and man. For this we recognize as a most peculiar property of the Person of Christ.

And so, we confess that even after the Incarnation He is the one Son of God, and we confess that the same is the

---

[1] σύνθετος ὑπόστασις, or compound hypostasis, an expression used by Leontius and meaning that the whole Christ is made up, as it were, of two parts or natures, is used in opposition to the Monophysite expression, 'one compound nature of Christ.'

Son of Man, one Christ, one Lord, the only-begotten Son and Word of God, Jesus our Lord. And we venerate His two begettings—one from the Father before the ages and surpassing cause and reason and time and nature, and one in latter times for our own sake, after our own manner, and surpassing us. For our own sake, because it was for the sake of our salvation; after our own manner, because He was made man from a woman and with a period of gestation; and surpassing us, because, surpassing the law of conception, He was not from seed but from the Holy Ghost and the holy Virgin Mary. And we do not proclaim Him God alone, stripped of our humanity, nor do we despoil Him of His divinity and proclaim Him man alone. Neither do we proclaim Him one and another; rather, we proclaim Him to be one and the same, at once both God and man, perfect God and perfect man, God entire and man entire—the same being God entire, even with His flesh, and man entire, even with His most sacred divinity. By saying 'perfect God and perfect man' we show the fullness and completeness of the natures, while by saying 'God entire and man entire' we point out the individuality and the indivisibility of the person.

Following the blessed Cyril,[2] we also confess one incarnate nature of the Word of God and by saying 'incarnate' intend the substance of the flesh. So, the Word was made flesh without giving up His own immateriality and He was wholly made flesh while remaining wholly uncircumscribed. With respect to His body He becomes small and contracted, while with respect divinity He is uncircumscribed, for His body is not co-extensive with His uncircumscribed divinity.

The whole He, then, is perfect God, but not wholly God, because He is not only God but also man. Likewise, the whole He is perfect man, but not wholly man, because He is not only man but also God. For the 'wholly' is indicative of nature, while the 'whole' is indicative of person, just as 'one thing' is of nature, while 'another one' is of person.

---

[2] Cf. Cyril of Alexandria, *Epistle* 44 and 46 (PG 77.225B and 241B).

One must know, moreover, that, although we say that the natures of the Lord are mutually immanent, we know that this immanence comes from the divine nature. For this last pervades all things and indwells as it wishes, but nothing pervades it. And it communicates its own splendours to the body while remaining impassible and having no part in the affections of the body. For, if the sun communicates its own operations to us, yet has no part in our own, then how much more so the Creator of the sun who is the Lord?

Chapter 8

Should anyone inquire regarding the natures of the Lord as to whether they are reducible to a continuous quantity or to a divided one, we shall reply that the Lord's natures are neither one solid, nor one surface, nor one line, nor are they place or time, so as to be reducible to a continuous quantity —for these are the things which are accounted to be continuous.

It must be known, moreover, that number belongs to things which differ and that it is impossible for things to be numbered which do not differ at all. It is by that in which they differ that things are numbered. For example, in so far as Peter and Paul are one, they are not numbered. Thus, since they are one by reason of their substance, they cannot be called two natures. However, since they do differ in person, they are called two persons. Hence, things which differ have number, and it is according to the manner in which they differ that they are numbered.

Now, whereas the Lord's natures are hypostatically united without confusion, they are divided without separation by reason and way of their difference. In so far as they are one, they have no number, for we do not say that Christ has two natures according to person. They are numbered, however, by way of their being divided without separation. For by reason and way of their difference the natures of Christ are two. Thus, being hypostatically one and mutually immanent, they are united without confusion with each one preserving its own natural difference. And so, since they are numbered by way of their difference only, it is in that way that they will be reducible to a divided quantity.

Christ, then, who is perfect God and perfect man, is one.[1] Him do we adore with the Father and the Spirit together with His immaculate body in one adoration. And we do not say that His body is not to be adored, because it is adored in the one Person of the Word who became Person to it. Yet we do not worship the creature, because we do not adore it as a mere body, but as being one with the divinity, because His two natures belong to the one Person and the one subsistence of the Word of God. I am afraid to touch the burning coal because of the fire which is combined with the wood. I adore the combined natures of Christ because of the divinity which is united to the body. Thus, I do not add a fourth person to the Trinity—God forbid!—but I do confess the Person of the Word of God and of His flesh to be one. For, even after the Incarnation of the Word, the Trinity remained Trinity.

To those who inquire as to whether the two natures are reducible to a continuous or divided quantity.[2]

The Lord's natures are neither one solid, nor one surface, nor one line, nor are they place or time, so as to be reducible to a continuous quantity—for these are the things which are accounted to be continuous. Moreover, the Lord's natures are hypostatically united without confusion and they are divided without separation by reason and way of their dif-

---

[1] Cf. Cyril of Alexandria, *Defense of the Anathemas against Theodoret* 8 (*PG* 76.429AB).
[2] This is found in most manuscripts after Book 4.9, but it is more logically placed here by Lequien.

ference. In so far as they are one, they have no number. For we do not say that Christ's natures are two Persons or that they are two according to Person. They are numbered, however, by way of their being divided without separation. For there are two natures by reason and way of their difference. Thus, being hypostatically one and mutually immanent, they are united without any confusion or transformation of one into the other and with each preserving its own natural difference for itself. For the created remained created and the uncreated uncreated. And so, since they are numbered by way of their difference only, it is in that way that they will be reducible to a divided quantity. For it is impossible for things to be numbered which do not differ at all. It is by that in which they differ that things are numbered. For example, in so far as Peter and Paul are one, they are not numbered. Thus, since they are one by reason of their substance, they neither are two natures nor are they so called. However, since they do differ in person, they are called two persons. And so their difference is the cause of their number.

Chapter 9

Now, although there is no nature without subsistence (ἀνυπόστατος) or substance without person, because both the substance and the nature are only to be found in subsistences and persons, it is unnecessary for natures hypostatically united to each other to be provided each with its own subsistence. For they can concur in one subsistence without being non-subsistent, yet not having each its own individuating subsistence, but both having one and the same.[1] Thus, since the same Person of the Word belongs to both natures, it does not allow one of them to lack subsistences, nor is it now the Person of one and now that of the other. On the contrary, it is always indivisibly and inseparably

---

1 Cf. Leontius, *On Sects* 7.2 (*PG* 86,1241BC).

Person of both, and is not distributed and divided by the allotment of one part of itself to the one nature and another part to the other, but belongs indivisibly and entirely all to one and all to the other. For the flesh of the Word of God was not independently subsistent nor was there any other person besides that of the Word of God. On the contrary, it was in the Person of the Word that the flesh subsisted, or, rather, had personality (ἐνυπόστατος), and it did not become an independently subsisting person in itself. For this reason, it neither lacks personality nor introduces another person into the Trinity.

Chapter 10

It follows from the preceding that we consider blasphemous the addition made to the Thrice-Holy Hymn[1] by that stupid Peter the Fuller, because it introduces a fourth person and makes the Son of God partly the subsistent power of the Father and partly the crucified One—as if this last were another than the Strong, or as if the Holy Trinity was held to be passible and the Father and the Holy Ghost to have been crucified along with the Son. Away with this blasphemous interpolated nonsense! We understand the 'Holy God' as referring to the Father, and yet we do not restrict the appellation of divinity to Him alone, but recognize the Son and the Holy Ghost to be God, also. The 'Holy Strong' we take as referring to the Son, yet we do not strip the Father and the Holy Ghost of their strength. And the 'Holy Immortal' we apply to the Holy Ghost without excluding the Father and the Son from immortality, but understanding all the divine attributes as referring to each of the Persons. In this we are faithfully imitating the Apostle when he says: 'Yet to us there is but one God, the Father, of whom are all things, and we of him: and one Lord Jesus Christ, by

---

[1] For the *Trisagion Hymn* see the Introduction and J. Bingham, *Antiquities of the Christian Church* (London 1865) 688-689.

whom are all things, and we by him: and one Holy Ghost, in whom are all things, and we in him,'[2] and in the same way Gregory the Theologian, who somewhere says: 'To us there is one God the Father, from whom are all things, and one Lord Jesus Christ, through whom are all things, and one Holy Ghost, in whom are all things.'[3] And the 'from whom,' 'through whom,' and 'in whom' do not divide the natures, for in that case the prepositions and the order of the names would not be changeable. Rather, they designate the properties of one unconfused nature. This is also clear from the fact that they are found brought together into one again, when one reads with attention that passage from the same Apostle that runs: 'Of him, and by him, and in him are all things: to him be glory for ever. Amen.'[4]

Moreover, the divine and holy Athanasius,[5] and Basil, Gregory, and the whole choir of inspired Fathers bear witness to the fact that the Thrice-Holy Hymn is not addressed to the Son alone, but to the Holy Trinity, saying that by the threefold sanctification the holy Seraphim are intimating to us the three Persons of the supersubstantial Godhead. And by the one dominion they are making known the one substance and kingdom of the divinely sovereign Trinity. Certainly, Gregory the Theologian says: 'Thus, then, the Holy of Holies, which is veiled by the Seraphim, is glorified with three sanctifications converging into one dominion and Godhead, which has also been most beautifully and sublimely discussed by a certain other of our predecessors.'[6]

Now, those who have compiled the history of the Church[7] relate how once, when Proculus was archbishop, the people of Constantinople were making public entreaty to avert some threat of the divine wrath, and it happened that a child was

---

2 1 Cor. 8.6.
3 Gregory Nazianzen, *Sermon* 39.12 (*PG* 36.348A).
4 Rom. 11.36.
5 Cf. Athanasius, *On the Text of Matthew* 11.27 6 (*PG* 25.217C-220A).
6 Gregory Nazianzen, *Sermon* 38.8 (*PG* 36.320BC).
7 Cf. Theophanes, *Chronography*, a.m. 5930 (*PG* 108.244ff.).

taken up out of the crowd and by some angelic choirmasters was taught the Thrice-Holy Hymn after the following fashion: 'Holy God, Holy Strong, Holy Immortal, have mercy on us.' When the child came back again and told what he had been taught, the whole crowd sang the hymn and the threat was averted. And it is traditional that the Thrice-Holy Hymn was also sung in this manner at the holy and great Fourth Ecumenical Council—that which was held in Chalcedon, I mean—for so it is reported in the acts of this same holy council.[8] So it is really a silly and childish thing for the Thrice-Holy Song, which was taught by the angels, confirmed by the averting of the disaster, ratified and guaranteed by the council of so many holy Fathers, and sung first of all by the Seraphim to express the Godhead in three Persons, to have been trampled upon, as it were, and supposedly corrected by the absurd conceit of the Fuller—as if he were greater than the Seraphim. Oh, what presumption—not to call it madness! However, though the demons may burst, we, too, will say in this way: 'Holy God, Holy Strong, Holy Immortal, have mercy on us.'

Chapter 11

The nature may either be taken purely theoretically, since it is not self-subsistent; or it may be taken as what is common to persons of the same species and connects them, in which case it is said to be a nature taken specifically; or the same, with accidents added, may be considered wholly in one person, in which case it is said to be a nature taken individually, which is the same as that taken specifically. Now, when God the Word became incarnate, He did not assume His human nature as taken in a purely theoretical sense—for that would have been no real incarnation, but a fraudulent and fictitious one. Nor did He assume it as taken specifically,

---

8 Cf. Mansi, *Sacrorum conciliorum nova et amplissima collectio* 6.936C.

because He did not assume all persons. But He did assume it as taken individually, which is the same as that taken specifically. For He assumed the first-fruits of our clay not as self-subsistent and having been an individual previously and as such taken on by Him, but as having its subsistence in His Person. Thus, this Person of the Word of God became Person to the flesh, and in this way 'the Word was made flesh,[1] and that without any change, and the flesh without transformation was made Word, and God was made man. For the Word is God, and man is God by virtue of the hypostatic union. It is therefore the same thing to say 'the nature of the Word' as it is to say 'the nature taken individually,' for it properly and exclusively shows not the individual, the Person, that is to say, nor that which is common to the Persons, but the common nature as found and discovered in one of the Persons.

Now, union is one thing and incarnation another. This is because union shows the joining, but not that with which the junction is made. Incarnation, however, is the same thing as is meant by saying becoming man, and it shows a joining with the flesh, that is, with man—just as the firing of the steel implies the union with fire. Thus, in explaining the expression 'one incarnate nature of the Word of God,' the blessed Cyril himself in his second letter to Succensus says as follows: 'If we were to speak of one nature of the Word but were to keep silent and not add the "incarnate," thus setting aside, as it were, the dispensation, then they perhaps would not be speaking entirely without reason who might pretend to ask: "If one nature is the whole, then where is the perfection in humanity?" or: "How did the substance which is like ours subsist?" However, since by saying "incarnate" both the perfection in humanity and the indication of the substance like ours have been introduced, let them cease to lean on their reedy staff.'[2] Here, then, he

---
1 John 1.14.
2 Cyril of Alexandria, *Epistle* 46 (*PG* 77.244A).

has used the 'nature' of the Lord in the sense of nature. This is evident because, if he had taken the nature in the sense of Person, it would not have been out of place to say it without the "incarnate," for we are not wrong when we simply say 'one Person of the Word of God.' What is more, Leontius of Byzance[3] has likewise understood the expression in the same way as meaning nature, but not nature in the sense of person. And the blessed Cyril himself, in his defense against Theodoret's attacks on the Second Anathema, speaks thus: 'The nature of the Word, that is to say, the Person, which is the Word Himself.'[4] Consequently, to say 'the nature of the Word' is not to signify the person alone, nor what is common to the Persons, but the common nature as considered wholly in the Person of the Word.

Now although it has been said that the nature of the Word became incarnate, that is, was united to the flesh, we have never heard up to now that the nature of the Word suffered in the flesh. We have, however, been taught that Christ suffered in the flesh. Consequently, saying 'nature of the Word' does not signify the Person. So it remains to say that to have become incarnate means to have been united to the flesh, and that the Word was made flesh means that without suffering change the very Person of the Word became Person of the body. And again, although it has been said that God was made man and man God—for the Word, while being God, was made man without suffering change, yet we have never heard at all that the Godhead was made man, or was incarnate, or put on human nature. We have, however, learned that the Godhead was united to humanity in one of Its Persons. It has also been said that God takes on another form, or substance—ours, that is to say. For the name God applies to each one of the Persons, but we cannot say Godhead in reference to a Person, because we

---
[3] Cf. Leontius, *On Sects* 8.2 (*PG* 86.1252D-1253A).
[4] Cyril of Alexandria, *Defense of the Anathemas against Theodoret* 2 (*PG* 76.401A).

have not heard that the Godhead is the Father alone, or the Son alone, or the Holy Ghost alone. This is because Godhead indicates the nature, whereas Father indicates the Person, just as humanity indicates the nature, and Peter the person. The name God, moreover, also signifies the community of nature and is applied to each of the Persons like a surname, just as the word man is. For God is one who possesses a divine nature, and man is one who possesses a human one.

Furthermore, in connection with all this one must know that the Father and the Holy Ghost in no way participate in the Incarnation of the Word, unless it be in miracles and by complaisance and will.[5]

Chapter 12

And we proclaim the holy Virgin to be properly and truly Mother of God (Θεοτόκος).[1] For, as He who was born of her is true God, so is she truly Mother of God who gave birth to the true God who took His flesh from her. Now, we do not say that God was born of her in the sense that the divinity of the Word has its beginning of being from her, but in the sense that God the Word Himself, who was timelessly begotten of the Father before the ages and exists without beginning and eternally with the Father and the Holy Ghost, did in the last days come for our salvation to dwell in her womb and of her was, without undergoing change, made flesh and born. For the holy Virgin did not give birth to a mere man but to true God, and not to God simply, but to God made flesh. And He did not bring His body down from heaven and come through her as through a channel, but assumed from her a body consubstantial with us

---

5 Cf. Pseudo-Dionysius, *Divine Names* 2.6 (*PG* 3.644BC).

1 Cf. Gregory Nazianzen, *Epistle* 101 (*PG* 37.177-178).

and subsisting in Himself. Now, had the body been brought down from heaven and not been taken from our nature, was there any need for His becoming man? God the Word was made man for this reason: that that very nature which had sinned, fallen, and become corrupt should conquer the tyrant who had deceived it. Thus should it be freed from corruption, as the divine Apostle says: 'For by a man came death: and by a man the resurrection of the dead.'[2] If the first was true, then so is the second.

If, however, he also says: 'The first Adam was, of earth, earthly: the second Adam, the Lord, from heaven,'[3] he is not saying that the body is from heaven.[4] But it is obvious that He is not a mere man, for notice how he called Him both Adam and Lord—thus indicating that He is both together. For Adam is interpreted as meaning born of earth, and it is obvious that man's nature is born of earth because it was formed from dust. On the other hand, the name Lord is expressive of the divine substance.

And again, the Apostle says: 'God sent his only-begotten Son, made of a woman.'[5] He did not say *by* a woman, but *of* a woman. Therefore, the divine Apostle meant that the one made man of the Virgin was Himself the only-begotten Son of God and God, and that the Son of God and God was Himself the one born of the Virgin. And he further meant that, in so far as He was made man, He was born corporeally and did not come to inhabit a previously formed man, as a prophet, but Himself substantially and truly became man, that is, He made flesh animated by a rational and intellectual soul subsist in His person and Himself became the Person to it. Now, that is what 'made of a woman' means, for how would the Word of God Himself have been

---

2 1 Cor. 15.21.
3 1 Cor. 15.47.
4 Cf. Gregory Nazianzen, *op. cit.* (PG 37.181BC).
5 Gal. 4.4.

made under the law, had it not been that He was made a man of the same substance as ourselves?

Hence, it is rightly and truly that we call holy Mary the Mother of God, for this name expresses the entire mystery of the Incarnation. Thus, if she who gave birth is Mother of God, then He who was born of her is definitely God and also definitely man. For, had He not become man, how could God whose existence is before the ages have been born of a woman? And that the Son of Man is a man is quite evident. Moreover, if He who was born of a woman is God, then it is quite evident that the very one who in respect to His divine and unoriginated nature was begotten of God the Father, and the one who in the last times was born of the Virgin in respect to his originated and temporal nature —His human nature, that is—are one. And this means that our Lord Jesus Christ has one Person, two natures, and two begettings.

However, under no circumstances do we call the holy Virgin Mother of Christ (Χριστοτόκος).[6] This is because that vessel of dishonor, that foul and loathsome Jew at heart, Nestorius, invented this epithet as an insult to do away with the expression Mother of God and—though he burst with his father Satan—to bring dishonor upon the Mother of God, who alone is truly worthy of honor above all creation. And David is 'Christ,' too, and so is the high priest Aaron, because the royal and priestly offices are both conferred by anointing. Furthermore, any God-bearing (Θεοφόρος) man may be called 'Christ,' yet he is not by nature God, which is why the accursed Nestorius was so insolent as to call Him who was born of the Virgin 'God-bearing.' But God forbid that we should ever speak or think of Him as God-bearing; rather, let it be as God incarnate.[7] For the very Word of God was conceived of the Virgin and made flesh, but continued to be God after this assumption of the flesh. And,

---

6 Cf. Cyril of Alexandria, *Epistle* 1 (*PG* 77.20ff.).
7 Cf. Cyril of Alexandria, *Against Nestorius* 2 (*PG* 76.60A).

simultaneously with its coming into being, the flesh was straightway made divine by Him. Thus three things took place at the same time: the assuming of the flesh, its coming into being, and its being made divine by the Word. Hence, the holy Virgin is understood to be Mother of God, and is so called not only because of the nature of the Word but also because of the deification of the humanity simultaneously with which the conception and the coming into being of the flesh were wondrously brought about—the conception of the Word, that is, and the existence of the flesh in the Word Himself. In this the Mother of God, in a manner surpassing the course of nature, made it possible for the Fashioner to be fashioned and for the God and Creator of the universe to become man and deify the human nature which He had assumed, while the union preserved the things united, just as they had been united, that is to say, not only the divinity of Christ but His humanity, also; that which surpassed us and that which was like us. Now, it was not first made like us and then made to surpass us. On the contrary, it was always both from its first beginning of being, because from the first instant of conception it had its existence in the Word Himself. Therefore, while by its own nature it is human, it is also of God and divine in a manner surpassing the course of nature. And what is more, it possessed the properties of the living flesh, since by reason of the Incarnation the Word received them as truly natural in the order of natural motion.

Chapter 13

Since we confess our Lord Jesus Christ to be at once both perfect God and perfect man, we declare that this same One has all things that the Father has, except the being unbegotten, and, with the sole exception of sin, all that the first Adam has; namely, a body and a rational and intellectual soul. We furthermore declare that corresponding to His two natures He has the twofold set of natural properties belonging to the two natures—two natural wills, the divine and the human; two natural operations, a divine and a human; two natural freedoms, a divine and a human; and wisdom and knowledge, both divine and human. For, since He is consubstantial with God the Father, He freely wills and acts as God. And, since He is also consubstantial with us, the same one freely wills and acts as man. Thus, the miracles are His, and so are the sufferings.

Chapter 14

Since, then, Christ has two natures, we say that He has two natural wills and two natural operations. On the other hand, since these two natures have one Person, we say that He is one and the same who wills and acts naturally according to both natures, of which and in which is Christ our God, and which are Christ our God. And we say that He wills and acts in each, not independently, but in concert. 'For in each form He wills and acts in communion with the other.'[1] For the will and operation of things having the same substance is the same, and the will and operation of things having different substances is different.[2] Conversely, the substance of things having the same will and operation is the same, whereas that of things having a different will and operation is different.

Thus, in Father and Son and Holy Ghost we discover the identity of nature from the identity of the operation and the will. In the divine Incarnation, on the other hand, we discover the difference of the nature from the difference of the wills and operations, and knowing the difference

---
1 Leo, *Epistle* 28.4 (*PG* 54.768B).
2 Cf. Maximus, *Disputation with Pyrrhus* (*PG* 91.313D-316A,337B).

of the natures we confess the difference of the wills and operations. For, just as the number of the natures piously understood and declared to belong to one and the same Christ does not divide this one Christ, but shows that the difference of the natures is maintained even in the union, neither does the number of the wills and operations belonging substantially to His natures introduce any division—God forbid—for in both of His natures He wills and acts for our salvation. On the contrary, their number shows the preservation and maintenance of the natures even in the union, and this alone. We do not call the wills and operations personal, but natural. I am referring to that very faculty of willing and acting by force of which things which will will and things which act act. For, if we concede these to be personal, then we shall be forced to say that the three Persons of the Holy Trinity differ in will and operation.

Now, one must know that *willing* is not the same thing as *how one wills*.[3] This is because willing, like seeing, is of the nature, since it belongs to all men. How one wills, however, does not belong to nature but to our judgment, just as does how one looks at something, whether it be favorably or unfavorably. All men do not will alike, nor do they see things alike. And this we shall also concede in the case of the operations, for how one wills or sees or acts is a mode of the use of willing or seeing or acting, and this mode belongs to the user alone and distinguishes him from the others in accordance with what is commonly called the *difference*.

Consequently, simple willing is called *will*, or the volitive faculty, which is a natural will and rational appetite. But how one wills, or the subject of the volition, is the object *willed* and will based on judgment. And that is *volitive* which has it in its nature to will. For example, the divine nature is volitive, and so is the human. And finally, he is *willing* who uses the volition, and that is the person; Peter, for example.

---

3 Cf. *ibid.* (*PG* 91.292C).

Thus, since Christ is one and has one Person, the divinely willing in Him and the humanly willing are one and the same.[4] Nevertheless, since He has two natures which are volitive because they are rational, for everything that is rational is both volitive and free, we shall say that in Him there are two volitions, or natural wills. For the same one is volitive in both of His natures, since He assumed the volitive faculty which is inherent in our nature. Furthermore, since Christ is one and it is the same who wills in either nature, we shall say that the thing willed is the same. In saying this, we do not mean that He willed only what He willed naturally as God, for it is not of the nature of God to will to eat, drink, and the like; we mean that He also willed the things which go to make up human nature, not by any contradiction of judgment, but in accordance with the pecularity of the natures. For, when His divine will willed and permitted the flesh to suffer and to do what was peculiar to it, He willed these things naturally.

Now, that the will naturally belongs to man is evident from the following consideration.[5] Not counting the divine, there are three kinds of life: the vegetative, the sensitive, and the intellectual. Proper to the vegetative are the motions of nutrition, growth, and reproduction; proper to the sensitive is the motion by impulse; and proper to the rational and intellectual is the free motion. Therefore, if the nutritive motion is proper to the vegetative life and the impulsive to the sensitive, then surely the free motion is proper to the rational and intellectual. But, freedom of motion is nothing else but the will. Consequently, since the Word was made flesh animate, intellectual, and free, He was also made volitive.

Again, things which are natural are not acquired by learning, for no one learns to reason or live or hunger or thirst

---

4 Cf. *ibid.* (*PG* 91.289 AC).
5 Cf. *ibid.* (*PG* 91.301).

or sleep. And neither do we learn to will. Hence, it is natural to will.

And again, if, while nature rules in irrational beings, it is ruled in man who is freely moved by his will, then man is by nature volitive.

Still, again, if man has been made after the image of the blessed and supersubstantial Godhead, then, since the divine nature is naturally free and volitive, man as its image is also free and volitive by nature. For the Fathers have defined free will as volition.

Furthermore, if to will is inherent in all men and not present in some while absent in others, then, since what is found to be common to all is a characteristic of a nature in the individuals possessing that nature, man is by nature volitive.[6]

And again, if the nature does not admit of more or less, and if to will is inherent in all and is not more in some while less in others, then man is by nature volitive. And so, if man is by nature volitive, the Lord, too, is by nature volitive, not only in so far as He is God but also in so far as He was made man. For, just as He assumed our nature, so also has He assumed our natural will. And it is in this sense that the Fathers say that He impressed our will in Himself.

If the will is not natural, it will either be personal or be against nature. But, if it is personal, then the Son will have a different will from that of the Father, because that which is personal is characteristic of the person alone. And if it is against nature, there will be a defect in the nature, because what is against nature is destructive of what is according to nature.

Now, the God and Father of all things either wills as Father or as God. But, if He wills as Father, His will will be other than that of the Son, because the Son is not the Father. If, however, He wills as God, and the Son is God

---

6 Cf. *ibid.* (PG 91.304CD).

and the Holy Ghost is also God, then the will will belong to the nature; that is to say, it will be natural.

Furthermore, if, as the Fathers say,[7] those things that have one will have one substance, and if Christ's divinity and humanity have one will, then the substance of the divinity and that of the humanity will be one and the same.

And again, if, as the Fathers say, the natural difference does not appear in the one will, we must either say that there is one will in Christ and no natural difference, or that there is a natural difference and more than one will.

And still again, as the holy Gospel relates, the Lord went 'into the coasts of Tyre and Sidon: and entering into a house, he would that no man should know it. And he could not be hid.'[8] So, if His divine will was all-powerful and yet He was unable to conceal Himself when He willed to, then it was when willing as man that He was unable to, and as man also He was volitive.

And again, it says: 'Coming to the place he said: I thirst. And they gave him wine to drink mixed with gall. And when he had tasted, he would not drink.'[9] Now, if it was as God that He thirsted and having tasted did not want to drink, then as God He was subject to passion, for thirst is a passion and so is taste. If, however, it was not as God, then it was entirely as man that He thirsted, and as man also He was volitive.

There is also the blessed Apostle Paul, who says: 'Becoming obedient unto death, even to the death of the cross.'[10] This obedience was a submission of what was really His will and not of what really was not, for we may not call an irrational being either obedient or disobedient. However, the Lord became obedient to the Father not in so far as He was God, but in so far as He was man. For, as God, He is neither

---
7 Cf. Gregory of Nyssa and others, cited by the Council of Constant. 3 (Oec. 6), Mansi, *op. cit.* 11.400ff.
8 Mark 7.24.
9 Matt. 27.33-34; cf. Maximus, *op. cit.* (PG 91.321AB).
10 Phil. 2.8.

obedient or disobedient, because obedience or disobedience belong to such as are subject to authority, as the inspired Gregory has said.[11] Then, as man also, Christ was volitive.

Moreover, when we speak of the natural will, we mean that it is not constrained but free—for, if it is rational, it is also absolutely free. For there is not only the uncreated divine nature which is not subject to constraint, but there is also the created intellectual nature which is not so either. And this is obvious, because, although God is by nature good and creative and God, He is not these things by necessity—for who was there to impose the necessity?

It is furthermore necessary to know that the term *freedom of will* is used equivocally—sometimes being referred to God, sometimes to the angels, and sometimes to men.[12] Thus, with God it is supersubstantial, but with the angels the execution coincides with the inclination without admitting of any interval of time at all. For the angel has freedom by nature and he is unhampered in its exercise because he has neither the opposition from a body nor has he anyone to interfere with him. With men, however, it is such that the inclination precedes the execution in point of time. This is because, though man is free and has this freedom of will naturally, he also has the interference of the Devil to contend with and the motion of the body. Consequently, because of this interference and the burden of the body, the execution comes after the inclination.

If, then, Adam willingly gave ear, and willed and ate, then the will was the first thing to suffer in us. But, if the will was the first thing to suffer, and if, when the Word became incarnate, He did not assume it, then we have not been made free from sin.

And still further, if the nature's power of free will is His work, and yet He did not assume it, it was either because He condemned His own creation as not being good or because

---

11 Cf. Gregory Nazianzen, *Sermon* 30.6 (*PG* 36.109BC).
12 Cf. Maximus, *op. cit.* (*PG* 91.234D-325A).

He begrudged us our being healed in it. And while He deprived us of perfect healing, He showed Himself subject to suffering without willing or without being able to save us perfectly.

It is furthermore impossible to speak of one thing composed of two wills in the same way that we speak of a person composed of its natures. This is because, in the first place, compounds are made of things that have their own subsistence and are not found to exist by virtue of another principle than their own; whereas, in the second place, if we are to speak of a composition of wills and operations, we shall be forced to admit a composition of the other natural properties, such as the uncreated and the created, the invisible and the visible, and so on. And besides, what will the will that is composed of the wills be called? For it is impossible for the compound to be given the name of the things of which it is composed, since in such a case we should call that which is composed of the natures a *nature* and not a *person*. And further, should we speak of one compound will in Christ, then we are making Him distinct from the Father in will, because the will of the Father is not compound. Accordingly, it remains for us to say that only the Person of Christ is compound, in so far as it is composed of His natures and His natural properties as well.

And, should we wish to speak literally, it would be impossible to speak of *opinion* (γνώμη) and choice in the Lord. For the opinion resulting from the inquiry and deliberation, or counsel and judgment, in respect to the unknown thing is a disposition toward the thing judged. After the opinion comes the choice which selects and chooses one thing rather than the other. Now, since the Lord was not a mere man, but was also God and knew all things, He stood in no need of reflection, inquiry, counsel, or judgment. He also had a natural affinity for good and antipathy for evil.[13] Thus, it is in this sense that the Prophet Isaias, too, says: 'Before

---

13 Cf. Basil, *Homily on Psalm 44.8* (PG 29.405B).

the child shall know to refuse the evil, he will choose the good. For before the child know to refuse the evil, and to choose the good, he will reject the evil by choosing the good.'[14] The 'before' shows that he made no inquiry or investigation in a human manner, but that, since He was God and divinely subsisted in the flesh—that is to say, was hypostatically united to the flesh—by the fact of His very being and His knowing all things He naturally possessed the good. Now, the virtues are natural, and they are also naturally inherent in all men, even though all of us do not act naturally. For, because of the fall, we went from what is according to nature to what is against it. But the Lord brought us back from what is against nature to what is according to it—for this last is what is meant by 'according to his image and likeness.'[15] Now, asceticism and the labors connected with it were not intended for the acquisition of virtue as of something to be introduced from the outside, but for the expulsion of evil, which has been introduced and is against nature—just as the steel's rust, which is not natural but due to neglect, we remove with hard toil to bring out the natural brightness of the steel.

Moreover, one must know that the word γνώμη, or opinion, is used in many ways and with many meanings. Thus, it sometimes means *advice,* as when the divine Apostle says: 'Now, concerning virgins, I have no commandment of the Lord: but I give counsel.'[16] Sometimes it implies *design,* as when the Prophet David says: 'They have taken a malicious counsel against thy people.'[17] Sometimes it means *judgment,* as when Daniel says: 'Why so cruel a sentence had gone forth.'[18] And sometimes it is used in the sense of *faith,* or *notion,* or of *intent*—to put it simply, the word γνώμη has twenty-eight different meanings.

---
14 Cf. Isa. 7.16.
15 Gen. 1.26.
16 1 Cor. 7.25.
17 Ps. 82.4.
18 Dan. 2.15.

Chapter 15

Now, we also say that in our Lord Jesus Christ there are two operations.[1] For, in so far as He was God and consubstantial with the Father, like the Father He had the divine operation; in so far as He was made man and consubstantial with us, He had the operation of the human nature.

However, one must know that operation is one thing, what is operative another, which is operated another, and still another the operator. *Operation,* then, is the efficacious and substantial motion of the nature. And that which is *operative* is the nature from which the operation proceeds. That which is *operated* is the effect of the operation. And the *operator* is the one who performs the operation; the person, that is. However, the term operation is also used for the effect, and the term for the effect for the operation, as 'creation' is used for 'creature.' For in that way we say 'all creation," meaning 'all creatures.'

One must know that the operation is a motion and that it is operated rather than operating, as Gregory the Theologian says in his sermon on the Holy Ghost: 'But if He is an operation, then He will obviously be operated and will not operate. And, as soon as He has been effected, He will cease.'[2]

It is further necessary to know that life itself is an operation, and the primary operation of the animal. So also is the whole vital process—the motions of nutrition and growth, or the vegetative;[3] the impulsive, or the sensitive; and the intellectual and free motions. Operation, moreover, is the perfection of a potentiality. So, if we find all these things in Christ, then we shall declare that He also has a human operation.

---

[1] The *operation,* or *energy,* is the capacity or power to act inherent in every nature.
[2] Gregory Nazianzen, *Sermon* 31.6 (*PG* 36.140A).
[3] By a misprint the Migne text has 'natural' for the 'vegetative' of Lequien's original text.

The first thought (νόημα) formed in us is called an operation. It is a simple unrelated operation by which the mind of itself secretly puts forth those thoughts of its own without which it could not rightly be called mind (νοῦς). And again, that is also called an operation which is the expression and explanation of what has been thought by means of speech utterance. This, however, is no longer unrelated and simple. On the contrary, since it is composed of thought and speech, it is found to be in a relation. And the very relation which the doer has to the thing done is also an operation. And the thing itself which is effected is called an operation. Now, the first of these belongs to the soul alone, the next to the soul as using the body, the next to the body as endowed with an intellectual soul, and the last of them is the effect. Thus, the mind first considers the thing to be done and then acts accordingly through the body. So, it 'is to the soul that the control belongs, since it uses the body as an instrument which it guides and directs. The operation of the body as guided and moved by the soul, however, is a different one. And as to the effect, while that of the body is, as it were, the touching, holding, and clasping of the thing made, that of the soul is the thing's formation and configuration. It was also the same with our Lord Jesus Christ. While the power of working miracles was an operation of His divinity, the work of His hands, His willing, and His saying: 'I will. Be thou made clean,'[4] were operations belonging to His humanity. And as to the effect, the breaking of the loaves, the hearing the leper, and the 'I will' belong to His human nature, whereas to His divine nature belong the multiplication of the loaves and the cleansing of the leper. Now, by both, that is, by the operation of the soul and that of the body, He showed His divine operation to be one and the same, akin and equal. And just as we know that the natures are united and mutually immanent and still do not deny their difference, but even number them, while we know

---

4 Matt. 8.3.

them to be indivisible; so also do we know the connection of the wills and operations, while we recognize their difference and number them without introducing any division. For, as the flesh was made divine, yet suffered no change in its own nature, in the same way the will and operation were made divine, yet did not exceed their proper limits. For He is one who is both the one thing and the other and who wills and acts in both one way and the other, that is to say, both in a divine and in a human fashion.

Accordingly, because of the duality of His nature, it is necessary to affirm two operations in Christ. For things having diverse natures have different operations, and things having diverse operations have different natures. And conversely, things having the same nature have the same operation, and things having one operation have also one substance, as the inspired Fathers declare. Consequently, we must do one of two things: either we shall say that there is one operation in Christ and then say that His substance is one; or, if we keep to the truth, we shall confess with the Gospels and the Fathers that there are two substances, and at the same time we shall be confessing that there are also two operations corresponding to these. For, since in His divinity He is consubstantial with God the Father, He will also be equal to Him in His operation. On the other hand, since in His humanity He is consubstantial with us, He will also be equal to us in His operation. Indeed, the blessed Gregory, who was Bishop of Nyssa, says: 'Things having one operation very definitely have the same potentiality, also.'[5] For every operation is the perfection of a potentiality. Moreover, it is impossible for there to be one nature, potentiality, or operation belonging both to an uncreated nature and to a created one. And, were we to say that Christ has one nature, we

---

5 Lequien assigns this to the *Oratio de natura et hypostasi* of Gregory of Nyssa, which is really Basil's *Epistle* 38 (*On the Difference between Substance and Hypostasis*), (PG 32.325-340), but which does not contain the present quotation. It probably is from Gregory's *Against Eunomius* 1 (cf. PG 45.373-CD).

should be attributing the passions of the intellectual soul to the divinity of the Word—fear, I mean, and grief, and anguish.

However, should they say that in discussing the Blessed Trinity the holy Fathers said: 'Things having one substance also have one operation, and things which have different substances also have different operations,' and that one must not transfer to the human nature what belongs to the divine, we shall reply as follows. If this was said by the Fathers in respect to the divinity only, then the Son does not have the same operation as the Father and He is not even of the same substance. And, what is more, to whom shall we attribute the words: 'My Father worketh until now, and I work'; and 'What things soever he seeth the Father doing, these things the Son also doth in like manner'; and 'If you do not believe me, believe my works'; and 'The works which I do give testimony of me'; and 'As the Father raiseth up the dead and giveth life: so the Son also giveth life to whom He will'?[6] For all these show that even after the Incarnation He is not only consubstantial with the Father but also has the same operation.[7]

And again, if the providence exercised over creatures belongs not only to the Father and the Holy Ghost, but also to the Son even after the Incarnation, and if this is an operation, then even after the Incarnation He has the same operation as the Father.

And if from His miracles we perceive Christ to be of the same substance as the Father, and if miracles are an operation of God, then even after the Incarnation He has the same operation as the Father.

And if His divinity and His flesh have one operation, it will be composite, and either He will have a different operation from that of the Father, or the Father's operation will

---

6 John 5.17,19; 10-38; 5.36,21.
7 Cf. Maximus, *op. cit* (*PG* 91.348D-349A).

be composite, too. But, if the Father's operation is composite, it is obvious that His nature will be, too.

And, if they were to say that the introduction of the operation requires that of a person along with it,[8] we should reply that, if the introduction of the operation requires that of a person along with it, then by logical conversion the introduction of the person will require that of an operation along with it. In such a case, since there are three Persons, or hypostases, in the Holy Trinity, there will also be three operations; or, since there is one operation, there will also be one Person and one hypostasis. But the holy Fathers were all agreed in declaring that things having the same substance also have the same operation.

What is more, if the introduction of the operation requires that of a person, then those who decreed that neither one nor two operations be affirmed in Christ[9] in doing so ordered that neither one nor two persons be affirmed in Him.

And then, just as the natures of both the fire and the steel are preserved intact in the red-hot knife,[10] so also are there two operations and their effects. For, while the steel has its cutting power, the fire has its power of burning; and the cut is the effect of the operation of the steel, while the burn is that of the operation of the fire. And the distinction between these is preserved in the burnt cut and the cut burn, even though the burning of the cut does not take place separately after the union, and the cut is not made separately from the burn. Neither do we say that because of the twofold natural operation there are two red-hot knives, nor do we destroy their substantial difference because of the singleness of the red-hot knife. In just the same way there is in Christ both the divine and all-powerful operation of His divinity, and that after our own fashion, which is that of His humanity.

---

8 Cf. ibid. (PG 91.337B).
9 The *Ecthesis*, published in 638 by Emperor Heraclius, forbade the use of the expression of one or two operations in Christ, but asserted one will. This precipitated the Monothelite schism (640-657).
10 Cf. Maximus, *op. cit.* (PG 91.337D-340A).

Thus, the child's being taken by the hand and drawn up[11] was an effect of His human operation, whereas her being restored to life was an effect of His divine operation. For the latter is one thing and the former another, even though they are inseparable in the theandric operation. What is more, if, because the Person of the Lord is one, His operation must also be one, then because of the one Person there must also be one substance.

Again, if we were to affirm one operation in the Lord, we should be saying that this was either divine or human or neither.[12] Now, if we say that it is divine, we shall be saying that He is only God and devoid of our humanity. And if we say that it is human, we shall be uttering the blasphemy that He is mere man. But, if we say that it is neither divine nor human, we shall be saying that He is neither consubstantial with the Father nor with us. For the identity of person came from the union, without in any way destroying the difference of the natures. And, if the difference of the natures is kept intact, their operations will plainly be kept so, also, because there is no nature without any operation.

If the operation of the Lord Christ is one,[13] then it will be either created or uncreated; for, just as there is no intermediate nature between the created and the uncreated, neither is there any such operation. Therefore, if it is created, it will show only a created nature; if it is uncreated, it will indicate an uncreated substance only. This is because the natural properties must correspond with the natures absolutely, since the existence of a defective nature is impossible. The natural operation, moreover, does not come from anything outside the nature and it is obvious that the nature can neither exist nor be known without its natural operation.

---

11 Cf. Luke 8.54.
12 Maximus, *op. cit.* (*PG* 91.340C).
13 Cf. *ibid.* (*PG* 91.341A).

For, by remaining invariable in its operations, each thing gives proof of its own nature.

If Christ's operation is one, then the same operation can do divine and human things. But, no being acting according to nature can do things which are contrary. Thus, fire does not make hot and cold, nor does water make wet and dry. How, then, did He, who is God by nature and who became man by nature, both work the miracles and experience the passions with one operation?

Now, if Christ assumed a human mind, that is to say, a rational and intellectual soul, He certainly thinks and will always think. But, thinking is an operation of the mind. Therefore, Christ acts as a man also and will always so act.

The most wise and great St. John Chrysostom in the second homily of his commentary on the Acts says this: 'No one should be wrong in calling His suffering an action. For by suffering all things He did that great and wonderful work of destroying death and working all the rest.'[14]

If every operation is defined as a substantial motion of some nature, as those who are well versed in these matters have clearly laid down, where has anyone seen a nature without a motion or without any operation at all, or where has anyone found an operation which is not a motion of a natural power? And, according to the blessed Cyril,[15] no one in his right mind would hold the natural operation of God and of a creature to be one. It is not the human nature that restores Lazarus to life, nor is it the power of the divinity that sheds tears. For tears are peculiar to humanity, whereas life belongs to the Subsistent Life. Nevertheless, by reason of the identity of the person each one of these actions is common to both natures.[16] For Christ is one, and one is His Person, or hypostasis. Nevertheless, He has two natures: that of His divinity and that of His humanity. Consequently,

---
14 *Homily 1 on the Acts* 3 (*PG* 60.18).
15 Cf. *Thesaurus* 32.2 (*PG* 75.453B).
16 Cf. Leo, *Epistle* 28.4 (*PL* 54.772A).

the glory which proceeds naturally from the divinity became common to both by reason of the identity of person, while the humble things proceeding from the flesh became common to both. For He is one and the same who is both the one thing and the other, that is, both God and man; and to the same one belong both what is proper to the divinity and what is proper to the humanity. Thus, while the divinity worked the miracles but not separately from the flesh, the flesh did the humble things but not apart from the divinity. Thus, also, while remaining impassible, the divinity was joined to the suffering flesh and made the sufferings salutary. And the sacred mind was joined to the acting divinity of the Word and thought and knew the things which were being done.

Therefore, the divinity communicates its excellences to the flesh while remaining with no part of the sufferings of the flesh. For His flesh did not suffer through the divinity in the same way that the divinity acted through the flesh, because the flesh served as an instrument of the divinity. So, even though from the first instant of conception there was no divisions whatsoever of either form, but all the actions of each form at all times belonged to one Person, we nevertheless in no way confuse these things which were done inseparably. On the contrary, from the nature of the works we perceive to which form they belong.

And so, Christ acts through each of His natures and in Him each nature acts in communion with the other.[17] The Word does whatever pertains to the kingdom and the principality, which is what belongs to Him by reason of the authority and the power of His divinity, while the body in accordance with the intent of the Word united to it does what has also become proper to it. Now, the body of itself had no inclination for physical suffering, nor yet did it avoid and refuse to accept what was painful. Neither was it affected by external influences; rather, it was moved in accordance

---

17 Cf. *ibid.* (*PL* 54.768B).

with the order of its nature, with the Word wisely willing and permitting it to suffer and do what was proper to it, so that through its works the truth of its nature might be guaranteed.

Moreover,[18] even as He was conceived of a virgin and put on substance in a way that transcended substance, so does He also do human things in a way that transcends the human—as when He walked with His earthly feet upon unstable water which had not become earth but by the supernatural power of His divinity was made firm and did not yield to the weight of material feet. He did not do human things in a human way, because He was not only man, but God, also, which is the reason why His sufferings were life-giving and saving. Neither did He do divine things in a divine way, because He was not only God, but man, also, which is the reason why He worked miracles by touch and word and other such things.

And should someone say[19] that we do not hold one operation in Christ because we do away with the human operation, but because the human operation as contrasted with the divine is called passion, and in this sense we say that there is one operation in Christ—should they say this: We shall reply that by this token they who hold one nature do not do so in the sense of doing away with the human nature, but because the human nature as contrasted with the divine is called passible. God forbid that we should call the human motion passion just because of its contrast with the divine operation. For, generally speaking, nothing is known or defined as having its real existence from contrast or comparison. In such a case, things which exist would be found to be mutually causative of each other. Thus if, because the divine motion is action, the human is passion, then it will definitely follow that, because the divine nature is good, the

---

18 Cf. Pseudo-Dionysius, *Divine Names* 2.10, *Epistle* 4 (*PG* 3.648-649; 1072).
19 Cf. Maximus, *op. cit.* (*PG* 91.349C).

human will be evil. Conversely, because the human motion is called passion, the divine is called action; and because human nature is evil, the divine will be good. What is more, all creatures will thus be evil, and he will be a liar who said: 'And God saw all the things that he had made, and they were very good.'[20]

Now we say that the holy Fathers gave the human motion a variety of names, depending upon the fundamental concept in question.[21] Thus, they called it both power, operation, difference, movement, property, quality, and passion. And they did not do this by way of contrast to the divine motion. On the contrary, they called it *power,* in so far as it is sustaining and unchangeable; *operation,* as being distinctive and showing the invariability in all things of the same species; *difference,* as being defining; *motion,* as being indicative; *property,* as being component and as belonging to this alone and not to some other; *quality,* as being specific; and *passion,* as being moved. For all things which are from God and after Him are subject to being moved, since they are not motion or force itself. Consequently, it was not so named by contrast, as has been said, but after the principle that was put in it at its creation by the cause which framed the universe. For this reason, it was called operation, even when mentioned together with the divine motion. For what else did he do, who said: 'For each form acts in communion with the other,'[22] than he who said: 'And he had fasted forty days and forty nights, afterwards he was hungry'[23]—for, when He wished, He permitted His nature to do what was proper to it? Or what else did he do than those who said that there was a different operation in Him, or a twofold operation, or one and another? For by the opposition of terms these expressions signify two natures, since the number is

---
20 Gen. 1.31.
21 Cf. Maximus, *op. cit.* (*PG* 91.325AB).
22 See above, note 17.
23 Matt. 4.2.

oftentimes indicated by the opposition of terms, just as well as it is by saying 'divine and human.' Thus, the difference is a difference of things which differ. And how can things differ which do not exist?

Chapter 16

Since each individual man is made up of two natures—that of the soul and that of the body—and has these unchanged in himself, it will be reasonable to say that he has two natures. For even after the union he retains the natural property of each. Thus, the body is not immortal but corruptible, and the soul is not mortal but immortal. Neither is the body invisible, nor is the soul visible to bodily eyes. On the contrary, the latter is rational and understanding and incorporeal, whereas the former is material and visible and irrational. Moreover, things which are distinct in substance do not have the same nature; consequently, the soul and the body are not of the same substance.

And again, if man is a rational mortal animal, and if every definition designates the natures defined, and if, furthermore, that which is rational is not the same as that which is mortal as respects the concept of nature, then by the norm of his own definition man will not have one nature.

Now, should man at times be said to have one nature, the term 'nature' is being taken in the sense of 'species.' Thus, we say that one man does not differ from another by any difference in nature, because, to the contrary, all men fall under the same definition, in so far as they all are composed of body and soul and have the same makeup, each individual being two constituent natures. And this is not unreasonable, because the divine Athanasius in his discourse against the blasphemers of the Holy Ghost said that all created things have the same nature, when he wrote to the effect that the Holy Ghost is over and above creation and that it is possible to see clearly that, while in relation to the nature of created things He is something else, to the divinity He is proper.[1] Everything that is found to be common to several things without being more in one and less in another is said to be essence. Therefore, since every man is made up of a soul and a body, in this sense men are said to have one nature. As regards the Person of the Lord, however, we cannot speak of one nature, because even after the union each nature retains its natural property and it is not possible to find a species of Christs. For there has been no other Christ made of divinity and humanity, the same being both God and man.

And again, the specific unity of man is not the same thing as the substantial unity of soul and body. For the specific unity of man shows the invariable element in all men, whereas the substantial unity of soul and body destroys their very being and reduces them to absolute non-existence. For either the one will be transformed into the substance of the other, or from two different things a third will be made, or they will remain within their proper limits and be two natures. For it is not by reason of its substance that the body is identical with that which is incorporeal. Consequently, when people speak of one nature in man, not on account of the identity of the substantial quality of the body with that of the soul, but on account of the invariability of the individuals falling under the species, they do not also have to say that in Christ, in whom there is no species comprising several persons, there is one nature.

And further, every composite is said to be composed of those things which have been put together directly. Thus, we do not say that the house is composed of earth and water, but of bricks and wood. Otherwise, we should also have to say that man is made up of five natures at least, of the four elements, that is, and of a soul. So also, in the

---

[1] Athanasius, *Epistle 1 to Serapion* 12,17,22 *et passim* (*PG* 26.561,569, 581, *et al.*).

case of our Lord Jesus Christ we do not consider the part or parts, but those which have been put together directly—the divinity and the humanity.

Further, if by saying that man is two natures we shall be forced to say that there are three natures in Christ, then you, too, by saying that man is of two natures will be teaching that Christ is of three natures. And it will be the same way with the operations, because the operation must correspond with the nature. Witness to the fact that man is said to and does have two natures is Gregory the Theologian, who says:[2] 'God and man are two natures, as, indeed, are soul and body.' Also, in his sermon on baptism he says as follows: 'Since we are twofold, being of soul and body—of the visible and of the invisible nature—so also is the purification twofold: by water and by the Holy Ghost.'

Chapter 17

One should know that it is not by a transformation of nature or by change or alteration or mingling that the Lord's flesh is said to have been deified and made identical with God and God, as Gregory the Theologian says: 'The one of whom did deify, while the other was made divine and, I may confidently say, identical with God. And that which anointed became man, and that which was anointed became God.'[1] This was by no transformation of nature but by the union through dispensation, the hypostatic union, I mean, by which the flesh is inseparably united to God, the Word, and by the mutual indwelling of the natures such as that we also speak of in the case of the heating of the steel. For, just as we confess that the Incarnation was brought about without transformation or change, so also do we hold that

---

2 *Epistle* 101 (PG 37.180A); *Sermon* 40.8 (PG 36.368AB).

1 *Sermon* 45.13 (PG 36.640D-641A).

the deification of the flesh was brought about. For the Word neither overstepped the bounds of His own divinity nor the divine prerogatives belonging to it just because He was made flesh; and, when the flesh was made divine, it certainly did not change its own nature or its natural properties. For even after the union the natures remained unmingled and their properties unimpaired. Moreover, by reason of its most unalloyed union with the Word, that is to say, the hypostatic union, the Lord's flesh was enriched with the divine operations but in no way suffered any impairment of its natural properties. For not by its own operation does the flesh do divine works, but by the Word united to it, and through it the Word shows His own operation. Thus, the steel which has been heated burns, not because it has a naturally acquired power of burning, but because it has acquired it from its union with the fire.[2]

And so the same flesh was mortal in itself and life-giving by its hypostatic union with the Word. Likewise, we say that the deification of the will was not by a transformation of its natural motion, but by its becoming united with His divine and almighty will and being the will of God made man.[3] It was for this reason that, when He wished to be hid, He could not of Himself,[4] because it pleased God the Word that it be shown that in Himself He had the weakness of the human will. However, it was by willing that He worked the cure of the leper,[5] and this because of the union with the divine will.

One must furthermore know that the deification of the nature and the will is very expressive and indicative of the two natures and the two wills. For, just as heating does not transform the nature of the thing heated into that of fire, but, rather, brings out both the thing heated and the thing heating and shows not one thing but two, so neither does

---
2 Maximus, *op. cit.* (*PG* 91.337D-340A).
3 Cf. Gregory Nazianzen, *Sermon* 30.12 (*PG* 36.117C-120A).
4 Cf. Mark 7.24.
5 Cf. Matt. 8.3.

the deification produce one compound nature, but, rather, the two natures and their hypostatic union. In fact, Gregory the Theologian says: 'The one of whom did deify, while the other was made divine,'[6] where by saying 'of whom' and 'the one' and 'the other' he showed that there were two.

Chapter 18

When we say that Christ is perfect God and perfect man we are attributing to Him absolutely all the natural properties which belong to the Father and to His Mother. For He became man in order that that which had been conquered might conquer. Now, it was not impossible for Him who can do all things to deliver man from the tyrant by His almighty power and might; but, had the tyrant after having conquered man been prevailed over by God, he would have had grounds for complaint. For this reason the compassionate and loving God wished to make the victor him who had fallen, and so He became man and restored like by like.

Moreover, no one will deny that man is a rational and intellectual animal. How, then, did He become man if He assumed a soulless body or a mindless soul? For that sort of thing is no man. Further, what profit do we have from the Incarnation if he who was the first to suffer has not been saved, renewed, or strengthened by being conjoined with the Godhead? For that which has not been assumed has not been healed. And so, He assumes the whole man, who had fallen through weakness, and his most noble part, in order that He might grace the whole with salvation.[1] What is more, there never could be a mind without wisdom and bereft of knowledge, for, were the mind without operation and motion, it would also be absolutely non-existent.

---

6 *Sermon* 45.9 (PG 36.633D).

---

1 Cf. Gregory Nazianzen, *Epistle* 101, *passim* (PG 37.176ff).

God the Word, then, wishing to restore that which was in His image, became man. But what is in His image, if it is not the mind? Did He, then, disregard what was better and assume what was worse? For mind stands midway between God and the flesh as being a companion of the flesh on the one hand and on the other an image of God. Thus, mind is associated with Mind and the mind holds the middle place between purity of God and the grossness of the flesh. And, had the Lord assumed a mindless soul, He would have assumed the soul of a brute animal.

Now, although the Evangelist did say that the Word was made flesh, one must know that in sacred Scripture man is sometimes called 'soul,' as when it says that 'all the souls of the house of Jacob, that entered into Egypt, were seventy-five,'[2] and sometimes 'flesh,' as when it says that 'all flesh shall see the salvation of God.'[3] So, the Lord was not made flesh without soul or mind, but He was made man. In fact, He says: 'Why do you seek to kill me, a man who have spoken truth to you?'[4] Therefore, He assumed a body animated by a rational and intellectual soul having dominion over the flesh, but itself being under the dominion of the divinity of the Word.

Consequently, while He had naturally the power of willing both as God and as man, the human will followed after and was subordinated to His will, not being motivated by its own opinion, but willing what His divine will willed. Thus, it was with the permission of the divine will that He suffered what was naturally proper to Him.[5] And when He begged to be spared death, He did so naturally, with His divine will willing and permitting, and He was in agony and afraid. Then, when His divine will willed that His human will choose death, the passion was freely accepted by it, because it was not as God alone that He freely delivered Himself over to

---

2 Gen. 46.27 (Septuagint).
3 Luke 3.6.
4 John 8.40.
5 Cf. Sophronius, Synodic Letter (*PG* 87.3173B).

death, but as man, also. Whence, He also gave us the grace of courage in the face of death. Thus, indeed, He says before His saving passion: 'Father, if it is possible, let this chalice pass from me.'[6] It was manifestly as man that He was to drink the chalice, for it was not as God. Consequently, it is as man that He wishes the chalice to pass, and these are words arising from a natural fear. 'But yet not my will, but thine be done,'[7] that is to say: 'In so far as I am of another substance than thine, but thine, which is mine and thine in so far as I am begotten consubstantial with thee.' Again, these are the words of courage. For, since by His good pleasure the Lord had truly become man, His soul at first experienced the weakness of nature and through sense perception felt a natural pain at the thought of its separation from the body; then it was strengthened by the divine will and faced death courageously. For, since He was entirely God with His humanity and entirely man with His divinity, He as man in Himself and through Himself subjected His humanity to God the Father and became obedient to the Father, thus setting for us a most noble example and pattern.

Moreover, He willed freely with His divine and His human will, for free will is absolutely inherent in every rational nature. After all, of what good can rationality be to a nature that does not reason freely? Now, the Creator has implanted a natural appetite in brute beasts which constrains them to act for the preservation of their own nature. For, since they lack reason, they cannot lead; rather, they are led by their natural appetite. Whence it is that the instinct to act arises simultaneously with the appetite, for they enjoy neither the use of reason nor that of counsel or reflection or judgment. For this reason they are neither praised and deemed good for practicing virtue nor punished for doing evil. The rational nature, however, has its natural appetite, which

---

6 Matt. 26.39.
7 Luke 22.42.

becomes aroused, but is guided and controlled by the reason in regard to what is for the maintenance of the natural order. This, namely free will, is an advantage of the power of reason and we call it a natural motion in the reasoning faculty. Wherefore, the rational nature is both praised and deemed good for practicing virtue and punished for practicing vice.

And so, the Lord's soul was freely moved to will, but it freely willed those things which His divine will willed it to will. For the flesh was not moved by the command of the Word in the same way that Moses and all the saints were moved by the divine command. On the contrary, since the same one was both God and man, He willed according to His divine and His human will. Wherefore, it was not in opinion that the Lord's two wills differed from each other, but in natural power. For His divine will was without beginning and all-creating and having the corresponding power, and it was impassible. But his human will had a beginning in time and was itself subject to natural and irreprehensible passions. Although by its own nature it was not omnipotent, it was so in so far as it had been made to belong truly and naturally to God the Word.

Chapter 19

When the blessed Dionysius said that Christ had used a certain new theandric operation with us,[1] he was not doing away with the natural operations and saying that there was one operation proceeding from the human and divine natures. For, if such were the case, we might also say that there was one new nature made from the human and the divine, because, according to the holy Fathers, things which have one operation also have one substance. On the contrary, he wanted to show that the new and ineffable manner of the

---
1 Cf. *Epistle* 4 (*PG* 3.1072C).

manifestation of the natural operations in Christ was consonant with the mutual indwelling of Christ's natures in each other, and that His living as a man was both unusual and incredible and unknown to the nature of things. He also wanted to show the manner of the exchange arising from the ineffable union. Thus, we do not say that the operations are separated and that the natures act separately, but we say that they act conjointly, with each nature doing in communion with the other that which it has proper to itself. He did not perform the human actions in a human way, because He was not a mere man, nor did He perform the divine actions in a divine way only, because He was not just God, but God and man together. And just as we understand both the union of the natures and their natural difference, so also do we understand that of the natural wills and operations.

So that one must know that while we sometimes speak as of two natures in our Lord Jesus Christ, we sometimes speak as of one person, and that both the former way of speaking and the latter refer to the same concept. For the two natures are one Christ and the one Christ is two natures. It is therefore the same thing to say that Christ acts according to each of His natures and to say that each nature in Christ acts in association with the other. Accordingly, when the flesh is acting, the divine nature is associated with it because the flesh is being permitted by the good pleasure of the divine will to suffer and do what is proper to it and because the operation of the flesh is absolutely salutary—which last does not belong to the human operation, but to the divine. And when the divinity of the Word is acting, the flesh is associated with it, because the divine operations are being performed by the flesh as by an instrument and because He who is acting at once in a divine and human way is one.

One should furthermore know that His sacred mind performs His natural operations, both understanding and knowing itself to be the mind of God and adored by all creation, but at the same time still mindful of His doings and sufferings on earth. It is, moreover, associated with the operation of the divinity of the Word by which the universe is ordered and controlled, understanding and knowing and ordering not as a mere human mind, but as one hypostatically united to God and reckoned as the mind of God.

Thus, the theandric operation shows this: when God became man, that is to say, was incarnate, His human operation was divine, that is to say, deified. And it was not excluded from His divine operation, nor was His divine operation excluded from His human operation. On the contrary, each is found in the other. Now, when one expresses two things with one word, this figure of speech is called circumlocution (περίφρασις).[2] Thus, while we speak of the cut burn and the burnt cut of the red-hot knife, we nevertheless hold the cutting to be one operation and the burning another, the one belonging to one nature and the other to the other—the burning to the fire and the cutting to the steel. In the very same way, when we speak of one theandric operation of Christ, we understand the two operations of His two natures: the divine operation of the divinity and the human operation of the humanity.

Chapter 20

Moreover, we confess that He assumed all the natural and blameless passions of man. This is because He assumed the whole man and everything that is his, except sin—for this last is not natural and it was not implanted in us by the Creator. On the contrary, it grew up in our will from the oversowing of the Devil, freely and not prevailing over us by force. Now, those passions are natural and blameless which are not under our control and have come into man's life as a result of the condemnation occasioned by his fall. Such, for example, were hunger, thirst, fatigue, pain,

---

[2] Cf. Maximus, *Opuscula* (PG 91.100D).

the tears, the destruction, the shrinking from death, the fear, the agony from which came the sweating and drops of blood, the aid brought by the angels in deference to the weakness of His nature, and any other such things as are naturally inherent in all men.

So, He assumed all that He might sanctify all. He was put to the test and He conquered that He might gain for us the victory and give to our nature the power to conquer the Adversary, so that through the very assaults by which the nature had been conquered of old it might conquer its former victor.

Now, the Evil One attacked from the outside, just as he had with Adam, and not through thoughts—for it was not through thoughts that he attacked Adam, but through the serpent. The Lord, however, repelled the attack and it vanished like smoke, so that by being conquered the passions which had assailed Him might become easy for us to conquer and the new Adam thus be restored by the old.

Actually, our natural passions were in Christ according to nature and over and above nature. Thus, it was according to nature that they were aroused in Him, when He permitted the flesh to suffer what was proper to it; whereas it was over and above nature, because in the Lord the things of nature did not control the will. For with Him nothing is found to be done under compulsion; on the contrary, everything was done freely. Thus, it was by willing that He hungered and by willing that He thirsted, by willing that He was afraid and by willing that He died.

Chapter 21

One should know that He did assume an ignorant and servile nature, and this is because man's nature is subservient to God who made it, and it does not have knowledge of future events. If, then, like Gregory the Theologian,[1] you distinguish what is seen from what is thought, then the flesh will be said to be servile and ignorant. However, by reason of the identity of person and the inseparable union, the Lord's soul enjoyed the knowledge of future events as well as the other signs of divinity. For, just as the flesh of men is not of its own nature life-giving, whereas that of the Lord, being hypostatically united to God the Word Himself, became life-giving by reason of its hypostatic union with the Word without losing its natural mortality, and we cannot say that it was not and is not always so; in the same way, while His human nature did not of its essence have knowledge of future events, the Lord's soul, by reason of its union with God the Word Himself and the identity of person, did, as I have said, enjoy, along with the other signs of divinity, the knowledge of future events, also.

One must furthermore know that we can by no means call Him servile, because the terms 'servitude' and 'mastery' are not indicative of nature, but of relationships, just as 'paternity' and 'filiation' are. These last do not belong to the essence, but are indicative of relation. Therefore, we say here, just as we did in the case of ignorance, that if you distinguish the created from the uncreated by tenuous thought processes, or subtle imaginings, then the flesh is servile as long as it is not united to God the Word. But, once it is hypostatically united, how will it be servile? For, since Christ is one, He cannot be His own servant and Lord, because these do not belong to the things predicated absolutely, but to them that are predicated relatively. So, whose servant will He be? The Father's? But then, if He is the servant of the Father, the Son does not have 'all things whatsoever the Father hath.'[2] And He certainly is not His own servant. And, if He is Himself a servant, how is it that in regard to us, who have been adopted through Him, the Apostle says: 'There-

---

[1] Cf. *Sermon* 30.15 (*PG* 36.124B).
[2] John 16.15.

fore, now thou art not a servant, but a son.'³ Therefore, although He is not a servant, He is commonly so called as having for our sake taken on the form of a servant, and together with us He has been called one. For, although He was impassible, He became subject to passion and was made minister of our salvation. Now, they who say that He is a servant divide the one Christ into two, just as Nestorius did. But we say that He is Lord and Master of all creation, the one Christ, the same being at once both God and man, and that He knows all things, 'for in him are hid all the treasures of wisdom and knowldege.'⁴

Chapter 22

He is said to have progressed in wisdom and age and grace,¹ because He did increase in age and by this increase in age brought more into evidence the wisdom inherent in Him; further, because by making what is ours altogether His own He made His own the progress of men in wisdom and grace, as well as the fulfillment of the Father's will, which is to say, men's knowledge of God and their salvation.² Now, those who say that He progressed in wisdom and grace in the sense of receiving an increase in these are saying that the union was not made from the first instant of the flesh's existence. Neither are they holding the hypostatic union, but, misled³ by the empty-headed Nestorius, they are talking preposterously of a relative union and simple indwelling, 'understanding neither the things they say, nor whereof they affirm.'⁴ For, if from the first instant of its existence the

---

3 Gal. 4.7 according to the Greek text.
4 Col. 2.3.

1 Cf. Luke 2.52.
2 Cf. Gregory Nazianzen, *Sermon* 43.38 (*PG* 36.548BC).
3 Through a misprint, the Migne text is incorrect here; cf. Lequien, *Opera* 247.
4 1 Tim. 1.7.

flesh was truly united to God the Word—rather, had existence in Him and identity of person with Him—how did it not enjoy perfectly all wisdom and grace? It did not share the grace and neither did it participate by grace in the things of the Word; rather, because the human and divine things had become proper to the one Christ by the hypostatic union, then, since the same was at once God and man, it gushed forth with the grace and the wisdom and the fullness of all good things for the world.

Chapter 23

The word *fear* has two meanings. Thus, there is natural fear when the soul is unwilling to be separated from the body because of the natural feeling of affinity and kinship implanted in it by the Creator from the beginning. On account of this it is naturally afraid and distressed and it shrinks from death. The definition of this kind of fear is: Natural fear is a force which clings to existence by withdrawal.[1] The reason for this is that, if all things have been brought into existence from non-existence by the Creator, they naturally do not have the desire for non-existence. Furthermore, a natural property of these things is their instinctive tendency toward those things by which they are sustained. So, when God the Word was made man, He, too, had this appetite. On the one hand, by desiring both food and drink and sleep and by being naturally acquainted with these He showed His inclination for the things which sustained His nature; on the other, He showed His disinclination for things destructive of His nature, as when He freely withdrew from death at the time of His passion. For, even though what happened came about by a law of nature, it was not by compulsion as with us, because He freely willed to accept what was natural. Hence, this kind of fear and fright and distress

---

1 Cf. Maximus, *Disputation with Pyrrhus* (*PG* 91.297D).

belongs to the passions which are natural and blameless and are not subject to sin.

There is still another kind of fear which arises from loss of reason, from mistrust, and from not knowing the hour of one's death—as when we are frightened at night by the making of some noise. This is unnatural, and we define it: *Unnatural fear* is an unreasonable withdrawal. This kind the Lord did not have. Wherefore, except at the time of His passion, He was never afraid—even though for good reason He would oftentimes hide himself. For He was not ignorant of the time.

That He truly experienced fear is affirmed by the divine Athanasius in his discourse against Apollinaris:[2] 'For this reason the Lord said: "Now is my soul troubled."[3] And the "now" means this, namely, at the time when He willed; but all the same it indicates the actuality, because He would not call actual that which was not, as if the events related only seemed to happen. For everything happened naturally and truly.' And further on: 'In no wise does divinity admit of suffering without a suffering body, nor of affliction and sorrow without a sorrowing and afflicted soul. Neither does it become troubled and pray without a mind which is troubled and prays. However, even though these things did not result from a defect of nature, they were done to show reality.' The words 'these things did not result from a defect of nature,' make it clear that He did not endure them involuntarily.

Chapter 24

Prayer is an ascent of the mind to God, or the asking God for things which are fitting. Then, how did the Lord pray in the matter of Lazarus, and at the time of His passion? For, since Christ is one and His sacred mind was once and

---

[2] *Against Apollinaris* 1.16; 2.13 (*PG* 26.1124A; 1153B).
[3] John 12.27.

for all united hypostatically to God the Word, it neither needed to ascend to God nor to ask of God. It was, rather, that He appropriated our appearance and impressed what was ours upon Himself. He became a model for us, He taught us to ask of God and to lift ourselves up to Him, and through His sacred mind He opened the way for us to ascend to God. For, just as He endured the passions and gave us victory over them,[1] so also does He pray and open up for us, as I said, the way to the ascent to God. And so, also, does He for our sake fulfill all justice, as He said to John,[2] and reconcile His own Father to us and honor Him as principle and cause, thus showing Himself to be not adverse to God. Thus, in the matter of Lazarus, when He said: 'Father, I give thee thanks that thou hast heard me. And I knew that thou hearest me always; but because of the people who stand about have I said it, that they may believe that thou hast sent me,'[3] was it not made quite plain to all that He had said this to show that He honored His own Father as His own cause and that He Himself was not adverse to God?[4]

When He said: 'Father, if it be possible, let this chalice pass from me. Nevertheless, not as I will but as thou wilt,'[5] is it not clear to everyone[6] that He is teaching us to ask help of God alone in times of trial and to put the divine will before our own, and that He is showing that He had truly made His own what is proper to our nature, and that He actually had two wills that are natural and correspond to His natures and are not mutually opposed? 'Father,' he says as being consubstantial, 'if it be possible,' not because He did not know[7]—and what is impossible for God?—but to instruct us to put the divine will before our own. For

---

[1] Cf. Gregory Nazianzen, *Sermon* 30.14 (*PG* 36.121-122).
[2] Cf. Matt. 3.15.
[3] John 11.41,42.
[4] Cf. John Chrysostom, *Homily 64 on John* 2 (*PG* 59.355).
[5] Matt. 26.39.
[6] Cf. John Chrysostom, *Homily 83 on Matthew* 1 (*PG* 58.746-747).
[7] Gregory Nazianzen, *Sermon* 30.12 (*PG* 36.117C).

this alone is impossible, namely, that which God does not wish and does not permit. 'Nevertheless, not as I will but as thou wilt,' He says as God, since He is of the same will as the Father, while at the same time He says it as man to show the natural will of His humanity, for this last naturally shrinks from death.

Now, the 'My God, my God, why hast thou forsaken me?'[8] He said because He had appropriated our appearance. For, unless by subtle imaginings a distinction should be made between what is seen and what is thought, God as His Father would not be called ours. Nor was He ever deserted by His divinity—on the contrary, it was ourselves who were left behind and overlooked. And so He appropriated our appearance and prayed these things.

Chapter 25

One should, moreover, know that there are two kinds of appropriation, the one being natural and substantial and the other apparent (προσωπική) and relative.[1] Now, the natural and substantial is that by which the Lord out of His love for man assumed both our nature and all that was natural to it, and in nature and in truth became man and experienced the things that are natural to man. It is apparent and relative, however, when one assumes the appearance (πρόσωπον) of another relatively, as out of pity or love, and in this other's stead speaks words in his behalf which in no way concern himself. It was by this last kind of appropriation that He appropriated our curse and dereliction and such things as are not according to nature, not because He was or had been such, but because He took on

---

8 Matt. 27.46.

1 Maximus, *Solution of Difficulties of Theodore to Marinus* (PG 91. 220BC).

our appearance and was reckoned as one of us. And such is the sense of the words, 'being made a curse for us.'[2]

Chapter 26

God's Word Himself, then, endured all things in His flesh, while His divine nature, which alone is impassible, remained unaffected. For, when the one Christ made up of both divinity and humanity suffered, the passible part of Him suffered, because it was of its nature to suffer, but the impassible did not suffer with it. Thus, since the soul is passible, it does feel pain and suffer with the body when the body is hurt, although it itself is not hurt. The divinity, however, being impassible, does not suffer with the body.

And it should be known that, although we speak of God having suffered in the flesh, we by no means speak of the divinity suffering in the flesh or of God suffering through the flesh. For if, when the sun is shining upon a tree, the tree should be cut down by an axe, the sun will remain uncut and unaffected, then how much more will the impassible divinity of the Word hypostatically united with the flesh remain unaffected when the flesh suffers. And just as if one should pour water upon a red-hot iron, that which is naturally disposed to be affected by the water—the fire, I mean—will be quenched, while the iron remains unharmed, because it is not of its nature to be destroyed by the water; how much less did the divinity, which is alone impassible, endure the suffering of the flesh and still remain inseparable from it. Now, examples do not have to be absolutely and unfailingly exact, for, just because it is an example, one must find in it that which is like and that which is unlike. For likeness in everything would be identity and not an example, which is especially true with divine things. So, in the matter

---
2 Gal. 3.13.

of theology and the Incarnation, it is impossible to find an absolutely perfect example.

Chapter 27

Since our Lord Jesus Christ was without sin, 'because he hath done no iniquity, he who taketh away the sin of the world, neither was there deceit in his mouth,'[1] He was not subject to death, even though death had by sin entered into the world.[2] And so for our sake He submits to death and dies and offers Himself to the Father as a sacrifice for us. For we had offended Him and it was necessary for Him to take upon Himself our redemption that we might thus be loosed from the condemnation—for God forbid that the Lord's blood should have been offered to the tyrant! Wherefore, then, death approaches, gulps down the bait of the body, and is pierced by the hook of the divinity. Then, having tasted of the sinless and life-giving body, it is destroyed and gives up all those whom it had swallowed down of old.[3] For, just as the darkness entirely disappears when light is let in, so is destruction driven away at the onset of life, and life comes to all, while destruction comes to the destroyer.

And so, even though as man He did die and His sacred soul was separated from His immaculate body, the divinity remained unseparated from both—the soul, I mean, and the body. Thus, the one Person was not divided into two persons. For from the beginning both had existence in the same way in the Person of the Word, and when they were separated from each other in death, each one of them remained in the possession of the one Person of the Word. Hence, the one Person of the Word existed as person both of the Word and of the soul and of the body, for neither

---

1 Isa. 53.9; John 1.29.
2 Cf. Rom. 5.12.
3 Cf. Gregory of Nyssa, *Catecheses* 24 (*PG* 45.65A).

the soul nor the body ever had any person of its own other than that of the Word, and the Person of the Word was always one and never two. Hence, the Person of Christ was always one, since, even though the soul was separated from the body in place, it still was hypostatically united to it through the Word.

Chapter 28

The word *destruction* (φθορά) has two meanings.[1] Thus, it means human sufferings such as hunger, thirst, weariness, piercing with nails, death—that is separation of the soul from the body—and the like. In this sense, we say that the Lord's body was destructible, because He endured all these things freely. Destruction, however, also means the complete dissolution of the body and its reduction to the elements of which it was composed. By many this is more generally called *corruption* (διαφθορά). This the Lord's body did not experience, as the Prophet David says: 'Because thou wilt not leave my soul in hell; nor wilt thou give thy holy one to corruption.'[2]

Therefore, it is impious to say with the insane Julian and Gaianus that before the resurrection the Lord's body was indestructible in the first sense. For, if it was thus incorruptible, then it was not consubstantial with us, and the things such as the hunger, the thirst, the nails, the piercing of the side, and death which the Gospel says happened did not really happen, but only seemed to. But, if they only seemed to happen, then the mystery of the Incarnation is a hoax and a stage trick; it was in appearance and not in truth that He was made man and in appearance and not in truth that we have been saved. But far be it, and let those who say this have no part of salvation.[3] We, however,

---
1 Cf. Leontius, *On Sects* 10 (*PG* 86.1260-1261).
2 Ps. 15.10.
3 Cf. Anastasius Sin., *The Guide* 23 (*PG* 89.300BD).

have gained and shall obtain the true salvation. Moreover, in the second sense of the word destruction, we confess that the Lord's body was indestructible, that is to say, incorruptible, even as has been handed down to us by the inspired Fathers. Nevertheless, we do say that after the Saviour's resurrection the body of the Lord is indestructible in the first sense, too. And through His body the Lord has granted the resurrection and consequent incorruptibility to our body, also, Himself becoming to us the first fruits of the resurrection and incorruptibility and impassibility.[4] 'For this corruptible must put on incorruption,' says the divine Apostle.[5]

Chapter 29

The deified soul went down into hell so that, just as the Sun of Justice rose upon those on earth,[1] so also might the light shine upon them under the earth who were sitting in darkness and the shadow of death;[2] so that, just as He had brought the good news of peace to those on earth, so also might He bring that of deliverance to captives and that of sight to the blind.[3] And to them that believed He became a cause of eternal salvation, while to them that had not He became a refutation of unbelief, and so also to them in hell,[4] 'That to him every knee should bow, of those that are in heaven, on earth, and under the earth.'[5] And thus, having loosed them that had been bound for ages, He came back again from the dead and made the resurrection possible for us.

---

4 Cf. 1 Cor. 15.20.
5 Cor. 15.53.

1 Cf. Mal. 4.2.
2 Cf. Isa. 9.2.
3 Cf. Luke 4.19.
4 Cf. 1 Pet. 3.19.
5 Phil. 2.10.

BOOK FOUR

Chapter 1

AFTER HIS RESURRECTION from the dead He put aside all His passions, that is to say, ruin, hunger and thirst, sleep and fatigue, and the like. For, even though He did taste food after His resurrection,[1] it was not in obedience to any law of nature, because He did not feel hunger, but by way of dispensation that He might confirm the truth of the resurrection by showing that the flesh which had suffered and that which had risen were the same. Moreover, He did not put aside any of the elements of His nature, neither body nor soul, but kept possession of the body and the rational, intellectual, willing and acting soul. And thus He sits at the right hand of the Father and wills our salvation both as God and as man. And, while He acts as God by working the providence, preservation, and government of all things, He acts as man in remembering His labors on earth and in seeing and knowing that He is adored by all rational creation. For His sacred soul knows that it is hypostatically united to God the Word and that it is adored not as an ordinary soul, but as the soul of God. And both the ascent from earth into heaven and the descending again are actions of a circumscribed body, for 'he shall so come to you,' it is said, 'as you have seen him going into heaven.'[2]

---
1 Cf. Luke 24.43.
2 Acts 1.11.

Chapter 2

Now, we say that Christ sat in His body at the right hand of the Father, yet we do not mean a physical right hand of the Father. For how would He who is uncircumscribed have a physical right hand? Right and left hands belong to those who are circumscribed. What we call the right hand of the Father is the glory and honor of the Godhead in which the Son of God existed as God and consubstantial with the Father before the ages and in which, having in the last days become incarnate, He sits corporeally with His flesh glorified together with Him, for He and His flesh are adored together with one adoration by all creation.[1]

Chapter 3

Together with the Father and the Holy Ghost we adore the Son of God, Him who was bodiless before the Incarnation, whereas the same is now become incarnate and has been made man while at the same time remaining God. Now, should you by subtle reasonings distinguish what is seen from what is thought, then according to its own nature His flesh is not adorable, in so far as it is created.[1] When, however, it has been united with God the Word, it is adorable because of Him and in Him. In the same way, a king is revered whether or not he be robed; and the purple robe, when it is just a purple robe, is trod upon and tossed about, but when it has become a royal vestment it is esteemed and held in honor, and should anyone treat it with contempt, he will most likely be condemned to death. And again, it is not impossible to touch an ordinary piece of wood, but,

---

1 Cf. Basil, *On the Holy Ghost* 6.15 (PG 32.89.92).

1 Cf. Athanasius, *Against Apollinaris* 1.6 (PG 26.1106C); *Epistle to Adelphius* (PG 26.1073D-1076A); Epiphanius, *Ancoratus* 51 (PG 43.105).

after it has been exposed to fire and become a burning coal, it becomes impossible to touch, not because of itself but because of the fire combined with it. And it is not the nature of the wood which is untouchable, but the coal, that is to say, the burning wood. In the same way, the flesh is not of its own nature adorable, but in the incarnate Word of God it is so; not because of itself, but because of the Word of God hypostatically united to it. Neither do we say that we adore ordinary flesh, but the flesh of God, that is to say, God incarnate.

Chapter 4

The Father is Father and not Son.[1] The Son is Son and not Father. The Holy Ghost is Spirit and neither Father nor Son. This is so because that which is a property is unalterable; else, how would it be a property were it to be altered and changed? For this reason the Son of God becomes Son of Man, namely, that His peculiar property may remain unaltered. For, while He was Son of God, He was incarnate of the holy Virgin and became Son of Man without giving up His property of filiation.

The Son of God became man in order that He might again grace man as He had when He made him. For He had made him to His own image, understanding and free, and to His own likeness, that is to say, as perfect in virtues as it was possible for human nature to be, for these virtues are, as it were, characteristics of the divine nature—freedom from care and annoyance, integrity, goodness, wisdom, justice, freedom from all vice. Thus, He put man in communion with Himself and through this communion with Himself raised him to incorruptibility, 'for He created man incorruptible.'[2] But, since by transgressing the commandment we obscured and canceled out the characteristics of the divine

---

[1] Cf. Gregory Nazianzen, *Sermon* 39.12 (*PG* 36.348B).
[2] Wisd. 2.23.

image, we were given over to evil and stripped of the divine communion. 'For what fellowship hath light with darkness?'[3] Then, since we had been removed from life, we fell subject to the destruction of death. But, since He had shared with us what was better and we had not kept it, He now takes His share of what is worse, of our nature I mean to say, that through Himself and in Himself He may restore what was to His image and what to His likeness, while also teaching us the virtuous way of life which He has made easy of ascent for us through Him, and that, having become the first fruits of our resurrection, He may by the communication of life free us from death and restore the useless and worn-out vessel, and so that, having called us to the knowledge of God, He may redeem us from the tyranny of the Devil and by patience and humility teach us to overthrow the tyrant.

Indeed, the worship of demons has ceased. Creation has been sanctified with the divine blood. Altars and temples of idols have been overthrown. Knowledge of God has been implanted. The consubstantial Trinity, the uncreated Godhead is worshiped, one true God, Creator and Lord of all. Virtue is practiced. Hope of the resurrection has been granted through the resurrection of Christ. The demons tremble at the men who were formerly in their power. Yes, and most wonderful of all is that all these things were successfully brought about through a cross and suffering and death. The Gospel of the knowledge of God has been preached to the whole world and has put the adversaries to flight not by war and arms and camps. Rather, it was a few unarmed, poor, unlettered, persecuted, tormented, done-to-death men, who, by preaching One who had died crucified in the flesh, prevailed over the wise and powerful, because the almighty power of the Crucified was with them. That death which was once so terrible has been defeated and He who was once despised and hated is now preferred before life. These are

---

3 2 Cor. 6.14.

the successes consequent upon the advent of the Christ; these are the signs of His power. For it was not as when through Moses He divided the sea and brought one people safely through out of Egypt and the bondage of Pharao. Rather, He delivered all humanity from death's destruction and the tyrant that was sin. It was not by force that He led sinners to virtue, not by having them swallowed up by the earth, nor by having them burnt up by fire, nor by ordering them stoned to death;[4] it was with gentleness and forbearance that He persuaded men to choose virtue and for virtue's sake to undergo sufferings with rejoicing. Sinners were formerly tormented, yet they clung to their sin, and sin was accounted a god by them; but now, for piety and virtue's sake, they choose torments, tortures, and death.

Well done, O Christ, O Wisdom and Power and Word of God, and God almighty! What should we resourceless people give Thee in return for all things? For all things are Thine and Thou askest nothing of us but that we be saved. Even this Thou hast given us, and by Thy ineffable goodness Thou art grateful to those who accept it. Thanks be to Thee who hast given being and the grace of well-being and who by Thy ineffable condescension hast brought back to this state those who fell from it.

Chapter 5

Before the Incarnation, the Person of God the Word was simple and uncompounded, bodiless and uncreated. But when it had assumed flesh, it became person to the flesh also, and it became compounded of the divinity, which it always had, and the flesh, which it took on in addition. Being thus found in two natures, it bears the properties of the two, so that the same one person is at once uncreated in its divinity and created in its humanity, both visible and invisible. Otherwise, we are obliged either to divide the one Christ and

---

4 Cf. Num. 16.31-33,35; Lev. 20.2.

say that there are two persons, or to deny the difference of the natures and thus introduce change and mingling.

Chapter 6

Not as some falsely hold was the mind united to God the Word before the taking on of flesh from the Virgin and from that time called Christ. This absurdity results from the nonsense of Origen's teaching of the pre-existence of souls.[1] We say that the Son and Word of God became Christ the instant that He came to dwell in the womb of the holy Ever-Virgin and was made flesh without undergoing change, the instant that the flesh was anointed with the divinity. For, as Gregory the Theologian says, there was such an anointing.[2] Likewise, the most holy Cyril of Alexandria, in writing to Emperor Theodosius, said as follows: 'I say that neither the Word of God as distinct from the humanity, nor the temple born of woman as not united to the Word, may be called Christ Jesus. The Word which is from God is considered to be Christ when ineffably brought together with the humanity in the union of the dispensation.'[3] And to the empresses he writes thus:[4] 'There are some who say that the name Christ properly belongs to the Word only as considered in Himself as existing begotten of God the Father. But we have not been taught to think or talk in that way, because it is when the Word was made flesh that we say that He received the name of Christ Jesus. For, since He was anointed with the oil of gladness,[5] that is to say, anointed with the Spirit by God the Father, for this reason is He called Christ, or Anointed. That the anointing was of the humanity no right minded person would doubt.' And the

---

1 Cf. *De principiis* 2.9.6 (*PG* 11.230 *et al.*).
2 Cf. Gregory Nazianzen, *Sermon* 30.21 (*PG* 36.132B).
3 Cyril of Alexandria, *To Emperor Theodosius* 28 (*PG* 76.1173C).
4 *Ibid., To the Empresses* 13 (*PG* 76.1220CD).
5 Cf. Ps. 44.8; Heb. 1.9.

renowned Athanasius says to this effect, somewhere in his discourse on the saving coming of Christ: 'God (the Word) as existing before coming to dwell in the flesh was not man but God with God, being invisible and impassible. But, when He became man, He took the name Christ, because the passion and death are consequent upon this name.'[6]

Now, even though sacred Scripture does say: 'Therefore God, thy God, hath anointed thee with the oil of gladness,' one must know that sacred Scripture frequently uses the past tense for the future, as, for example: 'Afterwards, he was seen upon earth and conversed with men,'[7] for God had not yet been seen by man nor had conversed with them when this was said. And again: 'Upon the rivers of Babylon, there we sat and wept,'[8] for these things had not yet taken place.

Chapter 7

'Αγένητον and γενητόν, written with one ν, belong to nature and mean 'uncreated' and 'created.'[1] On the other hand, ἀγέννητον and γεννητόν—that is to say 'unbegotten' and 'begotten'—being spelled with two ν's, belong not to nature, but to person. Thus, the divine nature is ἀγένητος, that is to say, uncreated, whereas all things except the divine nature are γενητά, that is to say, created. Now, in the divine and uncreated nature the unbegotten is found in the Father, for He was not begotten, whereas the begotten is found in the Son, since He is eternally begotten of the Father, and the procession is found in the Holy Ghost. Moreover, the first individuals of every species of living beings were unbegotten but not uncreated, because they were made by

---

6 Athanasius, *Against Apollinaris* 2.1-2 (PG 26.1133B).
7 Bar. 3.38.
8 Ps. 136.1.

1 Cf. above, Book I, ch. 8.

the Creator and not begotten of their kind. For, while γένησις is creation, γέννησις with God is the proceeding of the consubstantial Son from the Father alone, and with human beings the proceeding of a consubstantial person from the conjunction of male and female. Thus, we know that to be begotten belongs not to nature, but to person, for, if it did belong to nature, we should not find the begotten and the unbegotten in the same nature. So, the holy Mother of God engendered a Person who is known in two natures and who in His divinity was timelessly begotten of the Father, but who in the last days became incarnate of her and was born in the flesh.

Now, should they who are inquiring intimate that He who was begotten of the holy Mother of God is two natures, we shall say: Certainly He is two natures, for the same is both God and man. It is the same way with the crucifixion, resurrection, and ascension, too, because these things do not belong to nature, but person. Therefore, Christ, while being two natures, suffered in His passible nature and in it was crucified, for it was in the flesh that He hung on the cross, and not in the divinity. Should they say, while inquiring of us: Did two natures dies? We shall reply: No, indeed. Therefore, two natures were not crucified either, but the Christ was begotten, that is to say, the Divine Word was incarnate and begotten in the flesh, and He was crucified in the flesh, suffered in the flesh, and died in the flesh, while His divinity remained unaffected.

Chapter 8

He who has been born first is first-born, whether he is the only child or has preceded other brothers. So, if the Son of God were called 'first-born' without being called 'only-begotten,' then we should understand Him to be first-born of creatures as being a creature.[1] Since, however, He is called

---

[1] Cf. Gregory of Nyssa, *Against Eunomius* 4.3 (PG 45.636-637).

both first-born and only-begotten, we must maintain both of these as applying to Him. Thus, we say that He is 'the first-born of every creature,'[2] since He is from God, and creation is also from God. But, since He alone is begotten timelessly of the substance of God the Father, He has fittingly been called the only-begotten and first-born Son, and not first-created, since creation is not of the substance of the Father, but has been brought by His will from nothing into being.[3] He is, moreover, 'first-born amongst many brethren,'[4] for, while He was only-begotten, He was also born of a mother. For this very reason, that He shared flesh and blood along with us and then, also, that we were made sons of God through Him by being adopted through baptism, He who is by nature Son of God has become first-born among us who have by adoption and grace become sons of God and are accounted as His brethren. This is why He said: 'I ascend to my Father and to your Father.'[5] He did not say 'our Father', but 'my Father,' that is to say, by nature, and 'your Father', by grace. And He said 'my God and your God,' and He did not say 'our God,' but 'my God.' And should you by subtle reasonings distinguish what is seen from what is thought, then it is as Creator and Lord that He said 'your God.'

Chapter 9

We confess one baptism unto remission of sins and life everlasting. For baptism shows the death of the Lord.[1] Indeed, through baptism we are buried with the Lord, as the divine Apostle says.[2] Therefore, just as the death of the Lord happened but once, so is it necessary to be baptized but once. It is

---

2 Col. 1.15.
3 Cf. Athanasius, *Ecthesis* 3 (*PG* 25.204-205).
4 Rom. 8.29.
5 John 20.17.

1 Cf. Rom. 6.3.
2 Cf. Col. 2.12.

further necessary, in accordance with the Lord's word,³ to be baptized in the name of the Father and of the Son and of the Holy Ghost and thus to learn to confess Father and Son and Holy Ghost. Consequently, all those who have been baptized in the Father and the Son and the Holy Ghost and have thus been taught the one nature of the Godhead in three Persons, but who are baptized over again, these crucify the Christ again, as the divine Apostle says: 'For it is impossible for those who were once illuminated,' and so forth, 'to be renewed again to penance, crucifying again to themselves the Christ and making him a mockery.'⁴ All those, however, who have not been baptized in the Holy Trinity must be baptized again. For, even though the divine Apostle says that 'we have been baptized in Christ and in his death,'⁵ he does not mean that the baptismal invocation should be made thus, but that baptism is a figure of Christ's death. Indeed, by the three immersions baptism signifies the three days of the Lord's burial. Therefore, being 'baptized in Christ' merely means believing in Him and being baptized. Besides, it is impossible to believe in Christ without having been taught to confess the Father and the Son and the Holy Ghost. For Christ is the Son of the living God, whom the Father anointed with the Holy Ghost,⁶ as the divine David says: 'Therefore God, thy God, hath anointed thee with the oil of gladness above thy fellows,'⁷ and Isaias, speaking in the name of the Lord: 'The spirit of the Lord is upon me, because the Lord hath anointed me.'⁸ Indeed, it was to teach His own disciples the invocation that He said, 'Baptizing them in the name of the Father and of the Son and of the Holy Ghost.'⁹ For God had created us for immortality,¹⁰ but, since we disobeyed

---

3 Cf. Matt. 28.19.
4 Heb. 6.4-6.
5 Rom. 6.3.
6 Cf. Matt. 16.16; Acts 10.38.
7 Ps. 44.8.
8 Isa. 61.1.
9 Matt. 28.19.
10 Cf. Methodius, *On the Resurrection* (PG 18.268C).

His saving commandment, He condemned us to the destruction of death in order that what was evil might not be immortal. But because He is compassionate, He condescended to His servants and, becoming like us, redeemed us from destruction by His own suffering. He made a fountain of forgiveness gush out for us from His sacred and immaculate side,[11] both water unto regeneration and the washing away of sin and destruction, and blood as drink productive of life everlasting. Moreover, He has given us a commandment to be born again of water and the Spirit,[12] with the Holy Ghost coming upon the water through prayer and invocation. For, since man is twofold,[13] being of body and soul, the purification He gave us is also twofold, through water and the Spirit, with the Spirit renewing in us what is to His image and likeness and the water by the grace of the Spirit purifying the body from sin and delivering it from destruction—the water completing the figure of the death and the Spirit producing the guarantee of life.

For from the beginning 'the spirit of God moved over the waters',[14] and over and again Scripture testifies to the fact that water is purifying.[15] It was with water that God washed away the sin of the world in the time of Noe.[16] It was with water that every one who was unclean was purified in accordance with the Law, and even their garments were washed with water.[17] By burning up the holocaust with water Elias showed that the grace of the Spirit was mixed with the water.[18] And in accordance with the Law almost everything was purified with water, for the things which are perceptible to the eye are symbols of those which are perceptible to the mind. Indeed, it is in the soul that the regeneration is brought

---

11 Cf. John 19.34.
12 Cf. John 3.5.
13 Cf. Gregory Nazianzen, *Sermon* 40.8 (*PG* 36.368A).
14 Gen. 1.2.
15 Cf. Lev. 15.
16 Cf. Gen. 6.17.
17 Cf. Lev. 15.
18 Cf. 3 Kings 18.34,38.

about. Even though we be creatures, faith is capable of making us to be adopted through the Spirit and brought to our former state of blessedness.

By baptism, then, remission of sins is granted to all alike, but the grace of the Spirit is granted in proportion to the faith and the previous purification. Now, therefore, we receive the first fruits of the Holy Ghost through baptism, and this rebirth becomes the beginning of another life for us, a seal, a safeguard and an illumination.

It is furthermore necessary for us to make every effort to keep ourselves pure from filthy works, lest we return like the dog to his vomit[19] and once more make ourselves slaves to sin. For faith without works is dead; so, likewise, are works without faith, because true faith is proved by works.[20]

What is more, we are baptized in the Holy Trinity because the things that are baptized have need of the Holy Trinity for their preservation and permanence, and the three Persons cannot but be present together with each other, for the Holy Trinity is indivisible.

A first baptism was that of the flood unto the cutting away of sin. A second was that by the sea and the cloud,[21] for the cloud is a symbol of the Spirit, while the sea is a symbol of the water. A third is that of the Law, for every unclean person washed himself with water and also washed his garments and thus entered into the camp.[22] A fourth is that of John, which was an introductory baptism leading those thus baptized to penance,[23] so that they might believe in Christ. 'I indeed,' he says, 'baptize you in water: but he that shall come after me he shall baptize you in the Holy Ghost and fire.'[24] Thus, John purified with water in advance to prepare for the Spirit. A fifth is the Lord's baptism with which He Himself was bap-

---
19 Cf. 2 Pet. 2.22; Gregory Nazianzen, *Sermon* 39.14 (*PG* 36.352A).
20 Cf. James 2.22,26.
21 Cf. 1 Cor. 10.2; Gregory Nazianzen, *op. cit.* 17 (*PG* 36.353C).
22 Cf. Lev. 14.8.
23 Cf. Gregory Nazianzen, *loc. cit.*
24 Matt. 3.11.

tized. He, however, was baptized not that He Himself stood in any need of purification but that by making my purification His own He might 'crush the heads of the dragons in the waters,'[25] wash away the sin and bury all of the old Adam in the water, sanctify the Baptist, fullfill the Law, reveal the mystery of the Trinity, and become for us a model and example for the reception of baptism. And we, too, are baptized with the perfect baptism of the Lord, which is by water and the Spirit. Christ is said to baptize in fire, because He poured out the grace of the Spirit upon the holy Apostles in the form of tongues of fire, as the Lord Himself says: 'John indeed baptized with water; but you shall be baptized with the Holy Ghost and fire, not many days hence.'[26] Or it is because of the chastising baptism of the fire to come that He is said to baptize with fire. A sixth is that which is by penance and tears and which is truly painful.[27] A seventh is that which is by blood and martyrdom.[28] Christ Himself was also baptized with this for our sake.[29] It is exceedingly sublime and blessed in so far as it is not sullied by second stains. An eighth, which is the last, is not saving, but, while being destructive of evil, since evil and sin no longer hold sway, it chastises endlessly.

The Holy Ghost came down in bodily form as a dove to intimate the first fruits of our baptism and to give honor to His body, because it, that is to say, His body, was through its deification God.[30] And it was also because, earlier, it once was a dove that brought the good news of the cessation of the flood. And the Holy Ghost descended upon the holy Apostles in the form of fire, because He is God, and 'God is a consuming fire.'[31]

---

25 Ps. 73.13.
26 Acts 1.5.
27 Cf. Gregory Nazianzen, *op. cit.* (PG 36.356A).
28 Cf. *Ibid.*
29 Cf. Luke 12.50.
30 Cf. Gregory Nazianzen, *op. cit.* 16 (PG 36.353B).
31 Cf. Deut. 4.24; Gregory Nazianzen, *Sermon* 41.12 (PG 36.445A).

Oil is used at baptism to show our anointing and to make us Christs. It is also to proclaim God's mercy upon us through Holy Ghost, since the dove had also carried an olive branch to those who had been delivered from the flood.[32]

John was baptized when he placed his hand upon the divine head of the Lord. He was also baptized in his own blood.

When the faith of the candidates has been testified to by works, baptism should not be deferred.[33] Should, however, a candidate receive baptism fraudulently, he will be condemned rather than helped.

Chapter 10

Faith, indeed, is of two kinds. Thus, 'faith cometh by hearing,'[1] for, when we hear the sacred Scriptures, we believe in the teaching of the Holy Ghost. And this faith is made perfect by all those things which Christ has ordained; it believes truly, it is devout, and it keeps the commandments of Him who has renewed us. For he who does not believe in accordance with the tradition of the Catholic Church or who through untoward works holds communion with the Devil is without faith.

Then again, there is a faith 'which is the substance of things to be hoped for, the evidence of things that appear not.'[2] This is an undoubting and unquestioning hope both for the things promised us by God and for the success of our petitions. The first kind of faith comes from our faculty of judgment (γνώμη), whereas the second is one of the gifts of the Spirit.

Furthermore, one must know that by baptism we are cir-

---

32 Cf. Gen. 8.11. There is a sort of pun here, inasmuch as the Greek word for 'mercy' very closely resembles that for 'olive tree.'
33 Cf. Gregory Nazianzen, *Sermon* 40.11 (*PG* 36.372).

1 Rom. 10.17.
2 Heb. 11.1.

cumcised of the entire covering which we have borne from birth, sin that is, and become spiritual Israelites and a people of God.

Chapter 11

'The word of the cross, to them indeed that perish, is foolishness; but to them that are saved, that is, to us, it is the power of God.'[1] For 'the spiritual man judgeth all things, but the sensual man perceiveth not these things that are of the Spirit.'[2] For they are foolishness to such as do not receive them in faith and conclude to the goodness and omnipotence of God, but by human and natural reasoning inquire into divine things. For all the things of God are above the natural order and beyond speech and understanding. And should one consider how and why God brought all things from nothing into being and should he try to arrive at this by natural reasoning, he will not succeed. For such knowledge is sensual and devilish.[3] If, however, one is guided by faith and concludes to the goodness, omnipotence, truth, wisdom, and justice of the Godhead, then he will find all things to be smooth and even and the road straight. Without faith it is impossible to be saved,[4] since by faith all things endure, both human and spiritual. For a farmer does not plow a furrow in the earth without faith, nor a merchant entrust his life to a bit of wood on the raging high seas. Neither are marriages contracted nor anything else in life done without faith. By faith we understand that all things have been brought from nothing into being by the power of God, and by faith we prosper in all things, both human and divine. Faith is, moreover, an assent devoid of all curiosity.

Every action of Christ and all His working of miracles

---
1 1 Cor. 1.18.
2 1 Cor. 2.15,14.
3 Cf. James 3.15.
4 Cf. Heb. 11.6.

were truly very great and divine and wonderful, but of all things the most wonderful is His honorable cross. For by nothing else except the cross of our Lord Jesus Christ has death been brought low, the sin of our first parent destroyed, hell plundered, resurrection bestowed, the power given us to despise the things of this world and even death itself, the road back to the former blessedness made smooth, the gates of paradise opened, our nature seated at the right hand of God, and we made children and heirs of God. By the cross all things have been set aright. 'For all we who are baptized in Christ,' says the Apostle, 'are baptized in his death' and 'as many of us as have been baptized in Christ have put on Christ'; moreover, 'Christ is the power and wisdom of God.'[5] See how the death of Christ, the cross, that is to say, has clothed us with the subsistent wisdom and power of God! And the word of the Cross is the power of God, whether because by it God's might, His victory over death, that is, was manifested to us, or because, just as the four arms of the cross are made solid and bound together by their central part, so are the height and the depth, the length and the breadth, that is to say, all creation both visible and invisible, held together by the power of God.

This we have been given as a sign on our forehead, just as Israel was given the circumcision, for by it we faithful are set apart from the infidels and recognized. It is a shield and armor and a trophy against the Devil. It is a seal that the Destroyer may not strike us, as Scripture says.[6] It is a raising up for those who lie fallen, a support for those who stand, a staff for the infirm, a crook for the shepherded, a guide for the wandering, a perfecting of the advanced, salvation for soul and body, an averter of all evils, a cause of all good things, a destruction of sin, a plant of resurrection, and a tree of eternal life.

So, then, that honorable and most truly venerable tree

---

5 Rom. 6.3; Gal. 3.27; 1 Cor. 1.24.
6 Cf. Exod. 12.23.

upon which Christ offered Himself as a sacrifice for us is itself to be adored, because it has been sanctified by contact with the sacred body and blood. So also are the nails, the lance, the garments, and such sacred resting places of His as the manger, the cave, saving Golgotha, the life-giving tomb, Sion the citadel of the churches, and others. Thus, David the forefather of God says: 'We will go into his tabernacle: we will adore in the place where his feet stood,' and that he means the cross is evident from what follows: 'Arise, O Lord, into thy resting place'[7]—for the resurrection follows after the cross. Now, if the house, the bed, and the clothing of our loved ones are dear to us, then how much more the things of our God and Saviour by which we also have been saved!

And we also adore the likeness of the honorable and life-giving cross, even though it be made of another material, not that we honor the material—God forbid!—but the likeness as a symbol of Christ. Thus, when He explained to His disciples saying: 'Then shall appear the sign of the Son of man in heaven,'[8] He meant the cross. For this reason, also, the angel of the resurrection said to the women: 'You seek Jesus of Nazareth, who was crucified.'[9] Likewise, the Apostle: 'But we preach Christ crucified.'[10] Now, there are many Christs and Jesuses, but only one Crucified, and he did not say 'pierced by a lance' but 'crucified.' Therefore, the sign of Christ is to be adored, for, wherever the sign may be, there He, too, will be. If, however, the form should happen to be destroyed, the material of which the likeness of the cross was composed is not to be adored, even though it be gold or precious stones. Thus, we adore everything that has reference to God, although it is to Him that we direct the worship.

---

7 Ps. 131.7,8.
8 Matt. 24.30.
9 Mark 16.6.
10 1 Cor. 1.23.

The tree of life which was planted by God in paradise prefigured this honorable Cross, for, since death came by a tree, it was necessary for life and the resurrection to be bestowed by a tree. It was Jacob who first prefigured the cross, when he adored the top of the rod of Joseph.[11] And when he blessed Joseph's sons with his hands crossed,[12] he most clearly described the sign of the cross. [Then there were] the rod of Moses which smote the sea with the form of a cross and saved Israel while causing Pharao to be swallowed up; his hands stretched out in the form of a cross and putting Amalec to flight; the bitter water being made sweet by a tree, and the rock being struck and gushing forth streams of water;[13] the rod of Aaron miraculously confirming the dignity of the priesthood; a serpent raised in triumph upon a tree, as if dead, with the tree preserving those who with faith beheld the dead enemy,[14] even as Christ was nailed up in flesh of sin but which had not known sin; great Moses calling out: 'You will see your life hanging before your eyes on a tree';[15] and Isaias: 'I have spread forth my hands all day to an unbelieving and contradictory people.'[16] May we who adore this attain to the portion of Christ the crucified. Amen.

Chapter 12

It is not without any reason or by chance that we worship toward the east. On the contrary, since we are composed of a visible and an invisible nature, of an intellectual nature and a sensitive one, that is, we also offer a twofold worship to the Creator. It is just as we also sing both with our mind and with our bodily lips, and as we are baptized both in

---

11 Cf. Heb. 11.21; Gen. 47.31 (Septuagint).
12 Cf. Gen. 48.13-15.
13 Cf. Exod. 14.16ff.; 17.11ff.; 15.25; 17.6.
14 Cf. Num. 17.8; 21.9.
15 Deut. 28.66 (Septuagint, except for the phrase 'on a tree').
16 Isa. 65.2 (Septuagint).

water and in the Spirit, and as we are united to the Lord in two ways when we receive the sacrament and the grace of the Spirit.

And so, since God is spiritual light[1] and Christ in sacred Scripture is called 'Sun of Justice' and 'Orient,'[2] the East should be dedicated to His worship. For everything beautiful should be dedicated to God from whom everything that is good receives its goodness. Also, the divine David says: 'Sing to God, ye kingdoms of the earth: sing ye to the Lord; who mounteth above the heaven of heavens, to the east.'[3] And still again, Scripture says: 'And the Lord had planted a paradise in Eden to the east; wherein he placed man whom he had formed,' and whom He cast out, when He had transgressed, 'and made him to live over against the paradise of pleasure,'[4] or in the west. Thus it is that, when we worship God, we long for our ancient fatherland and gaze toward it. The tabernacle of Moses had the veil and the propitiatory to the east; and the tribe of Juda, as being the more honorable, pitched their tents on the east; and in the celebrated temple of Solomon the gate of the Lord was set to the east.[5] As a matter of fact, when the Lord was crucified, He looked toward the west, and so we worship gazing towards Him. And when he was taken up, He ascended to the east and thus the Apostles worshiped Him and thus He shall come in the same way as they had seen Him going into heaven,[6] as the Lord Himself said: 'As lightning cometh out of the east and appeareth even into the west: so shall also the coming of the Son of man be.'[7] And so, while we are awaiting Him, we worship toward the east. This is, moreover, the unwritten

---

[1] Cf. 1 John 1.5.
[2] Cf. Mal. 4.2; Zach. 3.8; Luke 1.78.
[3] Ps. 67.33,34.
[4] Gen. 2.8; 3.24 (Septuagint).
[5] Cf. Lev. 16.14; Num. 2.3; Ezech. 44.1-2.
[6] Cf. Acts 1.11.
[7] Matt. 24.27.

tradition of the Apostles, for they have handed many things down to us unwritten.[8]

Chapter 13

Because of the exceedingly great wealth of His goodness, the good, all-good, and exceedingly good God, who is all goodness, did not rest content that the Good, or His nature, should just be and not be shared by anything.[1] For this reason, He first made the spiritual and heavenly powers, and then the visible and sensible world, and then, finally, man of the spiritual and the sensible. Hence, all things He has made participate in His goodness by the fact that they have being. For He is being to them all, since 'in him are all things,'[2] not only because He has brought them from nothing into being, but because it is by His operation that all things He made are kept in existence and held together. Living things, however, participate more abundantly, because they participate in the good both by their being and by their living. But rational beings, while they participate in the good in the aforementioned ways, do so still more by their very rationality. For they are in a way more akin to Him, even though He is, of course, immeasurably superior.

Since man was made both rational and free, he received the power to be unceasingly united to God by his own choice, provided, of course, that he persevere in the good, that is to say, in obedience to his Creator. Then, when man became disobedient to the commandment of Him who had made him and thus became subject to death and corruption, the Maker and Creator of our kind, through the bowels of His mercy, likened Himself to us and became man in all things

---

8 Cf. Basil, *On the Holy Ghost* 27.66 (*PG* 32.188A).

1 Cf. Gregory Nazianzen, *Sermon* 45.5 (*PG* 36.629A).
2 Rom. 11.36.

except sin and was united to our nature. Thus, because we did not keep what He had imparted to us, His own image and His own spirit, He now participates in our poor weak nature so that He may render us pure and incorrupt and make us once more participators in His divinity.

It was moreover, necessary not only for the first fruits of our nature, but also for every man who so wished. And it was necessary that every such man should be born with a second birth and nourished with a new food fit for the new birth, and thus attain to the measure of perfection. Hence, by His own birth, or incarnation, and by His baptism and passion and resurrection, He freed our nature from the sin of our first parent, from death and corruption. And He became the first-fruit of the resurrection and set Himself to be a way, a model, and an example, so that we, too, might follow in His footsteps and become by adoption, as He is by nature, sons and heirs of God and joint heirs together with Him.[3] Thus, He gave us, as I have said, a second birth, so that, as we had been born of Adam and had been likened to him and had become heir to his curse and corruption, we might by being born anew of Him be likened to Him and become heir to His incorruption and blessing and glory.

Now, since this Adam is spiritual, it was necessary that there be a spiritual birth and also a spiritual food. But, since we are individuals of a twofold nature and compounded, it is necessary that the birth also be of a twofold nature and that the food likewise be compounded. Hence, the birth was given us by water and the Spirit, by holy baptism, I mean, while the food was the Bread of Life itself, our Lord Jesus Christ who had come down from heaven.[4] For, when He was about to suffer death freely for our sake, on the night in which He delivered Himself up, He made a new testament

---

[3] Cf. Rom. 8.17.
[4] Cf. John 6.48.

for His holy disciples and Apostles and, through them, for all that believe in Him. So, when He had eaten the old Pasch with His disciples in the upper chamber on holy and glorious Mount Sion and had fullfilled the old testament, He washed the feet of His disciples and thus showed a symbol of holy baptism.[5] Then, after He had broken bread, He gave it to them saying: 'Take ye and eat. This is my body, which is broken for you unto remission of sins.'[6] And in like manner He took also the chalice of wine and water and gave it to them, saying: 'Drink ye all of this. This is my blood of the new testament, which is shed for you unto remission of sins. This do in commemoration of me. For as often as you shall eat this bread and drink this chalice, you shall show the death of the Son of man and confess his resurrection, until he come.'[7]

If, then, 'the word of the Lord is living and effectual,'[8] and if 'whatsoever the Lord pleased he hath done';[9] if He said: 'Be light made, and it was made. Be a firmament made, and it was made';[10] if by the word of the Lord the heavens were established, and all the power of them by the spirit of his mouth';[11] if heaven and earth, water and fire, and air and the whole universe of these were made perfect by the word of the Lord, and this much famed living being, too, which is man; if by His will God the Word Himself became man and without seed caused the pure and undefiled blood of the blessed Ever-Virgin to form a body for Himself;—if all this, then can He not make the bread His body and the wine and water His blood? In the beginning He said: 'Let

---

5 Cf. John 13.1-15.
6 Cf. 1 Cor. 11.24. The 'which is broken for you' is not strictly Scriptural but belongs to the most ancient liturgical tradition and still survives in most eastern Liturgies.
7 Cf. 1 Cor. 11.25-26. This form, as well as that of the consecration of the bread just mentioned, is the form of the Liturgy of St. James which was commonly used in Syria and Palestine.
8 Heb. 4.12.
9 Ps. 134.6.
10 Gen. 1.3,6.
11 Ps. 32.6.

the earth bring forth the green herb,'[12] and even until now, when the rain falls, the earth brings forth its own shoots under the influence and power of the divine command. God said: 'This is my body,' and, 'This is my blood,' and, 'This do in commemoration of me,' and by His almighty command it is done, until He shall come, for what He said was 'until he come.' And through the invocation the overshadowing power of the Holy Ghost becomes a rainfall for this new cultivation. For, just as all things whatsoever God made He made by the operation of the Holy Ghost, so also it is by the operation of the Spirit that these things are done which surpass nature and cannot be discerned except by faith alone. 'How shall this be done to me,' asked the blessed Virgin, because I know not man?' The archangel Gabriel answered, 'The Holy Ghost shall come upon thee and the power of the Most High shall overshadow thee.'[13] And now you ask how the bread becomes the body of Christ and the wine and water the blood of Christ. And I tell you that the Holy Ghost comes down and works these things which are beyond description and understanding.

Now, bread and wine are used[14] because God knows human weakness and how most things that are not constantly and habitually used cannot be put up with and are shunned. With His usual condescension, therefore, He does through the ordinary things of nature those which surpass the natural order. And just as in the case of baptism, because it is the custom of men to wash themselves with water and anoint themselves with oil He joined the grace of the Spirit to oil and water and made it a laver of regeneration, so, because it is men's custom to eat bread and drink water and wine He joined His divinity to these and made them His body and blood, so that by the ordinary natural things we might be raised to those which surpass the order of nature.

---

12 Gen. 1.11.
13 Luke 1.34,35.
14 Cf. Gregory of Nyssa, *Catechesi* 37 (*PG* 45.93ff.).

This is the body which is truly united to the Godhead, the same which is from the blessed Virgin. This is not because that body which was taken up to heaven comes down from heaven, but because the very bread and wine are changed into the body and blood of God. However, should you inquire as to the manner in which this is done, let it suffice for you to hear that it is done through the Holy Ghost, just as it was through the Holy Ghost that the Lord made flesh subsist for Himself and in Himself from the blessed Mother of God..And more than this we do not know, except that the word of God is true and effective and omnipotent, but the manner in which it is so is impossible to find out. What is more, it is not amiss to say this, that just as bread by being eaten and wine and water by being drunk are naturally changed into the body of the person eating and drinking and yet do not become another body than that which the person had before, so in the same way are the bread of the offertory and the wine and water supernaturally changed into the body and blood of Christ by the invocation and coming down of the Holy Ghost, yet they are not two bodies, but one and the same.

Hence, it is unto remission of sins and eternal life and unto a safeguard for body and soul and for such as partake worthily thereof and with faith. But for such as receive unworthily and without faith it is unto chastisement and punishment. It is just as the Lord's death has become life and immortality for those who believe, whereas for those who do not and for those who killed the Lord it is unto chastisement and eternal punishment.

The bread and wine are not a figure of the body and blood of Christ—God forbid!—but the actual deified body of the Lord, because the Lord Himself said: 'This is my body'; not 'a figure of my body' but 'my body,' and not 'a figure of my blood' but 'my blood.' Even before this He had said to the Jews: 'except you eat of the flesh of the

Son of man and drink his blood, you shall not have life in you. For my flesh is meat indeed: and my blood is drink indeed.' And again: 'He that eateth me, shall live.'[15]

Wherefore, in all fear and with a pure conscience and undoubting faith let us approach, and it will be to us altogether as we believe and do not doubt. And let us honor it with all purity of body and soul, for it is twofold. Let us approach it with burning desire, and with our hands folded in the form of a cross[16] let us receive the body of the Crucified. With eyes, lips, and faces turned toward it let us receive the divine burning coal, so that the fire of the coal may be added to the desire within us to consume our sins and enlighten our hearts, and so that by this communion of the divine fire we may be set afire and deified. Isaias saw a live coal,[17] and this coal was not plain wood but wood joined with fire. Thus also, the bread of communion is not a plain bread, but bread joined with the Godhead. And the body joined with the Godhead is not one nature. On the contrary, that of the body is one, whereas that of the Godhead joined with it is another—so that both together are not one nature, but two.

It was with bread and wine that Melchisedech, the priest of the most high God, received Abraham, when he was returning from the slaughter of the alien tribes.[18] That altar prefigured this mystical altar, even as that priest was a type and figure of the true Archpriest who is Christ. For 'thou,' He says, 'art a priest forever according to the order of Melchidesech.'[19] This bread was figured by the loaves of proposition. This is quite plainly the pure and unbloody sacrifice which the Lord, through the mouth of the Prophet, said

---
15 John 6.54-58.
16 Cf. Cyril of Jerusalem, *Catechetical Discourse* 23.21 (*PG* 33.1124B-1125A); Council in Trullo (Quinisext), Can. 101, Hardouin, *Acta Conciliorum* 3 (Paris 1714), cols. 1696E-1697A.
17 Cf. Isa. 6.6.
18 Cf. Gen. 14.18; Heb. 7.1.
19 Ps. 109.4; Heb. 7.17.

was to be offered to Him from the rising of the sun even to its going down.[20]

It is Christ's body and blood entering into the composition of our soul and body without being consumed, without being corrupted, without passing into the privy—God forbid!—but into our substance for our sustenance, a bulwark against every sort of harm and a purifier from all uncleanliness—as if He were to take adultered gold and purify it by the discerning fire, so that in the life to come we shall not be condemned with the world. For He purifies by diseases and all sort of seizures, even as the divine Apostle says: 'But if we would judge ourselves, we should not be judged. But whilst we are judged, we are chastised by the Lord, that we be not condemned with this world.' And this is what he says: 'For he that partaketh unworthily of the Lord eateth and drinketh judgment to himself.'[21] When we are purified by it, we become one with the body of the Lord and with His spirit, and we become the body of Christ.

This bread is the first-fruits of the bread to come, which is the supersubstantial bread.[22] For *supersubstantial* either means that which is to come, that is, the bread of the world to come, or it means that which is taken for the sustenance of our substance. So, whether it be the one or the other, the term will be suitably applicable to the body of the Lord, because, since the flesh of the Lord was conceived of the life-giving Spirit, it is itself life-giving spirit—for 'that which is born of the Spirit is spirit.'[23] I say this not to detract from the nature of the body, but because I wish to show its life-giving and divine character.

Moreover, although some may have called the bread and wine *antitypes* of the body and blood of the Lord, as did the inspired Basil,[24] they did not say this as referring to

---

20 Cf. Mal. 1.11.
21 1 Cor. 11.31,32,29.
22 Cf. Matt. 6.11; Cyril of Jerusalem, *op. cit.* 15 (PG 33.1120B).
23 John 3.6.
24 Cf. Liturgy of St. Basil, prayer of the *epiclesis* (F. E. Brightman, *Liturgies Eastern and Western* 1 [Oxford 1896] 329).

after the consecration, but to before the consecration, and it was thus that they called the offertory bread itself.

It is called *participation* because through it we participate in the divinity of Jesus. It is also called *communion,* and truly is so, because of our having communion through it with Christ and partaking both of His flesh and His divinity, and because through it we have communion with and are united to one another. For, since we partake of one bread, we all become one body of Christ and one blood and members of one another and are accounted of the same body with Christ.

Let us then make every effort to guard against receiving communion from heretics or giving it to them. 'Give not that which is holy to dogs,' says the Lord, 'neither cast ye your pearls before swine,'[25] lest we become sharers in their false teachings and their condemnation. If there really is such a union with Christ and with each other, then we really become united deliberately with all those with whom we communicate together, for this union comes from deliberate choice and not without the intervention of our judgment. 'For we are all one body, because we partake of one bread,' as the divine Apostle says.[26]

They are called antitypes of the things to come, not because they are not really the body and blood of Christ, but because it is through them that we participate in the divinity of Christ now, while then it will be through the intellect and by vision alone.

Chapter 14

Since in what has gone before we have discussed to some extent the holy and most celebrated Ever-Virgin and Mother of God and have shown what is most important of all, how she is really and truly the Mother of God and is so called,

---

25 Matt. 7.6.
26 1 Cor. 10.17.

let us now supply what remains to be said. She was predestined in the eternal foreknowing counsel of God and she was prefigured by various figures and foretold by the Holy Ghost through the words of the Prophets. Then, at the predestined time, she sprang from the root of David in fulfillment of the promises which had been made to him. For it is written: 'The Lord hath sworn truth to David, and he will not make it void: Of the fruit of thy womb I will set upon thy throne', and again: 'Once have I sworn by my holiness: I will not lie unto David. His seed shall endure forever. And his throne as the sun before me, and as the moon perfect for ever: and a faithful witness in heaven.'[1] And Isaias: 'There shall come forth a rod out of the root of Jesse: and a flower shall rise up out of his root.'[2]

The most holy Evangelists Matthew and Luke have distinctly shown how Joseph is descended from the tribe of David. Matthew, however, traces the descent of Joseph from David through Solomon, whereas Luke traces it through Nathan. Yet both have passed over the lineage of the blessed Virgin in silence.

One should know, however, that it was not customary for the Hebrews, nor for sacred Scripture either, to give the pedigrees of women. But there was a law that one tribe should not marry into another.[3] And Joseph, who was descended from the tribe of David and was a just man, for the holy Gospel testifies to this in his regard,[4] would not have espoused the blessed Virgin illegally, but only if she were descended from the same tribe. Consequently, it was sufficient to show the descent of Joseph.

One should know this, too, that there was a law that the brother of a man dying without issue should marry the wife of the deceased and raise up seed for his brother.[5] Thus, the offspring belonged by nature to the second, that is to say,

---

1 Ps. 131.11; 88.36-38.
2 Isa. 11.1.
3 Cf. Num. 36.6.
4 Cf. Matt. 1.19.
5 Cf. Deut. 25.5.

to the one who had begotten it, but by law to the deceased.

Levi was born from the line of Nathan the son of David and he begot Melchi and Panther. Panther begot Barpanther, for such was he called. This Barpanther begot Joachim, and Joachim begot the holy Mother of God. Mathan, however, had a wife from the line of Solomon the son of David, and from her begot Jacob. Then, when Mathan died, Melchi, who was of the tribe of Nathan and the son of Levi and brother of Panther, married the wife of Mathan. It was she who was the mother of Jacob, and from her Melchi begot Heli. Thus, Jacob and Heli were born of the same mother, but Jacob was of the tribe of Solomon, while Heli was of the tribe of Nathan. Heli, however, who was of the tribe of Nathan, died childless, and his brother Jacob, who was of the tribe of Solomon, took his wife and raised up seed for his brother and begot Joseph. So, while Joseph was by nature a son of Jacob of the descent of Solomon, he was by law son of Heli, who was of the line of Nathan.

And so Joachim took the noble and praiseworthy Anna in marriage.[6] Then, even as the earlier Anna, although barren, had through prayer and a vow given birth to Samuel,[7] so did this Anna through supplication and a vow receive from God the Mother of God, so that not even in this should she be inferior to any of the illustrious mothers. Thus, Grace, for such is the interpretation of Anna, brings forth the Lady, for that is the meaning of the name Mary. And Mary really did become Lady of all created things, since she was accounted Mother of the Creator. And she was born in the house of Joachim at the Probatica and was brought to the Temple. From then on she grew up in the house of God, nourished by the Spirit, and like a fruitful olive tree[8] became and abode of every virtue with her mind removed from every worldly and carnal desire. And thus, as was fitting for

---

6 Cf. *Protevangelium of James* 1-2.
7 Cf. 1 Kings 1.11.
8 Cf. Ps. 51.10.

her who was to conceive God within herself, she kept her soul and body virginal, for He is holy and abides in holy ones. Thus, then, she sought holiness and was shown to be a holy and wondrous temple worthy of the most high God.

However, since the Enemy of our salvation was keeping an eye on virgins because of the prophecy of Isaias, who said: 'Behold a virgin shall be with child and bring forth a son: and they shall call his name Emmanuel, which being interpreted is, God with us,'[9] the maid was betrothed to Joseph by the priests as 'the sealed book is delivered to one that is learned,'[10] in order that He 'who catcheth the wise in their craftiness'[11] might ensnare him who ever glories in wisdom.[12] And the betrothal was at once a safeguard for the virgin and a deception for him who was keeping his eye on virgins. Now, when the fullness of time came, an angel of the Lord was sent to her with the good news of her conception of the Lord. And thus she conceived the Son of God, the subsistent power of the Father, 'not of the will of the flesh, nor of the will of man'[13]—that is to say, not of carnal conjunction and seed—but of the good pleasure of the Father and the co-operation of the Holy Ghost. To the Creator she gave that He might be created, to the Fashioner that He might be fashioned, and to the Son of God and God that He might from her innocent and undefiled flesh and blood put on flesh and become man. And thus she paid the debt for the first mother. For, as Eve was formed from Adam without carnal conjuction, so did this one bring forth the new Adam in accordance with the law of gestation but surpassing the nature of generation. Thus, He who is without a mother begotten of a father was without a father born of a woman. And because it was of a woman it was in accordance with the law of gestation; while, because it was without father, it surpassed the nature of generation.

---

9 Matt. 1.23; Isa. 7.14.
10 Isa. 29.11.
11 Job 5.13.
12 Cf. Jer. 9.23.
13 John 1.13.

And because it was at the normal time, for having completed the nine-month period He was born at the beginning of the tenth, it was in accordance with the law of gestation; while because it was without pain, it surpassed the established order of birth—for, where pleasure had not preceded, pain did not follow, as the Prophet said: 'Before she was in labor, she brought forth,' and again: 'before her time came to be delivered she brought forth a man child.'[14]

And so the Son of God became incarnate and was born of her. It was not as God-bearing man that He was born of her, but as God incarnate; not as a prophet anointed through the operation of the one anointing, but as one anointed with the entire presence of the one anointing—so that the one anointing became man and the one anointed became God; not by a change in nature, but by the hypostatic union. For, He was the same who anointed and who was anointed, as God anointing Himself as man. How, then, is she not Mother of God who from herself brought forth God incarnate? Actually, she is really and truly Mother of God, Lady, and Mistress of all created things, being accounted both handmaid and mother of the Creator. And just as at His conception He had kept her who conceived Him a virgin, so also at His birth did He maintain her virginity intact, because He alone passed through her and kept her shut.[15] While the conception was by hearing, the birth was by the usual orifice through which children are born, even though there are some who concoct an idle tale of His being born from the side of the Mother of God. For it was not impossible for Him to pass through the gate without breaking its seals.

Hence, the Ever-Virgin remained a virgin even after giving birth and never had converse with a husband as long as she lived. For, even though it is written: 'And he knew her not

---
14 Isa. 66.7.
15 Cf. Ezech. 44.2.

till she brought forth her firstborn son,'[16] one must know that the first child to be born is the firstborn, even though it may also be the only-begotten. Firstborn means having been born first, and does not by any means imply the birth of others; on the other hand, the 'till' signifies the fulfillment of the appointed time, without excluding the time after that. Thus, the Lord says: 'And behold I am with you all days, even till the consummation of the world,'[17] without meaning that He is to be separated after the consummation of the world. The divine Apostle certainly says: 'And so shall we be always with the Lord,'[18] meaning after the general resurrection.

How, indeed, would she have given birth to God and have known the miracle from the experience of subsequent events and then have allowed intercourse with a husband? Far be it! The thinking of such things is beyond the bounds of prudent thought, let alone the doing of them.

However, this blessed one, who had been found worthy of gifts surpassing nature, did at the time of the Passion suffer the pangs which she had escaped at childbirth. For, when she saw Him put to the death as a criminal, whom she knew to be God when she gave birth to Him, her heart was torn from maternal compassion and she was rent by her thoughts as by a sword. This is the meaning of 'And thy own soul a sword shall pierce.'[19] But her grief gave way to the joy of the resurrection, the resurrection which proclaimed Him to be God who had died in the flesh.

---

16 Matt. 1.25.
17 Matt. 28.20.
18 1 Thess. 4.16.
19 Luke 2.35.

Chapter 15

The saints must be honored as friends of Christ and children and heirs of God, as John the Theologian and Evangelist says: 'But as many as received him, he gave them the power to be made the sons of God.'[1] 'Therefore they are no longer servants, but sons: and if sons, heirs also, heirs indeed of God and joint heirs with Christ.'[2] And again, in the holy Gospels the Lord says to the Apostles: 'You are my friends. . . I will not now call you servants: for the servant knoweth not what his lord doth.'[3] Furthermore, if the Creator and Lord of all is called both King of kings and Lord of lords and God of gods,[4] then most certainly the saints, too, are both gods and lords and kings. God both is and is said to be their God and Lord and King. 'For I am,' He said to Moses, 'the God of Abraham, the God of Isaac, and the God of Jacob,' and God appointed Moses the God of Pharao.[5] However, I say that they are gods, lords, and kings not by nature, but because they have ruled over and dominated sufferings, and because they have kept undebased the likeness of the divine image to which they were made—for the image of the king is also called a king, and, finally, because they have freely been united to God and receiving Him as a dweller within themselves have through association with Him become by grace what He is by nature. How, then, should these not be honored who have been accounted servants, friends, and sons of God? For the honor shown the more sensible of one's fellow servants gives proof of one's love for the common Master.

These are become repositories and pure dwelling places of God, for 'I will dwell in them and walk among them,'

---
1 John 1.12.
2 Gal. 4.7; Rom. 8.17.
3 John 15.14,15.
4 Apoc. 19.16; Ps. 49.1.
5 Exod. 3.6; 7.1.

says God, 'and I will be their God.'⁶ So, indeed, sacred Scripture says that 'the souls of the just are in the hand of God: and death shall not touch them.'⁷ For the death of the saints is rather sleep than death, since 'they have labored unto eternity and shall live unto the end,' and 'precious in the sight of the Lord is the death of his saints.'⁸ What then is more precious than to be in the hand of God? For God is life and light, and they that are in the hand of God abide in life and light.

Moreover, because through their mind God has also dwelt in their bodies, the Apostle says: 'Know you not that your members are the temple of the Holy Ghost, who is in you?'; 'Now the Lord is the Spirit'; and again: 'If any man violate the temple of God, him shall God destroy.'⁹ How, then, should they not be honored, who are the living temples of God, the living tabernacles of God. These in life openly took their stand with God.

In the relics of the saints the Lord Christ has provided us with saving fountains which in many ways pour out benefactions and gush with fragrant ointment.¹⁰ And let no one disbelieve. For, if by the will of God water poured out of the precipitous living rock in the desert, and for the thirsty Sampson from the jawbone of an ass,¹¹ is it unbelievable that fragrant ointment should flow from the relics of the martyrs? Certainly not, at least for such as know the power of God and the honor which the saints have from Him.

In the Law, anyone who touched a corpse was accounted unclean.¹² But these of whom we speak are not dead. Because Life itself and the Author of life was reckoned amongst the

---

6 2 Ccr. 6.16; Lev. 26.12.
7 Wisd. 3.1.
8 Ps. 48.9,10; 115.15.
9 1 Cor. 6.19; 2 Cor. 3.17; 1 Cor. 3.17.
10 The special epithet *myroblytus*, or 'gushing ointment,' is applied to certain saints whose relics exude a fragrant oil. The two most famous *myroblytae* are St. Demetrius of Salonica and St. Nicholas of Bari.
11 Cf. Exod. 17.6; Judges 15.19.
12 Cf. Num. 19.11.

dead, we do not call these dead who have fallen asleep in the hope of resurrection and in the faith in Him. For how can a dead body work miracles? How, then, through them are demons put to flight, diseases driven out, the sick cured, the blind restored to sight, lepers cleansed, temptation and trouble driven away; and how through them does 'every best gift come down from the Father of lights'[13] to them who ask with undoubting faith? What would you not do to find a patron to present you to a mortal king and intercede with him in your behalf? Are not the patrons of the entire race to be honored who make petitions to God in our behalf? Yes, indeed; we must honor them by raising churches to God in their name, by making fruit-offerings, and by celebrating their anniversaries and taking spiritual joy in these, such as will be the very joy of our hosts, but taking care lest in endeavoring to do them honor we may give them annoyance instead. For by some things honor is given to God and they who serve Him rejoice in them, whereas by others He is offended and so, too, are His shield-bearers. 'In psalms and hymns and spiritual canticles,'[14] in compunction, and in compassion for the needy let us faithful do honor to the saints, through whom most especially is honor rendered to God. Let us set up monuments to them, and visible images, and let us ourselves by the imitation of their virtues become their living monuments and images. Let us honor the Mother of God as really and truly God's Mother. Let us honor the Prophet John as precursor and baptist, apostle and martyr, for 'there hath not risen among them that are born of women a greater than John,'[15] as the Lord said, and he was the first herald of the kingdom. Let us honor the Apostles as brethren of the Lord, as eye-witnesses and attendants to His sufferings, whom God the Father 'foreknew and predestinated

---

13 James 1.17.
14 Eph. 5.19.
15 Matt. 11.11.

to be made conformable to the image of his Son,'[16] 'first apostles, secondly prophets, thirdly shepherds and teachers.'[17] And let us honor the holy martyrs of the Lord who have been picked from every rank and whose corps commander is Christ's archdeacon, apostle, and protomartyr Stephen; let us honor them as soldiers of Christ who have drunk of His chalice and have then been baptized with the baptism of His life-giving death, and as participants in His sufferings and His glory. Let us also honor those sainted fathers of ours, the God-bearing ascetics who have struggled through the more drawn-out and laborious martyrdom of the conscience, 'who wandered about in sheepskins, in goatskins, being in want, distressed, afflicted: wandering in deserts, in mountains and in dens and in caves of the earth: of whom the world was not worthy.'[18] Let us honor the Prophets who preceded the Grace, the patriarchs and just men who announced beforehand the advent of the Lord. Let us carefully observe the manner of life of all these and let us emulate their faith, charity, hope, zeal, life, patience under suffering, and perseverance unto death, so that we may also share their crowns of glory.

Chapter 16

Since there are certain people who find great fault with us for adoring and honoring both the image of the Saviour and that of our Lady, as well as those of the rest of the saints and servants of Christ, let them hear how from the beginning God made man to His own image.[1] For what reason, then, do we adore one another, except because we have been made to the image of God? As the inspired Basil, who is deeply learned in theology, says: 'the honor paid to the

---

16 Rom. 8.29.
17 1 Cor. 12.28.
18 Heb. 11.37,38.

---

1 Cf. Gen. 1.26.

image redounds to the original,'[2] and the original is the thing imaged from which the copy is made. For what reason did the people of Moses adore from round about the tabernacle which bore an image and pattern of heavenly things, or rather, of all creation?[3] Indeed, God had said to Moses: 'See that thou make all things according to the pattern which was shewn thee on the mount.' And the Cherubim, too, that overshadowed the propitiatory, were they not the handiwork of men?[4] And what was the celebrated temple in Jerusalem? Was it not built and furnished by human hands and skill?[5]

Now, sacred Scripture condemns those who adore graven things, and also those who sacrifice to the demons. The Greeks used to sacrifice and the Jews also used to sacrifice; but the Greeks sacrifice to the demons, whereas the Jews sacrificed to God. And the sacrifice of the Greeks was rejected and condemned, while the sacrifice of the just was acceptable to God. Thus, Noe sacrificed 'and the Lord smelled a sweet savor'[6] of the good intention and accepted the fragrance of the gift offered to Him. And thus the statues of the Greeks happen to be rejected and condemned, because they were representations of demons.

But, furthermore, who can make a copy of the invisible, incorporeal, uncircumscribed, and unportrayable God? It is, then, highly insane and impious to give a form to the Godhead. For this reason it was not the practice in the Old Testament to use images. However, through the bowels of His mercy God for our salvation was made man in truth, not in the appearance of man, as He was seen by Abraham or the Prophets, but really made man in substance. Then He

---

2 Basil, *On the Holy Ghost* 18.45 (*PG* 32.149C).
3 Cf. Exod. 33.10.
4 Cf. Heb. 8.5; Exod. 25.40,20.
5 Cf. 3 Kings 6.
6 Gen. 8.21.

abode on earth, conversed with men,[7] worked miracles, suffered, was crucified, rose again, and was taken up; and all these things really happened and were seen by men and, indeed, written down to remind and instruct us, who were not present then, so that, although we have not seen, yet hearing and believing we may attain to the blessedness of the Lord. Since, however, not all know letters nor do all have leisure to read, the Fathers deemed it fit that these events should be depicted as a sort of memorial and terse reminder. It certainly happens frequently that at times when we do not have the Lord's Passion in mind we may see the image of His crucifixion and, being thus reminded of His saving Passion, fall down and adore. But it is not the material which we adore, but that which is represented; just as we do not adore the material of the Gospel or that of the cross, but that which they typify. For what is the difference between a cross which does not typify the Lord and one which does? It is the same way with the Mother of God, too, for the honor paid her is referred to Him who was incarnate of her. And similarly, also, we are stirred up by the exploits of the holy men to manliness, zeal, imitation of their virtues, and the glory of God. For, as we have said, the honor shown the more sensible of one's fellow servants gives proof of one's love for the common Master, and the honor paid to the image redounds to the original. This is the written tradition, just as is worshiping toward the east, adoring the cross, and so many other similar things.[8]

Furthermore, there is a story told[9] about how, when Abgar was lord of the city of Edessenes, he sent an artist to make a portrait of the Lord, and how, when the artist was unable

---

7 Cf. Bar. 3.38.
8 Cf. Basil, *op. cit.* 27.66 (*PG* 32.188B).
9 The earliest form of the Syriac legend of Abgar, the first Christian king of Edessa, is to be found in Eusebius (*Eccles. Hist.* 1.13). The later and more amplified version containing the incident of the portrait here referred to is to be found in the Syriac document known as the *Doctrine of Addai* (translated and published by G. Phillips, London 1876).

to do this because of the radiance of His face, the Lord Himself pressed a bit of cloth to His own sacred and life-giving face and left His own image on the cloth and so sent this to Abgar who had so earnestly desired it.

And Paul, the Apostle of the Gentiles, writes that the Apostles handed down a great many things unwritten: 'Therefore, brethren, stand fast: and hold the traditions which you have learned, whether by word or by our epistle'; and to the Corinthians: 'Now I praise you, brethren, that in all things you are mindful of me and keep my ordinances as I have delivered them to you.'[10]

Chapter 17

The God proclaimed by the Old Testament and the New is one He who is celebrated and glorified in Trinity, for the Lord said: 'I am not to come to destroy the law, but to fulfil.'[1] For He worked our salvation, for the sake of which all Scripture and every mysetry has been revealed. And again: 'Search the scriptures: for these give testimony of me.'[2] And the Apostle too, says: 'God, who, at sundry times and in diverse manners, spoke in times past to the fathers by prophets, last of all, in these days, hath spoken to us by his Son.'[3] Through the Holy Ghost, then, both the Law and the Prophets, the evangelists, apostles, pastors, and teachers spoke.

Therefore, 'all scripture, inspired of God, is quite profitable,'[4] so that to search the sacred Scripture is very good and most profitable for the soul. For, 'like a tree which is planted

---

10 2 Thess. 2.14; 1 Cor. 11.2.

1 Matt. 5.17.
2 John 5.39.
3 Heb. 1.1-2.
4 2 Tim. 3.16.

near the running waters,'⁵ so does the soul watered by sacred Scripture also grow fat and bear fruit in due season, which is the orthodox faith, and so is it adorned with its evergreen leaves, with actions pleasing to God, I mean. And thus we are disposed to virtuous action and untroubled contemplation by the sacred Scriptures. In them we find exhortation to every virtue and dissuasion from every vice. Therefore, if we are eager for knowledge, we shall also be rich in knowledge, for by diligence, toil, and the grace of God who grants it all things succeed. 'For he that asketh receiveth: and he that seeketh findeth: and to him that knocketh it shall be opened.'⁶ So let us knock at the very beautiful paradise of the Scriptures, the fragrant, most sweet and lovely paradise which fills our ears with the varied songs of inspired spiritual birds, which touches our heart, comforting it when grieving, calming it when angry, and filling it with everlasting joy, and which lifts our mind onto the back of the sacred dove, gleaming with gold and most brilliant,⁷ who bears us with his most bright wings to the only-begotten Son and heir of the Husbandman of the spiritual vineyard and through Him on to the Father of lights. Let us not knock casually, but with eagerness and persistence, and let us not lose heart while knocking, for so it will be opened to us. Should we read once and then a second time and still not understand what we are reading, let us not be discouraged. Rather, let us persist, let us meditate and inquire, for it is written: 'Ask thy father, and he will declare to thee: thy elders and they will tell thee.'⁸ For not all have knowledge.⁹ From the fountain of paradise let us draw everflowing and most pure waters springing up into life everlasting.¹⁰ Let us revel in them, let us revel greedily in them to satiety, for they contain the grace which cannot

---

5 Ps. 1.3.
6 Luke 11.10.
7 Cf. Ps. 67.14.
8 Deut. 32.7.
9 Cf. 1 Cor. 8.7.
10 Cf. John 4.14.

be exhausted. Should we, however, be able to get some profit from other sources, this is not forbidden. Let us be proved bankers and amass the genuine and pure gold, while we reject the spurious. Let us accept the best sayings, but let us throw to the dogs the ridiculous gods and unhealthy fables, for from the former we should be able to draw very great strength against the latter.

One must know that there are twenty-two books of the Old Testament, corresponding to the letters of the Hebrew alphabet,[11] for the Hebrews have twenty-two letters, of which five are doubled so as to make twenty-seven. Thus, *kaph, mem, nun, pe,* and *sade* are double. For this reason the books, too, are numbered this way and are found to be twenty-seven, because five of them are doubled. Ruth is combined with Judges and counted as one book by the Hebrews. Kings 1 and 2 make one book; 3 and 4 Kings, one book; 1 and 2 Paralipomenon, one book; and 1 and 2 Esdras, one book. Thus, the books fall into four groups of five, as follows. There are five books of the Law: Genesis, Exodus, Leviticus, Numbers, and Deuteronomy. This first group of five is also called the Law. Then, another group of five books called the Writings, or, by some, the Sacred Books, which are as follows: Josue, son of Nave; Judges, together with Ruth; 1 and 2 Kings making one book; 3 and 4 Kings making one book; and the two Paralipomenons making one book. This is the second group of five books. A third group of five is made up of the poetical books, namely: Job, the Psalter, the Proverbs of Solomon, Ecclesiastes of the same, and the Canticle of Canticles of the same. A fourth group of five books is the prophetic, which is made up of the twelve minor Prophets, making one book, Isaias, Jeremias, Ezechiel, Daniel, and then the two books of Esdras combined into one, and Esther. The All-Virtuous Wisdom, however, that is to say, the Wisdom of Solomon—and the Wisdom of Jesus, which the father of Sirach composed in

---

11 Epiphanius, *On Weights and Measures* (PG 43.244A).

Hebrew but which was translated into Greek by his grandson, Jesus son of Sirach—these are indeed admirable and full of virtue, but they are not counted, nor were they placed in the Ark.

In the New Testament there are: four Gospels, those according to Matthew, Mark, Luke, and John; the Acts of the holy Apostles by Luke the Evangelist; seven Catholic Epistles—one of James, two of Peter, three of John, and one of Jude; fourteen Epistles of the Apostle Paul; the Apocalypse of John the Evangelist; and the Canons of the Holy Apostles by Clement.[12]

Chapter 18

The things that are said about Christ fall into four general classes, for, while some apply to Him before the Incarnation, others do in the union, others after the union, and still others after the resurrection.

Of those applying before the Incarnation, there are six kinds. Thus, some show the union of nature and consubstantiality with the Father, as 'I and the Father are one'; 'He that seeth me seeth the Father also'; 'Who being in the form of God,'[1] and the like.

Others show the perfection of the hypostasis, as 'Son of God'; 'figure of his substance'; 'Angel of great counsel, Wonderful, Counsellor,'[2] and the like.

---

[12] The *Apostolic Canons* was a collection of eighty-five canons, mostly disciplinary and mostly taken from local Oriental councils of the fourth century. This collection was included in Book 8 of the *Apostolic Constitutions*, the whole being attributed to St. Clement. The Council in Trullo (692), while rejecting the *Constitutions*, retained and approved the *Canons*. The *Canons*, the Damascene not withstanding, were never generally considered to belong to the canon of Scripture.

[1] John 10.30; 14.9; Phil. 2.6.
[2] John 1.34; Heb. 1.3; Isa. 9.6.

Others show the mutual indwelling of the Persons in one another, as 'I am in the Father and the Father in me,'[3] and their inseparable indwelling, as Word, Wisdom, Power and Brightness. For the word, meaning the substantial word, while springing from the mind dwells in it inseparably from it; and also the wisdom in the mind, the power in the powerful, and the brightness in the light.

Others show how He is from the Father as from a cause, as 'the Father is greater than I'[4] for from Him He had His being and everything that He has—His being by generation, that is, not by creation,[5] as 'I came forth from the Father and I am come' and 'I live by the Father.'[6] Now, everything that He has He has not by communication and not by instruction but as from a cause, as 'the Son cannot do anything of himself, but what he seeth the Father doing.'[7] For, if there is no Father, then neither is there a Son, for the Son is from the Father, and in the Father and simultaneously with the Father and not after the Father. Similarly also, what He does He does of Him and with Him, for the will, operation, and power of the Father and of the Son and of the Holy Ghost are identical—not like, but the same.

Others show how things willed by the Father are fulfilled by Him, not as by an instrument or a servant, but as by His substantial and subsistent Word, Wisdom, and Power, because motion in Father and Son are seen to be one, as 'all things were made by him'; 'he sent his word, and healed them'; and 'that they may believe that thou hast sent me.'[8]

Some, finally, are said prophetically. Of these some are said as future, as, for example, 'he shall come manifestly'; the words of Zacharias: 'Behold thy King will come to thee'; and what was said by Micheas: 'For behold the Lord will

---

[3] John 14.10.
[4] John 14.28.
[5] Gregory Nazianzen, *Sermon* 30.7 (*PG* 36.112-113).
[6] John 16.28; 6.58.
[7] John 5.19.
[8] John 1.3; Ps. 106.20; John 11.42.

come forth out of his place: and he will come down and will tread upon the high places of the earth.'⁹ Others, however, refer to future events as past, as 'This is our God. . . .Afterwards, he was seen upon earth and conversed with men'; 'The Lord created me a beginning of his ways unto his works'; and 'Therefore God, thy God, hath anointed thee with the oil of gladness above thy fellows,'¹⁰ and the like.

Now, the things said of Him before the union may also be said of Him after the union, but those after the union may by no means be said of Him before the union, unless, indeed, it be by way of prophecy. Moreover, there are three kinds of things said of Him in the union. Thus, when we talk from the point of view of the more excellent, we speak of 'deification of the flesh,' 'becoming the Word,' 'exaltation,' and the like, showing the wealth accrued to the flesh by its union and intimate conjunction with the sublime Divine Word. When, on the other hand, we talk from the point of view of the less excellent, we speak of the 'Incarnation' of God the Word, His 'being made man,' 'emptying Himself out,' 'poverty,' 'abasement,' because these things and their like are attributed to God the Word on account of His being compounded with the humanity. But, when we talk with both in mind, we speak of 'union,' 'communication,' 'anointing,' 'intimate conjunction,' 'conformation,' and the like. Thus, by this third kind of things said the first two already mentioned are implied, for by the union there is shown what each one had from the junction and mutual indwelling of the one co-existing with it.

Because of the hypostatic union the flesh is said to have been deified, to have become God and of the same divinity with the Word;¹¹ at the same time God the Word is said to have been made flesh, to have become man, to be declared a creature and called last.¹² This is not because the two

---

9 Ps. 49.3; Zach. 9.9; Mich. 1.3.
10 Bar. 3.36,38; Prov. 8.22 (Septuagint); Ps. 44.8.
11 Cf. Gregory Nazianzen, *Sermon* 39.16 (*PG* 36.353B).
12 Cf. Isa. 53.3.

natures were transformed into one compound nature—it is impossible for contradictory natural qualities to exist together in one nature—but because they were hypostatically united and indwell mutually one in the other without confusion or transformation. The mutual indwelling, however, did not come from the flesh, but from the divinity, because it is inconceivable that the flesh should indwell the divinity—rather, at once the divine nature indwelt the flesh, it gave the flesh this same ineffable mutual indwelling, which, indeed, we call union.

One must furthermore know that in the first and second kinds of things said in the union the reverse is found. For, when we talk about the flesh, we speak of 'deification,' 'becoming the Word,' 'exaltation,' and 'anointing,' for, while these come from the divinity, they are to be found in the flesh. When, on the other hand, we talk about the Word, we speak of 'emptying out,' 'incarnation,' 'becoming man,' 'abasement,' and the like, which as we have said, are attributed to God the Word because He endured them willingly.

There are three kinds of things said about Christ after the union. The first is indicative of the divine nature, as 'I am in the Father and the Father in me' and 'I and the Father are one.'[13] Then, everything that is attributed to Him before the union may also be attributed to Him after the union, with the exception of the fact that He has not yet assumed the flesh and its natural properties.

The second is indicative of the human nature, as 'Why do you seek to kill me, a man who have spoken the truth to you,' and 'so must the Son of man be lifted up,'[14] and the like.

Now, there are six kinds of these things which have been said and written about Christ the Saviour in His human quality, whether they were of things said or of things done.

---

13 John 14.10; 10.30.
14 John 7.20; 8.40; 3.14.

Thus, some of them were done and said naturally through the dispensation. Such, for example, were His birth of the Virgin; His growing and advance in age; His hunger, thirst, weariness, tears, sleeping, being pierced with the nails, death; and all such other things as are natural and blameless passions. He might show that besides being God He was truly man. For, although there is indeed a mingling of the divinity with the humanity in all of these things, it is understood that they truly belong to the body and that the divinity suffered none of them, but through them worked our salvation.

Others are after the manner of a fiction, as, for example, His asking 'Where have you laid Lazarus?' His coming to the fig tree; His retiring, that is to say, withdrawing; His praying; and when 'he made as though he would go farther.'[15] For, these things and others of the same sort He did not need to do, either as God or as man; He was merely assuming a human way of acting as required by the advantage and profit to be gained thereby. For example, He prayed to show that He was not at variance with God and also to show that He honored the Father as His own cause. He asked questions, not because He did not know, but that He retired, in order that He might teach us not to be reckless and not to betray ourselves.

Others are by appropriation and said relatively, as 'My God, my God, why hast thou forsaken me?'; and 'him, who knew no sin, he hath made sin for us'; and 'being made a curse for us'; and 'the Son also himself shall be subject unto him that put all things under him.'[16] For neither as God nor as man was He ever forsaken by the Father;[17] neither was He made a sin or a curse, nor did He need to be subject to the Father. And as God He is equal to the Father and in no way at variance with Him or subject to Him, while as man He was never at any time so deaf to

---

15 John 11.34; Matt. 21.19; 12.15; 26.39; John 11.41; Luke 24.28.
16 Matt. 27.46; 2 Cor. 5.21; Gal. 3.13; 1 Cor. 15.28.
17 Gregory Nazianzen, *Sermon* 30.5 (PG 36.109A).

His Begetter that He should stand in need of subjection. So it was in appropriating our appearance and classing Himself with us that He said these things, for it was we who were subject to sin and curse, because we were disobedient and unhearing and thus forsaken.

Others are by distinction of reason. Thus, if you make a distinction in your mind between things which are really inseparable, that is to say, between the flesh and the Word, then He is said to be a servant and ignorant.[18] This is so because He was of a servile and ignorant nature, and unless the flesh has been united to God the Word it would have been servile and ignorant. However, because of its hypostatic union with God the Word, it was not servile and it was not ignorant. In the same way, also, He called the Father His God.

Others are for our enlightenment and assurance, as 'Glorify thou me, O Father, with thyself, with the glory which I had, before the world was.'[19] For He had indeed been glorified and is so, but His glory had not been made plain and certain to us. And then, that which was said by the Apostle: 'Who was predestinated the Son of God in power, according to the spirit of sanctification, by resurrection from the dead,'[20] for by His miracles and resurrection and by the descent of the Holy Ghost it was made plain and certain to the world that He was the Son of God.[21] And also: 'He advanced in wisdom and grace.'[22]

Others are in accordance with His appropriation of the appearance of the Jews and His counting Himself as one of them, as when He said to the Samaritan woman: 'You

---

18 Cf. *ibid.* 29.18 (PG 36.97A).
19 John 17.5.
20 Rom. 1.4.
21 Cf. John Chrysostom, *Homily 1 on Epistle to the Romans 2* (PG 60.397).
22 Luke 2.52.

adore that which you know not: we adore that which we know. For salvation is of the Jews.'²³

The third kind of things said about Christ after the union is that which is indicative of the one Person and displays both natures, as, for example: 'I live by the Father: so he that eateth me, the same also shall live by me'; and 'I go to the Father: and you shall see me no longer'; and 'They would never have crucified the Lord of glory'; and 'no man ascended into heaven, but he that descended from heaven, the Son of man who is in heaven,'²⁴ and the like.

And now, finally, some of the things which are said about Christ after the resurrection pertain to the divinity, as 'baptizing them in the name of the Father and of the Son and of the Holy Ghost,' which is indicative of God the Son; and 'Behold I am with you all days, even to the consummation of the world,'²⁵ and the like, because He is with us as God. Others, however, pertain to the humanity, as 'they took hold of his feet,' and 'There they shall see me,'²⁶ and the like.

There are furthermore, several kinds of things said about Christ after the resurrection which pertain to the humanity. Some of these, although quite actual, are not according to nature, but by dispensation, to give assurance that it was the same identical body that had suffered that rose again. Such are the wounds, and the eating and drinking after the resurrection. Others, however, are both actual and according to nature, as the passing easily from place to place and the entering through closed doors. Still others are after the manner of a fiction, as 'he made as though he would go farther.'²⁷ Others pertain to both natures, as 'I ascend to my Father and to your Father, to my God and to your God'; and 'the

---

23 John 4.22.
24 John 6.58; 16.10; 1 Cor. 2.8; John 3.13.
25 Matt. 28.19,20.
26 Matt. 28.9,10.
27 Luke 24.28.

King of Glory shall enter in'; and 'Who sitteth on the right hand of the majesty on high.'[28] And still others are said as if He were classing Himself with us by a mere distinction of reason, as 'my God and your God.'

Therefore, we must attribute the sublime things to the divine nature, which is naturally superior to passions and the flesh, whereas we must attribute the lowly ones to the human nature.[29] But those which are common to both we must attribute to the composite, that is to say to the one Christ who is God and man. And we must understand that both belong to one and the same, our Lord Jesus Christ. For, if we know what is proper to each and see that both are done by one, we shall believe rightly and not be deceived. From all of these things the distinction between the united natures is known, as well as the fact that, as the most divine Cyril says,[30] although divinity and humanity are not identical in their natural quality, there is definitely one Son and Christ and Lord. And since He is one, then His Person (πρόσωπον) is also one, and no division whatsoever will be introduced into the hypostatic union by our recognition of the difference between the natures.

Chapter 19

One should know that it is customary for sacred Scripture to call God's permission His action, as when the Apostle says in his Epistle to the Romans: 'Or hath not the potter power over the clay, of the same lump, to make one vessel unto honour and another unto dishonour?'[1] He does indeed make both the one and the other, because He is the sole

---

28 John 20.17; Ps. 23.7; Heb. 1.3.
29 Cf. Gregory Nazianzen, *Sermon* 29.18 (*PG* 36.97B).
30 Cf. Cyril of Alexandria, *Epistle* 40 (*PG* 77.183BC).

1 Rom. 9.21.

Creator of all things, but it is the own deliberate choice of each and not He that makes them honorable or dishonorable.[2] This is also clear from what the Apostle himself says in his Second Epistle to Timothy: 'In a great house there are not only vessels of gold and silver, but also of wood and of earth: and some indeed unto honour, but some unto dishonour. If any man therefore shall cleanse himself from these, he shall be a vessel unto honour, sanctified and profitable to the Lord, prepared unto every work.'[3] It is clear that this cleansing is done freely, for he says 'if any man shall cleanse himself,' the converse of which rejoins that, if he does not cleanse himself, he will be a vessel unto dishonor, of no use to Lord, and only fit to be broken. Thus, the foregoing quotation and that which reads: 'God hath concluded all in unbelief' and 'God hath given them the spirit of insensibility; eyes that they should not see and ears that they should not hear,'[4] are none of them to be taken in the sense of God acting, but in that of God permitting because of free will and because virtue is not forced.

It is, then, customary for sacred Scripture to speak of His permission as an action and deed, but even when it goes so far as to say that God 'creates evil' and that 'there is not evil in a city, which the Lord hath not done,'[5] it still does not show God to be the author of evil. On the contrary, since the word *evil* is ambiguous, it has two meanings, for it sometimes means what is by nature evil, being the opposite of virtue and against God's will, while at other times it means what is evil and painful in relation to our sensibility, which is to say, tribulation and distress. Now, while these last seem to be evil, because they cause pain, actually they are good, because to such as understand them they are a source of conversion and salvation. It is these last that Scripture says

---

2 Cf. Basil, *That God Is Not Author of Evils* (PG 31.340BC).
3 2 Tim. 2.20,21.
4 Rom. 11.32,8.
5 Isa. 45.7; Amos 3.6.

are caused by God. Moreover, one must know that we, too, cause them, because involuntary evils spring from voluntary ones.

This also must be known, that it is customary for Scripture to speak of some things as causes which really are chance effects, as: 'To thee only have I sinned, and have done evil before thee: that thou mayst be justified in thy words, and mayst overcome when thou art judged.'[6] Now, he who sinned did not do so in order that God might overcome, and neither did God have any need of our sin for Him to appear as victor over it. For God incomparably bears off the prize of victory over all, and even over such as do not sin, because He is Creator, and beyond understanding, and uncreated, and He has glory which comes from His nature and not from without. However, because it is not unjust of Him to inflict His wrath, when we sin, or to forgive, when we repent, He is proclaimed victor over our evil. And it is not because of this that we sin, but because the matter turns out that way. For instance, should one be sitting at work and a friend drop in, then he will say: 'My friend has come to visit and so I shall not work today.' The friend did not come to keep him from working, but just happened to drop in. So he, being taken up with the entertainment of his friend, does not work. Such things are called chance effects, because the matter happens that way. What is more, God does not want to be the only one that is just, but wishes that all be like Him in so far as they are able.

Chapter 20

We shall now see that there are not two principles, the one good and the other evil.[1] For good and evil are mutually

---

6 Ps. 50.6.

---

1 Cf. Athanasius, *Against the Pagans* 6 (PG 25.12-13).

opposed and mutually destructive and they cannot exist in or with each other. In this last case, each would be a part of the whole and, consequently, each would be circumscribed not only by the whole but by a part of the whole.

Then, who is there to apportion the space to each? For they will say that they can neither agree nor be reconciled, since evil would not be evil if it made peace by becoming reconciled with the good, nor would good be good if it were on friendly terms with evil. If, however, there were to be a third, who had marked out for each its own sphere, then he would more likely be God.

Moreover, one of the two alternatives would be necessary. Either they would have to be in contact with each other and thus destroy each other, or there would have to be something between them in which there was neither good nor evil and which would separate them like a sort of partition. Then there would no longer be two principles, but three.

And again, one of the following alternatives would be necessary. Either they would have to be at peace, which evil cannot do, because, should it be at peace, it would not be evil. Or they would have to fight, which good cannot do, because, should if fight, it would not be perfectly good. Or the evil would have to fight and the good not fight back and either be destroyed by the evil or always be in a state of affliction and distress, which is not a characteristic of good. Consequently, there must be one principle removed from all evil.

But, they say, if such is the case, where does the evil come from? For it is inconceivable that evil should originate from good. Then we reply that evil is no more than a negation of good[2] and a lapse from what is natural to what is unnatural, for there is nothing that is naturally evil. Now, as they were made, all things that God made were very good.[3] So, if they remain as they were created, then they are very

---

2 Cf. Basil, *op. cit.* (PG 31.341B).
3 Cf. Gen. 1.31.

good. But, if they freely withdraw from the natural and pass to the unnatural, then they become evil.

All things, then, by nature serve and obey the Creator. So, whenever any creature freely rebels and becomes disobedient to Him who made him, he has brought the evil upon himself. For evil is not some sort of a substance, nor yet a property of a substance, but an accident, that is to say, a deviation from the natural into the unnatural, which is just what sin is.

Then, where does sin come from?[4] It is an invention of the free will of the Devil. Then, is the Devil evil? As he was made he was not evil, but good, because he was created a shining and most bright angel by the Creator, and free because rational. And he freely departed from his natural virtue, fell into the darkness of evil, and was removed far from God, the only Good and the only Giver of life and light. For from Him every good has its goodness, and in proportion as one is removed from Him in will—not, of course, in place—one becomes evil.

Chapter 21

God in His goodness brings into being from nothing the things that are made, and He foreknows what they are going to be. Now, if they were not going to be, they would never be evil in the future, nor would they be foreknown. For the object of knowledge is existing things; and that of foreknowledge, absolute futures. Also, being comes first and, afterwards, being good or evil. However, had God kept from being made those who through His goodness were to have existence, but who by their own choice were to become evil, then evil would have prevailed over the goodness of God. Thus, all things which God makes He makes good, but each one becomes good or evil by his own choice. So, even

---

4 Cf. Basil, *op. cit.* (PG 31.345D).

if the Lord did say: 'It were better for him if that man had not been born,'[1] He did not say so in deprecation of His own creature, but in deprecation of that creature's choice and rashness. For it was the rashness of his own will that made the Creator's benefaction useless to him. It is just as if someone who had been entrusted with wealth and authority by a king should tyrannize over his benefactor, and His benefactor, seeing that he is to persist in his tyranny to the end, should rightly bring him to hand and punish him.

Chapter 22

Good and more than good is the Divinity, and so also is His will, for what God wishes, that is good. The commandment which teaches us this is a law, so that we may abide in Him and be in light.[1] And the violation of this commandment is sin. Sin results from the Devil's suggestion and our own unconstrained and free acceptance of it. And this, too, is called a law.[2]

The law of God, then, acts upon our mind by drawing it to Him and spurring on our conscience. And our conscience is also called the law of our mind. The suggestion of the Devil, or the law of sin, also acts upon the members of our flesh and through it attacks us. For, once we succumbed to the suggestion of the Evil One and freely violated the law of God, we allowed this suggestion to gain entrance and sold ourselves to sin. For this reason our body is easily brought to sin. Hence, the odor and sense of sin which is inherent in our body, that is to say, the concupiscence and pleasure of the body, is also called a law in the members of our flesh.

---

1 Mark 14.21.

1 Cf. 1 John 1.7.
2 Cf. Rom. 7.23.

Accordingly, the law of my mind—my conscience, that is to say—rejoices in the law of God, or His commandment, and wills it. On the other hand, the law of sin—that is to say, the suggestion that comes through the law in our members, or the concupiscence and base tendency and movement of the body and the irrational part of the soul—fights against the law of my mind, that is to say, my conscience, and captivates me. It does this by insinuating itself, even though I do will the law of God and love it and do not will to sin, and it deceives me and persuades me to become a slave to sin through the softness of pleasure and the concupiscence of the body and the irrational part of the soul, as I have said. However, 'what the law could not do, in that it was weak through the flesh, God, sending his own Son in the likeness of sinful flesh'—for, while He assumed flesh, He by no means took on sin—'hath condemned sin in the flesh. That the justification of the law might be fulfilled in us who walk not according to the flesh, but according to the spirit,' for 'the Spirit also helpeth our infirmity,' and gives strength to the law of our mind against the law which is in our members. 'For we know not what we should pray for as we ought: but the Spirit himself asketh for us with unspeakable groanings,'[3] that is to say, He teaches us what we should pray for. Hence, it is impossible to observe the commandments of the Lord except by patience and prayer.

Chapter 23

The seventh day was called the Sabbath and it means rest, for on it God 'rested from all his work,'[1] as sacred Scripture has it. And it is for this reason that the numbering of the days goes up as far as seven and then starts over

---

3 Rom. 8.3,4,26.

1 Gen. 2.2.

again from one. This number is held in honor by the Jews, because God prescribed that it be honored—not in any casual way, but under the most severe sanctions in case of violation.[2] What is more, He did not prescribe this arbitrarily, but for certain reasons which are perceptible in a mystic sense to spiritual and discerning men.[3]

At any rate, to start with the inferior and grosser things, as my unlearned self understands it, when God saw the grossness and sensuality of the people of Israel and their absolute propensity for material things, as well as their indiscretion, then first of all He prescribed that 'the man-servant and the ox should rest,'[4] as it is written. This was because 'the just regardeth the lives of his beasts,'[5] but at the same time it was in order that they might rest from the distraction of material things and congregate to God to spend the entire seventh day 'in psalms, hymns and spiritual canticles,'[6] in the study of sacred Scripture, and in taking rest in God. For, when there was no law or divinely inspired Scripture, neither was the Sabbath consecrated to God; but when the divinely inspired Scripture was given through Moses, then the Sabbath was consecrated to God, so that on that day such might have leisure to study it as do not consecrate their entire lives to God nor with longing serve the Lord as Father but like unfeeling servants—the kind who, if ever they do allot some short and very small part of their lives to God, do so from fear of the punishment and chastisement attendant upon its violation. For 'the law is not made for the just man but for the unjust.'[7] Moses was the first to wait upon God for forty days fasting, and again for another forty days,[8] and, when he did so, he most certainly mortified

---

2 E.g., Num. 15.32-36.
3 Cf. Gregory Nazianzen, *Sermon* 41.2 (*PG* 36.429).
4 Deut. 5.14.
5 Prov. 12.10.
6 Col. 3.16.
7 1 Tim. 1.9.
8 Cf. Exod. 24.18; 34.28.

himself with fasting on the Sabbaths, although the law prescribed that they should not mortify themselves on the Sabbath day. However, should they say that this happened before the Law, then what will they have to say about Elias the Thesbite who made a forty-day journey on one meal?[9] For this man broke the Sabbath by afflicting himself on the Sabbaths of those forty days not only with fasting, but with traveling, and God, who had given the Law, was not angry with him, but on the contrary appeared to him on Horeb as a reward for virtue. And what will they say about Daniel? Did he not go for three weeks without food?[10] And what about all Israel? Do they not circumcise a child on the Sabbath, if the eighth day happens to fall on it? And also, do they not keep the great fast, which is ordained by law, if it comes on the Sabbath? And also, do not the priests and levites profane the Sabbath in the works of the tabernacle, yet remain without blame?[11] More than that, should a beast fall into a pit on the Sabbath, he who pulls it out is without blame, while he who neglects it is condemned.[12] And what about all Israel? Did they not circle about the walls of Jericho carrying the ark for seven days, on one of which the Sabbath most certainly fell?[13]

And so, as I said, for the sake of leisure time for God, in order that they might devote at least a minimum portion to Him and that their man-servant and beast might rest, the observance of the Sabbath was imposed upon them while still 'children and serving under the elements of the world,'[14] carnal and unable to understand anything beyond the body and the letter. 'But when the fulness of time was come, God sent His only-begotten Son, made man of a woman, made under the law; that he might redeem them who are

---
9 Cf. 3 Kings 19.8.
10 Cf. Dan. 10.2,3.
11 Cf. Matt. 12.5.
12 Cf. Luke 14.5.
13 Cf. Josue 6.4.
14 Gal. 4.3.

under the law: that we might receive the adoption of sons.'[15] For as many of us as received Him, He gave power to be made the sons of God, to those that believe in Him.[16] And so we are no longer servants, but sons.[17] We are no longer under the Law, but under grace.[18] We no longer give the Lord just partial service out of fear, but we are bound to dedicate the whole space of our life to Him and constantly to make the man-servant, by which I mean anger and desire, desist from sin, while at the same time turning him to the service of God. And while we constantly raise up all our desire to God, our anger we arm against His enemies. And the beast of burden, that is to say, our body, we release from the servitude of sin, while at the same time we urge it onto the fullest observance of the divine commandments.

These things the spiritual law of Christ enjoins upon us, and they who keep this law are become superior to the Law of Moses. For, since 'that which is perfect is come, that which is in part is done away,' and since the covering of the Law, the veil, that is to say, was rent because of the crucifixion of the Saviour and the Spirit was radiant with tongues of fire,[19] the letter is done away, the things of the body have ceased, the law of servitude has been fulfilled, and the law of freedom has been given us. And we celebrate the complete adjustment of human nature, by which I mean the day of the resurrection upon which the Lord Jesus, the Author of life and Saviour, admitted us to the portion promised them that worship God in the spirit, into which He entered as our precursor when He rose from the dead and, with the gates of heaven opened to Him, sat down corporeally at the right hand of the Father, where they also shall enter who keep the law of the Spirit.

---

15 Gal. 4.4,5.
16 John 1.12.
17 Cf. Gal. 4.7.
18 Cf. Rom. 6.14.
19 1 Cor. 13.10; Matt. 27.51; Acts 2.3.

We, then, who follow the spirit and not the letter must put aside all things of the flesh and worship in the spirit and be joined with God. For circumcision is really the putting aside of bodily pleasure and superfluous unnecessary things, since the foreskin is nothing more than a piece of skin, a superflous part of the pleasurable member. Moreover, any pleasure which is not from God and in God is a pleasure, the figure of which is the foreskin. The Sabbath, moreover, is the desisting from sin. Hence, both amount to the same thing, and when both are observed together in this way by those who are spiritual, they induce no violation of the law whatsoever.

One must furthermore know that the number seven signifies all the present time,[20] as the most wise Solomon says: 'Give a portion to seven, and also to eight.'[21] Also, when the inspired David was singing a psalm for the octave, he sang of the state of things to be after the resurrection from the dead.[22] Therefore, when the Law prescribed that bodily things be refrained from on the seventh day and time devoted to the spiritual, it intimated to the true Israel, the Israel which has a mind that sees God, that it should devote itself to God at all times and rise up above the things of the body.

Chapter 24

Men who are carnal and given to pleasure belittle virginity and offer by way of testimony the saying, 'Cursed be every man who raiseth not up seed in Israel.'[1] But we, made confident by the fact that God the Word took flesh of a virgin, declare that virginity is from above and was implanted in men's nature from the beginning. Thus, man

---

20 Cf. Gregory Nazianzen, *Sermon* 45.15 (*PG* 36.644C).
21 Eccle. 11.2.
22 Cf. Ps. 6.11.

1 Cf. Deut. 25.5-10.

was formed from the virgin earth. Eve was created from Adam alone. Virginity was practiced in paradise. Indeed, sacred Scripture says that 'they were naked, to wit, Adam and Eve: and were not ashamed.'[2] However, once they had fallen, they knew that they were naked and being ashamed they sewed together aprons for themselves.[3] After the fall, when Adam heard 'Dust thou art, and unto dust return,' and death entered into the world through transgression, then 'Adam knew Eve his wife: who conceived and brought forth.'[4] And so to keep the race from dwindling and being destroyed by death marriage was devised, so that by the begetting of children the race of men might be preserved.[5]

But they may ask: What, then, does 'male and female' mean, and 'increase and multiply'?[6] To which we shall reply that the 'increase and multiply' does not mean increasing by the marriage union exclusively, because, if they had kept the commandment unbroken forever, God could have increased the race by some other means. But, since God, who knows all things before they come to be, saw by His foreknowledge how they were to fall and be condemned to death, He made provision beforehand by creating them male and female and commanding them to increase and multiply. So let us continue along the road and see what the increments from virginity are, which is nothing else than to talk about chastity.

When Noe was ordered to enter the ark and was entrusted with the safeguarding of the seed of the earth, he was given this command, which reads: 'Go in thou and thy sons, and thy wife, and the wives of thy sons.'[7] He separated them from their wives, so that with the help of chastity they

---

2 Gen. 2.25.
3 Cf. Gen. 3.7.
4 Gen. 3.19; cf. Rom. 5.12; Gen. 4.1.
5 Cf. Gregory of Nyssa, *On the Making of Man* 17 (*PG* 44.188-189).
6 Gen. 1.27,28.
7 Gen. 7.1; 6.18.

might escape the deep and that world-wide destruction. However, after the cessation of the flood, the command was: 'Go out thou and thy wife, thy sons, and the wives of thy sons.'[8] Here, see how marriage was again permitted for the sake of increase. And, then, did not Elias, who rode up to heaven in a fiery chariot,[9] embrace celibacy and was not approval of this shown by his being endowed with a superiority over men? Who closed the heavens? Who raised the dead? Who divided the Jordan?[10] Was it not Elias the virgin? And did not Eliseus, his disciple, ask for the grace of his spirit in double, and receive it, when he displayed equal virtue?[11] And what about the three children? Was it not by practicing virginity that they became stronger than the fire, because by virginity their bodies had become impregnable to fire? Was there not a Daniel, whose body the teeth of wild beasts could not penetrate, because it had been hardened by virginity?[12] When God was about to appear to the Israelites, did He not enjoin them to keep their bodies pure?[13] Did not priests purify themselves and thus enter the sanctuary and offer sacrifices?[14] Did not the Law proclaim chastity to be a great vow?

Thus, the prescription of the Law must be taken in the more spiritual sense. For there is a spiritual seed which through charity and the fear of God is conceived in the womb of the soul, which in turn travails and brings forth the spirit of salvation. It is in this sense that the passage is to be taken which reads: 'Blessed is he who has seed in Sion and kindred in Jerusalem.'[15] What, indeed! Even though one be a fornicator, a drunkard, or an idolater, will he be

---
8 Gen. 8.16.
9 Cf. 4 Kings 2.11.
10 Cf. 3 Kings 17.1; 17.22; 4 Kings 2.8.
11 Cf. 4 Kings 2.9,14.
12 Cf. Dan. 3.50; 6.22.
13 Cf. Exod. 19.15.
14 Cf. Lev. 21.
15 Isa. 31.9 (Septuagint).

blessed, provided only that he has seed in Sion and kindred in Jerusalem? No one in his right mind would say that.

Virginity is the habitual state of the angels, the peculiar characteristic of every incorporeal nature. We are not saying all this to decry marriage, God forbid, because we know that the Lord blessed marriage by His presence,[16] and we know the passage which says: 'marriage honorable and the bed undefiled.'[17] We do, however, know that virginity is better than good. For with the virtues, as well as with the vices, there are greater and lesser degrees. We do know that, with the exception of the first parents of the race, all mortals are offspring from marriage, for our first parents were the work of virginity and not of marriage. Celibacy, however, is an imitation of the angels, as we have said. So, virginity is as much more honorable than marriage as the angel is superior to man. But what am I saying—an angel? Christ Himself is the glory of virgintiy, not only because He was begotten of the Father without beginning, without change, and without coition, but also because, when He became man like us, He for our sake took flesh of a virgin without any carnal union and exhibited in Himself the true and perfect virginity. But He did not make this a law for us, because 'all men take not this word,'[18] as He Himself said. He did, however, instruct us by His example and give us the strength to keep virginity, for to whom is it not clear that virginity is being observed among men now?

The begetting of children which results from marriage is certainly good. Marriage, too, is good, because it does away with fornication and by licit intercourse prevents the frenzy of concupiscence from being excited to illicit actions.[19] Marriage is good for those for whom continence is impossible, but virginity is better, because it increases the fecundity of

---
16 Cf. John 2.2.
17 Heb. 13.4.
18 Matt. 19.11.
19 Cf. 1 Cor. 7.2.

the soul and offers prayer to God as a seasonable fruit. 'Marriage honourable, and the bed undefiled. For fornicators and adulterers God will judge.'[20]

Chapter 25

The circumcision was given to Abraham before the Law, after the blessings and after the promise, as a sign to set him and those born of him and those of his household apart from the Gentiles in whose midst he was living.[1] And this is obvious, because, when Israel spent forty years alone by themselves in the desert without mixing with any other nation, all those who were born in the desert were not circumcised.[2] However, when Josue brought them across the Jordan, they were circumcised and a second law of circumcision was made. For, under Abraham a law of circumcision was given, and then it was inoperative for forty years in the desert. Then, after the crossing of the Jordan, God again gave the law for a second time, as is written in the book of Josue, son of Nave: 'At that time the Lord said to Josue: make thee knives of stone from the sharpest rock, and sitting down circumcise the second time the children of Israel'; and a little further on: 'for during forty-two years Israel dwelt in the wilderness of Midbar, and for this reason very many were uncircumcised of the sons of the fighting men who had come out of Egypt, who had disobeyed the commandments of God and to whom he declared that they should not see the good land which he had sworn to give to their fathers, the land flowing with milk and honey. The children of these he made to succeed in their place whom Josue circumcised

---

20 Heb. 13.4.

---

1 Cf. Gen. 12; 13; 15; 17.10-14.
2 John Chrysostom, *Homily 39 on Genesis* 4 (PG 53.366).

because of their not having been circumcised in the way.'³ Hence, circumcision was a sign by which Israel was set apart from the Gentiles among whom they lived.

Now, this was a figure of baptism,⁴ for, just as circumcision cuts off from the body a part which is not useful, but a useless superfluity, so by holy baptism are we circumcised of sin. It is obvious that sin is a superfluity of concupiscence and of no use. For it is impossible for anyone not to have any concupiscence at all or to be entirely without any taste for pleasure, but the useless part of pleasure, that is to say, the useless concupiscence and pleasure, this is the sin which holy baptism circumcises. And holy baptism gives us the sign of the venerable cross upon our forehead but does not set us apart from the Gentiles, for all the Gentiles have attained baptism and have been sealed with the sign of the cross. It does, however, distinguish the faithful in each nation from the infidel. Therefore, now that the truth has been made manifest, its figure and shadow is of no use. And so, to be circumcised is now superflous and a contradiction of holy baptism, for 'he who circumciseth himself is a debtor to the whole law.'⁵ The Lord, however, was circumcised that He might fulfill the Law. He also kept the Law in all things and observed the Sabbath that He might fulfill the Law and make it stand. But from the time when He was baptized and men saw the Holy Ghost coming down upon Him in the form of a dove, from that time on the spiritual worship and polity and the kingdom of heaven have been proclaimed.

Chapter 26

One should know that the Antichrist must come. Antichrist, to be sure, is everyone who does not confess that the Son of

---
3 Josue 5.2; 5.6-7 (Septuagint).
4 Cf. Athanasius, *On Sabbaths and the Circumcision* (PG 28.141BC)
5 Gal. 5.3.

God came in the flesh, is perfect God, and became perfect man while at the same time He was God.[1] In a peculiar and special sense, however, he who is to come at the consummation of the world is called Antichrist.[2] So, it is first necessary for the Gospel to have been preached to all the Gentiles, as the Lord said,[3] and then he shall come unto conviction of the impious Jews. For the Lord said to them: 'I am come in the name of my Father, and you receive me not: if another shall come in his own name, him you will receive.'[4] And the Apostle: 'Because they receive not the love of the truth, that they might be saved. Therefore God shall send them the operation of error, to believe lying: that all may be judged who have not believed the truth but have consented to iniquity.'[5] Hence, the Jews did not receive the Lord Jesus Christ and God, although He was the Son of God, but the deceiver who says that he is God they will receive.[6] For, that he will call himself God the angel who taught Daniel thus declares: 'He shall make no account of the gods of his fathers.'[7] And the Apostle: 'Let no man deceive you by any means; for unless there come a revolt first, and the man of sin be revealed, the son of perdition, who opposeth and is lifted up above all that is called God or that is worshipped, so that he sitteth in the temple of God, shewing himself as if he were God.'[8] 'In the temple of God,' he says—not, however, in ours, but in the former one, that of the Jews, for he will not come to us, but to the Jews—not for the sake of Christ and Christ's, for which reason, also, he is called Antichrist.[9]

The Gospel, then, must first be preached in all nations,

---

1 Cf. 1 John 4.3.
2 Cf. Cyril of Jerusalem, *Catechetical Discourse 15* 12 (PG 33.885AB).
3 Cf. Matt. 24.14.
4 John 5.43.
5 2 Thess. 2.10,11.
6 Cf. John Chrysostom, *Homily 4 on 2 Thessalonians* 1 (PG 62.487).
7 Dan. 11.37 (Septuagint).
8 2 Thess. 2.3,4.
9 Cf. Cyril of Jerusalem, *op. cit.* 11 (PG 33.884-885).

'and then that wicked one shall be revealed: whose coming is according to the working of Satan, in all power and signs and lying wonders, in all seduction of iniquity to them that perish: whom the Lord shall kill with the words of his mouth and shall destroy with the coming of his brightness.'[10] Thus, the Devil does not himself become man after the manner of the incarnation of the Lord—God forbid!—but a man is born of fornication and receives into himself the whole operation of Satan, for God permits the Devil to inhabit him, because He foresees the future perversity of his will.[11]

So, he is born of fornication, as we said, and is brought up unnoticed; but of a sudden he rises up, revolts, and rules. During the first part of his reign—of his tyranny, rather—he plays more the part of sanctity; but when he gains complete control, he persecutes the Church of God and reveals all his wickedness. And he shall come 'in signs and lying wonders'[12]—sham ones and not real—and he will seduce those whose intention rests on a rotten and unstable foundation and make them abandon the living God, 'inasmuch as to scandalize (if possible) even the elect.'[13]

And Enoch and Elias the Thesbite will be sent and they shall 'turn the heart of the fathers to the children,'[14] that is to say, turn the synagogue to our Lord Jesus Christ and the preaching of the Apostles. And they will be destroyed by him. Then the Lord will come from heaven in the same way that the holy Apostles saw Him going into heaven, perfect God and perfect man, with glory and power; and He shall destroy the man of iniquity, the son of perdition, with the spirit of His mouth.[15] So, let no one expect the Lord to come from the earth, but from heaven, as He Himself has positively assured us.

---

10 2 Thess. 2.8-10.
11 Cf. John Chrysostom, *Hom. 3 on 2 Thess.* 2, (*PG* 62.482).
12 2 Tness. 2.9.
13 Matt. 24.24.
14 Mal. 4.6.
15 Cf. Acts 1.11; 2 Thess. 2.8.

Chapter 27

Furthermore, we also believe in the resurrection of the dead, for there really will be one, there will be a resurrection of the dead. Now, when we say resurrection, we mean a resurrection of bodies. For resurrection is a raising up again of one who has fallen. But, since souls are immortal, how shall they rise again? Well if death is defined as a separation of soul from body, the resurrection is the perfect rejoining of soul and body, and the raising up again of the dissolved and fallen animal.[1] Therefore, the very body which is corrupted and dissolved will itself rise up incorruptible. For He who formed it in the beginning from the slime of the earth is not incapable of raising it up again after it has again been dissolved and returned to the earth whence it was taken by the decision of its Creator.

Now, if there is no resurrection, let us eat and drink[2] and lead a life of pleasure and enjoyment. If there is no resurrection, then how do we differ from brute beasts? If there is no resurrection, let us call the beasts of the field blessed, because their life is free from care. If there is no resurrection, there is no God and no providence, and all things are being driven and carried along by mere chance. For just consider how very many just men we see in need and suffering injury, yet getting no recompense in this present life, whereas we see sinners and wicked men possessing wealth and every luxury in abundance. Who in his right mind would understand this to be the work of righteous judgment or wise providence? Therefore, there will be, there certainly will be, a resurrection. For God is just and He rewards those who await Him in patience. Now, if the soul had engaged alone in the contest for virtue, then it would also be crowned alone; and if it alone had indulged in pleasures, then it alone

---

1 Cf. Epiphanius, *Ancoratus* 88 (PG 43.180); Methodius, *On the Resurrection* (PG 18.285).
2 Cf. 1 Cor. 15.32; Isa. 22.13.

could be justly punished. However, since the soul followed neither virtue nor vice without the body, it will be just for them to receive their recompense together.

Moreover, sacred Scripture, too, testifies to the fact that there will be a resurrection of the body. Indeed, God says to Noe after the flood: 'Even as the green herbs have I delivered them all to you: saving that flesh with blood of its life you shall not eat. And I will require your blood of your lives, at the hand of every beast I will require it. And at the hand of every man I will require the life of his brother. Whosoever shall shed man's blood, for that blood his blood shall be shed: for I made man to the image of God.'[3] How can He require the blood of man at the hand of every beast, unless He raise the bodies of men who die? For beasts will not die in the place of men.

And again to Moses: 'I am the God of Abraham and the God of Isaac and the God of Jacob.'[4] God 'is not the God of the dead,'[5] of those who have died and will never be again. Rather, He is the God of the living, whose souls live in His hand,[6] and whose bodies will by the resurrection live again. And David, the ancestor of God, says to God: 'Thou shalt take away their breath, and they shall fail, and shall return to their dust.' See how it is a question of their bodies. Then he adds: 'Thou shalt send forth thy spirit, and they shall be created: and thou shalt renew the face of the earth.'[7]

And Isaias also: 'The dead shall rise and those in their graves be awakened.'[8] And it is obvious that it is not the souls that are put in the tombs but the bodies.

And the blessed Ezechiel also: 'And it came to pass as I prophesied, and behold a commotion. And the bones came

---
3 Gen. 9.3-6 (Septuagint).
4 Exod. 3.6.
5 Matt. 22.32.
6 Cf. Wisd. 3.1.
7 Ps. 103.29,30.
8 Isa. 26.19 (Septuagint).

together, bone to bone, each one to its joint. And I saw, and behold the sinews and the flesh came upon them, and spread over them, and the skin was stretched out over them.'[9] Then he relates how the spirits were commanded and returned.

And the divine Daniel, also: 'And at that time shall Michael rise up, the great prince, who standeth for the children of thy people: and a time of tribulation shall come such as never was from the time that nations began on the earth even until that time. And at that time shall thy people be saved, every one that shall be found written in the book. And many of those that sleep in the dust of the earth shall awake: some unto life everlasting, and others unto reproach and everlasting shame. And they that are learned shall shine as the brightness of the firmament, and from the many just, as stars for all eternity and still they shall shine.'[10] When he says 'many of those that sleep in the dust of the earth shall awake,' it is clear that he means the resurrection of their bodies, for I do not suppose that anyone would speak of souls sleeping in the dust of the earth.

There is, moreover, no doubt that the Lord, too, has very clearly shown in the holy Gospels that there is a resurrection of the body, for 'they that are in the graves,' He says, 'shall hear the voice of the Son of God. And they that have done good things shall come forth unto the resurrection of life: but they that have done evil, unto the resurrection of judgment.'[11] Now, no person in his right mind would ever say that it was the souls that were in the graves.

And it was not only in word that He brought out the resurrection, but also in deed. First of all, He raised Lazarus who was four days dead and already putrified and stinking.[12] It was not a soul devoid of a body that He raised, but a

---

9 Ezech. 37.7,8 (Septuagint)
10 Dan. 12.1-3 (Septuagint).
11 John 5.28,29.
12 Cf. John 11.

body with its soul—not another body, but the same one which had putrified. For how would one know or believe in the resurrection of one who had died, were it not for the proof offered by his characteristic peculiarities? Moreover, He also raised Lazarus, who was to return to death again, to show His own divinity and to give assurance of His and our resurrection. And then the Lord Himself became the first-fruits of the perfect resurrection which will never be subject to death. That is why the divine Apostle Paul said: 'If the dead rise not again, neither is Christ risen again. And if Christ be not risen again, our faith is vain, for we are yet in our sins'; and: 'Because Christ is risen, the first-fruits of them that sleep'; and 'firstborn from the dead'; and again: 'For if we believe that Jesus died and rose again: even so them who have slept through Jesus, will God bring with him.'[13] 'Even so,' he said, 'as the Lord has risen.'

And it is plain that the resurrection of the Lord was the uniting of a soul with an incorrupted body, for these had been separated, because He said: 'Destroy this temple; and in three days I will raise it up.'[14] And the holy Gospel is a trusty witness to the fact that He was here speaking of His own body. 'Handle me and see,' the Lord said to His own disciples, who thought that they were seeing a spirit, 'that it is myself, and that I am not different, for a spirit hath not flesh and bones, as you see me to have.' And when He had said this, He showed them His hands and His side and He held them out to Thomas to touch.[15] Now, are not these things a sufficient guarantee of the resurrection?

Again, the divine Apostle says: 'For this corruptible must put on incorruption: and this mortal must put on immortality'; and again 'It is sown in corruption: it shall rise in incorruption. It is sown in weakness: it shall rise in power. It is sown in dishonour: it shall rise in glory. It is sown a

---

13 1 Cor. 15.16,17,20; Col. 1.18; 1 Thess. 4.13.
14 John 2.19,21.
15 Luke 24.39,40; John 20.27.

natural body (which is to say, gross and mortal): it shall rise a spiritual body.'[16] Such was the body of the Lord after the resurrection, the same which entered through the closed doors without difficulty and which needed neither food, nor sleep, nor drink. 'For they shall be,' says the Lord, 'like the angels of God,'[17] and there shall no longer be marriage or begetting of children. Indeed, the divine Apostle says: 'But our conversation is in heaven: from whence also we look for the Saviour, our Lord Jesus Christ, who will reform the body of our lowness, unto its being made like to the body of his glory,[18] not meaning a transformation into another form—far be it!—but rather a change from corruption to incorruption.

'But some man will say: How do the dead rise again?' Oh, what lack of faith! Oh, what stupidity! He who just by His will changed dust into a body and ordained that a little drop of seed should grow up in the womb to make this complex and multiform organ which is the body, will He not much more be able to raise up again the body which has already been made and then wasted away, just by willing it? 'Or with what manner of body shall they come?' Senseless man, if thou art callous enough not to believe the words of God, then at least believe His works, for 'that which thou sowest is not quickened, except it die first. And that which thou sowest, thou sowest not the body which shall be: but bare grain, as of wheat, or some of the rest. But God giveth it a body as he will: and to every seed its proper body.'[19] Consider, then, the seeds that are buried in the furrows as in graves. Who is it that engrafts roots upon them, stem and leaves and ear and those most delicate tassels. It is not the Creator of them all? Is this not done by the command of Him who fashioned all things? Then believe thus: that the

---

16 1 Cor. 15.53,42-44.
17 Mark 12.25.
18 Phil. 3.20,21.
19 1 Cor. 15.35-38.

resurrection of the dead also will come about by the divine will and sanction. For He has the power to correspond with His will.

And so, with our souls again united to our bodies, which will have become incorrupt and put off corruption, we shall rise again and stand before the terrible judgment seat of Christ.[20] And the Devil and his demons, and his man, which is to say, the Antichrist, and the impious and sinners will be given over to everlasting fire,[21] which will not be a material fire such as we are accustomed to, but a fire such as God might know. And those who have done good will shine like the sun together with the angels unto eternal life with our Lord Jesus Christ, ever seeing Him and being seen, enjoying the unending bliss which is from Him, and praising Him together with the Father and the Holy Ghost unto the endless ages of ages. Amen.

---

20 Cf. Rom. 14.10.
21 Cf. Matt. 25.41.

INDEX

INDEX

abandonment, 262
Abgar of Edessa, 372, 373
Abimelech (Abd-al-Malik), ix, xii
Abraham, 113, 156, 157
Abrasax, 117
accident, 13, 14, 19, 43; compared with difference 52, with genus 51, with property 54, with species 54; etymology of, 64
accidental, defined, 101
Acephali, xviii, xix
Aconites, or Manichaeans, 127
act, 90
action, 61, 84, 85, 247
acts, natural, 252
Adam, fall of, 265
Adamians, 124
adorableness, of Christ's human nature, 336, 337
Aerians, 129
Aerius of Pontus, 129
Aetians, 130
Aetius, 130
aevum, 203 n.
affection (pathos), 83
affirmation, 97
affirmations, about Christ, 376ff
Agarenes 153
age, 203
ageneton and *agenneton*, 181
Agnoetae, 148, 149
Agonyclites, 150
air, 108, 222, 223
Alogians, 124
alteration, 108
Al-Walid, ix, xii, xiv
Ammonius, xxvii

analysis, logical, 107
Anastasius the Sinaite, xxxiv
Angelici, 126
angels, 205ff., 234; fallen, 209, 210; freedom of, 259; place of, 198
anger, 241
anhypostaton, 55, 69, 174
Anna and Joachim, 363
Annunciation, 269, 270
anointing, of humanity of Christ, 272, 340, 365
Anomoeans, 130
Antichrist, 398ff.
Antidicomarianites, 131
antiparastasis, 100
antitypes, 360, 361
Apellians, 122
Aphrodite of the Arabs, 153
Aphthartodocetae, 103
Apollinarists, 131
Aposchistae, 103
Apostolici, or Apotactici, 126
appropriation, 330f.
Arbiter, The, of John the Tritheite, 140ff.
Archontics, 121
Arians, 127
Ariomanites, 127
Aristotle, xxvii, 96
Artotyrites, 123
Asceticus, a book of the Massalians, 131
Ascodrugites, 123
astrology, 219
Athanasius, xxxiv, 281, 314

Audians, 128
370
Autoproscoptae, 152
autumn, 109

Babel, Tower of, 111
Bahira, friend of Mohammed, 153 n.
baptism, 343ff., 356, 357, 398
barbarism, 111
Barbelo, 118
Bardesanites, 125
Barsanouphites, 149
Basil, St., xxxiv, 58, 288, 360,
Basilidians, 117
bee, method of, 5
being, 13, 14; division of, 69
Bero, 118
Blasphemers, or Theocatagnostae, 150
Borborites, 118

Cainites, 121
Camel of God, Book of the, 158
canon (liturgical poem), xxiv n.
Canons of Apostles, 376
Carpocratians, 118
Cataphrygians, 123
categories, ten, xxvii, 61, 73
Cathari, 125
Caulacau, 118
Cerdonians, 121
Cerinthians, 118
Chalcedon, Council of, 139
Christ, affirmations about, 376-

ff.; anointed, 272, 340 341, 365; appropriation by, 330; begotten in His human nature, 341, 342; fear in, 327, 328; genealogy, 361ff.; ignorance in, 324ff.; natural passions in, 323, 324; natures, 270ff., 275ff., 277 ff., 284-286, 295, 296; deification of His human nature, 316ff.; His human nature adorable, 336, 337; union of natures in, 217-ff.; passibility and impassibility, 331, 332; one Person of, 332, 333; portrait of, 372, 373; prayer of, 328ff.; progress in, 326, 327; servitude in, 324ff.; sitting at the right hand of the Father, 336; two wills and freedoms, 296ff.; free will of, 319ff.; after Resurrection, 335
Christianocategori, xxxi, 160
Christolytae, 150
Christotokos, 294
circumcision, 397, 398
circumincession, 187
circumstances (parts of speech), 254
Coddians, 118
Colarbasaeans, 120
Collyridians, 131
comet, 109
common, defined, 100
conjugates, 60
conscience, 389
continuous things, 73

contradictions, 97
contraries, 88, 89
corruption, 108, 333, 334
Cosmas of Maiuma, 3
Cosmas the Monk, vi, viii, xxv
creation, 205, 264; visible, 210
Cyril of Alexandria, xxxiv, 281, 283, 310, 340
Cyril of Jerusalem, xxxiv
Cyrus of Alexandria, 152

darkness, 172, 215
day, 109
decrease, 108
definition, 26; differs from term, 28; descriptive, 27; of philosophic terms, 99ff.
deification, of Christ's human nature, 316 ff.
deliberation, 249, 250
demonstration, 107
derivative, 22, 24, 25, 59
description, 27
destruction, 108, 333
Devil, the, 209, 229, 265, 266, 387
dew, 110
dialectical methods, four, 107
dialogue form, 100
Diatomites, or Arians, 127
difference, 17, 19, 41; compared with accident, 52; with genus, 50; with property, 52; with species, 52; dividing and constituent, 35, 40; essential, 42, 70; generic, 62; natural, 70;

non-essential, 42; numerical, 73; specific, 18, 62, 72
different, thing which are, 60
Dimoerites, 131
Diodorus of Taesus, 273
Dionysius the Pseudo-Areopagite, 321
Dioscorus of Alexandria, 149
Dioscurus, 273
discrete things, 73
Dispensation, the, 166
disposition, 80
division, 20, 23, 107
doing (and making), 101
domestic economy, 12
Donatists, 150
Dosthenes, 114, 115
Doxarii, 160

earth, 108, 227ff.
earthquake, 110
East, worship to, 352, 353
Easter, celebration by Quartodecimans, 124
Ebionites, 119
eclipse, 220
Ecthesis, 308 n.
Eden, 230
Egyptians, 138, 139
element, 108
elements, 236, 237
Elkesaites, 124
Elxas, 124
Encratites, 123
enhypostaton, 54, 68, 174
Enthusiasts, 136

Epicureans, 114
Epiphanes, 119
Epiphanius, St., xxix, xxxi
equivocals, 56, 57
equivocal prediction, 47
Esdras, 114
Essenes, 114
essential difference, 42
essential terms, 16
ether, 211
Ethicoproscoptae, 151
ethics, 12
Ethnophrones, 150
Eucharist, the, 354ff.
Euchites, 131, 135ff.
Eudoxius, arian heretic, 130
Eunomians, 130
Euphemites, 131
Eustathians, 151
Eustathius of Sebaste, 129
Eutychians, 138, 273
evil, 384, 387; God not author of, 387ff; no principle of, 385 ff.
excogitation, 101
expressions relating to natural phenomena, 108

faculties, cognitive, 247; natural, 237ff.; vital or appetitive, 247
faith, 348ff.; profession of, 161-168
fear, 240, 241, 327, 328
fifth body, 171
fire, 108, 215

fire-ball, 109
first-born, 342, 343
Flavian of Antioch, 136
Flora, 120
form, 18, 56, 65
Fount of Knowledge, reason for title, 10
fountain, 110
freedoms in Christ, 296ff.
free will, 255ff.; of Christ, 319ff.
frost, 110

Gaianites, 148
Gaianus of Alexandria, 148
genera, ten most general, 61
genus, 18, 29, 36; compared with accident 51; with difference, 50; with property, 51; with species, 50; most general, 32, 37; inferior and superior, 30; subaltern, 32, 37
George, Arian bishop of Alexandria
Gnostics, 118
Gnosimachi, 149
God, attributes, 201f.; bodily attributes, 191; incomprehensible essence, 170ff.; what He is, 170f.; proof of existence, 168ff.; foreknowledge of, 263, 387, 388; spoken of in human terms, 167; incomprehensible, 165ff.; names, 189f.; 193ff.; place of, 197f.; unity of, 172.; the Father, 200
Gorthenes, 114

Greeks, divisions of, 113; philosophers of, 5
Gregory Nazianzen, xxxiv, 5, 288, 316, 325, 340
Gregory of Nyssa, xxxiv, 311

habit, 80, 90
hail, 110
having, 87, 96, 97
hearing, 242
heavens, 210ff.
Heifer, Book of the, 159
Hemerobaptists, 116
Helen, companion of Simon Magus, 117
Heliotropites, 149
hell, the descent into, 334
Hellenes, 112
Hellenism, 111, 112
Heracleonites, 120
heresy, defined, 110; origin, 111
Herodians, 116
Hetaeriasts, 155
heterohypostaton, 68
heteronymous things, 60
Hicetae, 149
Hieracites, 127
Hierax of Leontopolis, 127
Holy Ghost, 174, 175, 183, 200; procession of, 181, 188, 196
homoiousion, 129
homoousion, 129
hour, 109
humors, 217, 218, 237
hypostasis, 54, 56, 66-68, 141ff.
hypostatic union, 103, 104

ice, 110
Iconoclasts, xii, 160
identity, generic, 62; specific, 62, 72; hypostatic, 73
ignorance in Christ, 324ff.
images, veneration of, 370ff.
imagination, 241, 242
Incarnation, of Word, 268ff.; and union, 290, 291
incorporeal, 236
increase, 108
individual, 41, 56, 67, 68, 141ff.
indivisibles, 141
inquiry, and interrogation, 100
intelligence, 248
interrogation, and inquiry, 100
involuntary, 253, 254
Ionians, 112
iris, 109
Isagoge of Porphyry, xxvii
Ishmaelites, 153ff.
Isidore, 119

Jacobites, xviii
James of Syria (Baradeus), 139
Javan, 112
Jews, seven heresies of the, 115
Joachim and Anna, 363
John Chrysostom, xxii
John, of Jerusalem and of Antioch, v
John the Tritheite (or Grammarian), 139, 140
Juda, 113
Judaism, 113
Julian of Halicarnassus, 148

Justin, 123

Ka'ba, sacred place of Mecca, 156
Khabar, Aphrodite of Arabs, 153
knife, red-hot, 308, 323
knowledge, 7
Koran, 153ff.

lake, 110
Lampetians, 151
law, of God and of sin, 388, 389
lemma, 100
Leo the Great, St., xxxiv; *Tome* of, 138
Leo the Isaurian, vi, ix, xii
Leontius of Byzance, xxix
Lequien, Michel, xxx
lightning, 110
likeness, division, 58; origin, 57
Litoius of Melitene, 136
Lucianists, 122
lyre, 110

Maiuma, Cosmas of, 3
making (and doing), 101
man, 234, 235, 237
Manes the Persian, 127
Manichaeans, xix, 127
Mansur, ix
Mar Saba, xv
Marcellina, 118
Marcellians, 128
Marcionites, 121
Morcoseans, 120

Mark the Gnostic, 120
Maronites, xix n.
marriage, 396, 397
Marthina, 124
Marthus, 124
Marthyrians, 131
Mary, genealogy of, 361ff.; divine maternity of, 292ff.; perpetual virginity of 365, 366
Massalians, xxix; or Euchites, 131; the Asceticus, 131 ff.
mathematics, 12
Maximus the Confessor, xxxiv
Melchisedechians, 125
Meletians, 127
memory, 245
Menander, 117
Menandrianists, 117
Merinthians, 118
Meropes, 112
meteor, 109
method, analytical, 107; dialectical, 107; mathematical, 108
mind, 305, 319
mist, 110
Mohammedans, xxxi, 153ff.
Monophysites, xviii, 138, 139
Monothelites, xix, 152
Montanists, 123
month, 109
moon, 220ff.
Moses, 3, 113
Mother of God, 292ff.
motion, 94, 108
multinominals, 59
myroblytae, 368 n.

Nasaraeans, 116
natural phenomena, terms relating to, 108
nature, 18, 55, 65, 141ff., 289ff.
Nazarenes, 119
necessity, 108
negation, 97
Nemesius, xxxiv
Nestorians, xviii, xix, 138
Nestorius, 145, 272, 273, 294, 326
Nicolaitans, 117
Nicolas, 117
night, 109
Noe, 111
Noetians, 125
non-essential difference, 42; terms, 16
Novatus, 125

objection, 100
ocean, 225
Oeconomia, 166 n.
Oktoikhos, xxiv
Omayyads, ix, x, xii
one, 63
operation, 304, 305; in Christ, 304ff.; theandric, 321ff.
Ophites, 121
opinion, 248f, 349; common, defined, 100
opposites, 88
Origen, xxxiv, 126, 235
origination, 108
Ossenes, 116
other, 18

pain, 240
Panarion, xxix
paradise, 230ff.
Parermeneutae, 151
parhelion, 109
passion, 246; and action, 84, 85; affection, 83; one of ten most general genera, 61; natural passions in Christ, 323, 324
pathos, 83
Paulianists, 126
Pepuzians, 123
Peripatetics, 113
Peter Lombard, xxxii
person, 56, 67, 68, 141ff., 275, 276; of Christ, 332, 333; of God the Word, 281ff., 339, 340; in Trinity, 277ff.
Phaleg, 111
Pharisees, 115
Phibionites, 118
Philoponus, John, 139, 140
philosophers, Greek, 5
philosophy, speculative and practical, 12; definitions of, 11, 105, 106
Photinians, 128
physiology, 12
place, 61, 87
planets, 212, 216ff.
Platonists, 113
pleasures, 239, 240
Pneumatochi, 129
poetry, xxiv
politics, 12
Porphyry, xxvii

position, 61, 86
posterior, 93
potency, in, 90
prayer, of Christ, 328ff.
predestination, 263
predicable, 46
predicate, 45, 46
predication, 46-48
premise, 98, 99
principles, that there are not two, 385ff.
prior, 91, 92; by nature, 25
Priscilla, 123, 124
privation, 90, 91
Proclus of Constantinople, 288
progress, in Christ, 326, 327
property, 18, 19, 41, 44; characteristic, 56; compared with accident, 54; with difference, 52; with genus, 51; with species, 53
Providence, 257, 260ff.
Prunicus, 118
Pseudo-Dionysius, xxxiv
Ptolemaeans, 120
Pythagoreans, 113

quality, 41, 61, 80
quantity, 61, 73
quantum, 73, 76
Quartodecimans, 124
question, 99, 100
Quintillians, 123

Ragau, 111
rainstorm, 110

redivision, 20, 23
redundance, 101, 102
relation, 61, 102
relative, 22, 24, 25, 59
relatives, 77
relics, veneration of, 368ff.
Renuntiants, 126
Resurrection, 401ff.
rotation, 108
Sabbas, St. Monastery of, vii, xi, xii, xvff.
Sabbath, the, 389 ff.
Sabellians, 126
Sadduccees, 115, 116
Sadoc, 116
saints, veneration of, 367ff.
Samaritans, 114
Sampsaeans, 124
Saracens, 153
Sarug, 111
Satanians, 131
Saturnilians, 117
Schematics, 138, 139
scindapsus, 15
Scribes, 115
Scripture, 373-376; canon of, 375, 376
Scythism, 111
Seas, the, 226
seasons, 217, 218
Sebyaeans, 114
Secundians, 119
self-motion, 109
Semiarians, 128
Semidalites, 149
senses, 242ff.

Sergius of Constantinople, 152
Sergius ibn Mansur, ix
servitude in Christ, 324ff.
Sethians, 121
Severians, xviii, 122
Severus of Antioch, 139
Severus the Gnostic, 122
shape, 82
sight, 242
Simon Magnus, 116, 117
Simonians, 116
simultaneous, 93
smell, 243
snow, 110
Socratites, 118
Son, 200; why He became man, 337ff.
sort, being such a, 80
soul, 235, 236, 238; place of, 198
species, 17, 19, 31, 36, 38; compared with accident, 54; with difference, 52; with genus, 50; with property, 53; most specific, 31, 38, 66
specific difference, 18
speculation, 101
Spirit, Divine, 174, 175
spring, 109
star, barbed, 109
state, 61, 87
Stoics, 114
Stratiotics, 118
subalterns, 37, 70
subdivision, 20, 23
subject, of existence and predication, 47

417

subsistence, 286
substance, 13, 14, 18, 55, 61, 64; division, 70; properties, 71
summer, 109
syllogism, 98, 99, 107
syzygies, 119

Table, Book of the, 159
taste, 243
Tatianists, 123
term, 15 ff., 28, 49; of premise, 98, 99
Thare, 112
Themistians, 148, 149
Theocatagnostae, 150
Theodore of Mopsuestia, 273
Theodoret, xxx, xxxii; on Massalians, 135ff.
Theodosius of Alexandria, 139
Theodotians, 124
theology, 12
Theophanes, ix, xiii, xiv
Theotokos, 292ff.
thinking faculty, 244, 245
Thnetopsychites, 150
thunderbolt, 109
Thymoleontes (or Iconoclasts), 160
time, 61, 109; seasonable, 109; solar and lunar, 221
Timothy of Constantinople, xxx
tradition, 166
tree, of knowledge and of life, 232, 233
Trinity, 177, 178, 182ff.; Persons in, 277, 278

Trisagion, 287ff.
typhoon, 109

uncircumscribed, 198
union, hypostatic, 102, 103
universal, 101
universals, five, xxvii, 18
univocal predication, 46
univocals, 59
unseasonableness, 109

Valentinians, 119
Valesians, 125
veneration of images, 370ff.; of relics 367ff.; of saints, 367ff.
virginity, 365, 366, 393ff.; of Mary, 365, 366
volcanic crater, 110
voluntary, 253
water, 108, 224ff.
water-spout, 109
will, 248, 251; free, 255ff.
wills, of Christ, 296ff.
winds, the, 223
wishing, 248, 251
Woman, Book of, 157
Word, the, 174, 201; Incarnation, 268ff.; Person, 339, 340; procession of, 178ff.

Yazid, ix
year, 109

Zanchaeans, 118
Zeid, 157
Zodiac, 218, 221, 222

INDEX OF SCRIPTURE TEXTS

OLD TESTAMENT

Genesis
1.1, 227
1.2, 223, 224, 226, 228, 345
1.3, 215, 356
1.5, 215
1.6, 356
1.7, 224
1.8, 211, 213
1.9-10, 225
1.11, 357
1.14, 217
1.26, 303, 370
1.27-28, 394
1.28, 229
1.31, 209, 386, 313
2.2, 389
2.8, 353
2.9, 231
2.10, 225
2.16, 232, 233
2.17, 233
2.25, 231, 394
3.1, 229
3.7, 267, 394
3.1, 229
3.7, 267, 394
3.18, 229
3.19, 229, 394
3.21, 267
3.24, 353
4.1, 394
6.13, 267
6.17, 345
6.18, 394
7.1, 394
8.11, 348

8.16, 395
8.21, 371
9.3-6, 402
11.7, 267
12, 397
13, 397
14.18, 359
15, 397
17.10-14, 397
18.1ff., 267
19.1ff., 267
46.27, 319
47.31, 352
48.13-15, 352

Exodus
3.6, 367, 402
3.14, 189
7.1, 367
12.23, 350
14.16ff., 352
15.25, 352
17.1ff., 352
17.6, 352, 368
19.15, 395
20.2-3, 172
24.18, 390
25.20, 371
25.40, 371
33.10, 371
33.10, 371
34.28, 390

Leviticus
14.8, 346
15, 345

16.14, 353
20.2, 339
21, 395
26.12, 368

Numbers
2.3, 353
15.32-36, 390
16.31-33,35, 339
17.8, 352
19.11, 368
21.9, 352
36.6, 362

Deuteronomy
4.24, 189, 347
5.14, 390
6.4, 172
25.5, 362
25.5-10, 393
28.66, 352
32.7, 374

Josue
5.2,6-7, 398
6.4, 391

Judges
15.9, 368

1 Kings
1.11, 363

3 Kings
1.34, 116
6, 371

17.1, 395
17.22, 395
18.24,38, 345
19.8, 391

4 Kings
2.8, 395
2.9, 395
2.11, 395
2.14, 395

1 Paralipomenon
29.22, 116

Tobias
12.19, 207

Job
1.1, 275
1.12, 209, 261, 263
2.6, 209
5.13, 364
26.7, 227
33.4, 176

Psalms
1.3, 374
6.11, 393
8.4, 216
13.1, 168
15.10, 333
18.2, 214
23.2, 227
23.7, 383
32.6, 176

32.8, 356
44.8, 340, 344, 378, 275
48.9-10, 368
48.13, 229, 265
49.1, 367
49.3, 378
50.6, 385
51.10, 363
54.23, 231
67.14, 374
67.33-34, 353
73.13, 347
74.4, 227
82.4, 303
88.36-38, 362
89.2, 203
95.11, 214
101.27, 214
103.2, 213
103.4, 205
103.29-30, 402
103.30, 176
106.20, 176, 377
109.4, 359
113.3,5,6, 214
113.16, 211
115.15, 378
118.89, 176
131.11, 362
134.6, 176, 260, 356
135.6, 227
136.1, 341
138.6, 233
145.6, 210
148.4, 211
148.5-6, 213

Proverbs
8.22, 378
12.10, 390
22.28, 166

Ecclesiastes
11.2, 393

Wisdom
1.13, 259
2.23, 337
3.1, 368, 402
13.5

Ecclesiasticus
34.11, 265

Isaias
6.6, 359
7.14, 364
7.16, 303
9.2, 334
9.6, 376
11.1, 362
22.13, 401
26.19, 402
29.11, 364
31.9, 395
40.22, 211, 213
43.10, 173
45.7, 384
53.3, 378
53.9, 332
61.1, 344
65.2, 352
66.1, 197

66.7, 365

Jeremias
9.23, 364
23.24, 171

Baruch
3.36, 277, 378
3.38, 197, 277, 341, 372, 378

Ezechiel
37.7-8, 403
44.1-2, 353, 365

Daniel
2.15, 303
3.50, 395
3.80, 213
6.22, 395
10.2-3, 391
11.37, 399
12.1-3, 403
13.42, 189, 202

Amos
3.6, 384

Micheas
1.3, 378

Zacharias
3.8, 353
9.9, 378

Malachias
1.11, 360

4.2, 334, 353
4.6, 400

2 Machabees
9.5, 189

NEW TESTAMENT

Matthew
1.9, 362
1.23, 364
1.25, 366
3.11, 346
3.15, 329
4.2, 313
5.4, 230
5.17, 373
6.11, 360
6.25, 231
6.33, 231
6.33, 231
7.6, 361
8.3, 305, 317
11.11, 369
11.27, 165
12.5, 391
12.15, 380
12.32, 203
16.16, 344
19.11, 396
21.19, 380
22.32, 402
23.5, 115
24.14, 399
24.24, 400

24.27, 353
24.30, 35;
25.41, 210, 406
26.39, 320, 329, 380
27.33-34, 300
27.46, 330, 380
27.51, 392
28.9-10, 382
28.19, 177, 344, 382
28.20, 382, 366

Mark
5.13, 263
7.4, 115, 300, 317
12.25, 405
14.21, 388
16.6, 351

Luke
1.28-38, 270
1.34-35, 357
1.78, 353
2.35, 366
2.52, 326, 381
3.6, 319
4.19, 334
8.54, 309
10.41, 231
10.41-42, 231
11.10, 374
12.50, 347
14.5, 391
16.19ff., 261
18.12, 115
22.42, 320
24.28, 380, 382

423

24.39-40, 404
24.43, 335

John
1.1, 268
1.3, 377
1.12, 367, 392
1.13, 364
1.14, 290
1.18, 165, 268
1.29, 332
1.34, 376
2.2, 396
2.19, 404
2.21, 404
3.5, 345
3.6, 360
3.13, 274, 382
3.14, 379
4.14, 374
4.22, 382
5.17, 307
5.19, 307, 183, 377
5.21, 307
5.22, 199
5.28-29, 403
5.30, 200
5.36, 307
5.39, 373
5.43, 399
6.41, 200
6.48, 355
6.54-58, 359
6.58, 377, 382
7.20, 379
8.40, 319, 379

9.3, 261
10.30, 376, 379
10.38, 307
11, 403
11.34, 380
11.41, 380
11.41-42, 329
11.42, 377
12.27, 328
13.1-5, 356
14.9, 376
14.10, 377, 379
14.11, 187
14.28, 92, 377
15.14-15, 367
16.10, 382
16.15, 325
16.28, 377
17.3, 173
17.5, 381
19.34, 345
20.17, 383
20.22, 188
20.27, 404

Acts
1.5, 347
1.11, 335, 353, 400
2.3, 392
10.38, 344
17.31, 199

Romans
1.4, 381
1.20, 166, 200, 233
1.25, 220

5.12, 332, 394
6.3, 343, 344, 350
6.14, 392
7.23, 388
8.3-4, 389
8.9, 188
8.17, 355, 367
8.26, 389
8.29, 343, 370
9.19, 260
9.21, 234, 383
10.17, 348
11.8, 384
11.32, 384
11.36, 288, 354
14.10, 406

1 Corinthians
1.15, 178
1.18, 349
1.23, 351
1.24, 178, 350
2.8, 274, 276, 382
2.11, 165
2.14-15, 349
3.17, 368
6.19, 368
7.2, 396
7.25, 303
8.6, 288
8.7, 374
10.2, 346
10.17, 361
11.2, 373
11.24, 356
11.25-26, 356

11.29, 360
11.31-32, 360
12.28, 370
13.10, 392
15.16-17, 404
15.20, 334, 404
15.21, 293
15.28, 380
15.32, 401
15.35-38, 405
15.42-44, 405
15.47, 293
15.53, 334, 405

2 Corinthians
3.17, 368
5.21, 380
6.14, 338
6.16, 368
12.2, 211, 213
12.7, 261

Galatians
3.13, 331, 380
3.27, 350
4.3, 391
4.4, 293
4.4-5, 392
4.7, 326, 367, 392
5.3, 398
6.15, 113

Ephesians
2.6, 281
3.14-15, 182
5.19, 369

Philippians
2.6, 376
2.8, 300
2.10, 334
5.20-21, 405

Colossians
1.15, 343
1.17, 194
1.18, 404
2.3, 326
2.9, 279
2.12, 343
3.11, 113
3.16, 390

1 Thessalonians
4.13, 404
4.16, 366

2 Thessalonians
2.3-4, 399
2.8-10, 400
2.9, 400
2.10-11, 399
2.14, 373

1 Timothy
1.7, 326
1.9, 390
2.4, 262
3.6, 265

2 Timothy
2.20-21, 384
3.16, 373

Hebrews
1.1-2, 373
1.2, 182, 203
1.3, 178, 180, 376, 383
1.9, 340
1.11-12, 214
4.12, 356
5.12, 231
6.4-6, 344
7.1, 359
7.13,14, 269
7.17, 359
8.5, 371
11.1, 348
11.6, 349
11.21, 352
11.37-38, 370
13.4, 396

James
1.17, 369
2.22,26, 346
3.15, 349

1 Peter
3.19, 334

2 Peter
2.22, 346

1 John
1.5, 353
1.7, 388
4.3, 399

Apocalypse
19.16, 367
21.1, 214, 230

www.ingramcontent.com/pod-product-compliance
Lightning Source LLC
Chambersburg PA
CBHW032022290426
44110CB00012B/629